Men's Artistic Gymnastics Handbook

by Gerald Carr

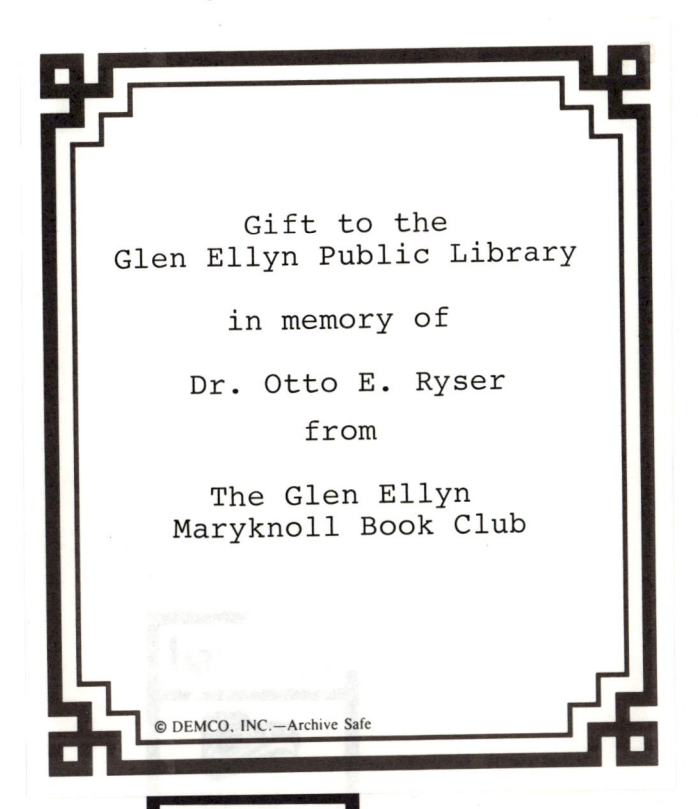

Gift to the
Glen Ellyn Public Library

in memory of

Dr. Otto E. Ryser

from

The Glen Ellyn
Maryknoll Book Club

HANCOCK HOUSE PUBLISHERS

GLEN ELLYN PUBLIC LIBRARY
Glen Ellyn, IL 60137

ISBN 0-88839-046-7 pa.

Copyright © 1981 Carr, Gerald A.

These books have been prepared for the Ministry of Education, Province of British Columbia, under the direction of the Secondary Physical Education Curriculum Revision Committee (1980)

    James Appleby   John Lowther
    Alex Carre   Mike McKee
    Madeline Gemmill   Norman Olenick
    Gerry Gilmore   David Turkington
    George Longstaff

Handbook Consultant: F. Alex Carre, Ph.D.

Canadian Cataloguing in Publication Data
Carr, Gerald A., 1936-
    Men's artistic gymnastics and curriculum guide
(Physical education series)

    Bibliography: p.
    ISBN 0-88839-046-7 pa.
    1. Artistic Gymnastics - Study and
teaching. I. Title. II. Series: Physical Education
Series (Hancock House)
GV461.C37   796.4'1'07'   C81-091141-8

All rights reserved. No part of this publication may be reproduced, stored in a retrieval system or transmitted in any form or by any means, electronic, mechanical, photocopying, recording or otherwise without the prior written permission of Hancock House Publishers.

Editor Margaret Campbell
Design Donna White
Production Manager Peter Burakoff
Cover Photo Paul Bond
Typeset by Donna White & Sandra Sawchuk *in Megaron type on an AM Varityper Comp/Edit*

Printed in Canada

Published by
HANCOCK HOUSE PUBLISHERS LTD.
#10 Orwell St. North Vancouver, B.C. Canada V7J 3K1

Table of Contents

Acknowledgments 8

Chapter One
Format and Purpose of the Handbook
    A. What is Artistic Gymnastics 9
    B. Purpose of the Handbook 9
    C. Handbook Format 9
    D. Objectives of the Program 10
    E. Description of the Levels Approach 10
    F. Explanation of Activity Sequence Chart 10
    G. Activity Sequence Chart 11
    H. Relationship of Men's Artistic Gymnastics to goals and
        Learning Outcomes 12

Chapter Two
Preparation
    A. Conditioning for Gymnastics 13
    B. Safety Techniques and Spotting 21
    C. The Warm-Up 26
    D. Readiness 26
    E. From Basics to the Refined Performance 27

Chapter Three
Skill Development and Teaching Techniques
    A. Floor Exercises and Tumbling 30
        General Safety 30
        Level I Skills 31
        1. Tip-Up (Elbow Balance)-(3 seconds) 31
        2. Headstand (3 seconds) 31
        3. Handstand (with assistance) 33
        4. V-Sit (3 seconds) 35
        5. Front Scale (3 seconds) 36
        6. Forward Roll-Tuck 37
        7. Backward Roll-Tuck 38
        8. Backward Roll-Straddle 40
        Level II Skills 41
        9. Momentary Headstand-Forward Roll 41
        10. Press to Headstand from Straddle Stand 42
        11. Backward Roll in Piked Position (Piked Backward Roll) 43
        12. Forward Roll-Jump-Pirouette 44

13. Momentary Handstand-Forward Roll 45
14. Cartwheel 47
   Level III Skills 50
15. Cartwheel Forward Roll 50
16. Forward Roll in Straddled Position (Straddled Forward Roll) 51
17. Standing Dive Forward Roll 52
18. Backward Roll to Handstand (Back Extension) 54
19. Handstand (without assistance)-(3 seconds) 55
20. Handstand Quarter Turn 56
21. Round-Off 57
22. Headspring from a rolled mat or box-top 59
23. Tucked Press to Handstand (with flexed arms) 62
   Level IV Skills 63
24. Straddle Press to Handstand 63
25. L-Support (3 seconds) 64
26. Headspring on the Floor 65
27. Handspring 66
28. One-Armed Cartwheel 70
29. Backhandspring 71
30. Handstand Forward Roll in Piked Position
    (Handstand Piked Forward Roll) 75
31. Combinations and Routines 77

B. Pommel Horse (Side Horse) 79
   General Safety 79
   Level I Skills 80
   1. Front Support Swings 80
   2. Rear Support Swings 81
   3. Stride Support Swings 82
   Level II Skills 83
   4. Support Travel 83
   5. Single Leg Half Circle 84
   6. Flank Dismount 85
   Level III Skills 86
   7. Single Leg Full Circle 86
   8. Double Leg Half Circle 87
   9. Rear Pick-Up Flank Both Legs to Rear Support 89
   Level IV Skills 90
   10. Front Pick-Up Flank Both Legs to Front Support 90
   11. Front Scissors 91
   12. Back Scissors 92
   13. Rear Dismount 94
   14. Double Leg Circle 95
   15. Combinations and Routines 98

C. Rings 100
- General Safety 100
- Rope Activities as Lead-Ups to the Rings............................101
- Level I Skills 102
  1. Straight Inverted Hang..102
  2. Piked Inverted Hang 102
  3. Cross Support (3 seconds) 103
  4. Skin the Cat..104
  5. Swings 105
- Level II Skills 106
  6. Tucked Support (3 seconds) 106
  7. Backward Tuck Dismount 107
- Level III Skills...108
  8. Muscle-Up 108
  9. L-Support (3 seconds) 109
  10. Tucked Shoulder Balance (3 seconds)..............................110
  11. From Cross Support-Half Backward Roll to Piked Inverted Hang...111
  12. Flyaway (Backward Dismount with Straight Body) 112
  13. Backward Straddle Dismount......................................113
- Level IV Skills..114
  14. From Cross Support-Half-Forward Roll to Piked Inverted Hang....114
  15. Shoulder Balance (3 seconds) 115
  16. Inlocate 116
  17. Back Uprise...118
  18. Combinations and Routines 120

D. Vault 121
- General Safety 121
- Characteristics of Vaulting Apparatus...............................121
- Suggestions on How To Teach Vaulting 124
- Orientation To Vaulting...124
- Use of the Beat Board for Vaulting 125
- Level I Skills 127
  1. Front Vault (Side Horse) 127
  2. Flank Vault (Side Horse)...129
- Level II Skills 130
  3. Rear Vault (Side Horse)..130
  4. Squat Vault (Side Horse) 132
- Level III Skills..133
  5. Straddle Vault (Side Horse).....................................133
  6. Straddle Vault (Long Horse) 135
  7. Stoop Vault (Side Horse) 136
- Level IV Skills...138
  8. Squat Vault (Long Horse)..138

       9. Stoop Vault (Long Horse) 140
     10. Headspring Vault (Side Horse) 141
     11. Handspring Vault (Side Horse) 144
  E. Parallel Bars 146
    General Safety 146
    Examples of Basic Positions on the Parallel Bars 148
    Level I Skills 149
      1. Cross Support-Hop Travel 149
      2. Cross Support Swings 149
      3. Dismount from a Forward Swing (Rear Vault Dismount) 150
      4. Underarm Support Swings 151
      5. Glide Swing and Return 152
    Level II Skills 153
      6. Glide Swing to Piked Inverted Hang 153
      7. Dismount from a Backswing (Front Vault Dismount) 154
      8. L-Support (3 seconds) 155
    Level III Skills 153
      9. Shoulder Balance (3 seconds) 155
     10. Forward Roll from a Momentary Shoulder Balance 157
     11. Back Uprise 158
     12. Underarm Kip to Cross Support 159
    Level IV Skills 161
     13. Front Uprise 161
     14. Glide Kip 163
     15. Drop Kip 165
     16. Momentary Handstand Quarter Turn Dismount
         at the End of the Parallel Bars 167
     17. Combinations and Routines 168
  F. Horizontal Bar 170
    General Safety 170
    Examples of Basic Positions on the Horizontal Bar 172
    Level I Skills 173
      1. Front Support Swings (Simple Cast) 173
      2. Front Support-Forward Roll Dismount 174
      3. Front Support to Stride Support 175
      4. Single Knee Swing Up 176
    Level II Skills 177
      5. Pullover Mount 177
      6. Backward Hip Circle (Back Hip Circle) 179
      7. Underswing Dismount 180
      8. Glide Swing and Return 181
    Level III Skills 182
      9. Stride Inverted Swings 182

    10. Forward Stride Circle (Front Stride Circle) 184
    11. Forward Hip Circle (Front Hip Circle) 185
    12. Piked Inverted Swings 187
  Level IV Skills 187
    13. Glide-Stride Inverted Swing to Stride Support 187
    14. Cast-Straddle Sole Dismount 189
    15. Glide-Kip 190
    16. Glide-Piked Inverted Swing to Rear Support 191
    17. Combinations and Routines 193

Chapter Four
Planning the Program

  A. How to Progress to Group Activities 195
    1. Introducing Apparatus 195
    2. From Floor to Apparatus 196
  B. Sample Lesson Plans 196
  Lesson One: Introduction to Floor Exercises and Tumbling 199
  Lesson Two: Floor Exercises and Tumbling—Continued 200
  Lesson Three: Introduction to Vaulting 201
  Lesson Four: Continuation of Instruction in Vaulting 202
  Lesson Five: Introduction to the Low Horizontal Bar 204
  Lesson Six: Low Horizontal Bar—Continued 205
  Lesson Seven: Introduction to the Parallel Bars (males) and Further Work
                    On The Horizontal Bar (females) 206
  Lesson Eight: Introduction to New Apparatus 207

Chapter Five
Evaluation

  A. Individual Evaluation 209
  B. Program Evaluation 209

Appendix I   Reference Materials 211
Appendix II   Glossary 212
Notes   214

Acknowledgments

To the Ministry of Education Curriculum Development Branch, Province of British Columbia for initiating and developing the Secondary Physical Education Curriculum and Resources Guide. This gymnastics handbook is an integral part of the Secondary Physical Education Curriculum and Resources Guide.

To Gordon Gannon the Provincial Coordinator for Gymnastics for his invaluable help in the organization and evaluation of the skills selected for this handbook, and to all the teachers who provided input.

To the gymnasts of the School of Physical Education at the University of Victoria for performing the skills illustrated in this handbook.

To Margaret Loos and Preston Denny for the graphics, and Roger Keeping as research assistant.

Chapter One
Format And Purpose Of The Handbook

A. Introduction: What is Artistic Gymnastics

Nowadays it is confusing to speak simply of gymnastics. What was originally a stylized form of calisthenics, tumbling, and apparatus gymnastics has developed into a sport with many different forms. In Canada and the United States one sees most frequently Artistic Gymnastics, Rhythmic Gymnastics, Trampoline, and Educational Gymnastics. A new type of gymnastics which is now growing in popularity is Acrobatics, a form of partner balancing and tumbling.

Artistic Gymnastics is a relatively new name given to what was previously called Apparatus or Olympic Gymnastics. It is the most commonly taught form of gymnastics in British Columbia Secondary schools. It consists of four events for women (vault, uneven bars, balance beam, and floor exercises) and six events for men (floor exercises, pommel horse (side horse), rings, vault, parallel bars, and the horizontal bar (high bar)

Rhythmic Gymnastics, like Artistic Gymnastics, has its roots in Europe. This beautiful flowing form of gymnastics is for women only and is characterized by its use of balls, hoops, clubs, and ribbons. It is performed only on the floor.

Educational Gymnastics is well known in British Columbia. This form of gymnastics originally gained great popularity in Great Britain where it was felt that it satisfied the child's need for freedom and individual expression. Educational Gymnastics uses the concepts of force, space, time and flow and allows the child's fertile imagination to develop an appreciation for movement in all its forms. Cues given by the instructor help the child to progress from simple to more complex movement patterns. Today, Educational Gymnastics is often used as a foundation for Artistic Gymnastics. Using the discovery approach of Educational Gymnastics, the instructor then progresses to the more specific skills of Artistic Gymnastics.

The unique contributions of Artistic Gymnastics become quickly apparent to anyone whose background in physical education has been strictly in team sports and games. Artistic Gymnastics develops power, flexibility, and coordination to a degree that is frequently absent in other activities, and it emphasizes, in particular, the upper body, an area which is frequently overlooked and neglected. Coupled with the strong cardiovascular emphasis that occurs in many team sports, Artistic Gymnastics helps to produce a balanced physical development which is an important goal of a physical education program.

B. Purpose of the Handbook

This handbook is an extension of the B.C. Physical Education Curriculum and Resource Guide (1980). The information included in this handbook is intended to provide the gymnastics instructor with a comprehensive guide for the teaching of Men's Artistic Gymnastics.

C. Handbook Format

Men's Artistic Gymnastics is a sport made up of a tremendous number of skills on the floor and on five other pieces of apparatus. For the instructor, it demands an extensive knowledge of class organization, safety techniques, selection of skills, and the careful choice of teaching progressions. For many instructors the sheer size and complexity of Artistic Gymnastics is overwhelming, and the need for a guide to assist them in their instruction has been apparent for a long time. This handbook has been planned specifically to fill this need. It contains the following:

1. Information on conditioning for gymnastics. This section helps the instructor select activities for the improvement of power, flexibility, coordination, balance, endurance, and so on.
2. Information on safety techniques and spotting. This section discusses the common principles of safety and spotting. Common spotting errors are illustrated and methods given for their correction. Each event is also given an introductory section which discusses specific safety regulations relative to the event.
3. Information on teaching progressions. Suggestions are given on how to progress from basic motor patterns to the refined gymnastic performance.
4. A series of suggested skills for each event. These skills are set out in four levels (I-IV) ranging from skills for the beginner through to those that suit the more advanced performer. (See Section E for a more detailed explanation of the Levels approach).
   Each skill is treated in the following manner:
   a) a large number of illustrations show the skill, its lead-ups and methods of spotting;

b) a written description gives the following:
   i) recommended lead-ups for the skill
   ii) what the skill leads to, i.e. further related skills
   iii) teaching points for the skill
   iv) teaching points for safety and spotting
   v) common errors in the performance of the skill (and its related safety technique) and how to correct them.
5. Information on planning the program. This chapter offers suggestions on organizing the gymnastic program, and on planning each individual lesson. Sample lesson plans are given and methods of evaluation are discussed.
6. Information on terminology, resources, and national and provincial organizations.

D. Objectives of the Program

The objectives of a gymnastic program in any school should be considered in three ways:

1. Psychomotor Objectives

a) Participants should develop a physically fit body.
b) Participants should develop effective motor skills through power, flexibility, balance, coordination, agility, and endurance.
c) Participants should develop rhythm, timing and body awareness.

2. Cognitive Objectives

a) Participants should develop an understanding and appreciation of the sport of Artistic Gymnastics.
b) Participants should develop control, discipline, perseverance, courage, initiative, and creativity.
c) Participants should develop an understanding and appreciation of human movement as an expressive art form.

3. Affective Objectives

a) Participants should develop a positive attitude through enthusiastic involvement in Artistic Gymnastics.
b) Participants should learn to work in a responsible manner and strive for individual perfection and originality.
c) Participants should be encouraged to work with partners in a manner which is cooperative and responsible.
d) Participants should observe safety precautions at all times and demonstrate responsibility and cooperation.
e) Participants should learn to provide and accept direction as specified by the instructor.

E. Description of the Levels Approach

Skills listed under Levels I and II are intended for the average student and are offered as reasonable skills for the general gymnastic class. Level III and IV skills are intended as objectives for the better performer: whether these skills are taught in a class situation will depend upon the instructor and the performance level of the students. In most cases these skills will be beyond the average performer and are more appropriate as suggested skills for members of a school gymnastics club.

The objective of the levels approach is to offer the instructor a series of suggested skills ranging from Level I through to Level IV. These skills progress in difficulty and incorporate most of the fundamental movement patterns that are found in Artistic Gymnastics, notably body positions, rotation, swinging, springing, orientation to height, flight, and landing.

The instructor should not discard all other gymnastic skills and concentrate solely on those listed in Levels I-IV. Rather, he should use these recommended skills as a framework for a program and a suggestion for a standard at which to aim.

It is to be expected that there will be criticism of the selection of certain skills and of their placement at a particular level. Some skills do not fit perfectly into any one level. Furthermore, progress on some pieces of apparatus, such as the pommel horse, is more difficult and slower than on other apparatus.

Nevertheless, considerable attention has been given to the selection and accurate placement of skills. *The majority have been placed at their particular level as though performed with technically correct form and with no assistance.* However, the instructor should feel free to place the skill at a lower level if it is performed technically well with assistance. For instance, in Floor Exercises and Tumbling, a handstand performed with assistance has been placed at Level I, but without assistance, and held for a count of three seconds, this same skill has been placed at Level III. Similarly a headspring on the floor without assistance is set at Level IV. With assistance from one spotter this skill could become Level III and with two spotters, possibly Level II.

These skills relate closely to the Merit and Bronze levels of the Canadian Gymnastic Federation's Development Program. An instructor who is interested in having direction in the selection of skills prior to Levels I-IV should consult Book I of the Canadian Gymnastic Federation's Development Program (see Appendix I). By working through the Red, White and Blue levels of Book I, the instructor then leads directly into Levels I-IV of this handbook. From there the final target is the Silver and Gold levels of Book II (Men's Achievement) of the Canadian Gymnastic Development Program.

F. Explanation of the Activity Sequence Chart

The Activity Sequence Chart lists skills in each of the six events by level. All the Level I Floor Exercise and Tumbling skills are placed together, as are Levels II, III, and IV. This duplicates the method by which the skills are laid out in the handbook. In this way the instructor has an overview of all the skills contained in each level for each event.

Combinations and Routines

With the exception of vaulting, all events offer suggestions for combinations and routines of skills. These progress in difficulty in the following manner:

1. Combinations and routines of skills from Level I.
2. Combinations and routines of skills from Level I and Level II.
3. Combinations and routines of skills from Levels I, II, and III.
4. Combinations and routines of skills from Levels I, II, III, and IV.

It is expected that the instructor will use spotting, and will modify these routines to suit the needs of the individual.

G. Activity Sequence Chart

SKILLS	I	II	III	IV
A. Floor Exercises				
1. Tip-up (elbow balance) (3 seconds)	●			
2. Headstand (3 seconds)	●			
3. Handstand (with assistance)	●			
4. V-sit (3 seconds)	●			
5. Front scale	●			
6. Forward roll-tuck	●			
7. Backward roll-tuck	●			
8. Backward roll-straddle	●			
9. Momentary headstand - forward roll		●		
10. Press to headstand from straddle stand		●		
11. Backward roll-pike		●		
12. Forward roll-jump-pirouette		●		
13. Momentary handstand forward roll		●		
14. Cartwheel		●		
15. Cartwheel forward roll			●	
16. Forward roll straddle			●	
17. Standing dive roll			●	
18. Backward roll-extension			●	
19. Handstand without assistance (3 seconds)			●	
20. Handstand quarter-turn			●	
21. Round-off			●	
22. Headspring on a rolled mat or box-top			●	
23. Tucked press to handstand (flexed arms)			●	
24. Straddle press to handstand				●
25. L-support (3 seconds)				●
26. Headspring on the floor				●
27. Handspring				●
28. One-arm cartwheel				●
29. Backhandspring				●
30. Handstand - forward roll in piked position				●
31. Combinations and routines	●	●	●	●
B. Pommel Horse				
1. Front support swing	●			
2. Rear support swing	●			
3. Stride support swing	●			
4. Support travel		●		
5. Single leg half circle		●		
6. Flank dismount		●		
7. Single leg full circle			●	
8. Double leg half circle			●	
9. Rear pick up flank both legs to rear support			●	
10. Front pick up flank both legs to front support				●
11. Front scissors				●
12. Back scissors				●
13. Rear dismount				●
14. Double leg circle				●
15. Combinations and routines	●	●	●	●
C. Rings				
1. Straight inverted hang	●			
2. Piked inverted hang	●			
3. Cross support (3 seconds)	●			
4. Skin the cat (from standing)	●			
5. Swings (low amplitude)	●			
6. Tucked support (3 seconds)		●		
7. Backward tuck dismount		●		
8. Muscle-up			●	
9. L-support (3 seconds)			●	
10. Tucked shoulder balance (3 seconds)			●	
11. From support half backward roll to piked inverted hang			●	
12. Flyaway (backward dismount with straight body)			●	
13. Backward straddle dismount			●	
14. From cross support half forward roll to piked inverted hang				●
15. Shoulder balance (3 seconds)				●

SKILLS	I	II	III	IV
16. Inlocate				•
17. Back uprise				•
18. Combinations and routines	•	•	•	•
D. Vault				
1. Front vault - side horse	•			
2. Flank vault - side horse	•			
3. Rear vault - side horse		•		
4. Squat vault - side horse		•		
5. Straddle vault - side horse			•	
6. Straddle vault - long horse			•	
7. Stoop vault - side horse			•	
8. Squat vault - long horse				•
9. Stoop vault - long horse				•
10. Headspring vault - side horse				•
11. Handspring vault - side horse				•
E. Parallel Bars				
1. Cross support hop travel	•			
2. Cross support swings	•			
3. Dismount from forward swing	•			
4. Underarm support swing	•			
5. Glide swing and return	•			
6. Glide swing to piked inverted hang		•		
7. Dismount from backward swing		•		
8. L-support (3 seconds)		•		
9. Shoulder balance (3 seconds)			•	
10. Forward roll from momentary shoulder balance			•	
11. Back uprise			•	
12. Underarm kip to cross support			•	
13. Front uprise				•
14. Glide kip				•
15. Drop kip at end of bars				•
16. Momentary handstand quarter-turn dismount at end of bars				•
17. Combinations and routines	•	•	•	•
F. Horizontal Bars (chest height throughout)				
1. Front support swings (simple cast)	•			
2. Front support-forward roll dismount	•			

SKILLS	I	II	III	IV
3. Front support to stride support	•			
4. Single knee swing up	•			
5. Pullover mount		•		
6. Backward hip circle		•		
7. Underswing dismount		•		
8. Glide swing and return		•		
9. Stride inverted swing			•	
10. Forward stride circle			•	
11. Forward hip circle			•	
12. Piked inverted swing			•	
13. Glide-stride inverted swing to stride support				•
14. Cast-straddle sole dismount				•
15. Glide kip				•
16. Glide-piked inverted swing to rear support				•
17. Combinations and routines	•	•	•	•

H. Relationship of Men's Artistic Gymnastics to Goals and Learning Outcomes

A series of Goals and Learning Outcomes for physical education were developed for the Secondary Physical Education Curriculum and Resource Guide (1980). The relationship of Men's Artistic Gymnastics to the four major goals of this Curriculum Guide is indicated below.

From involvement in Men's Artistic Gymnastics:
1. Participants should demonstrate a greater degree of fitness with visible improvements in power, flexibility, coordination and endurance.
2. Participants should demonstrate a development of efficient and effective motor skills.
3. Participants should demonstrate a greater understanding of the sport of Artistic Gymnastics as an expressive art form.
4. Participants should demonstrate improvement in such qualities as discipline, courage, initiative and creativity. They should demonstrate improved responsibility and should be able to work within a group setting in a manner which is cooperative and which develops a positive and enthusiastic attitude toward Artistic Gymnastics.

Chapter Two
Preparation

A. Conditioning for Gymnastics

Progress in gymnastics occurs not only through practicing gymnastic skills but through the development of certain physical attributes such as power (strength and speed), flexibility, balance, orientation, coordination, rhythm and endurance.

By learning gymnastic skills these qualities are improved, and conversely, by developing power, flexibility, etc. the level of gymnastics performance is improved.

No gymnast can hope to progress far in his sport if all he does is attempt skills on the floor and on apparatus. He will eventually find that he has insufficient power for one skill—that his legs refuse to straddle wide enough in another—that a series of skills leave him exhausted—or that he is unable to coordinate the movements of his body in the necessary manner. These are messages indicating that his body is ill-prepared and that his physical preparation has been insufficient.

The physical attributes mentioned above can be improved not only in the gymnastics lesson, but also in other classes. Conditioning for a variety of sports can complement the preparation necessary for raising gymnastic performance. However, the overall effect of an emphasis on conditioning is improvement in all sports and not only in gymnastics.

In any school gymnastics program the instructor is faced with severe time limitations. Because of this restriction the following suggestions are made:

  a) Concentrate on improving power and flexibility, as the two most important items in gymnastic conditioning.
  b) Understand the principles for increasing power and flexibility and prepare a wide repertoire of activities which will develop these qualities.
  c) Repetition (without boredom) is the key to improvement.

1. Power

Power is a combination of strength and speed and is one of the most important physical attributes necessary in gymnastics performance. Most gymnastic skills depend on an ability to move the body or body parts fast, and this demands the simultaneous application of strength and speed. Any strength activity performed quickly is thus more beneficial (in a gymnastics sense) than the same activity performed slowly. In this way power and explosiveness is developed which is important in so many gymnastic skills. Simply stated a push-up (or press-up) should be performed with as much punch and vigor as possible—never slowly.

What should occur if participants cannot perform a single pull-up or push-up? In this case, the exercises must be modified so that the same muscle-groups are being worked in an easier manner.

It is unfortunate that, for some youngsters, such exercises must be adjusted to the point where the resistance placed on the muscles is minimal. But at least it is a start and by progressively increasing the demand placed on the muscles, progress can be made.

Illustrations #1, #2, and #3 on page 14 show pull-ups being performed in three ways. The most difficult is #3 where the legs are unsupported and the gymnast has to pull his full weight. Obviously modifications have to be made for those unable to perform a single repetition in this manner. Suggestions are shown in illustrations #1 and #2.

One of the characteristics of gymnastics is the emphasis it places on the upper body. With the exception of vaulting and tumbling which also demand power in the legs, events such as the rings, parallel bars, horizontal bar, and pommel horse stress the upper body. These events also emphasize the need to have a favorable power-bodyweight ratio. In simple terms every extra kilogram of bodyweight has to be counteracted by a considerable increase in power.

Diet is also very important. The motto for all gymnastics is "Thin is in" which for the average student means that a loss of 2-5 kilograms in bodyweight translates into improved gymnast performance. An increase in power coupled with a loss in bodyweight brings many more skills within reach and also improves safety. Amongst other things a stronger gymnast has better control and will fall less dangerously than a weaker and heavier gymnast.

An instructor who is restricted by time and is forced to choose certain body "areas" to emphasize in the conditioning program, should concentrate on the following:

  a) Improve participants' "pull-push power" (i.e. triceps, biceps, latissimus, pectorals, deltoids, etc.)
  b) Improve the power of their abdominal muscles.

Any additional time should be spent working on other areas of the body, particularly the legs and back.

Illustrations #'s 1-18 offer some suggestions for increasing strength and power. There are limitless other methods and exercises by which the same muscle groups can be strengthened, for example by weight training, partner combatives where one pulls against the resistance of another, or by repetitions of gymnastic skills. The following is offered as a guide in planning an exercise schedule.

a) Modify the exercise so that the individual can repeat it 6-8 times in a row. Of these repetitions the last 2-3 are performed with difficulty but with good form. Rest (no more than a minute) and repeat each set of repetitions two times. As the gymnast improves in power adjust the exercise so that it is more difficult. Controlled overload is the key. This means progressively increasing the repetitions, reducing the rest pause, and increasing the number of sets.
b) Whenever possible work the muscle groups through their full range of movement.
c) Never neglect flexibility in favor of power, or vice versa. Too much work on power alone has a tendency to reduce flexibility and range of movement. The gymnast must be powerful *and* limber. Few gymnastic skills demand one without the other.

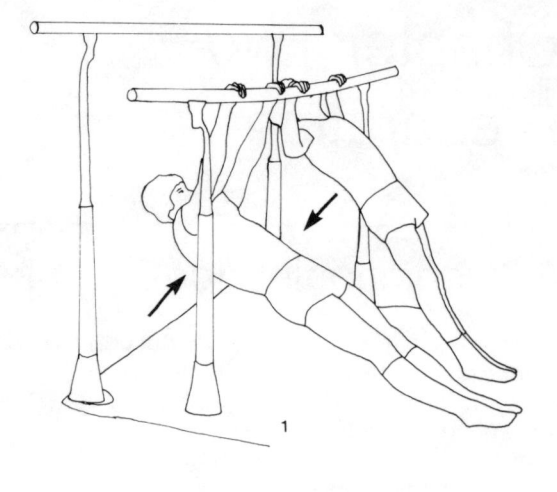

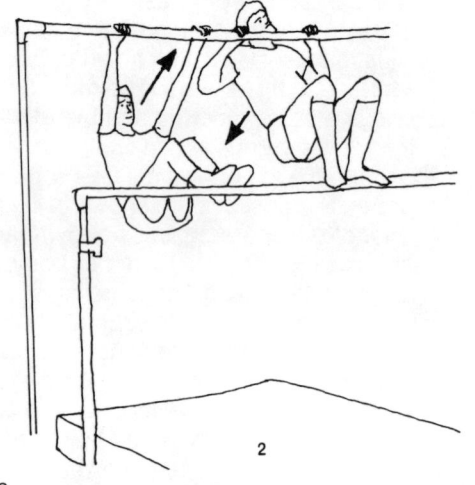

Illustrations #1, 2, 3
Exercises for developing pulling power. Illustrations #1 and 2 show a modification of the pull-up (illustration #3). Further adjustments can be made by changing the hand hold to undergrip.

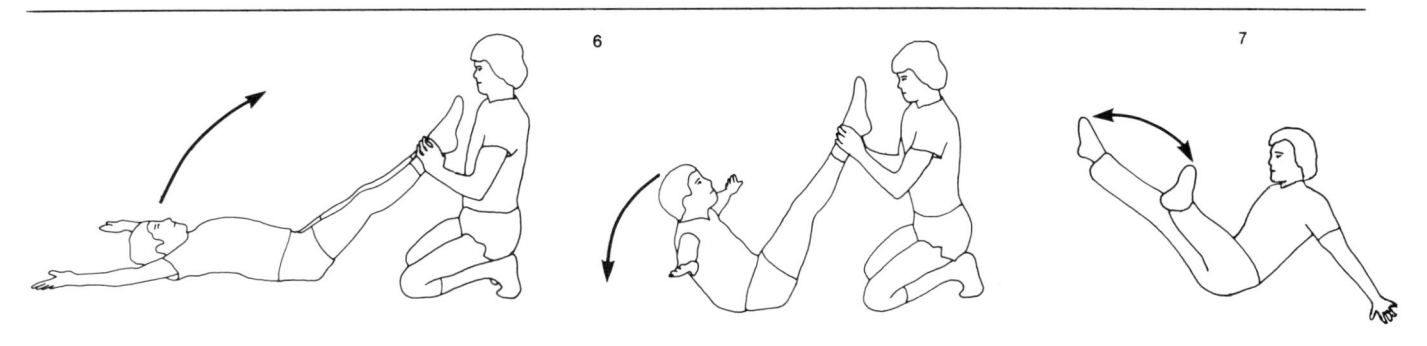

Illustrations #4, 5, 6, 7.
Variations in developing abdominal strength. Illustrations #4 and 5 can be modified by bending the legs. Illustration #6 shows repetitions of V-Sit. In #7 the performer holds a V position and opens and closes the legs. Lower the legs to 3" from the floor and repeat. Increase the number of repetitions.

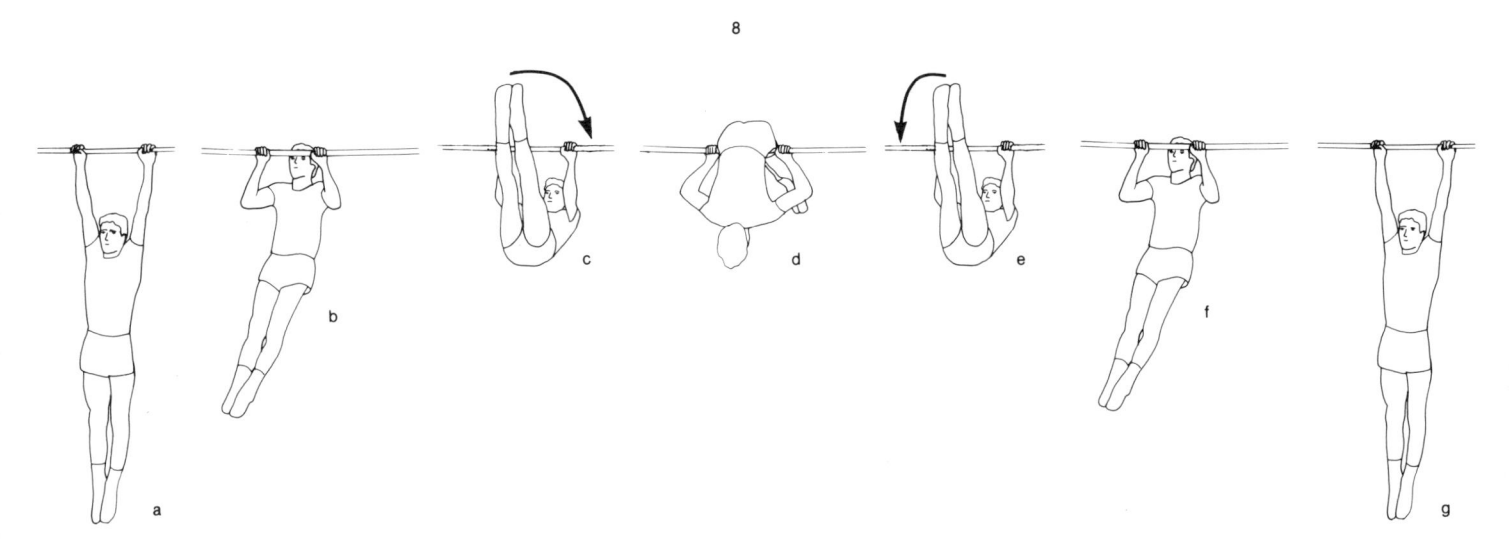

Illustration #8
This is a real challenge. Pull up-pull over to position 'd', lower down forward and repeat. Modify the exercise by bending the legs, or lower the bar and allow a slight push from the floor.

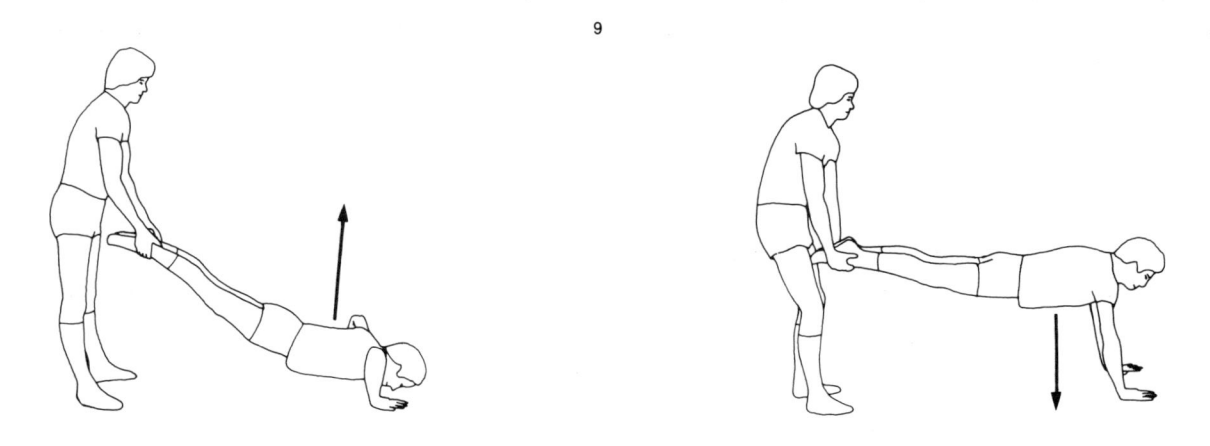

Illustration #9
Push-ups. Raise the legs to make it more difficult. Push-ups in the handstand position will provide the greatest challenge.

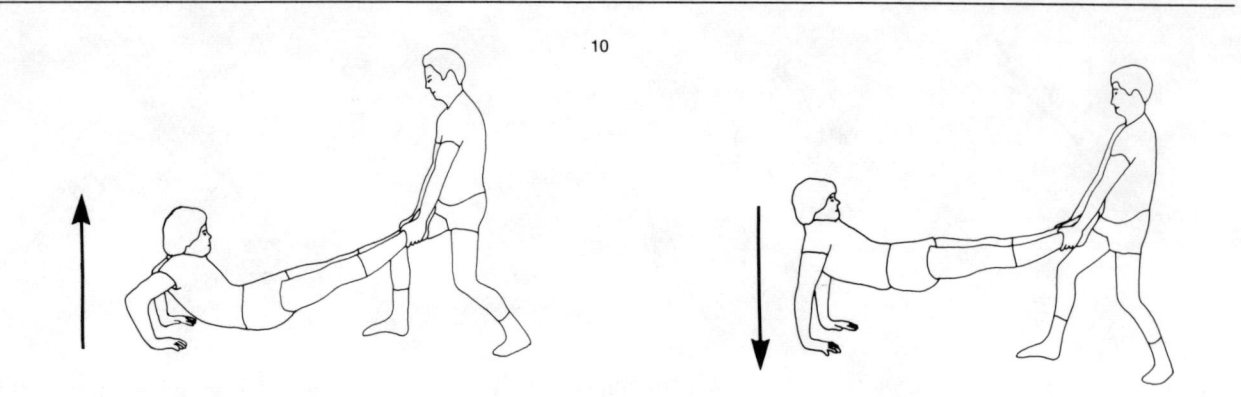

Illustration #10
A variation of the push-up. This also improves shoulder flexibility.

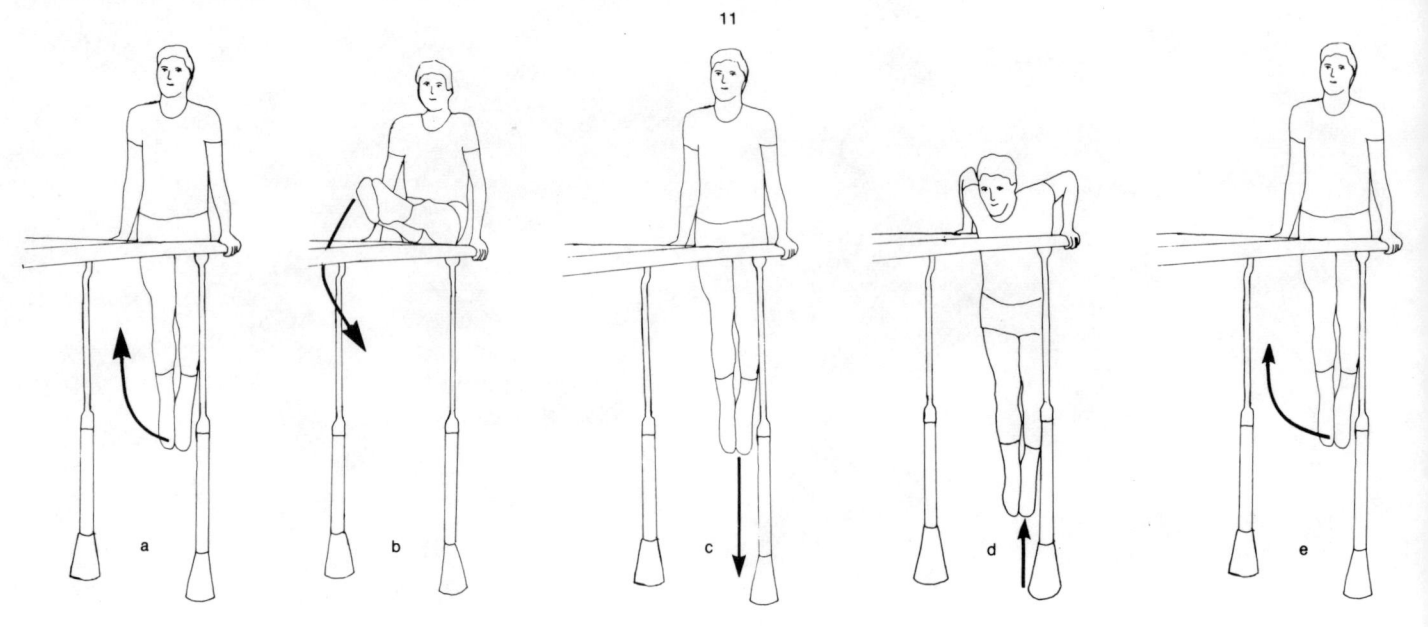

Illustration #11
An exercise for developing pushing power and abdominal strength. Raise the legs, lower the legs, dip, return to cross support, and repeat the whole sequence. To increase the difficulty hold the L-Sit position for a count of three during each repetition.

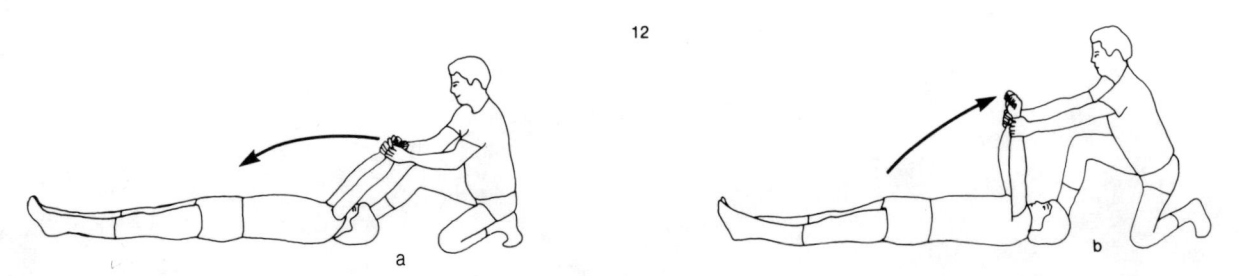

Illustration #12
A partner exercise for developing shoulder strength. In illustration 'a' the partner resists the downward pull of the arms. In illustration 'b' the partner resists the upward press of the arms. This form of shoulder strength is particularly important in gymnastics.

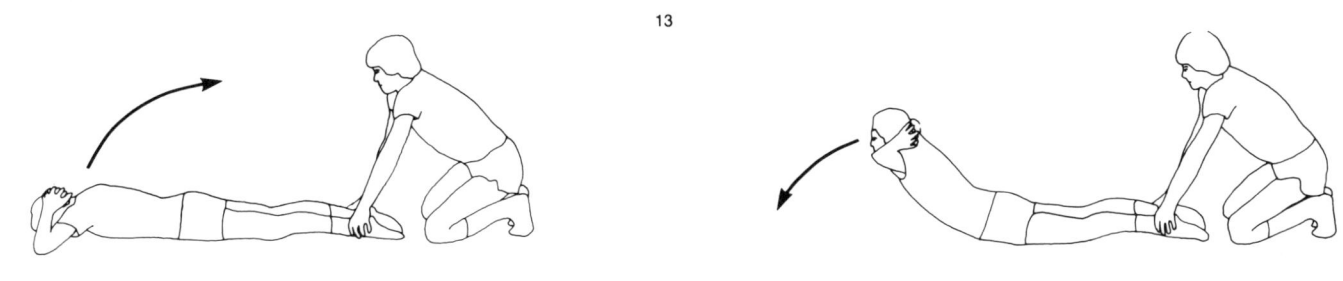

Illustration #13
A partner exercise for developing the muscles of the back. Perform the same exercise over a bench to increase the range of movement.

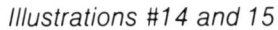

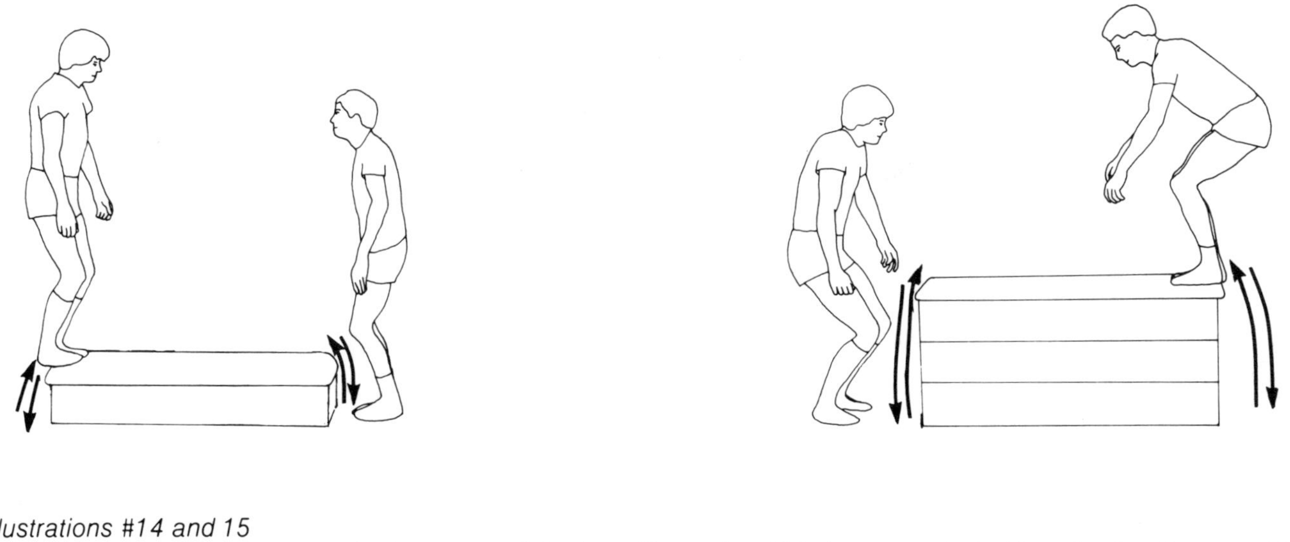

Illustrations #14 and 15
Exercises for developing the explosive power of the legs. Illustration #14 shows two-footed jumping for distance. All jumping activities particularly those used by triple jumpers are excellent for developing leg power. Illustration #15 shows a partner competition for repetition two-footed jumping on and off a box. The box is progressively increased in height.

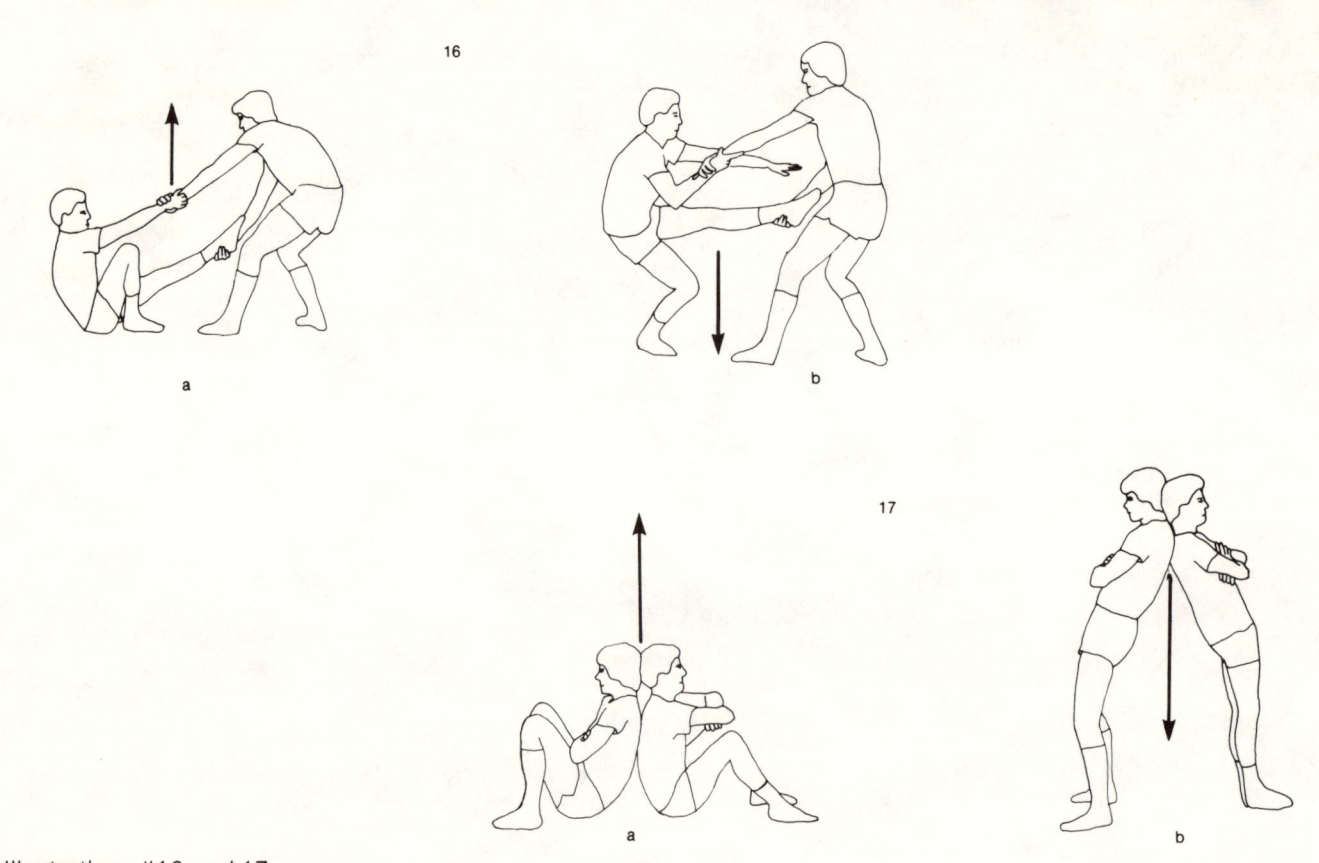

Illustrations #16 and 17
Partner activities for increasing leg strength. How many times can you raise and lower using one leg without a partner assisting?

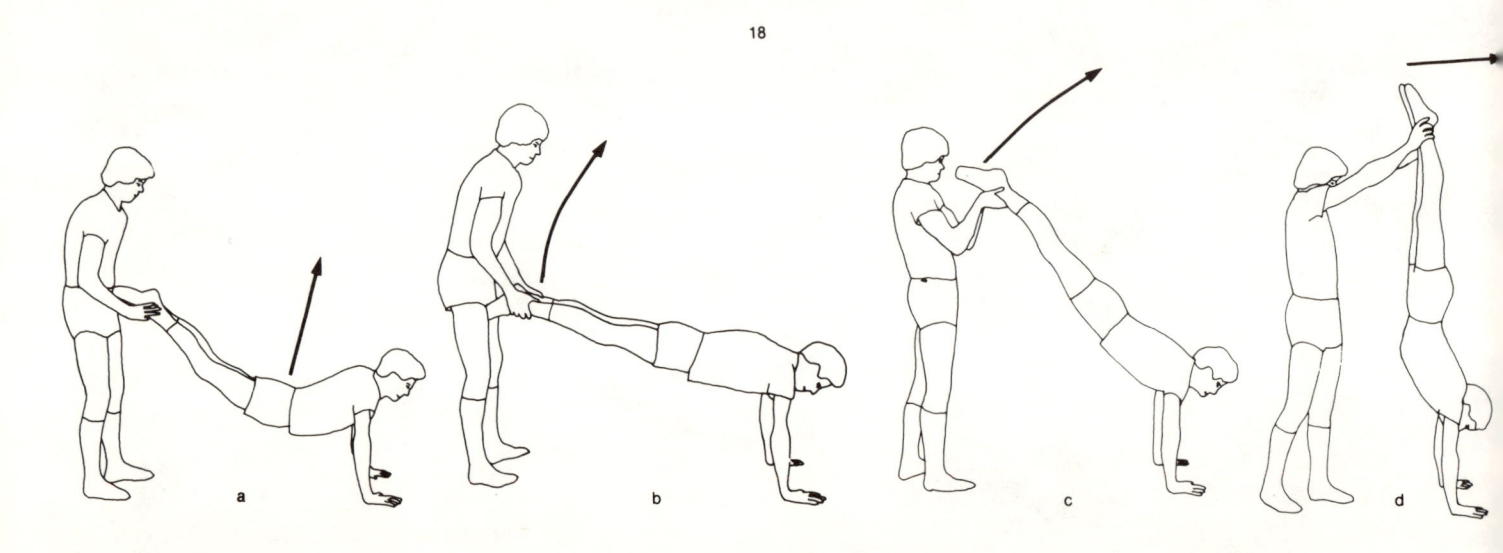

Illustration #18
This is an activity for improving the ability to maintain body position. Illustration 'a' shows the performer with the hips sagging low to the ground. Illustration 'b' shows the hips elevated and the body brought into alignment. The performer must now maintain this alignment while his partner lifts him into the handstand position. This activity also teaches control and orientation.

2. Flexibility

Like power, flexibility is extremely important in gymnastics. Many gymnastic skills simply cannot be performed without a high level of flexibility. In addition, flexibility adds to the aesthetic quality of a gymnastic performance, and equally important, provides the gymnast with an added margin of safety against injury.

The following are three basic methods of improving flexibility:

a) Static Stretching

In static stretching the performer assumes a position which stretches a group of muscles and their associated ligaments and maintains that position for a set time period. In a class situation 10-15 seconds is adequate.

b) Dynamic or Ballistic Stretching

This method requires repeated movements (often bouncing) in and out of the stretched position such as using repeated high kicks in the fashion of a can-can dancer. Although known to increase flexibility, ballistic stretching is not recommended in a school situation because of the difficulty in controlling the vigor of the ballistic action.

c) Partner Assisted Stretching

This method incorporates the use of a partner to assist in stretching. Assistance can be provided in three ways.

i Passive Stretching
In this method the partner helps by providing additional pressure on the area being stretched. Illustration #5 shows the performer in a straddle-sit position working to increase flexibility in the hip-groin and lower back area. His partner assists by providing pressure in the middle and lower back.

ii Stretch and Maintain
Using the exercise shown in illustration #5, the partner assists in pressing the performer forward, and at the greatest range of movement the performer attempts to hold that position without his partner's assistance.

iii Press and Relax
Using the exercise shown in illustration #5, the performer relaxes forward as far as possible. The partner now provides resistance at that point as the performer attempts to press *back* and out of the stretched position. After pressing backward the performer relaxes forward to a new and greater stretch position, and the sequence of pressing back and relaxing forward is repeated anew.

With the exception of the ballistic method, stretching is usually performed slowly. All types of stretching require an excellent warm-up of lighter, non-stressful activities, and during stretching a definite effort must be made to relax and breath normally.

Of the methods described above the "Press and Relax" technique is considered the most effective for increasing flexibility. Its disadvantage lies in the time taken to work through a series of exercises. Those exercises in which an individual works alone can be performed much faster and this largely compensates for their lack of effectiveness in relation to the "Press and Relax" method.

Work on flexibility demands good organization and seriousness on the part of gymnastics students. Flexibility exercises should not become an opportunity for wasting time or an activity loathed by every member of the class. The instructor must aim for variety and instill in the students a genuine interest in improving their individual level of flexibility.

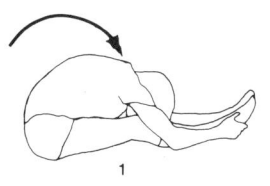

Illustrations #1 and 2
Exercises for developing hip flexion. Hold the ankles or feet. Pull-hold-relax and repeat.

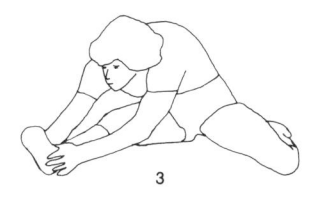

Illustration #3
The familiar hurdler's exercise. The angle between the legs should be 90 degrees. Stretch forward to the leading leg, stretch toward the knee of the flexed trailing leg. Change legs and repeat.

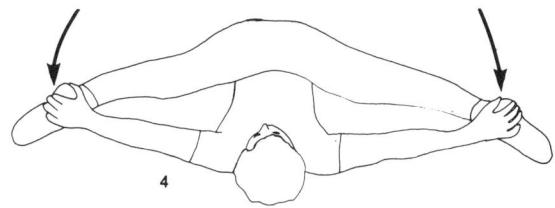

Illustration #4
A straddle stretch in back lying position. Keep the legs straight. Press the legs apart and pull the ankles downward.

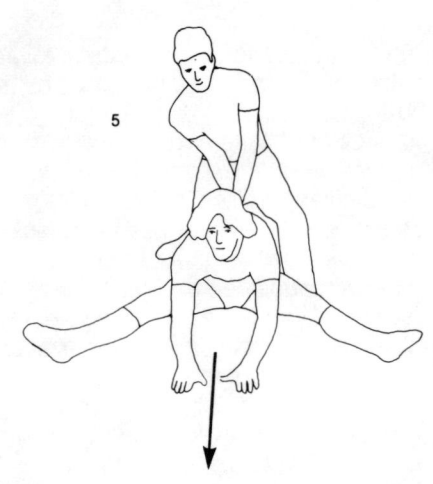

Illustration #5
Straddle as wide as possible and press forward with partner assistance. Use the "Press and Relax" method described on page 19.

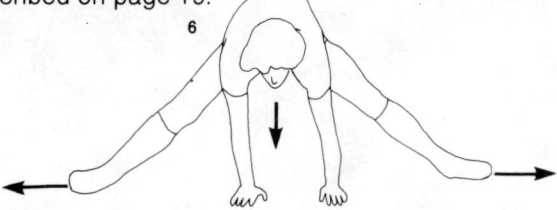

Illustration #6
Straddle splits sideways. Press the feet sideways, hold and relax. Then repeat. Use the arms to control the lowering of the body.

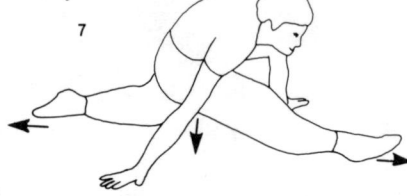

Illustration #7
Stride splits forward and backward. Press the legs forward and backward. Hold the position, relax, and repeat. Use the arms to control the lowering of the body. Change legs.

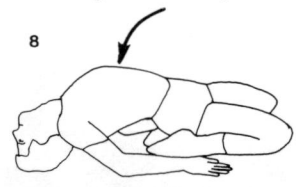

Illustration #8
An exercise for stretching the quadriceps. Control the lowering of upper body backward with the arms.

Illustration #9a and 9b
The "bridge" or "back arch". This exercise increases shoulder and hip flexibility. Assume the position shown in illustration #9a. Drop the head backward and press upward. Keep the feet flat. Press the body in the direction of the arrow.

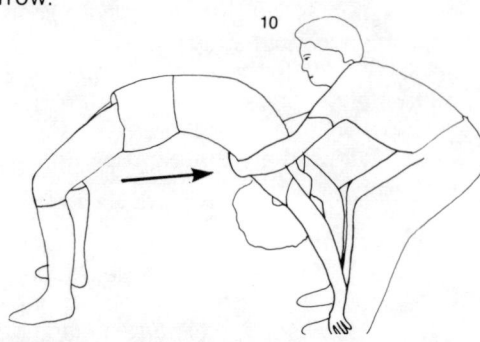

Illustration #10
The same exercise as #9a-9b but with partner assistance. The partner supports under the shoulders and pulls the performer GENTLY toward him. Emphasis is on increasing shoulder flexibility.

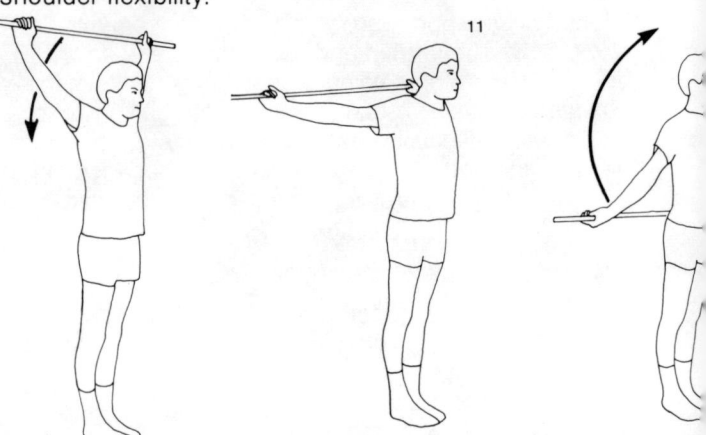

Illustration #11
A simple exercise for improving shoulder flexibility. With each session work the hands closer together.

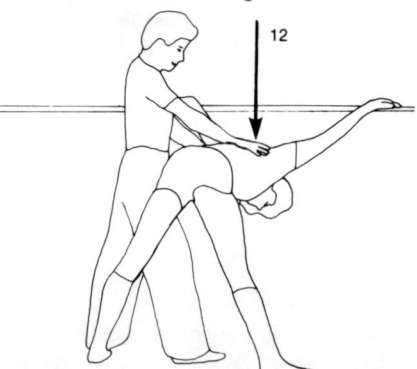

Illustration #12
The performer places his wrists on a bar or any apparatus set at chest height. The partner presses down between the shoulder blades. This exercise improves shoulder flexibility.

The flexibility exercises illustrated above are no more than a sample of the many exercises that are available. For further references see Appendix I.

3. Balance

The ability to balance is continuously being challenged in gymnastics. In its simplest form the performer must maintain stability during and at the completion of a skill. In its advanced form the competitive gymnast must be able to swing to a handstand on the rings and hold the handstand with as little motion as possible. Whatever the level of performance, the maintenance of balance demands considerable concentration and practice. Examples for the development of balance for beginners are listed below:

a) Run, jump, or, hop forward and backward on a bench or low beam.
b) Complete four forward rolls in succession and follow these immediately by standing at attention.
c) Stand erect and rotate five times around the long axis of the body and follow this immediately by balancing on one foot.
d) Hold a V-Sit for 2-3 seconds, lower legs to new position and repeat.
e) Hold a headstand and slowly lower the legs to horizontal and then return to vertical.

4. Orientation and Coordination

One of the demands of gymnastics is the ability to control the body even when it is placed in unfamiliar positions, such as with the feet above the head. Frequently we are required to move the arms and legs simultaneously in different directions. The ability to "know where one is" and to control body movements comes only with considerable practice. There are many activities for developing the basic elements of orientation and coordination. Some examples are given below:

a) Carry out a series of warm-up activities to the beat of the latest popular music. This can be done by making up a tape of music in which allowance is made for explanation and demonstration of the required exercise. Vary the music and the exercises.
b) Place groups of elementary skills together in a series. The students must roll, stand, half-turn, balance and so on according to a prescribed beat.
c) Practice a series of light strength and power activities to the beat of music. Demonstrate the sequence and in particular indicate the number of beats taken by the change from one activity to the next. Adjust each activity so that all can join in.

5. Endurance

Endurance is more readily associated with the long distance runner yet it is an important factor in gymnastics. The gymnast with endurance is able to train longer without becoming exhausted, and is able to perform a single or series of skills without losing control because of fatigue. In a nutshell, the gymnast with endurance needs less rest and consequently is able to train or perform at a higher level for a greater length of time.

Endurance is developed in a number of ways. Each method is characterized by repetitious exercise and continuous movement. Like power, endurance demands an "overload," placed not only on the muscles of the legs, chest, arms, etc. but also on the heart and lungs. Deep breathing is characteristic of endurance exercises. Some examples:

1. Relay races in which team members repetitiously carry each other. (Make them fun but make them safe.)
2. Power exercises in which the work load is reduced so 15-20 repetitions can be performed quickly and with good technique. The last five repetitions are performed under moderate stress. Repeat three times with minimal rest in between each set.
3. Rope climbing one to one and a half meters above arms reach and traveling back and forth from one rope to the next. A set of six ropes makes this a good endurance activity.

B. Safety Techniques and Spotting

It is the responsibility of the instructor to make the teaching environment as safe as possible. This is done by:

1. Making sure that equipment is in good order and used in a manner that reduces risk to a minimum.
2. Using carefully selected progressions for the teaching of each gymnastic skill.
3. Teaching safety techniques and spotting as an integral part of each gymnastic lesson.

It demands effort and organization to teach not only the progressions for a skill but also the spotting. In effect two jobs are being done at once. The performer is shown what he must do. His partners are then given their duties so that the performer can attempt the skill, or lead-up safely and without risk.

Spotting techniques vary from skill to skill and are modified as the performer becomes more accomplished. The beginner is initially given firm physical aid. The advanced performer, however, may be given help which is little more than a light touch at a critical phase of the skill. At all levels of performance, support can occur while the performer is in the air, on the floor, or in contact with the apparatus.

Basic spotting techniques (in which the spotters grasp the performer and give firm support) can be taught progressively to a class at the same time as they learn the related gymnastic skill. The basic principles of these spotting techniques are simple, easy to grasp, and often repeated from skill to skill and from apparatus to apparatus. Spotting improves if certain principles are followed. The most important of these are outlined below:

1. Repetition is the key to learning

This statement does not imply that participants are bored with endless repetitions of one skill and its associated spotting technique. Rolling and balancing, for example, can be taught as separate skills, and then reinforced in simple combinations and "routines" of two or three skills. Spotting techniques are reinforced as assistance is given in these "routines." The task of the spotter will be made easier by the fact that spotting techniques vary far less than the movements required in gymnastic skills. Reinforcement of support and hand positions will also occur as the instructor works from one lead-up to the next in the teaching progression.

At the initial stages of instruction, the physical demands of skills will be minimal. In those cases where support is given, there will be no danger if the spotter makes an error because the skill will have minimal risk. Like the person performing the skill, the spotter can try again and learn correctly.

It is insufficient for an instructor to demonstrate a gymnastic skill and then casually remark that spotters "lift here and here. . . ." Even though it takes additional time, spotting techniques must also be demonstrated so that the entire flow of skill and spotting technique is well understood. Spotters should understand where to stand or kneel in relation to the performer, where to hold, and what their duties are until the skill is fully complete.

Good spotting habits are established through practice on elementary skills. The instructor should supervise the whole class as it works in pairs or threes. Skill and spotting technique are repeated and spotters and performers rotate until both skill and spotting technique are well understood. At this level an understanding of the responsibility of the spotter is developed.

2. Introducing Spotting

The mechanics of spotting can be introduced in warm-ups and game situations. The instructor does not have to be teaching gymnastics in order to introduce spotting techniques. Many games and partner activities require participants to lift, move, roll, and carry one another. By selecting activities which progress from static lifting to supporting and resisting a moving body, students quickly learn timing, body positioning, and the correct mechanics of lifting. This experience is then carried over into spotting in gymnastics.

3. Working in Groups

The formation of groups should maximize the learning of both skill and spotting technique. Whether the students work in pairs or form larger groups, certain factors such as height, weight, sex, and reliability must be taken into account. The following are good general "rules" to follow:

a) Partner tall with tall, small with small.

Tall students spotting a shorter classmate will often support at too great a height and in a skill such as a handspring can pitch the performer forward onto his face.

b) Partner heavy performers with those who are capable of supporting them.

A heavyweight will collapse the support of lighter, weaker spotters, and a tall spotter partnered with someone much shorter produces unbalanced and unstable support.

c) Where possible have females spot females and males spot males.

Males are usually stronger than females and although two males will provide good spotting for a female, a male and a female will frequently provide unbalanced spotting (too much support on the male's side) causing the performer to twist sideways. In most cases two females will not be strong enough to support heavier males but give adequate support for those who are lighter.

d) Avoid partnering or grouping several poor performers together.

Poor performers will often be stimulated to greater effort by being partnered with others of better ability, whereas grouping poor performers together can produce less progress.

e) Avoid partnering or grouping students who are known discipline problems.

Poorly disciplined students placed together in a group invite horse-play and accidents. Where possible groups should be formed in which a poorer performer will be encouraged by those who are of better ability. A single undisciplined student is less likely to disrupt a group of enthusiastic learners than if he were set in a group with more of his kind.

Obviously an instructor cannot hope to satisfy all these suggestions in any one class. However, he should change partners and shift students from one group to the next until satisfactory arrangement has been made and optimal progress is achieved.

4. Class Control

Team spirit should be promoted within groups and good spotting rewarded by the instructor. Too often the task of spotting is an excuse for a casual attitude to develop and an opportunity for horse-play. How often is the performer in an inverted position made the butt of practical jokes! Such situations stem in part from a lack of value placed on spotting as well as poor class control. The instructor who has poor control when working with the whole class will have greater disorganization when the class is split into groups. Learning is minimal and there is an increase in the likelihood of accidents. A high value placed on spotting increases the level of safety, and need not in any way detract from the enjoyment of gymnastic performance.

Spotting can be increased in value in two ways:

a) By de-emphasizing the need to perform skills alone and instead, insisting that skills are correctly performed with assistance.

b) By using a system of reward based on the performance of the group, performer, and spotters combined. (See Chapter Five - Evaluation).

These regulations do not mean that young gymnasts are denied the ultimate thrill of performing a skill alone. Rather they are encouraged to perform a skill alone only when they are considered ready and capable of doing so. The decision should be made only by the instructor. This removes a "devil-may-care" or "kamakazi" approach which always causes accidents.

5. Common Spotting Errors

If spotters frequently commit major errors the instructor must immediately determine the cause. Possibly the instructor's teaching progressions were weak. The instructor should ask Did I rush through the teaching progessions for the skill and the spotting technique? Is the skill and its related spotting method beyond their physical ability? Are the students playing around when they spot each other because my class control is weak, or because I have not emphasized good spotting sufficiently? Is the equipment set at the correct height, that is *low* enough to allow the student to attempt the skill with the maximum of safety! At the risk of repetition, if the instructor establishes good control, and uses well conceived teaching progressions for the skill and the spotting technique, the gymnastics class will become virtually accident free. There is always an element of risk in sport, but good teaching removes all but the most inopportune error.

The following illustrations show common spotting errors. These mistakes will be successfully eliminated if correct spotting techniques are emphasized throughout the program.

a) *Leaning away from the performer and offering weak support. No real commitment to the performer*

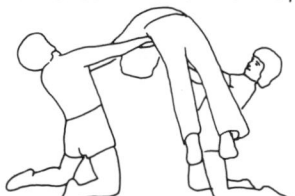

Illustration #13
In this handspring the spotters are leaning away from the performer. The further away they place themselves the weaker their support. Spotters should lean the head away but keep close to the performer and support on the upper arm where they have more strength.

Illustration #14

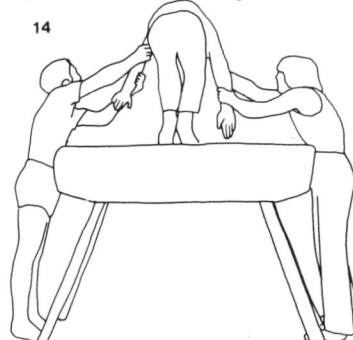

Illustration #14
Spotters standing at the end of the vaulting horse cannot spot satisfactorily. They must get as close to the performer as possible, in this case, on the post-flight side of the horse. This illustration also demonstrates a mix-up in handholds used by the spotters.

Uncertainty often causes spotters to shift away from the performer. Yet the further away the spotters place themselves, the weaker and more inefficient their support. In reverse, the closer the spotter to the performer, the stronger the support. The mechanics of lifting apply to spotting as much as they do to lifting and carrying any heavy object: namely, where possible, the spotters should straddle their legs, have an erect spine, and get as close to the performer as possible. This must be done without disturbing the flow of the skill. Spotters standing at the ends of the vaulting horse cannot be expected to provide adequate support to a performer passing over the center of the horse. If the performer makes an error, the spotters are in a weak position and too far away to provide adequate assistance.

b) *Forgetting handhold or support positions*

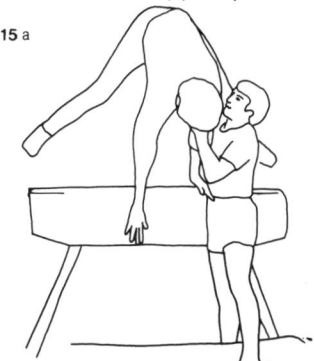

Illustration #15a
The spotter has forgotten how to spot for a straddle vault and in his confusion is spotting for a squat vault. An error such as this can also occur through lack of communication between spotter and performer.

Illustration #15b
Spotters in illustration #1 are providing support for a shoulder balance-forward roll on the parallel bars. Should they forget to shift their support position they will suffer a painful learning experience. Once they have spotted the shoulder balance they must shift their

support so that their arms are beneath the bars (illustration #2). In this way they can comfortably spot the forward roll.

Some of the more advanced spotting techniques demand a quick shift of handholds on the part of the spotters and require considerable repetition before they become familiar. However, most spotting techniques follow a common pattern:
  i) Support is given near the performer's center of weight.
  ii) The upper body is controlled and protected. This usually means that one hand supports near the middle of the body (often under the seat), and the other grips the upper arm or shoulder, and supports and controls the movement of the upper body. Though these common principles appear in most spotting techniques, variations do occur and spotters can forget their duties.

Spotters are liable to forget handholds if:
  i) Too many spotting variations have been taught in too short a time period.
  ii) The performer enters the skill at too great a speed. The spotter then becomes flustered and confused.
  iii) Constant changes from spotting on the right side to spotting on the left side of the performer confuse the spotter.
  iv) The performer begins the approach run without communicating to the spotters exactly what skill is going to be attempted.
  v) The spotters stand too far away from the correct spotting position and are forced to rush to apply handholds.
  vi) The spotters have only a vague idea of what is entailed in the actual skill.

c) *Failing to move with the performer through the skill*

Illustration #16
In this squat vault, the spotters have made no allowance for the post-flight of the vault (that is, that the vaulter will travel through the air and cover distance from above the horse to the landing). By gripping the performer and not moving with him during the post-flight they place severe strain on the performer's shoulder joints.

Spotters must realize that the performer is moving quickly and covers distance into and out of a skill. To grip the performer on the vaulting box and not move through the post-flight, means that the upper part of the performer's body is arrested suddenly, often painfully. Spotters must step along the mat making allowance for the performer's movement. In this way they control the performer comfortably and safely. The same principle applies on the floor and for all apparatus where there is considerable movement in and out of the skill.

d) *Over-estimating the performer's ability*

Illustration #17
The spotter in this illustration is applying an advanced spotting technique used to help the performers who have minor problems with a handspring (see page 69). The performer has not yet learned to maintain an extended body position which destroys the effectiveness of the spotting technique. In this case the spotter has badly over-estimated the ability of the performer.

Errors in spotting often occur when spotters are unfamiliar with the performer's ability. One spotter may provide support when there should have been two, or a technique is used which does not give adequate support relative to the performer's ability. The gymnast who has a poor body position in the handspring—ducking the head and rolling—cannot be supported adequately by a single spotter. Spotting techniques vary in the degree of support they provide and must be appropriate to the level of performance. The simplest method to apply in a situation where there is some uncertainty about the performer's ability is to work through the lead-up stages applying the appropriate spotting.

e) *Over-spotting*

Illustration #18
Spotters in this handspring have supported the performer at too great a height. As a result her feet are not set down

correctly and she is thrown forward.

Over-spotting can occur in several ways. Tall spotters can rotate a small performer through a handspring at such a height that the performer is still well above the ground when the skill is completed. If better balanced groups cannot be set up, tall spotters must straddle their legs wide so that the performer is supported at the correct level. Spotters must remember that their duty is to provide the right amount of support and not to accelerate the performer through the skill or to vigorously lift upward. A good rule of thumb is to keep the beginner's approach run short, and speed of movement to a minimum. As a result spotters work more slowly, with greater control, and with great confidence.

f) *No regard for the final stabilization of the performer*

Illustration #19
Spotters have tossed the performer through the handspring with no regard for his landing position. The duties of the spotters do not cease halfway through the skill. The correct landing position of the performer is as important as any other part of the skill.

The duties of the spotters are not over until the skill is complete and the performer has ceased moving. Many spotters content themselves with supporting the first portion of a skill and care little for the final section. Spotters must maintain contact with the performer throughout the skill and stabilize him at its completion. In vaulting this may mean that there is a transference of responsibility from spotters on the pre-flight side of the box to those on the post-flight side.

g) *Poor arrangement of spotters*

Illustration #20
In this illustration spotters are badly arranged for supporting a handspring. The spotter on the right is much taller and the performer is liable to twist or slide toward the left side. Where possible spotters should be balanced in height in order to provide comfortable and efficient support.

A student of basketball-player proportions is always difficult to support adequately by classmates who are considerably shorter in height. Similarly a heavyweight moving quickly through a skill can generate momentum sufficient to collapse the support provided by lighter and weaker spotters. A tall spotter who is partnered with someone much shorter must squat lower or straddle his legs to reduce the extra height in order to give balanced support with his partner. If this is not done, the performer is inevitably twisted or pushed to one side. As much as possible, the instructor should form groups which are fairly equal in height and weight. A reasonable substitute is to place a light but stronger student in a group with heavier students on the basis that he has the strength to support their weight.

h) *Lack of communication between spotters and performer*

Illustration #21
The performer attempting the handspring has placed his hands on the floor several feet ahead of the spotters. In a kneeling support, spotters cannot correct an error of this nature. Spotters and performer must be taught to work as a team making sure that each member knows what is expected of him.

Poor communication between spotters and performer can occur in several ways. It commonly occurs in vaulting where spotters prepare themselves for one skill and the performer attempts another. Occasionally the spotter on the left side of the performer will provide support in a manner which is different from the partner on the right. With certain spotting techniques, particularly those where the spotters kneel, there is little time for the spotters to adjust their positions. The performer must know the exact position on the mat to attempt the skill if adequate support is to be received.

i) *Spotting on the lower back*

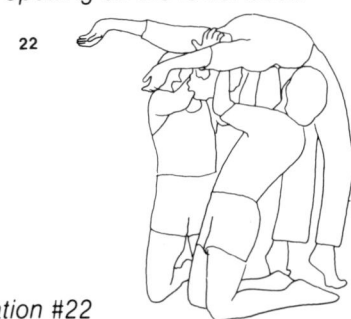

Illustration #22
This illustration shows two spotters supporting a

performer in a handspring. Support has been given in the lower back which has forced the performer's back into a painful hyper-extended position.

So much of spotting requires that support be given at the mid-point of the body, near the center of gravity. Often a spotter will support in the lower back without realizing that this can be extremely painful to the performer. Support should be given under the seat and in this way the performer's back is not forced into an extreme arch.

j) *Setting up the equipment at a height beyond the requirements of the skill or the ability of the performer*

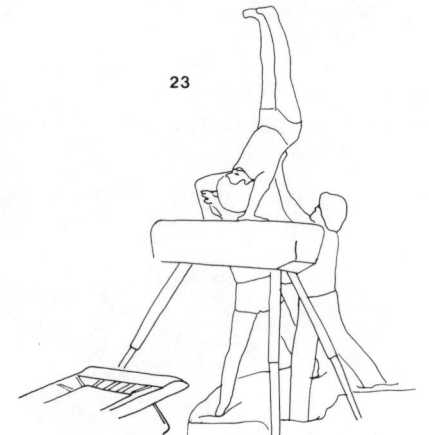

Illustration #23
The performer is attempting a handspring vault on equipment set far too high for his ability. This makes it difficult for both performer and spotters and greatly increases risk.

The height of the equipment should always be controlled by the instructor. In all cases it should be set *as low* as will satisfy the requirements of the skill and the individual build of the performer. Bars, rings, and vaulting horses should adjust in height. Both performance and spotting become increasingly difficult when equipment is set high. Low equipment, good spotting, and adequate matting provide a considerable margin of safety.

Finally the instructor should not give students safety duties which they are incapable of performing because of inexperience. The ability to provide adequate support has to be developed at the same time as the skill is being taught. Spotting is a technique that needs progressive development. In this sense it does not differ from the teaching of gymnastic skills.

C. The Warm-up

The warm-up is a particularly important part of each gymnastics lesson. Its duties are three-fold:
1. It sets the tone of the lesson.
2. It improves the level of safety by warming up muscles, ligaments and joints.
3. It provides the instructor with an opportunity for working through specific conditioning activities with the whole class as a unit.

A gymnastics lesson can be made or destroyed by the spirit and interest developed during the warm-up. By being the first item that occurs in the lesson it can generate enthusiasm by the variety and type of activities chosen. Nothing is more soul-destroying than jumping jacks and push-ups repeated from one lesson to the next, or two or three flexibility exercises which are repeated over and over to the point where participants dread the start of the class. Warm-ups should contain games, combatives, single and partner balances, and strength and power activities which change with each lesson and challenge and excite the students. Flexibility exercises should be developed in intensity from lesson to lesson and never take up the whole warm-up. This applies equally to strength activities.

A warm-up will also improve the level of safety by preparing participants for the dynamic actions that follow during the main part of the class. It is often jokingly said that the warm-up is more important for the instructor than for the students. The demands of spotting place considerable stress on the instructor's "aging" body and it is preferable to lead students through warm-up activities rather than slide into the habit of simply giving verbal commands. This prepares both students and instructor together.

Finally the warm-up will give the instructor the opportunity to work through skills that previously had been part of the main lesson. As the students improve, elementary floor skills can be used as part of the warm-up. This provides continuity to related skills being taught in the main part of the lesson.

D. Readiness

Readiness refers to the individual's capability for performing a particular skill. A typical situation in gymnastics is as follows: A gymnast is attempting a glide kip on the horizontal bar (pages 190-191). Two spotters are assisting. The gymnast is successful and gets up to the final front support position. The spotters remove their assistance and the gymnast now finds he cannot even bring his legs to the bar at the end of the glide. There are three possible reasons for this situation:
1) The gymnast has insufficient strength and flexibility to perform the skill alone.
2) The gymnast has a poor understanding of the movement pattern required.
3) The gymnast lacks in both #1 and #2 above.

Continuous repetition of a skill with two spotters assisting provides an understanding of the movement pattern of the skill. Other than an increase in orientation, little else is provided. When spotters are removed, the inadequacies of the performer simply show themselves again. Such a situation occurs most frequently when an instructor rushes ahead from one skill to the next. Consequently the importance of adequate preparation cannot be overemphasized. The instructor must:
1) Prepare students physically.

2) Work systematically through lead-ups and elementary skills.
3) Teach the movement pattern of the complex skill with full assistance.
4) Systematically remove assistance.
5) Go back and re-work weaknesses in technique and physical preparation where necessary.
6) *Never* give the learner the benefit of the doubt in relation to "readiness."

If the instructor follows these suggestions, a class may not progress as far as the instructor would wish, but students will not experience the frustration of continuous failure which comes from attempting skills which are beyond their ability. Risk also becomes minimal because the young gymnasts are working on skills within their capacity and rate of learning.

E. From Basics To The Refined Performance

The importance of well planned progressions in the teaching of skills and spotting cannot be stressed too highly. Each skill, whatever its level, must be built up carefully from basic movement patterns to the final objective which is a refined and technically correct performance of the skill. Complex skills such as a headspring or handspring should be first broken down into component parts, and the easiest and most basic movements taught first. From these fundamental movements, the instructor carefully works toward the final skill by progressively teaching the more complex actions that are entailed in its performance. Each lead-up is systematically linked to the previous one. Any weakness in the teaching progression will show in the final product. If, for example, the instructor fails to teach a piked headstand with the hips passing well beyond the head and shoulders (see pages 59-62), then this error will inevitably appear when the performer attempts the headspring.

The same principle of careful progression occurs in the use of spotting. Spotters are used to provide the performer with a comfortable, non-injurious attempt at the skill or lead-up. As the performer progresses and learns the movement patterns required, spotters are progressively removed. If, for example, the standard of performance drops dramatically with the shift from two spotters to one spotter (and it is not the fault of the spotter), then the next logical step is to *return* to the two spotter stage and re-practice the skill with the extra assistance. Many students may never progress beyond the two spotter level in some of the more advanced skills. This should not lessen the fun and enjoyment obtained from completing the skill even if it is with the help of two classmates.

Illustrations A#1-7 and the sequences B, C, D, E, and F show the progressive development of two skills, a front vault and a handspring assisted by one spotter.

The front vault is developed from running and jumping over a low box to a front vault in which the body is fully extended and vertical at the mid-point of the skill. At each stage in the progression, the box is gradually built up and the performer works from a low tucked position to one in which the hips are well above the shoulders. Finally the legs are extended for the last stage in the progression. Spotters are used throughout to assist and support the performer.

The sequences B-F show a progression from a handstand through to a handspring assisted by one spotter. In this progression the performer initially works on a handstand which is assisted by two spotters (illustrations B#1-3). He then progresses to a handstand which he enters at speed from a one or two pace approach. A single spotter is now providing assistance (illustrations C#1-3).

Orientation to the handspring movement pattern is initially provided by three spotters who cradle the performer through the complete skill. (illustrations D#1-4) Using the fast entry to the handstand which was learnt earlier, the performer now practices the complete handspring with two spotters assisting (illustrations F#1-3) With an improvement in technique one spotter is removed and the remaining spotter adjusts his position to assist the performer through the skill.

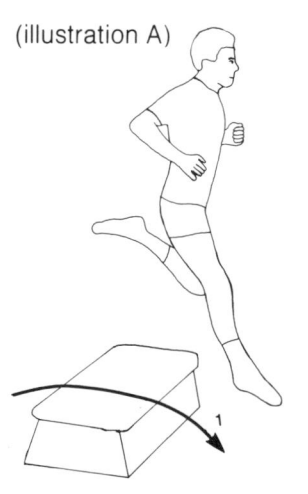

(illustration A)

A Progression of Skills Leading to a Front Vault

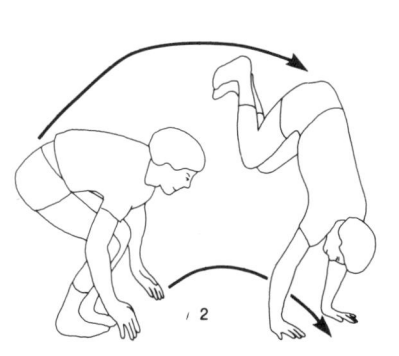

1. Running and jumping over a low box
2. Momentary tucked handstand
3. Jumping back and forth over a low box
4. Tucked front vault over a low box-high hip position

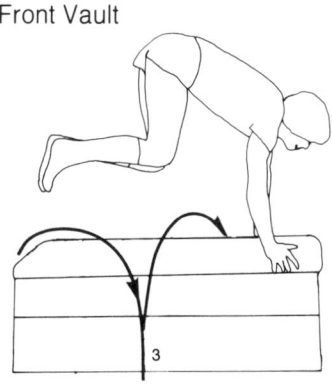

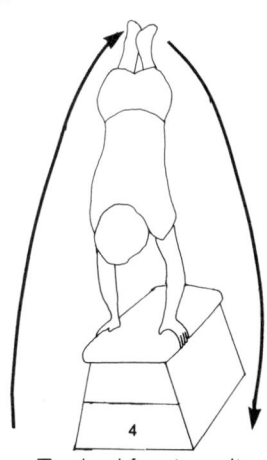

Tucked front vault– higher box–low hip position

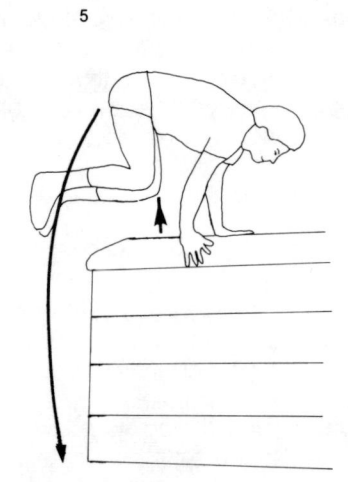

Tucked front vault high hip position

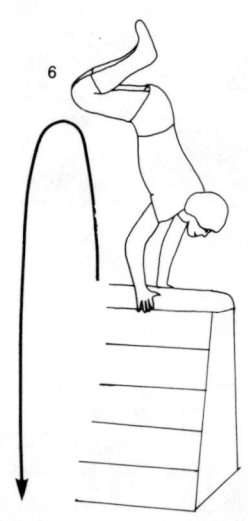

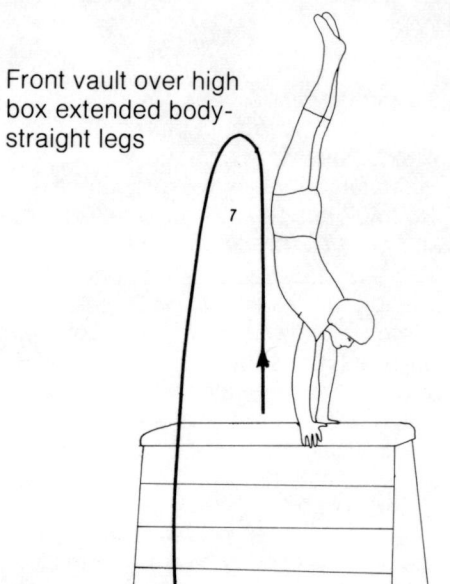

Front vault over high box extended body– straight legs

From a Handstand With Maximum Support to a Handspring Assisted By One Spotter

A Handstand Assisted by Two Spotters

(illustration B)

A Fast Entry Into A Handstand With One Spotter Assisting

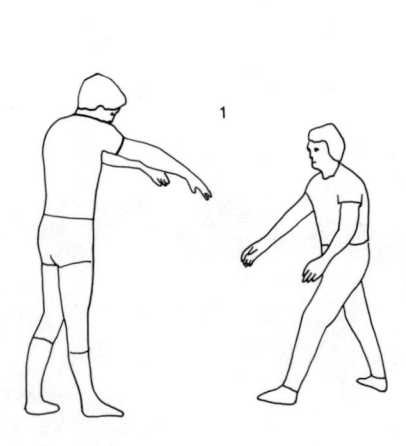

(illustration C)

Orientation to the Handspring Movement Pattern

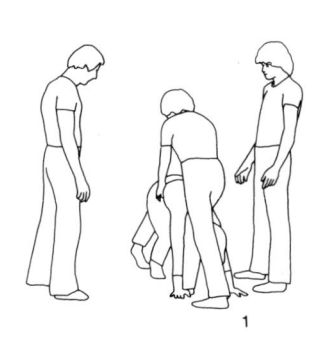

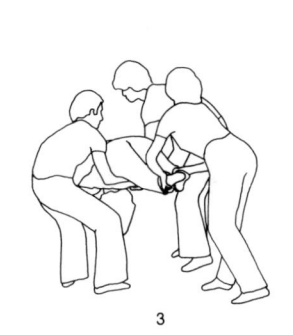

(illustration D)

A Handspring With Two Spotters Assisting.

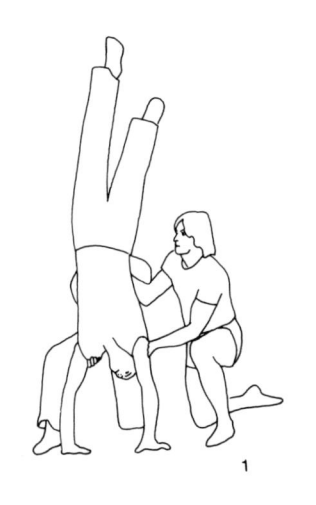

(illustration E)

A Handspring With One Spotter Assisting

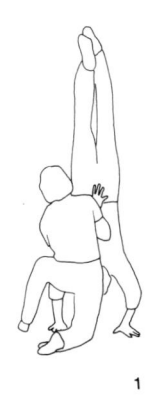

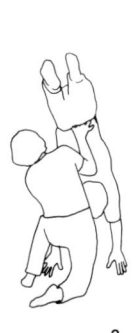

(illustration F)

Chapter Three
Skill Development and Teaching Techniques

A. Floor Exercises and Tumbling

General Safety

Note: **It is imperative to study the sections entitled "Lead-up skills" and "This skill leads to" before reading the material headed "Teaching Techniques and Observation Points."**

TEACHING TECHNIQUES AND OBSERVATION POINTS

1. As a general rule, floor exercise areas should have firm matting with soft absorbent mats or crash pads for landings. Old fashioned fiber mats are more of a detriment than an aid, and can cause burns and abrasions. Similarly, mats in which the filling has shifted are dangerous and are often responsible for twisted ankles. When mats are placed together no gaps should remain and they should not slide on the gymnasium floor. Once the gymnastics class is over, mats should be carried rather than dragged, and stacked carefully. This increases their life expectancy.
2. The crash pad has greatly increased safety in gymnastics. However even the best crash pad can produce instability and spotters will often stumble when trying to move quickly on them. It is a good policy to put a thin but stiff mat on top of the crash pad. This provides a more stable surface, yet does not reduce its absorbent qualities. Netting with rubber chip filling should be avoided. This gives an uneven surface with no guarantee of the same degree of support in an area particularly on the outer edges.
3. The main floor area should be free from apparatus, particularly cables and the protruding ends of leg supports. If possible, traffic should move around the outside of this area. In this way, approaches and dismounts from floor and apparatus do not cross one another and cause collisions.
4. The instructor should ensure that participants are dressed appropriately for each gymnastics class. Clothing should allow freedom of movement. Running shoes should not be worn and preference should be given to gymnastic slippers. With bare feet there is always a possibility of twisting or stubbing toes.
5. Jewelry such as rings, decorative combs, and watches should be removed and stored prior to the class. Hair should be tied back, and nails kept short. These regulations safeguard spotters as well as the performer.
6. Floor space is the largest single item available to the instructor and usually the only place where the whole class can work together. Consequently it is in floor exercises and tumbling where foundations of gymnastic skills and their related safety techniques are established. In schools, the greater part of the gymnastics program should occur on the floor. Good safety habits taught well during floor exercises and tumbling with the whole class carry over into group work on apparatus. Consequently the importance of an excellent foundation of skills and safety habits taught during floor exercises and tumbling cannot be over-emphasized.

| SKILL | TEACHING TECHNIQUES AND OBSERVATION POINTS |

Level I Skills

1. Tip-up (Elbow Balance)

(3 seconds)

This skill leads to:
1. tucked and straight-legged headstand (pages 31-32)

Lead-up skills:
1. No specific lead-up skills

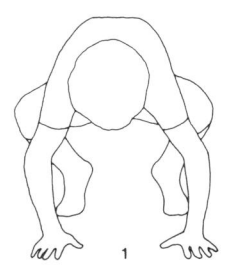

Starting Position (Front View)    Balance Position (Side View)

Teaching Points for the Skill:
1. Begin in a squatting position with the hands on the ground, shoulder width apart. Turn the knees out and rest them on the elbows (illustration #1).
2. Tilt forward and raise the seat until a balance point is found (illustration #2).
3. After balancing for 2-3 seconds, return to a squatting position and repeat.

Safety and Spotting:
1. Perform the skill toward a mat so that the head is cushioned if the performer over-balances.
2. No spotting is necessary.

Common Errors:
Errors in Performance:
1. Not flexing the arms sufficiently so that the thighs can be rested on the elbows. *Correction:* Lower the upper body forward by bending and flexing the arms. The thighs are then easily supported on the upper arms.
2. Losing balance and falling forward. *Correction:* Resist the forward motion by pressing down with the finger tips on the floor.

2. Headstand

(3 seconds)

This skill leads to:
1. headspring (pages 59-62)
2. neckspring (pages 65-66)
3. the piked headstand page 59), is a specific lead-up for the headspring and neckspring.

Lead-up skills:
1. tip-up (elbow balance) above.
2. tucked headstand (illustrations A#1-4, below).

Teaching Points for the Skill:
Tucked Headstand (illustrations A#1-4)
1. Form an equilateral triangle with the forehead and hands. (Note: This differs from the position necessary for a headspring where the head and hands are placed in a straight line.)
2. Keep the back as straight as possible, and without curving the neck (or rolling the head under), "walk" toward the spotter until the hips are vertically above the head and hands (illustration A#3).
3. Lift the legs off the ground keeping them flexed (bent) throughout (illustration A#4).
4. Lower slowly.

Lead-up Tucked Headstand

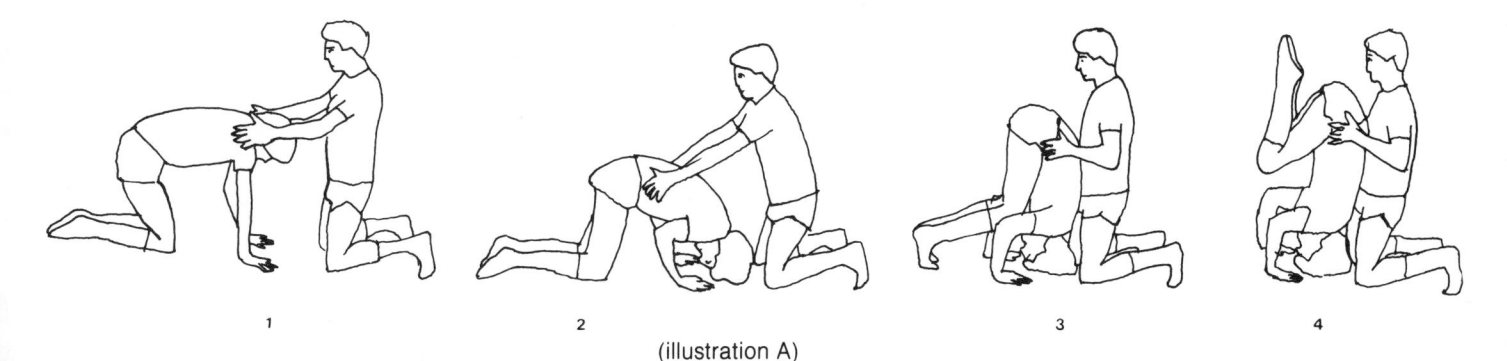

(illustration A)

SKILL
Headstand With Straight Legs

1

2

(illustration B)

3

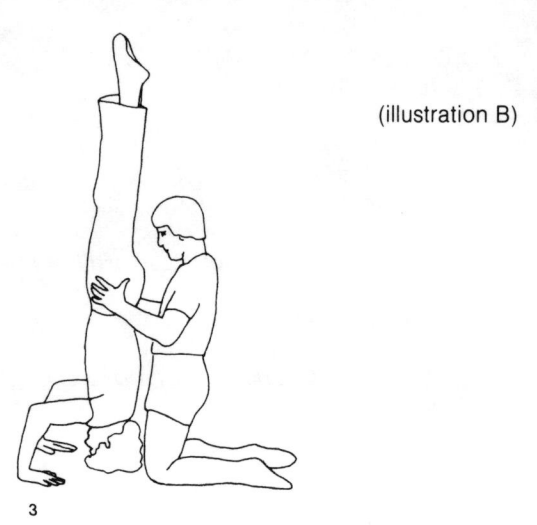

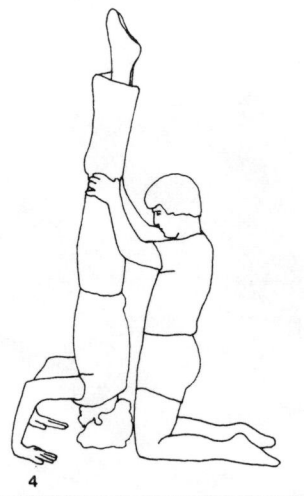

4

TEACHING TECHNIQUES AND OBSERVATION POINTS

Headstand with straight legs
A headstand with straight legs can be performed in two ways:
1. Straighten the legs from the tucked headstand position, and then lower to the tucked position again. (This is the easier method).
2. Form a triangle with the forehead and hands (illustration B#1). Straighten the legs and "walk" forward using the feet only until the hips are pushed forward above the head and hands (illustration B#2). Keeping the legs straight, raise them to the vertical position (illustrations B#3-4). Lower the legs slowly with control. Try not to bend them.
3. *Optional Activity:*
   Lower the legs until they are parallel to the floor. Hold the position for three seconds and lower.

Safety and Spotting:
1. Perform the headstand on a soft mat.
Spotting
1. Kneel facing the performer's back. Grip around the waist (illustration B#1).
2. Help the performer to raise the hips above the head and hands (illustration B#2).
3. Stabilize the final position (illustration B#3-4).
4. Control the return of the legs to the ground. Do not allow them to be dropped hard onto the mats.

Common Errors:
Errors in Performance:
1. The performer's hands and forehead do not form an equilateral triangle. *Correction:* Re-align the positioning of the head and hands. Make sure that the forehead (not the top of the head) is placed on the mat. The fingers must point forward (illustration B#1).
2. The performer's back and neck is curved. *Correction:* The back must be kept straight and the muscles of the neck tightened. The spotter can assist by kneeling close to the performer. He then lifts the performer's hips upward and simultaneously pushes his stomach toward the performer. This action will straighten out the back and correct the alignment of the body (illustrations A #3-4).
3. Dropping down heavily out of the headstand. *Correction:* Beginners must bend their legs and lower slowly out of the headstand. Lowering the legs with no bend at the knees is more difficult to perform.

Errors in Spotting:
1. The spotter positions himself facing the side of the performer instead of toward his back. *Correction:* This is not a major error. However by facing the performer's back the spotter is then able to stop the performer from rolling or falling onto his back. This is more difficult to do when spotting the performer from the side.

SKILL		TEACHING TECHNIQUES AND OBSERVATION POINTS

3. Handstand
(With assistance)

This skill leads to:
All skills in which an extended inverted position occurs, such as:
1. handstand (pages 55-56)
2. handspring (pages 66-70)
3. backspring (pages 71-75)
4. back roll to handstand (back extension) (pages 54-55)

Teaching Points for the Skill:
The Handstand with one or two spotters (illustrations C#1-4 and D#1-5)
1. Place the hands shoulder width apart on the floor and straighten the arms so that there is no bend at the elbows. Vision is on the ground between the hands or just ahead of the fingertips. Bend one leg forward and leave the other straight (illustrations C#1 and D#1).
2. Swing the extended leg directly upward and at the same time push from the floor with the flexed leg (illustration C#2).
3. Do not attempt to bring both legs together in the vertical position until the lead leg is "pointing" directly upward.
4. Bring both legs together in the vertical position (illustrations C#3 and D#3).
5. Press upward, pull in the stomach and point the toes (illustrations C#4 and D#4).
6. Step down one leg at a time. Keep the legs straight during this action and bend at the waist (illustration D#5).

Lead-up Jump to Tucked Handstand (Two-footed Take-off)

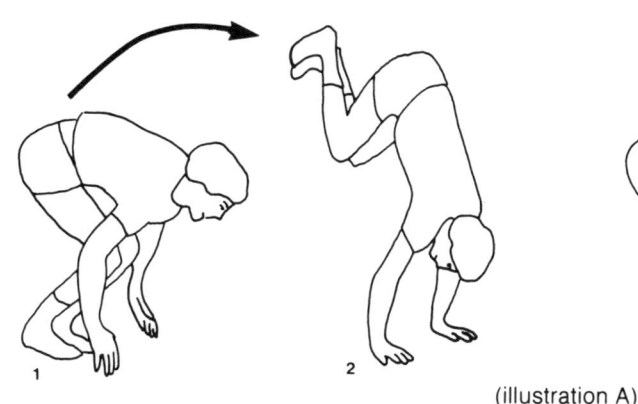

(illustration A)

Lead-up skills:
1. Jump to tucked handstand (illustrations A#1-4). This teaches the performer to raise the hips and take his weight momentarily on the hands. A two-footed take-off is used. Perform on or toward mats.
2. "Kick and point" (illustrations B#1-5). This teaches the performer to raise the hips by swinging one leg up and pointing the foot vertically upward. The trailing leg pushes from the floor, but is not raised to the vertical position. Perform on or toward mats.

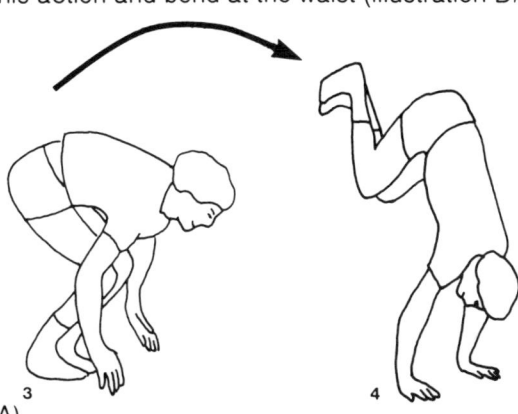

Safety and Spotting:
Two Spotter Method (illustrations C#1-4)
Spotter on the *right* (as reader views illustrations)
1. Step forward with one leg and place the thigh against the performer's shoulder. The performer's head can be placed on either side of this leg.
2. Grip on either side of the waist (illustration C#1). As the performer kicks upward, assist by lifting forward and upward (illustrations C#2-3).
3. When the performer is in the handstand position, step back and raise the hands to the performer's ankles (illustration C#4).

Spotter on the *left* (as reader views illustrations)
1. Place one hand under the leading (or swing-up) leg and help to raise it to a vertical position (illustrations C#1-3).
2. With both hands help to stabilize and align the performer in the handstand position (illustration C#4).

SKILL	TEACHING TECHNIQUES AND OBSERVATION POINTS

Lead-up Kick and Point

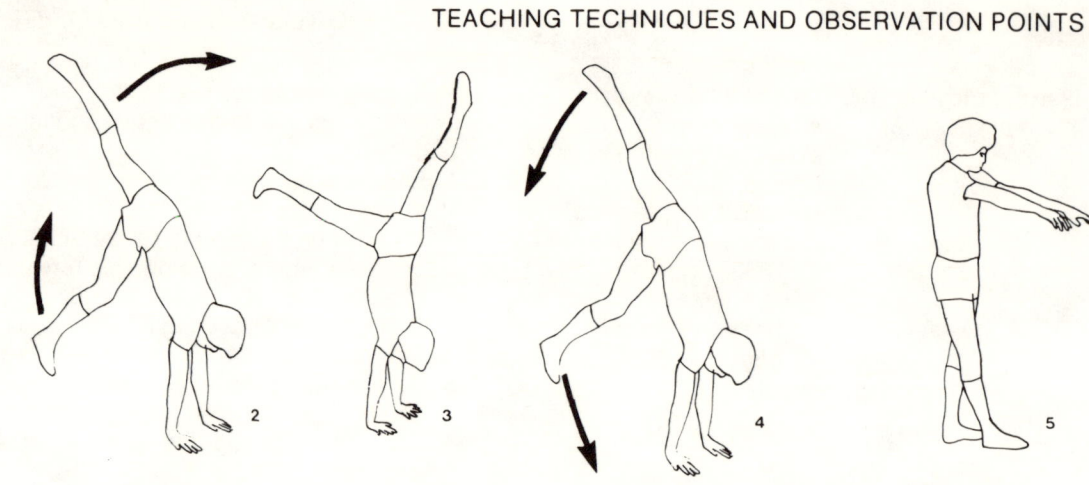

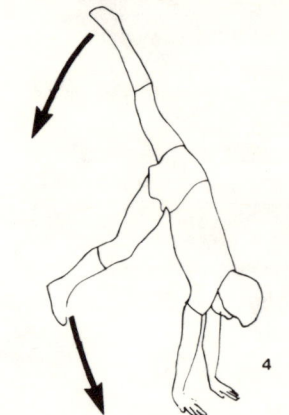

(illustration B)

Single Spotter Method (illustrations D#1-5)
1. The actions of a single spotter repeat those of the spotter on the right in illustrations C#1-4.
2. To assist the performer in stepping down from the handstand, the spotter grips around one ankle or thigh and pushes the free leg down toward the floor. This prevents the performer from bringing both legs down to the ground together (illustration D#5).

Handstand (Two Spotters)

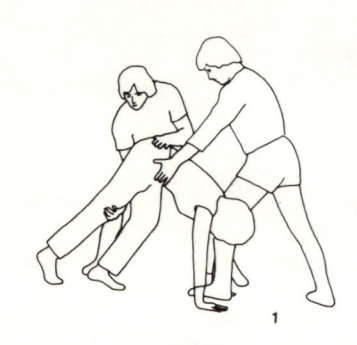

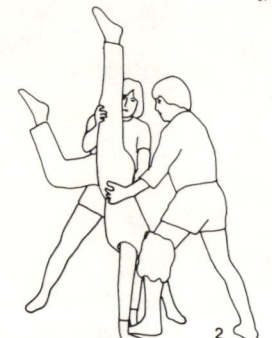

(illustration C)

Common Errors:
Errors in Performance:
1. Bending the arms. *Correction:* The arms must be straight throughout the handstand. The performer should be told to "rest on his bones." There is no flexion at the elbows.
2. Lifting the trailing leg off the floor too soon. *Correction:* This is a very common error. Kick the leading leg as close to the vertical position as possible before raising the trailing leg from the floor. Practice "kick and point" (illustrations B#1-5).
3. Sagging the shoulders forward and curving the back (called a "banana" handstand). *Correction:* Pull the stomach in and press upward from the shoulders. (The spotter can help significantly by using his thigh to stop the performer's shoulders from sagging forward. He can also lift upward on the performer's ankles or thighs and help in straightening the body.

SKILL	TEACHING TECHNIQUES AND OBSERVATION POINTS

Handstand (One Spotter)

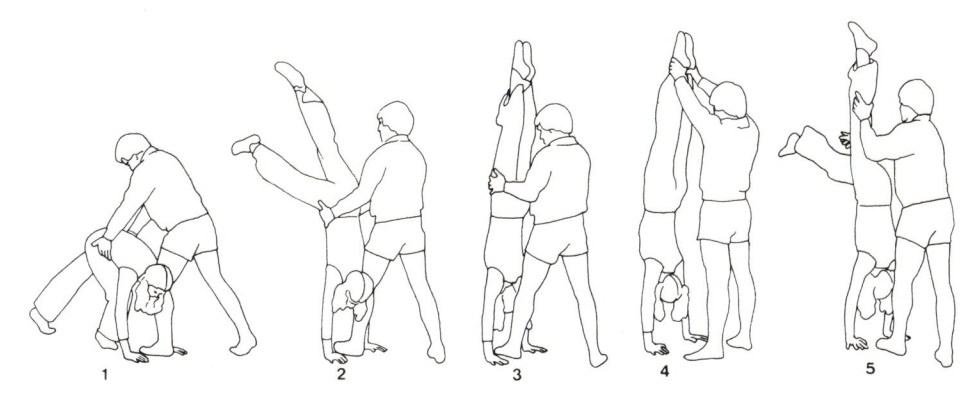

(illustration D)

Errors in Spotting:
1. Inability to hold the performer in a handstand position or being knocked backward when the performer kicks into the handstand.
   Correction:
   a) Check that the spotter is not under-sized and is physically capable of assisting the performer.
   b) Make sure that the performer is attempting the handstand with "reasonably" correct technique. The arms should be straight, the shoulders should not sag forward. The leading leg should be kept straight and kicked vertically upward. If the performer is still having trouble with these elements of the skill, then the lead-ups must be re-practiced.
   c) Check that the performer is kicking into the handstand with moderate force rather than with extreme vigor. The latter will knock the spotter backward.
   d) The spotter must make sure that he has a good stable base and is able to withstand the movement of the performer toward him (see illustration D#3). If there is a problem with the single spotter method, return to the two spotter method. In most cases poor actions by the performer make it very difficult for a single spotter to assist adequately.

4. V-Sit

(3 seconds)

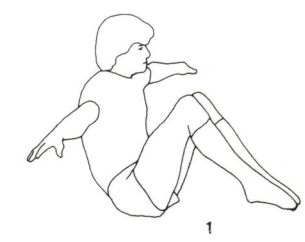

V-Sit in Tucked Position

This skill leads to:
1. All skills demanding abdominal strength and hip flexion; for example, backward roll to handstand (back extension) (pages 54-55), and piked backward roll (pages 43-44).

Lead-up skills:
Participants can attempt the v-sit without prior lead-up experience; however, the following will be of assistance:

Teaching Points for the Skill:
Tucked V-Sit (illustration #1)
1. Begin in a sitting position, with the hands at the side on the floor. Draw the legs inward to bring the heels close to the seat.
2. Lean back slowly to lift the feet from the floor. Raise the arms sideways until they are horizontal (illustration #1).
3. Hold the balance momentarily and then relax to sitting position. Repeat.

| SKILL | TEACHING TECHNIQUES AND OBSERVATION POINTS |

1. exercises to improve abdominal strength (pages 14-16)
2. exercises to improve hip flexion (page 19)
3. the tucked v-sit (illustration #1)

V-Sit with Straight Legs (illustration #2)
1. Begin in a sitting position with the legs extended and resting on the floor.
2. Hold the arms out sideways so that they are parallel to the floor.
3. Tighten the stomach muscles and lean back slowly so that the legs are lifted from the floor. Hold the feet 6" from the floor for three seconds and relax. Repeat.

Safety and Spotting:
None necessary.

Common Errors:
Errors in Performance:
1. Holding the upper body vertical throughout. *Correction:* Tighten the stomach muscles and lean backward until a balance point is found. Do not attempt a tight v-sit with the legs held high. This will come later when the stomach is stronger and flexion at the hips is improved.

5. Front Scale
(3 seconds)

This skill leads to:
1. More advanced balancing skills, such as side scale. The front scale develops control, coordination, and strength.
2. The high elevation of the rear leg in the front scale can be used as a lead-up skill to the handstand (pages 33-35)

Lead-up skills:
1. No specific lead-up skills are necessary to attempt a front scale. However for a good performance in the front scale, the flexibility and strength exercises shown on pages 14-20 should be practiced.

Teaching Points for the Skill:
1. Step forward with one leg and lift both arms forward or to the side. In both cases they are held parallel to the floor.
2. Lift the rear leg back and upward as high as possible.
3. Slowly lower the upper body meanwhile holding the arms in their horizontal position.
4. Keep the supporting leg straight and maintain balance by working hard with the supporting foot.
5. Relax and repeat.

Safety and Spotting:
A spotter can help the performer achieve the correct body position (illustration #1).

Common Errors:
Errors in Performance:
1. Attempting to raise the rear leg too high. *Correction:* Raise the rear leg only as far as flexibility will comfortably allow. Do not struggle to raise it higher since this will disturb balance.
2. Insufficient use of the supporting foot in maintaining balance. *Correction:* The toes of the supporting foot must be used to control balance. Do not move the arms or the elevated leg once they have been placed in position.

Front Scale (With Assistance)

Optional St Arms to S (T-Scale

| SKILL | TEACHING TECHNIQUES AND OBSERVATION POINTS |

6. Forward Roll - Tuck

This skill leads to:
1. straddle forward roll (pages 51-52)
2. piked forward roll (pages 75-77)

Lead-up skills:
Forward roll down an incline. Illustrations A#1-3 show the use of an incline to elevate the hips and make the rolling action easier to perform. The head is well tucked under and the back is curved. A push from the floor helps the performer to a squatting position. Spotting assistance can be given in the manner shown in illustrations B#1-4.

Teaching Points for the Skill:
Forward Roll from Standing (illustrations B#1-4)
1. Begin in a semi-crouch position (illustration B#1). Reach forward with the hands and place them on the mat shoulder width apart. The fingers point forward.
2. To enter the roll extend the legs, tuck the head under and curve the back (illustrations #2).
3. Keep the legs extended and the body piked as the hips pass above the head. Then tuck quickly and reach forward (illustrations B#2-4).

Lead-up Forward Roll Down an Incline

(illustration A)

Safety and Spotting:
Perform the roll on mats
Spotting
1. Kneel "ahead" of the performer in order to be in line with the shoulders during the roll (illustrations B#1-2).
2. Tuck the performer's head under and press down on the thighs so that the body is piked at the mid-point of the roll (illustration B#2).
3. Quickly shift both hands to either side of the waist to help the performer forward into a squatting position (illustrations B#3-4).

Tucked Forward Roll From Standing

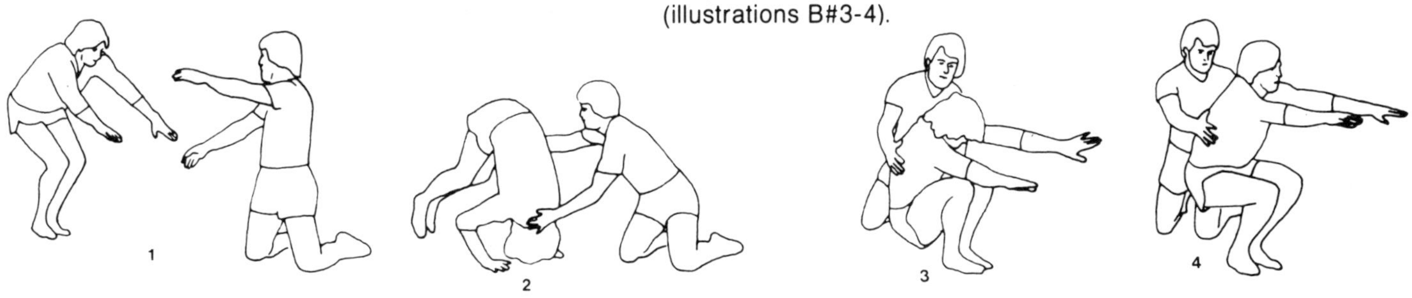

(illustration B)

Common Errors:
Errors in Performance:
1. Rolling onto a flat back. *Correction:* Tuck the head under at the entry to the skill and bring the thighs into the chest so that the back is curved. Hold a relaxed pike position until the lower back contacts the floor. Then tuck quickly. (The spotter can help beginners in the timing of this action).
2. Inability to move into a squatting position at the end of the roll. *Correction:* Practice the forward roll with a final push from the floor to move into a squatting or standing position. Then practice the forward roll with the arms reaching forward horizontally at the end of the roll. As confidence increases, enter the skill with more speed.

SKILL	TEACHING TECHNIQUES AND OBSERVATION POINTS

Errors in Spotting:
1. Poor positioning of the spotter relative to the performer. *Correction:* The spotter must position himself so that he is able to lift the performer forward and upward out of the roll. This means kneeling at least one full pace ahead of the performer at the start of the skill (illustration B#1).

7. Backward Roll - Tuck

This skill leads to: More advanced skills using a rolling action backward, for example, piked backward roll (pages 43-44), backward roll to handstand (i.e. back extension-pages 54-55)

Lead-up skills: the "rocking horse" practice (illustrations A#1-5).

Lead-up "Rocking Horse"

Teaching Points for the Skill:
"Rocking Horse" lead-up (illustration A#1-5)
1. In a tucked sitting position, roll back and forth.
2. Curve the back and on each roll backward place the hands in position on either side of the head (illustration A#3). Place the fingers parallel to the direction of the roll.
3. At the furthest point backward in the rolling action extend the legs into a relaxed pike position. Point the elbows directly upward (illustration A#3)

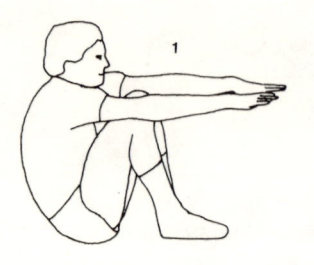

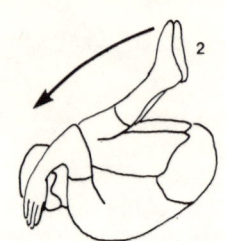

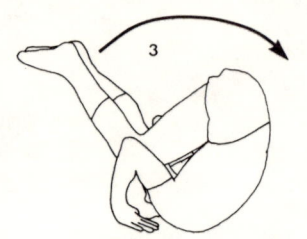

(illustration A)

Backward roll from a Back Lying Position (illustrations B#1-4)
1. Lie on the back with the hands in a ready position on either side of the head (the hand positions are best shown in illustration A#3). Check that the elbows point upward.
2. Roll backward slowly. Press the feet down toward the floor (illustration B#3).
3. As the seat passes over and beyond the head and the feet approach the floor, press up to a squatting position (illustration B#4).

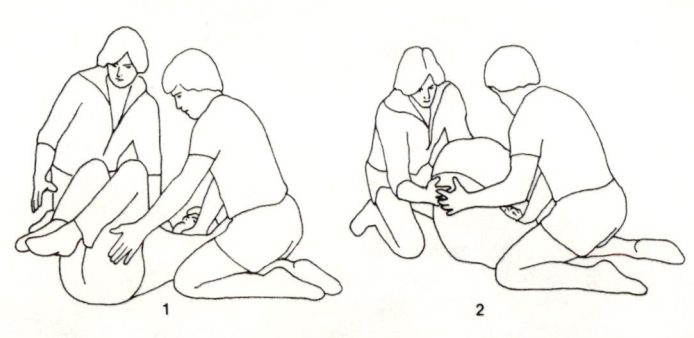

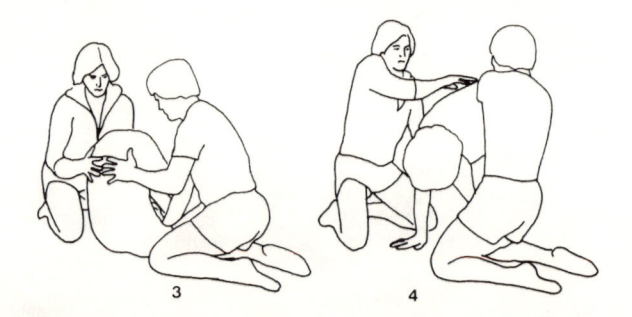

Backward Roll From a Back-Lying Position

(illustration B)

Backward Roll from a Squatting Position (illustrations C#1-4)
1. Begin in a squatting position (illustration C#1).
2. Roll backward. Allow the legs to relax from their flexed position as the feet are pushed backward to the floor. (This means that the performer will move from a tucked position to a "loose" pike position (illustration C#2)—and then back to a squatting position (or standing position at the end of the skill)

| SKILL | TEACHING TECHNIQUES AND OBSERVATION POINTS |

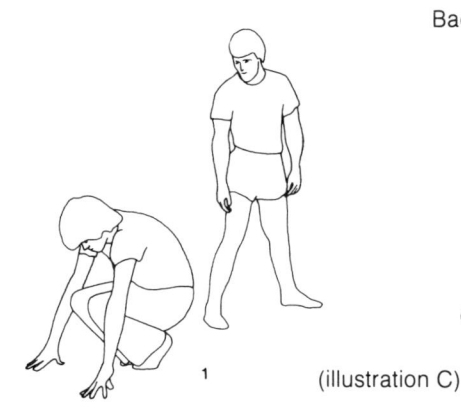

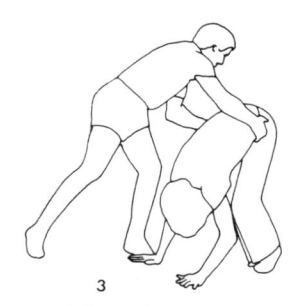

Backward Roll From a Squatting Position

(illustration C)

Safety and Spotting:
The backward roll should be practiced on mats.
Backward Roll from a Back Lying Position
Spotting
1. Kneel with your partner on either side of the performer's shoulders.
2. As the performer rolls backward reach around the seat and help with the backward motion (illustration B#2).
3. When the performer's seat passes over his head and shoulders, lift upward with the hand gripping under the shoulder (illustration B#3-4).

Backward Roll from a Squatting Position
Spotting
1. Stand ahead of the performer in order to be in line with his shoulders during the roll (illustration C#1).
2. As he rolls backward, turn toward his feet and grip either side of the waist (illustration C#2).
3. Lift upward. This will help the performer to roll over and "past" the head and makes it easier for him to press up to a standing or squatting position (illustration C#2-4).

Common Errors:
Errors in Performance:
1. The hands are placed too close to the head. *Correction:* The hands must be placed on the mat shoulder width apart. The fingers must be parallel to the direction of the roll. The elbows must point upward.
2. Pushing with the arms before the feet are on or near to the floor (or-before the hips have passed over the head). *Correction:* Reach for the floor with the feet as soon as the backward roll is initiated. Make sure that the feet are on or near to the floor before any push is initiated. This means performing a "loose" or relaxed pike action at the mid-point of the skill.

Errors in Spotting:
1. Failing to lift in the direction of the skill. *Correction:* The spotters must realize that the performer is moving along the floor as he rolls backward. The lift must be both upward and in the direction of the roll.

| SKILL | TEACHING TECHNIQUES AND OBSERVATION POINTS |

8. Backward Roll - Straddle

This skill leads to:
1. piked backward roll (pages 43-44)
2. backward roll to handstand (back extension - pages 54-55)

Lead-up skills;
1. a wide straddle sit position (pages 19-20)
2. v-sit (pages 35-36)
3. tucked backward roll (pages 38-39)

Teaching Points for the Skill:
Straddle Backward Roll from Sitting
1. Sit in a straddled position on the floor, hands held in ready position (illustration A#1).
2. Roll backward holding the straddled position. Keep the hips flexed (that is, maintain the sitting position). Curve the back as much as possible (illustration A#2).
3. As the hips pass over the head and the feet touch the mat, press the body upward to a straddle standing position (illustration A#3).

Straddle Backward Roll From Sitting

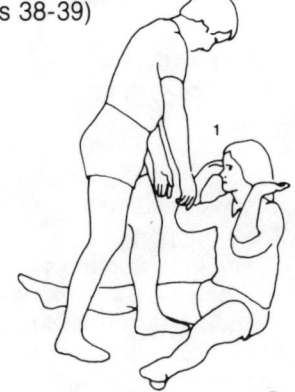

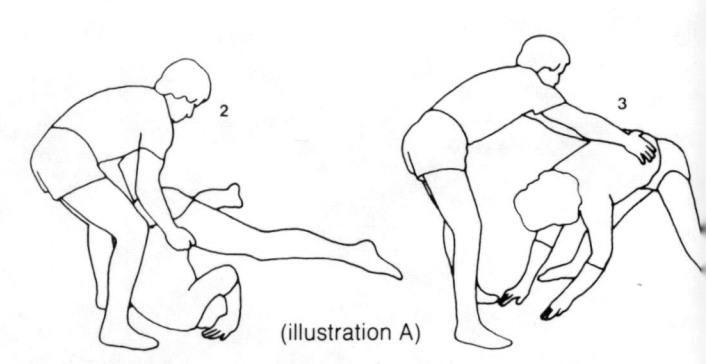

(illustration A)

Straddle Backward Roll from Standing (more difficult than from sitting position)
1. Begin standing in a straddle position (illustration B#1).
2. Sit backward, simultaneously bending as far forward as possible. Reach between the legs with the hands to cushion the landing (illustration B#2).
3. As the hips pass over the head and the feet touch the mat, press the body upward to straddle stand position (illustrations B#4-6).

Straddle Backward Roll From Standing

(illustration B)

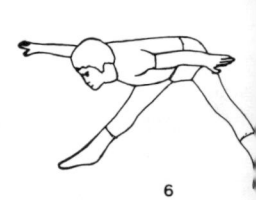

Safety and Spotting:
The straddle backward roll should be performed on mats.
Spotting
1. Stand between the performer's straddled legs (illustration A#1).
2. Follow the motion of the backward roll. Grip on either side of the waist and under the thighs (illustration A#2).
3. Lift upward to help the performer's hips pass over and beyond the line of the head and shoulders (illustrations A#2-3).
4. Move quickly. Remember the performer is rolling away from the spotter.

SKILL	TEACHING TECHNIQUES AND OBSERVATION POINTS

Common Errors:
Errors in Performance:
1. Failing to maintain a wide straddle position throughout the skill. *Correction:* Press the legs as far apart as possible. Maintain this position particularly during the mid-phase of the skill. Do not bend at the knees.
2. Failing to maintain a piked position throughout the skill. *Correction;* During the roll backward bring the legs as close to the chest as possible (illustration A#2). Hold this position until the feet touch the ground.
3. Straightening the arms too soon. *Correction:* Wait until the hips have passed over the head and the feet touch the mat before extending the arms.

Errors in Spotting:
1. Moving too slowly to be of help to the performer. *Correction:* The spotter must remember that the performer is rolling away from him. Step quickly forward and obtain hand positions as quickly as possible. The performer should succeed with a straddle backward roll from sitting before attempting the same skill from standing.

Level II Skills

9. Momentary Headstand - Forward Roll

This skill leads to:
1. More advanced balance-roll combinations, for instance the handstand-forward roll (pages 45-46).
2. The headstand is a lead-up to the piked headstand and headspring (pages 59-62).
3. The tucked forward roll leads to the straddle forward roll and the piked forward roll (pages 51-52 and 75-77).

Lead-up skills:
1. headstand (pages 31-32)
2. tucked forward roll (pages 37-38)

Teaching Points for the Skill:
The teaching points for the headstand and the tucked forward roll as individual skills are outlined on pages 31-32 and 37-38.
The shift from the headstand into the tucked forward roll
1. Overbalance in the direction of the roll.
2. As the body is over-balancing, press the body upward by pushing down on the floor. This will make it easier to tuck the head under, and generates speed into the roll.
3. Curve the back and bend the legs.
4. Stretch forward with the arms to shift to a squatting position.

Safety and Spotting:
Use a mat to cushion the headstand and tucked forward roll.
Spotting
1. Kneel to one side of the performer. Grip on the thighs and help the performer into the headstand (illustrations #1-2).
2. As the performer rolls forward, reach around the back and assist him out of the roll (illustrations #4-5).

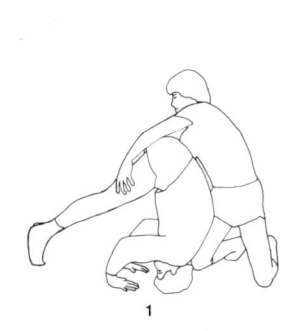

Momentary Headstand - Forward Roll

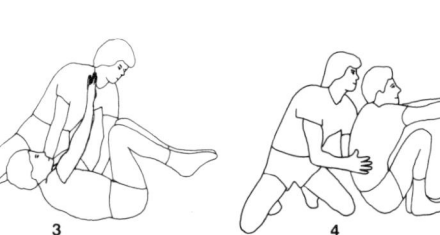

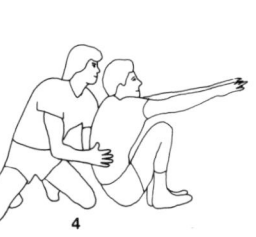

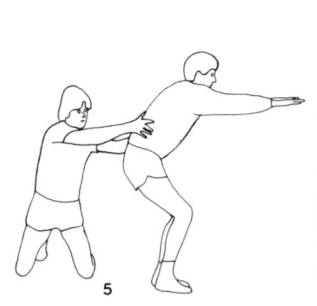

SKILL	TEACHING TECHNIQUES AND OBSERVATION POINTS

Common Errors:

Errors in Performance:

Errors in the headstand and the forward roll as individual skills are discussed on pages 31-32 and 37-38.

1. Insufficient momentum out of the headstand and into the forward roll. *Correction:* Overbalance in the direction of the roll and press down with the hands. This will give sufficient speed into the roll and also make it easy to tuck the head under. Delay the tuck into the forward roll until the last possible instant.

Errors in Spotting:

1. Poor positioning relative to the performer. *Correction:* Spotting for this skill must be given from the side of the performer. This allows for the headstand to be followed by a forward roll. The spotter must kneel slightly "ahead" of the performer so that he is able to assist with the headstand (illustration #2) and then quickly shift support to assist with the forward roll. The spotter must realize that the performer is rolling away from him during the forward roll and make allowance for this action.

10. Press to Headstand from Straddle Stand

This skill leads to:
1. tuck press to handstand (flexed elbows) (pages 62-63).
2. straddle press to handstand (pages 63-64)

Lead-up skills:
1. tucked headstand (page 31)
2. headstand with straight legs (page 32)

Teaching Points for the Skill:
1. From a straddle stand position lower the head and hands to form an equilateral triangle on the mat (illustration #1).
2. Place the head and hands as close to midway between the feet as possible.
3. Press down hard on the floor with the hands to raise the seat upward and the legs to the vertical position (illustrations #2-4).

Safety and Spotting:
Use a mat.

Press to Headstand From Straddle Stand

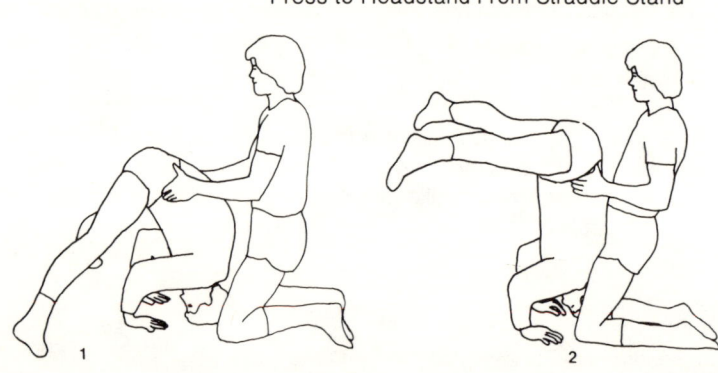

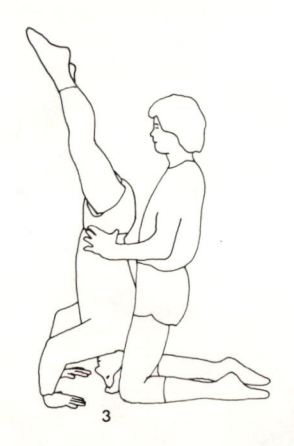

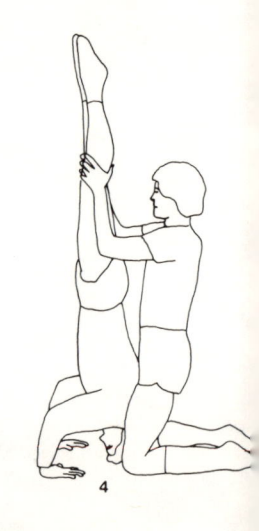

Spotting:
1. Kneel facing the performer's back (illustration #1).
2. Grip on either hip and help to raise the seat upward (illustration #2).
3. Once the performer has his legs in the vertical position, shift the grip to the ankles (illustrations #3-4).
4. Reverse the procedure when the performer is lowering the legs.

SKILL	TEACHING TECHNIQUES AND OBSERVATION POINTS

Common Errors:
Errors in Performance:
1. Placing the hands and head too far ahead of a line between the feet. *Correction:* Flex as much as possible at the hips so that the head and the hands can be placed as close to midway between the feet as possible. Do not curve the back.
2. Lifting the legs upward before the seat is above the head and hands. *Correction:* The seat must be directly above the head before raising the legs. Press the seat into this position before elevating the legs.

11. Backward Roll in Piked Position (Piked Backward Roll)

This skill leads to:
1. backward roll to handstand (back extension)(pages 54-55).

Teaching Points for the Skill:
Piked Backward Roll from Sitting
1. Begin sitting with the legs extended (illustration A#1).
2. Roll backward placing the hands on the mat either side of the head. The hands are shoulder width apart. Keep the legs straight and bring them as close to the chest as possible by flexing strongly at the hips (illustration A#2).
3. When the hips have passed over the head and the feet touch the mat, press the body upward by extending the arms (illustrations A#3-4).

Piked Backward Roll From Sitting

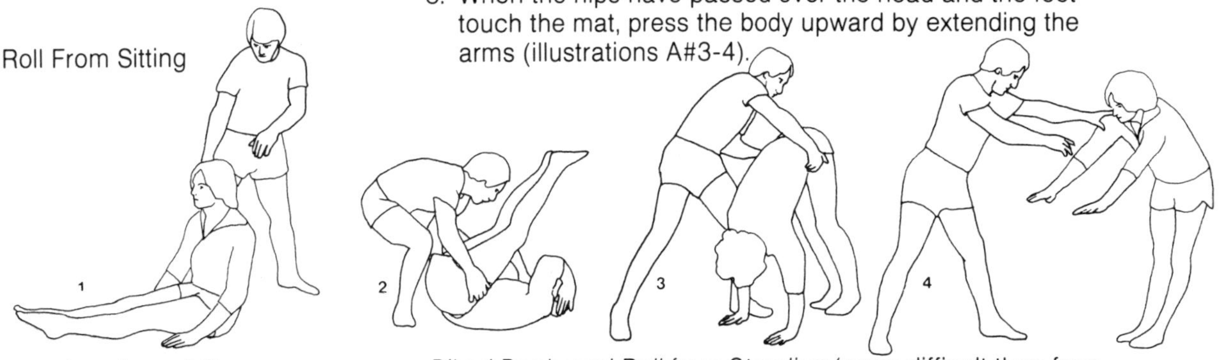

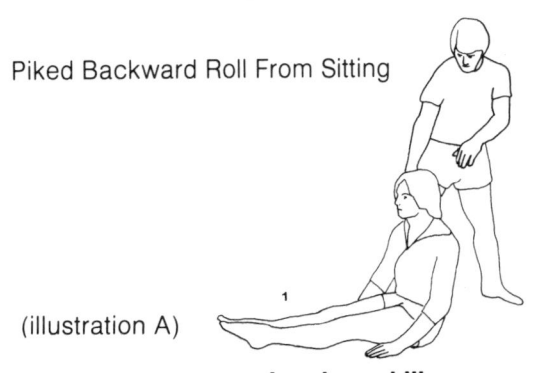

(illustration A)

Lead-up skills:
1. exercises for hip flexion (page 19) and arm extension (i.e. triceps strength, pages 15-16)
2. tucked backward roll (pages 38-39)
3. straddle backward roll (pages 40-41)
4. piked backward roll from sitting (illustrations A#1-4)

Piked Backward Roll from Standing (more difficult than from sitting)
1. Bend forward (pike) as far as possible and reach back behind the body to cushion the landing with the hands (illustrations B#1-2).
2. Cushion the landing and roll backward. Keep the legs as close to the chest as possible.
3. Shift the hands quickly to their positions either side of the head (illustration B#1). Be sure to maintain the piked position.
4. When the hips pass beyond the head and shoulders, press the body upward to standing position.

Piked Backward Roll From Standing

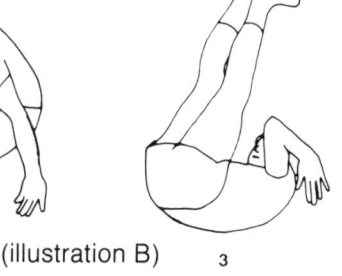

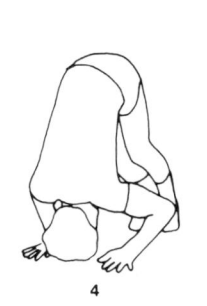

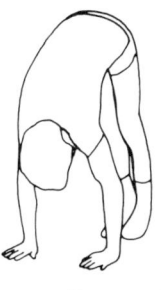

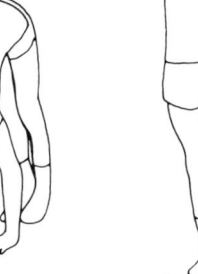

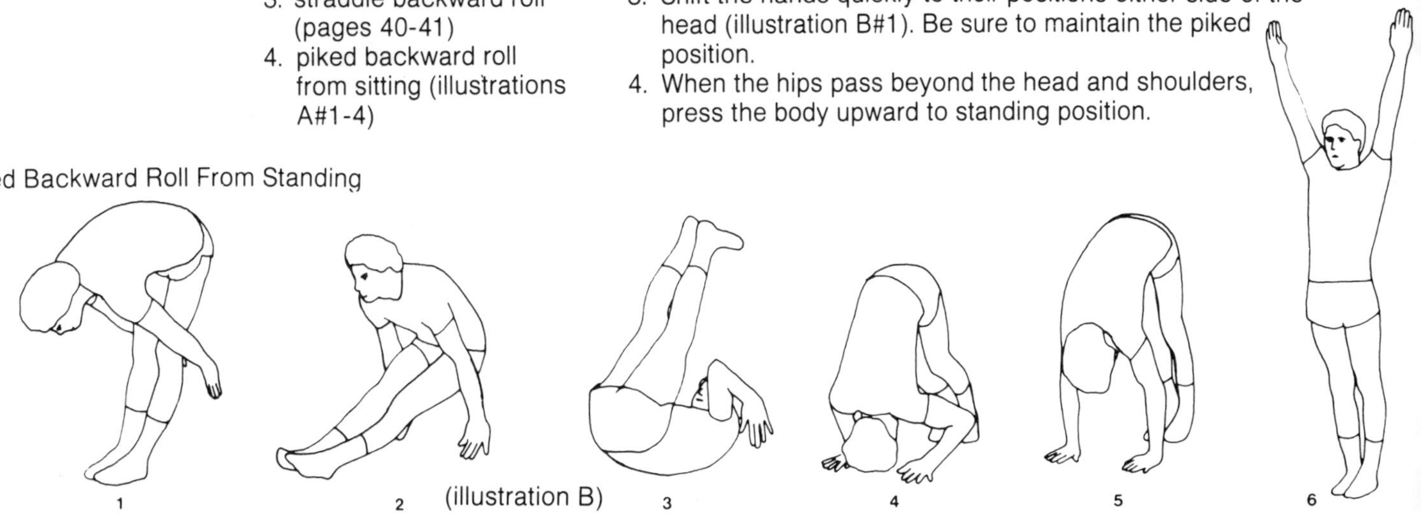

(illustration B)

SKILL	TEACHING TECHNIQUES AND OBSERVATION POINTS

Safety and Spotting:
Use mats throughout.
Spotting: (piked backward roll from sitting)
1. Stand in a straddle stance "ahead" of the performer so that assistance can be given at the midpoint of the skill (illustrations A#1-2).
2. As the performer's legs pass by, turn toward his feet and grip under either thigh (illustration A#2).
3. Lift upward in the direction of the roll (illustration A#3).

Spotting: (piked backward roll from standing)
1. Spotting is the same as for the piked backward roll from sitting. If the piked backward roll from sitting is mastered first, there will be no need to provide spotting for the same skill initiated from a standing postion. Practice the backward sitting action onto soft mats.

Common Errors:
Errors in Performance:
1. Failing to maintain a piked position. *Correction:* As the roll backward is initiated draw the legs as close to the chest as possible. If the performer is not flexible enough to succeed in this action additional hip flexion exercises must be practiced (pages 19-20).

Errors in Spotting:
1. Poor positioning relative to the performer. *Correction:* The spotter must make allowance for the backward roll. He must stand at least one full pace "ahead" of the performer in order to provide assistance at the midpoint of the skill.
2. Insufficient speed in providing assistance. *Correction:* The spotter must fully understand what he has to do. If the performer rolls back slowly from the sitting position, the spotter can then practice his handholds without trouble. If support is provided for the piked backward roll from standing, the spotter must move very quickly and provide accurate support.

---

12. Forward Roll-Jump-Pirouette

This skill leads to:
1. Improved orientation and coordination.
2. An understanding of rotation around the vertical and horizontal axes. These forms of rotation occur in numerous advanced floor exercises and apparatus skills.

Lead-up skills:
1. tucked forward roll (pages 37-38)
2. quarter, half and full pirouettes performed without the addition of the tucked forward roll.

Teaching Points for the Skill:
1. Practice quarter, half, and full pirouettes. Jump upward on the spot. There are several ways of obtaining rotation. The illustrations show one method:
   a) Jump upward keeping the body erect.
   b) Obtain some rotation by pushing around from the floor.
   c) Raise the arms directly upward with the jump and turn the palms of the hands in the direction of the rotation.
   d) Use vision as a means of orientation and control. Keep vision at the same level during the pirouette.
   e) Cushion the landing by bending the legs slightly.
2. Other methods of arm action to generate rotation employed by springboard divers and ballet performers can also be attempted.
3. Add the tucked forward roll to:
   a) a quarter-turn
   b) a half-turn
   c) a full pirouette (illustrations #1-8)

SKILL	TEACHING TECHNIQUES AND OBSERVATION POINTS

Safety and Spotting:
Practice the skill on mats. No spotting assistance is necessary.

Common Errors:
1. Failing to jump directly upward during the pirouette. *Correction:* Perform the forward roll slowly. Drive directly upward in the pirouette. If the roll is performed quickly, allowance will have to be made for the forward motion occurring out of the roll. In this case the pirouette will have to be performed with the vertical axis tilted slightly forward.
2. Dropping the head during the pirouette. *Correction:* Keep the vision at the same level and "spot" the pirouette by looking ahead and around for a spot which would be at eye level on completion of the full rotation.

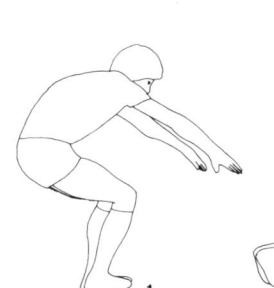

Forward-Roll-Jump-Pirouette

13. Momentary Handstand-Forward Roll

This skill leads to:
1. The handstand leads to all skills which use an inverted position, notably handspring, backhandspring, back extension.
2. The tucked forward roll leads to the straddle and piked forward roll.
3. The ability to roll out of an inverted position is an important safety device particularly for handstand practice.

Lead-up Handstand - Forward Roll

Teaching Points for the Skill:
1. Practice the handstand (with spotting) and the tucked forward roll as separate skills (pages 33-35 & 37-38).
2. An important series of actions occur during the transition from handstand to forward roll. During this phase the performer should:
   a) look at the floor and continue to do this while bending the arms and lowering the body,
   b) at the last moment tuck the head under,
   c) curve the back and bend the legs (in that order).
3. Spotting assistance is important because a spotter can slow the whole action down so that the performer can become oriented to the above sequence of actions (illustrations A#1-6).
4. Practice the handstand forward roll into a crash pad (if available). A good crash pad will provide sufficient cushioning for poor performances.

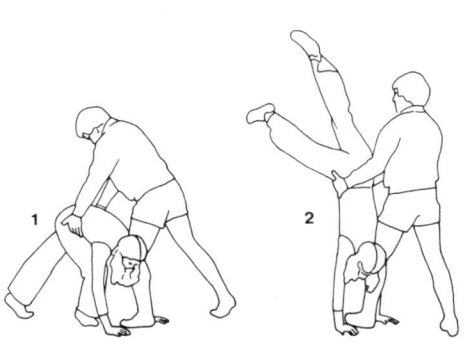

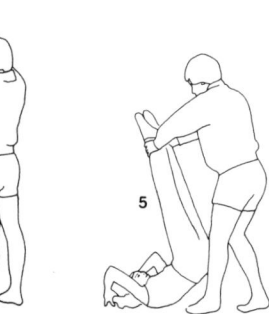

(illustration A)

| SKILL | TEACHING TECHNIQUES AND OBSERVATION POINTS |

Lead-up skills:
1. the handstand (with assistance, (pages 33-35)
2. tucked forward roll (pages 37-38).

Safety and Spotting:
1. Practice the handstand forward roll:
   a) by using a spotter (illustrations A#1-6),
   b) with or without spotting assistance into a crash pad (illustrations B#1-8).

Spotting: (illustrations A#1-6)
1. Help the performer into the handstand (a full description of the spotting assistance is given on pages 34-35). Grip the ankles (or lower down the legs if this is more comfortable and lower the performer slowly into the forward roll. Step backward or to the side as the performer rolls forward (illustrations A#5-6).
2. If spotting is provided for a handstand forward roll into a crash pad, it is provided from the side of the performer. Assistance is given at the ankles or lower on the legs.

Momentary Handstand - Forward Roll (onto crash pad)

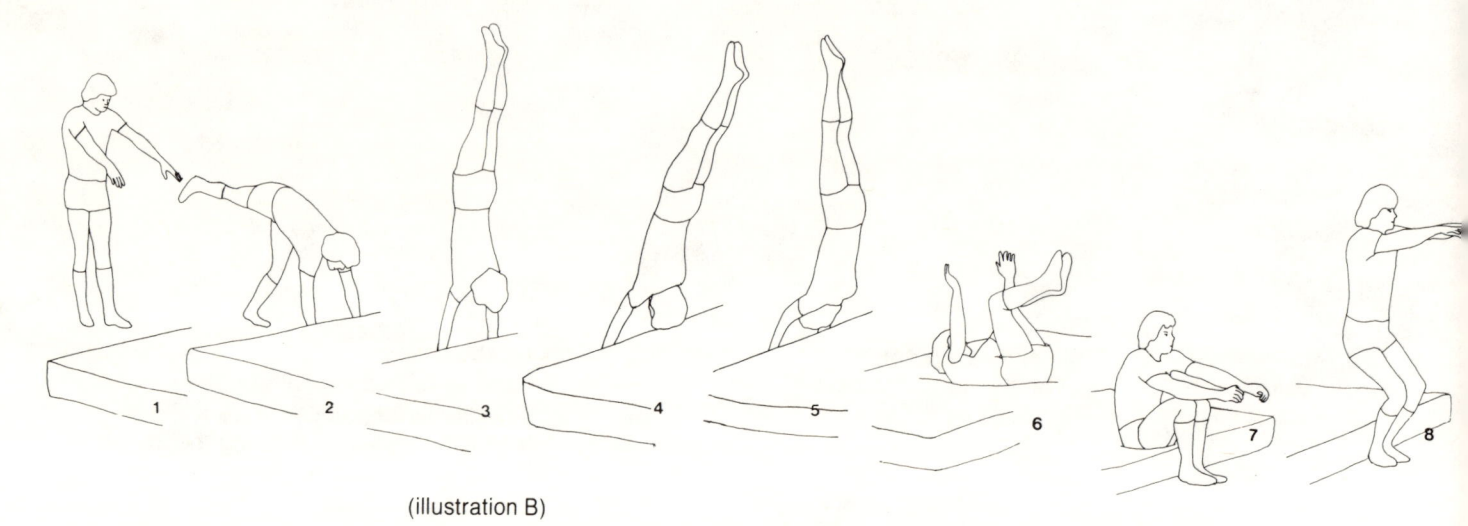

(illustration B)

Common Errors:
Errors in Performance:
1. Tucking the head under too soon and falling flat on the back. *Correction:* The sequence of actions outlined in the Teaching Points for the Skill must be followed closely. The vision is an important means of assessing distance from the floor. The sequence of bending the arms, curving the back, and bending the legs, cannot be altered.

Errors in Spotting:
1. Failing to step backward as the performer enters the forward roll. *Correction:* Give firm support at the ankles. Lower the performer slowly. At the same time step backward. A variation is to step to the side and give support at the ankles from that position. See cartwheel, forward roll (pages 50-51).

| SKILL | TEACHING TECHNIQUES AND OBSERVATION POINTS |

14. Cartwheel

Lead-up Method #1
Cartwheel Around Small Circle

This skill leads to:
1. one-armed cartwheel (pages 70-71).
2. round-off (pages 57-58).
3. cartwheel-forward roll (pages 50-51)
4. advanced skills which incorporate sideways rotation (side salto)
5. cartwheel skills on apparatus (cartwheel vaults).

Teaching Points for the Skill:
The cartwheel can be introduced in more than one way.
1. Illustrations A#1-8 and B#1-3 show one method in which the performer uses circles of increasing size to:
    a) progressively elevate the hips above the hands,
    b) work toward a cartwheel performed along a straight line.
2. Illustrations C#1-6 show a method by which the performer learns the first half of the cartwheel. The second half is then added on with assistance given by a spotter.

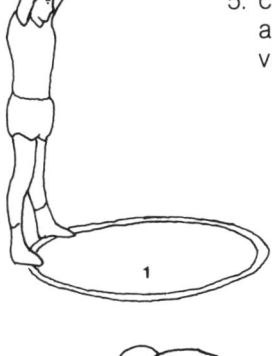

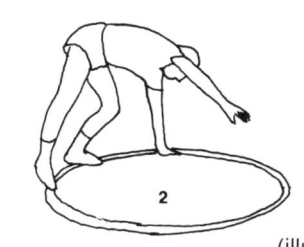

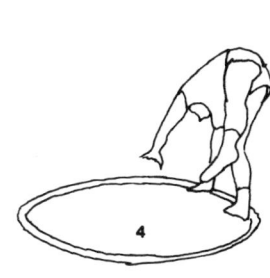

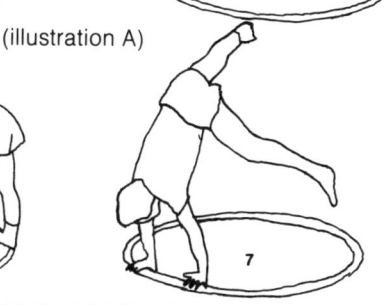

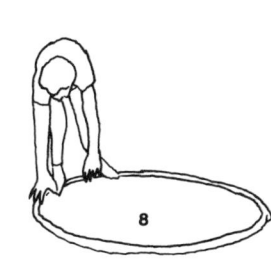

(illustration A)

Lead-up Method #1 Continued
Cartwheel Around a Larger Circle

(illustration B)

Lead-up skills:
1. the handstand (pages 33-35).
2. the lead-ups to the cartwheel shown in illustrations A#1-8, B#1-3, and C#1-6.

Learning the Cartwheel Around a Circle
1. Using a small circle (two meters in diameter) work around in a sequence of hand-hand-foot-foot.
2. Raise the hips as high as possible.
3. Do not attempt to raise the legs more than halfway to vertical.
4. Concentrate on working around the circle placing the hands and the feet on the circle each time.
5. Progress to a larger circle and again work around in the sequence of hand-hand-foot-foot.
6. Place the hands and feet on the circle each time.
7. Raise the legs as high as possible.
8. Increase the size of the circle.
9. Move to a straight line and attempt the cartwheel. Place the hands and the feet along the line. A single spotter can assist. See spotting methods illustrated in E#1-3 and F#1-4.

SKILL

Lead-up Method #2
Straddled Handstand From Side Approach
(First Half of Cartwheel) (illustration C)

Cartwheel - 2 Spotter and Spotting Belt

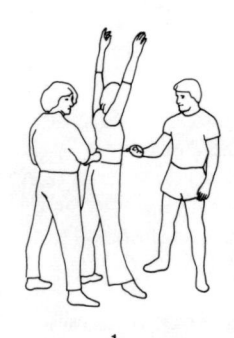

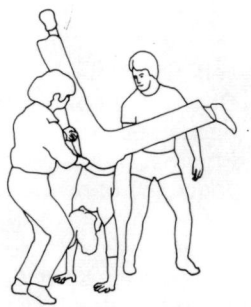

(illustration D)

TEACHING TECHNIQUES AND OBSERVATION POINTS

Learning the First Half of the Cartwheel (illustrations C#1-6)
1. Kick to a handstand directly toward the spotter (see page 35).
2. With each successive attempt work the initial stance around to the side of the spotter (illustration C#1).
3. Step *slowly* into a straddle handstand. Be sure the hips are above the shoulders (illustrations C#1-3).
4. Bring the legs together and step down (illustrations C#4-6).
5. Attempt the full cartwheel with a single spotter providing assistance chosen from the methods illustrated in E#1-3 and F#1-4.

Safety and Spotting:
Perform the cartwheel on mats.
Straddled Handstand from a Sideways Approach (first half of cartwheel)
Spotting
1. Stand in a stable straddled position (illustration C#1).
2. Reach around the performer's body and grip under the shoulder (illustration C#3).
3. Keep the head to one side to avoid the performer's legs (illustration C#3).
4. Stabilize the handstand (illustration C#4).
5. Allow the performer to step down (illustration C#5-6)

Cartwheel with Assistance from Two Spotters and Spotting Belt
1. Shift the spotting belt around the performer's body to allow for sideways rotation (illustration D#1).
2. Step with the performer and stabilize his movement through the vertical position (illustration D#2).
3. Lift upward to help elevate the performer's upper body (illustration D#3).

SKILL

Cartwheel - One Spotter

(illustration E)

Cartwheel - One Spotter

(illustration F)

Cartwheel

(illustration G)

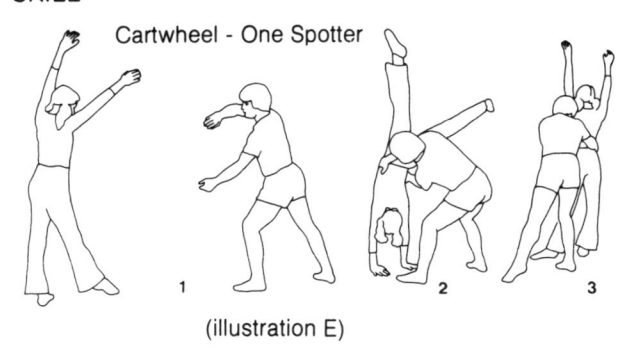

TEACHING TECHNIQUES AND OBSERVATION POINTS

Cartwheel with Assistance from One Spotter (illustrations E#1-3)
1. Stand ahead of the performer in order to be in line with the handstand position (illustration E#1).
2. Bend to the side and "reverse" the grip to hold on either side of the performer's waist (illustration E#2).
3. Stabilize the movement of the performer from the inverted to the standing position (illustrations E#2-3).

Cartwheel with Assistance from One Spotter (illustrations F#1-4)
1. Stand ahead of the performer to be in line with the handstand position.
2. Grip under the shoulder and around the waist (illustration F#3).
3. Maintain support under the waist and lift upward under the shoulder (illustration F#4).

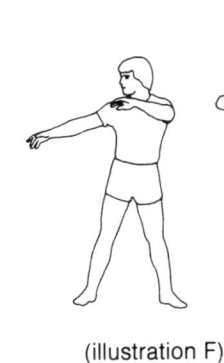

Cartwheel without Assistance
The complete cartwheel action without assistance is shown in illustrations G#1-5

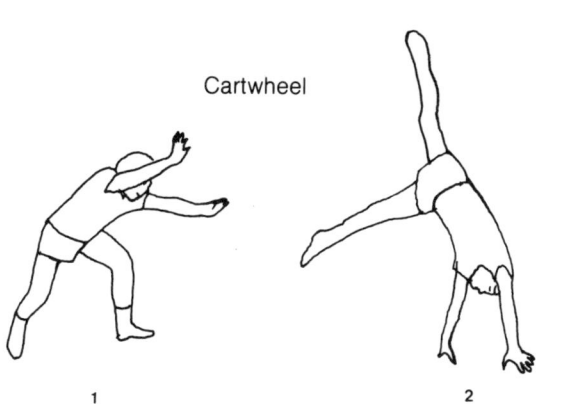

Common Errors:
Errors in Performance:
1. The hips and legs do not pass above the hands in the inverted position. *Correction:* Practice the straddled handstand from direct through to the side-approach

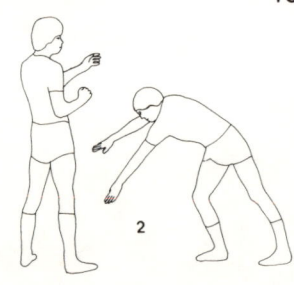

SKILL	TEACHING TECHNIQUES AND OBSERVATION POINTS

(illustrations C#1-6). Return to the full cartwheel when the body alignment is correct.
2. Bending the legs. *Correction:* Practice the straddled handstand from the side approach. Maintain straight legs throughout. Return to the full cartwheel when the leg action is correct.
3. Collapsing to the side in the final half of the skill. *Correction:* Make sure that the hips pass directly over the hands. Maintain the straddled position. (Do not let the legs come together.) Make sure the feet are placed along a straight line.

Errors in Spotting:
1. Insufficient support during the final half of the skill. *Correction:* This problem is caused more by the performer than by the spotter. Check whether the performer should return to earlier lead-ups (sideways approach to straddled handstand). For more assistance in the latter half of the cartwheel use the method shown in illustrations F#1-4.

Level III Skills

15. Cartwheel Forward Roll

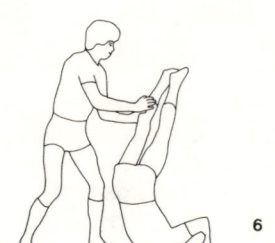

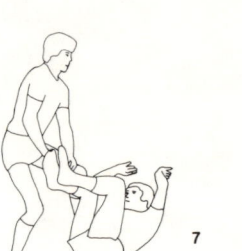

This skill leads to:
1. cartwheel-piked forward roll
2. cartwheel-straddled forward roll
3. Further advanced skills incorporating a cartwheel.

Lead-up skills:
1. handstand (pages 33-35)
2. cartwheel (pages 47-50)
3. tucked forward roll (pages 37-38)
4. handstand tucked forward roll (pages 45-46)

Cartwheel - Forward-Roll

Teaching Points for the Skill:
1. Step *slowly* into the first half of the cartwheel (illustrations #1-4).
2. Bring the legs together (illustration #5).
3. Keep the vision on the floor between the hands. Bend the arms and tuck the head under at the last instant. Curve the back and then bend the legs (illustrations #5-7).
4. Reach forward to stand up (illustration #8).

Safety and Spotting:
Perform the cartwheel-forward roll on mats.
Spotting
1. Stabilize the performer in the straddled handstand position (illustrations #3-4).
2. Step quickly to the side (illustration #6).
3. Provide support if necessary in the final part of the forward roll (illustration #8).

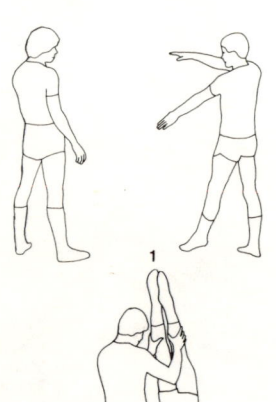

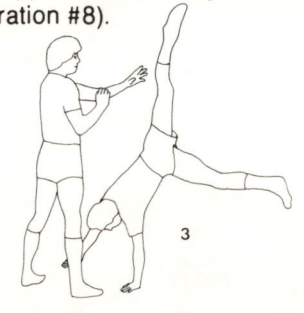

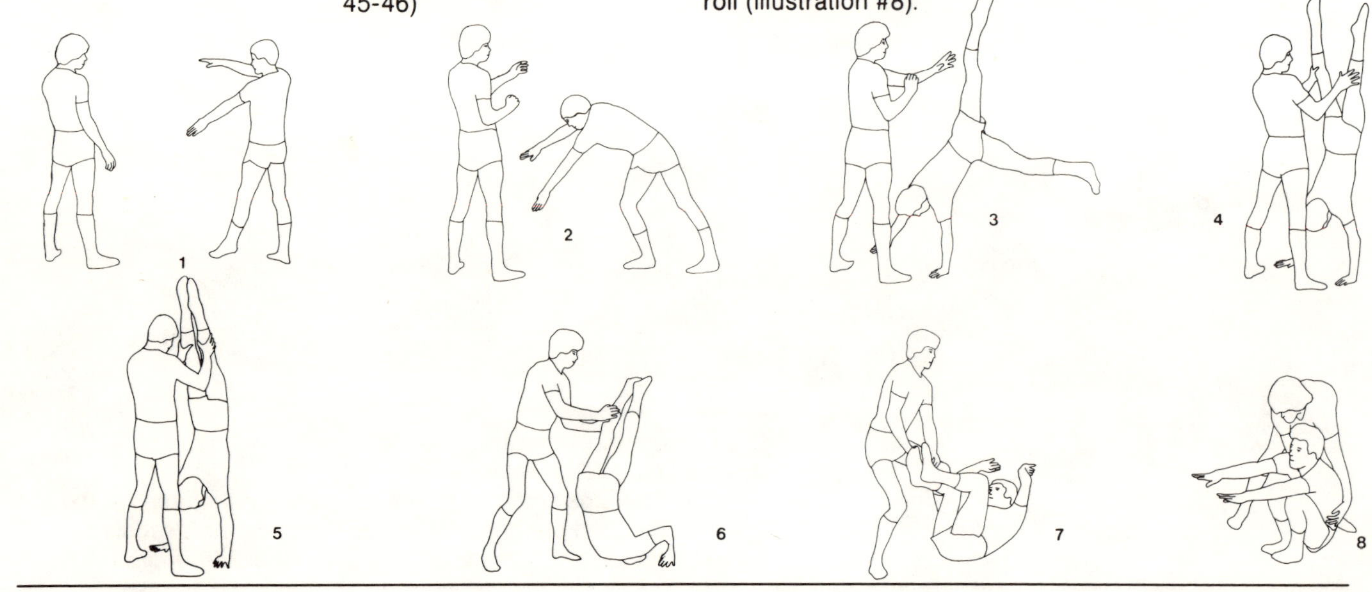

SKILL	TEACHING TECHNIQUES AND OBSERVATION POINTS

Common Errors:

Errors in Performance:

1. Failing to step into the straddled handstand with the hips above the shoulders. *Correction:* In order to initiate the forward roll out of the straddled handstand, it will be necessary to move the center of gravity slightly ahead of the hands i.e. toward the direction of the forward roll. If the hips are to the rear of the hands, it becomes more difficult to move out of the handstand position into the roll.
2. Entering the cartwheel with too much speed. *Correction:* Slow down and aim for control. The direction of movement changes in this skill. Too much speed in a sideways direction makes the entry into the forward roll extremely difficult. With less speed it is also easier for the spotter to give help.
3. Anticipating the forward roll. *Correction:* The performer who is thinking only of the forward roll will lean too much in that direction and be unable to achieve the correct body position in the cartwheel (with the hips above the shoulders). Try to complete the cartwheel in a vertical position, then simultaneously bring the legs together and over balance into the forward roll.

Errors in Spotting:

1. Failing to step out of the way of the performer who is entering the forward roll. *Correction:* The spotting for this skill combines many of the spotting techniques used for spotting the handstand and the forward roll. However, the spotter must realize that once he has provided support for the straddled handstand (or first half of the cartwheel), he must quickly shift to the side of the performer (illustrations #5-6). This action puts the spotter into position to assist with the forward roll (if necessary).

16. Forward Roll in Straddled Position (Straddled-Forward Roll)

Straddled - Forward Roll

This skill leads to:
1. piked forward roll (pages 75-77).
2. The straddle action occurs in many skills and on other apparatus, such as straddle vaults, and straddle mounts and dismounts on rings, parallel bars, and the horizontal bar.

Teaching Points for the Skill:
1. Stand in a wide straddle stance. Drive up, out, and then down toward the mats (illustrations A#1-3 and B#1-4).
2. Begin the roll and maintain a straddled position with the legs. Bend the upper body as far forward as possible (illustrations A#2 and B#2-3).
3. As the heels touch the mat, reach between the legs and press down and back on the floor as strongly as possible (illustrations A#4 and B#4-5).
4. When the hips and seat are above the feet and balance is obtained, stand up (illustration A#5).

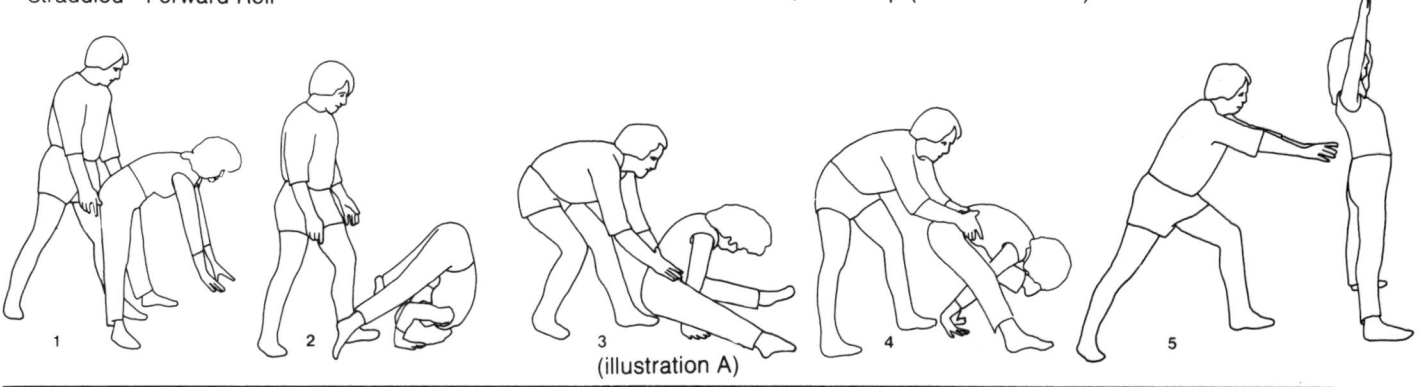

(illustration A)

| SKILL | TEACHING TECHNIQUES AND OBSERVATION POINTS |

Lead-up skills:
1. tucked forward roll (pages 37-38)
2. flexibility in a straddled position (pages 19-20)

Straddled-Forward Roll From Straddle Balance

Safety and Spotting:
Perform the straddle forward roll on a mat.
Spotting
1. Step forward as the performer rolls and quickly grip around the waist. Lift up and forward, timing the lift to occur with the performer's push from the floor (illustrations A#3-4).

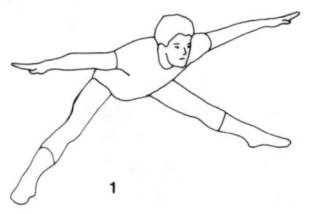

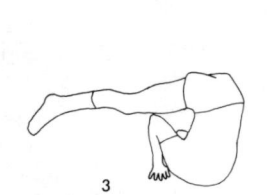

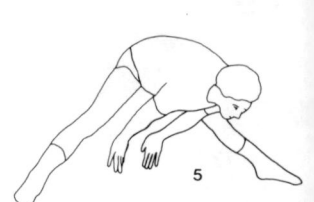

(illustration B)

Common Errors:
Errors in Performance:
1. Insufficient flexibility in a straddled position or poor hip flexion. *Correction:* Improve flexibility in these areas (see pages 19-20). Practice the skill with as much speed as possible.

Errors in Spotting:
1. Moving too slowly to be of any assistance to the performer. *Correction:* Be ready to step after the performer the moment the roll is initiated. Time the lift around the waist to occur the moment the performer pushes from the floor.

17. Standing Dive Forward Roll

This skill leads to:
1. running dive forward roll
2. front salto

Lead-up skills:
1. tucked forward roll (pages 37-38)
2. handstand-forward roll (pages 45-46)
3. dive forward roll with assistance (illustrations A#1-6)

Teaching Points for the Skill:
Standing Dive Forward Roll with and without assistance
1. Drive forward and up into the skill using the legs and arms to obtain lift. Extend the body (illustrations B#1-3)
2. Flex the arms, tuck the head under, curve the back, and bend the legs (in that sequence only) (illustrations B#3-5).
4. Hold the tuck and reach forward to stand up (illustration B#7).

Safety and Spotting:
Use a crash pad or thick soft mats.

Lead-up Standing Dive Forward Roll With Assistance

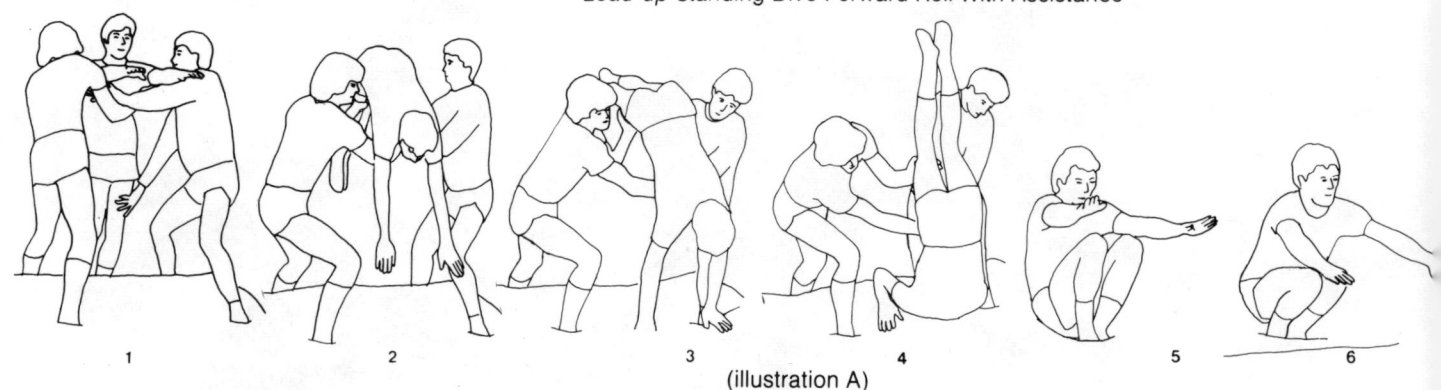

(illustration A)

SKILL	TEACHING TECHNIQUES AND OBSERVATION POINTS

Spotting
1. Reach across the chest and support in the front of the thigh (illustration A#1).
2. Cradle the performer as he drives up into the skill (illustration A#2).
3. Lower the performer gently into the roll (illustration A#3).

Standing Dive Forward Roll (onto crash pad)

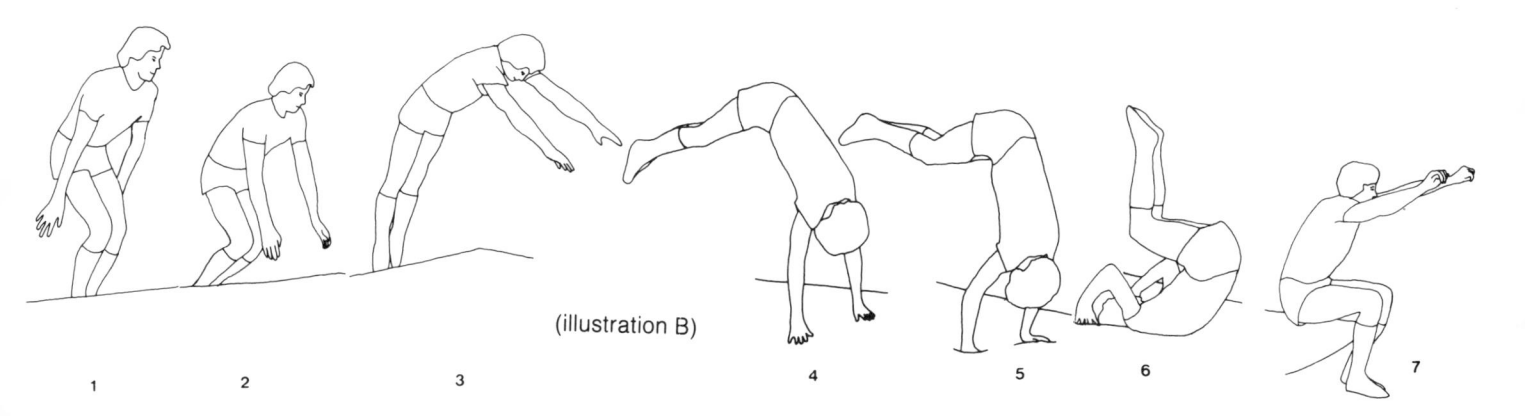

(illustration B)

Common Errors:

Errors in Performance:
1. Tucking the head under too early. *Correction:* Keep the vision on the mat and tuck the head under at the last instant. Use the arms as initial shock absorbers for the landing.
2. Keeping the body straight and as a result dropping onto the flat of the back. *Correction:* Lower into the roll in the following sequence - bend the arms, tuck the head under, curve the back, bend the legs. If this sequence is altered the performer will land too heavily. If the heavy landing continues to occur, re-practice the sequence of lowering the body into a forward roll from a handstand. Concentrate on the correct sequence of actions. When this sequence is well established, return to the standing dive forward roll.

Error in Spotting:
1. Overspotting. *Correction:* When two spotters are assisting the performer in the dive forward roll, they should take care not to throw the performer over onto his back. Assistance should be sufficient to elevate the performer upward and then lower him onto his outstretched arms. The performer then rolls out of this momentary handstand.

| SKILL | | TEACHING TECHNIQUES AND OBSERVATION POINTS |

18. Backward Roll to Handstand (Back Extension)

This skill leads to:
1. Other skills in which a vigorous extension at the hips occurs, e.g. headspring, neckspring as floor skills and as vaults (pages 65-66 and 141-144).
2. The back extension can also be performed from a straddle backward roll. The legs are brought together at the midpoint of the skill.

Lead-up skills:
1. all variations of the backward roll (see pages 38-41 & 43-44)
2. handstand (pages 33-35)
3. backward roll extend at 45 degrees (illustrations A#1-4), and back extension from piked position with two spotters assisting (illustrations B#1-3)
4. back extension from sitting (illustrations C#1-3).

Teaching Points for the Skill:
Backward Roll - extend at 45 degrees (illustrations A#1-4)
1. Roll backward either from straight legged sitting, or from tucked position (illustration A#1).
2. As the hips pass over and beyond the shoulders, extend the body and push strongly backward at 45 degrees (illustrations A#2-3).

Backward Roll - extend to 45°

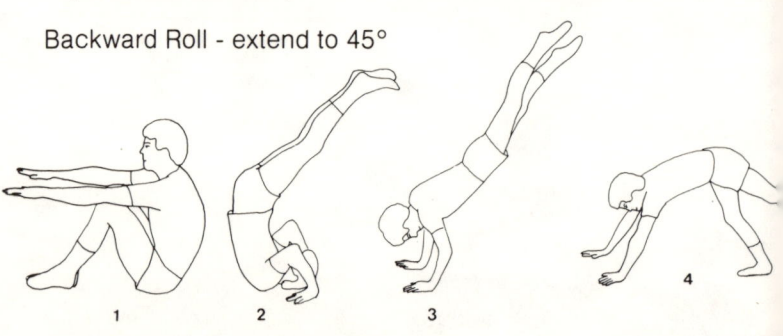

(illustration A)

Back Extension from Piked Position (illustrations B#1-3)
1. Begin in a back piked position on the floor (illustration B#1).
2. Extend at the hips and drive the legs directly upward. As the legs are extended push vigorously with the arms (illustrations B#2-3).

Back Extension From Piked Position

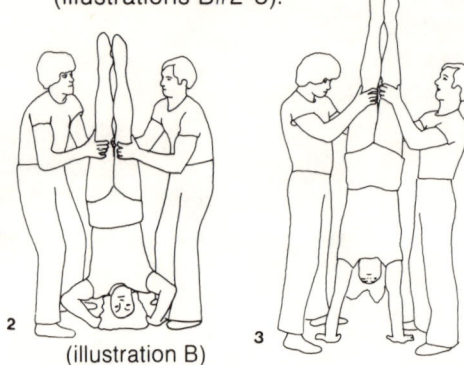

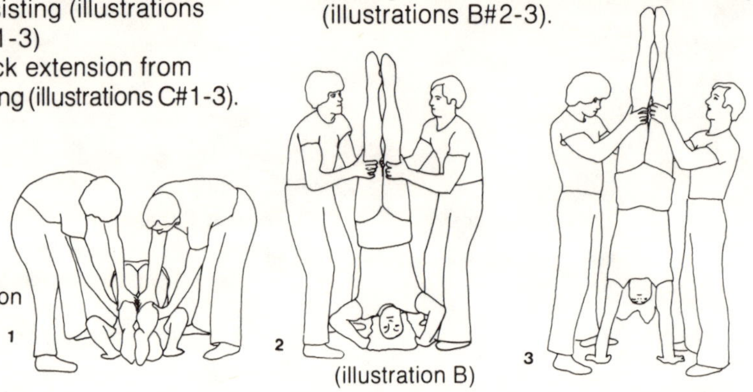

(illustration B)

Back Extension From Sitting

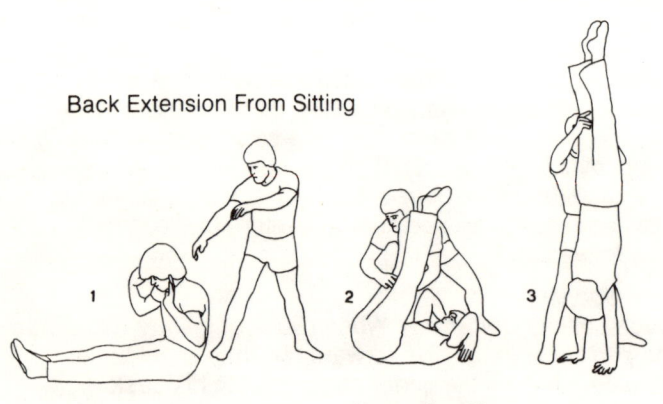

(illustration C)

Back Extension from Sitting (illustrations C#1-3)
1. Begin in a straight-legged sitting position with the arms held ready (illustration C#1).
2. Roll back in a piked position until the hips are above the shoulders.
3. Extend upward, straightening the body and pushing strongly with the arms (illustration C#3).

Back Extension from Standing (illustrations D#1-4)
1. While standing, pike forward. Reach as far back as possible to the rear of the body. Sit backwards (illustrations D#1-2).
2. Use the arms to cushion contact with the floor (illustration D#2).
3. Maintain the pike until the hips are above the head. Then extend vigorously upward from the hips. At the same time extend the arms as powerfully as possible (illustration D#3-4).

| SKILL | TEACHING TECHNIQUES AND OBSERVATION POINTS |

Back Extension From Standing

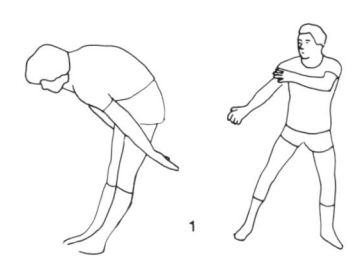

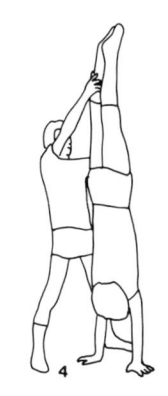

(illustration D)

Safety and Spotting:
Perform the back extension on mats.
Spotting
1. Spotters grip around the knee and elevate the performer upward timing this lift with his extension (illustration B#2).
2. If the performer is rolling backward from a standing or sitting start, allowance must be made for the distance covered in the roll and the increased speed of action (see illustrations D#1-4).

Common Errors:
Errors in Performance:
1. Extending upward too early or too late. *Correction:* The performer must wait until the hips are above or slightly past the line of the head and shoulders before extending upward.

Errors in Spotting:
1. Mistiming the lift upward. *Correction:* Spotters must time their lift upward to coincide exactly with the performer's extension. They must be prepared to lift upward quickly as the performer's extension from the hips can be extremely fast.

19. Handstand (without assistance)

(3 seconds)

This skill leads to:
1. handstand quarter turn (pages 56-57)
2. cartwheel-forward roll (pages 50-51)
3. advanced balances (e.g. one-handed handstand)

Lead-up skills:
1. jump to tucked handstand (page 33)
2. "kick and point" (page 34)
3. handstand with one spotter (page 35)
4. handstand-forward roll (pages 45-46)

Teaching Points for the Skill:
1. Stand in the ready position, one leg forward and the arms extended (illustration #1).
2. Step forward into the handstand, swinging one leg upward and pushing off the floor with the trailing leg. Do not allow the shoulders to sag forward (illustrations #2-3).
3. Bring both legs together in the vertical position. Extend the body upward and try not to arch the back. Keep the vision between or just ahead of the hands (illustration #5).
4. To maintain balance, press down on the floor with the fingertips if the bodyweight moves forward over the hands. Bend the elbows slightly if the bodyweight moves backward. Keep working in this fashion to maintain balance.
5. Step back down out of the handstand or forward roll out of the handstand.

Safety and Spotting:
Place a mat ahead of the fingertips to cushion a forward roll out of the handstand.
Spotting
Spotting techniques are explained on pages 34-35.

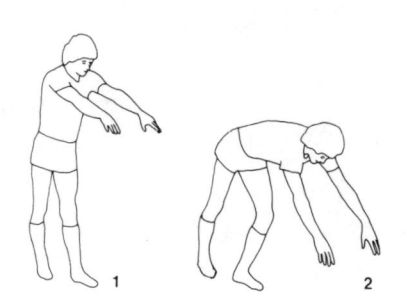

SKILL	TEACHING TECHNIQUES AND OBSERVATION POINTS

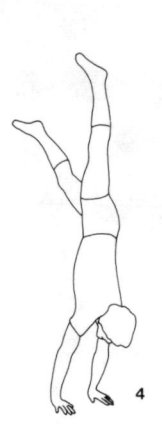

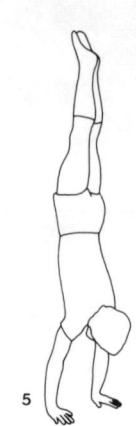

Handstand Without Assistance (3 seconds)

Common Errors:
Errors in Performance:
1. Bending the arms and arching the back. *Correction:* Practice pressing the body upward in the handstand and pulling the stomach in so that all body parts are in alignment. Use a spotter for assistance in achieving the correct body position.
2. Incorrect line of vision and tucking the head under. *Correction:* Look at the floor between the hands or just ahead of the fingertips. Do not roll the chin onto the chest or look too far ahead of the fingertips. This will cause the back to arch and it will disturb body alignment.

20. Handstand-Quarter Turn

This skill leads to:
1. handstand-half turn (half-pirouette)
2. handstand-full turn (full pirouette)
3. handstand-pirouette on apparatus; for example, parallel bars, and horizontal bar

Teaching Points for the Skill:
1. Kick to a handstand position with the body straight and erect.
2. For a quarter turn on the left hand, shift the weight slightly onto the left hand and move the right hand to its new position (illustrations A#3-4).
3. Shift weight slightly to the right hand and re-position and align the left hand (illustration #5).

Lead-up Handstand - Quarter Turn With Assistance

(illustration A)

Lead-up skills:
1. a well controlled handstand (2-3 seconds) (pages 55-56)
2. ability to step down or roll forward out of the handstand without

Safety and Spotting:
This skill is easier to perform on a hard surface rather than mats. Complete the quarter turn toward a mat so that the forward roll will be adequately cushioned.
Spotting
1. Stabilize the performer in the handstand. Support around hips rather than ankles (illustrations A#1-3).

SKILL	TEACHING TECHNIQUES AND OBSERVATION POINTS

assistance (see pages 33-35 and 45-46)

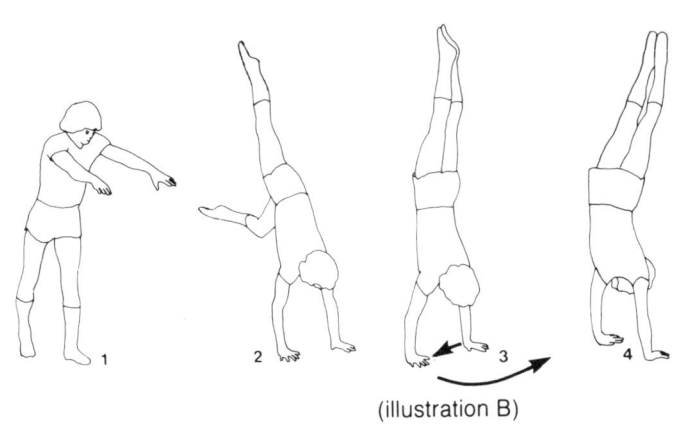

Handstand - Quarter Turn

(illustration B)

2. Guide and stabilize the performer through the quarter turn (illustrations A#3-5).
3. If the performer can roll out of the handstand then assistance will be unnecessary.

Common Errors:
Errors in Performance:
1. Failing to maintain a straight body. *Correction:* Press up from the shoulders and pull the stomach in. Avoid arching the back. Keep the body as straight as possible.
2. Attempting the quarter turn without a shift in bodyweight. *Correction:* If the turn is to the left, shift the bodyweight (center of gravity) over the left hand to lessen the weight on the right. When the right hand is shifted to its new position, align the left and move the bodyweight back between the hands.

Errors in Spotting:
1. Pulling the performer out of alignment (balance). *Correction:* Spotting should be used solely as a form of orientation to the movement and change of hand positions. After they have been established the performer should attempt the skill alone. It is difficult for a spotter to keep the performer's center of gravity in the correct position throughout the quarter turn. As a result spotting can become a hindrance.

21. Round-Off

This skill leads to:
The round-off is a lead-up or connecting skill, changing forward motion into backward motion. It is used most frequently in routines as a lead-up to backhandsprings and back saltos.

Lead-up skills:
1. handstand (pages 33-35)
2. cartwheel (pages 47-50)

Teaching Points for the Skill:
Beginners should initially attempt the round-off along a box top. This gives more height (particularly in the latter half of the skill) and gives more time for rotation of the body and "snapping" the legs downward.
1. Step into the round-off along the box top as though entering a cartwheel. (Note: the hurdle entry to the round-off, which is similar to that of the handspring, will be used when the round-off is performed on the floor with a running approach.)
2. Place the lead hand on the box top in a line directly ahead of the leading leg. As this hand is being placed down, turn the shoulders to initiate the rotation of the body (illustrations A#2-3).
3. Place the trailing hand on the box top. Rotate the hand prior to its placement to continue the rotation of the body. The actual placement of the trailing hand will vary for each individual.
4. Bring the legs together in the vertical position (illustrations A#3-4).
5. Complete the rotation and "snap" the legs down by piking vigorously at the waist (illustration A#4).
6. Push away from the box top (illustration A#5).
7. After practicing along a box top, without spotters (illustrations B#1-5) work on the round-off at floor level.

Safety and Spotting:
Practice the round-off on mats.

SKILL

Lead-up Round-Off Along a Box-Top (With Assistance)

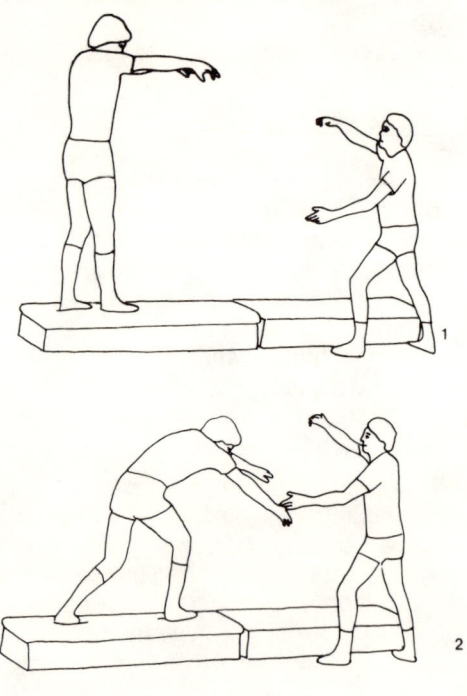

(illustration A)

Round-Off Along a Box-Top

(illustration B)

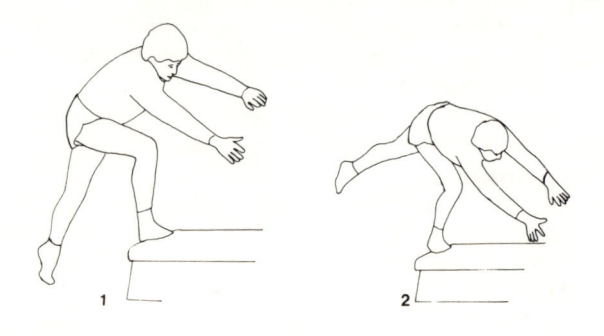

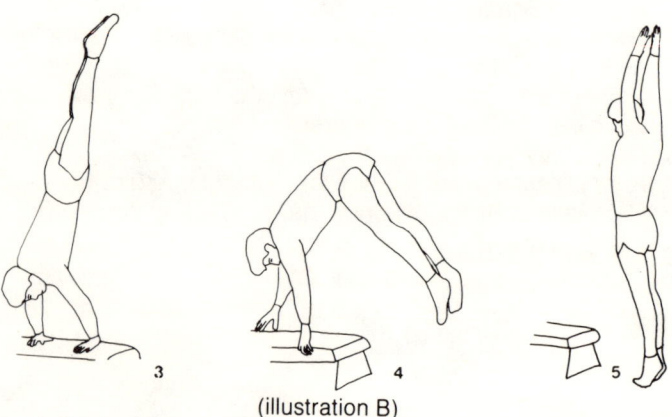

TEACHING TECHNIQUES AND OBSERVATION POINTS

Spotting
If the performer can manage a cartwheel (good technique - with hips passing over the shoulders), the round-off can be practiced without spotting.

Recommended spotting method if assistance is given
1. Stand "ahead" of the performer in order to obtain a strong grip on each hip (illustrations A#1-3).
2. Assist in rotating the performer through the half turn of the round-off (illustrations A#3-5).
3. When the round-off is performed with reasonable accuracy - remove spotting assistance.

Common Errors:
Errors in Performance:
1. Insufficient rotation so that the performer does not make a full half turn. *Correction:* Initiate the rotation by turning the shoulders prior to the placement of the first hand. Keep turning the body. Rotate the final hand placement so that it will assist in turning the body. Bring the legs together quickly. This will help the body to rotate.
2. The hips do not pass over the shoulders and the hand positions. *Correction:* Kick up and forward and not to the side during the entry to the round-off. Be sure the final hand placement is close to the line of direction and not out to the side.
3. The take-off and push away from the floor is too slow. *Correction:* The benefit of practicing the round-off along a box top is that it can be attempted slowly. With each attempt the skill should then become more dynamic and vigorous. When attempted on the floor it should be performed as quickly as possible. Kick strongly upward, bringing the feet together in the inverted position. Push away from the floor and snap the legs down. The hands should be well off the ground when the feet make contact.

SKILL	TEACHING TECHNIQUES AND OBSERVATION POINTS

22. Headspring from a rolled mat or box-top

This skill leads to:
1. headspring on the floor (pages 65-66)
2. headspring as a vault (pages 141-144)
3. other advanced forms of the headspring on the floor and on apparatus.

Lead-up Piked Headstand

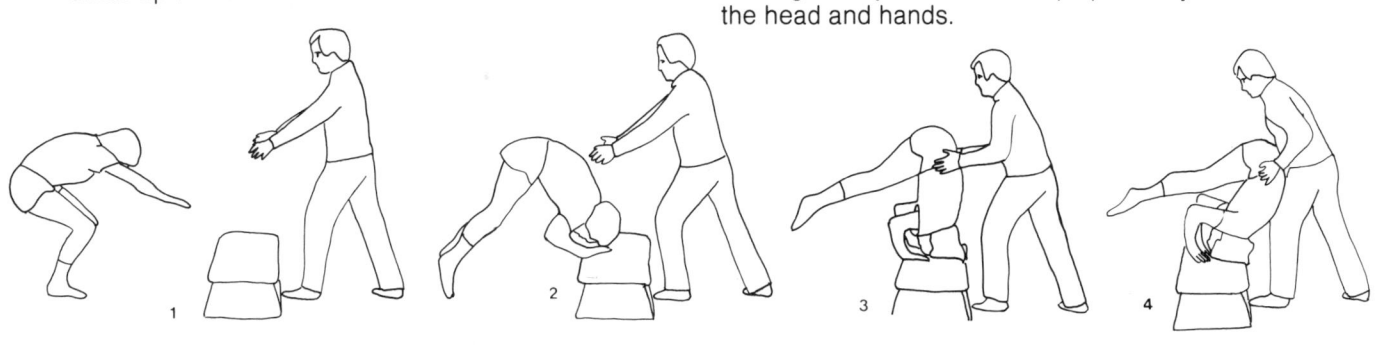

(illustration A)

Lead-up skills:
1. headstand (pages 31-32)
2. handstand (pages 33-35)
3. the back arch of bridge-flexibility exercise (page 20)
4. a fast entry to a piked handstand (illustrations A#1-4)
5. piked headstand to handstand (illustrations B#1-5)
6. headspring controlled by 3 spotters (illustrations C#1-4)

Lead-up Piked Headstand to Handstand (illustration B)

Teaching Points for the Skill:
Fast entry to a piked headstand (illustrations A#1-4)
1. Begin in a semi-squatting position (illustration A#1).
2. Extend forward toward the box top by straightening the legs. Place the forehead and hands in a line on the box top (illustration A#2).
3. Push forward into the piked headstand. Keep the back straight and the legs extended. The feet should be below the height of the seat (illustrations A#3-4). Perform this skill vigorously. Be sure the hips pass beyond the line of the head and hands.

Piked Headstand to Handstand (illustrations B#1-5)
This lead-up is best performed on the floor and not on a box top.
1. Extend forward into a piked headstand position (illustration B#3).
2. When the hips have moved above and slightly past the head, extend upward into the handstand. Push hard with the hands on the floor (illustrations B#3-5).

Headspring Controlled by Three Spotters (illustrations C#1-4)
1. The standing spotter lifts and pushes the performer's body into the piked headstand position (illustration C#1). The performer's hips are pushed well beyond the line of the head and hands (illustration C#1).
2. On a pre-determined count of "one-two-and-three" the spotter throws the performer's legs into the final portion of the headspring.

SKILL	TEACHING TECHNIQUES AND OBSERVATION POINTS

3. The performer will be listening to the count. On "three" the performer extends vigorously at the hips and pushes hard with the hands on the box top (illustration C#3).
4. The arms remain extended in the final landing position (illustration C#4).

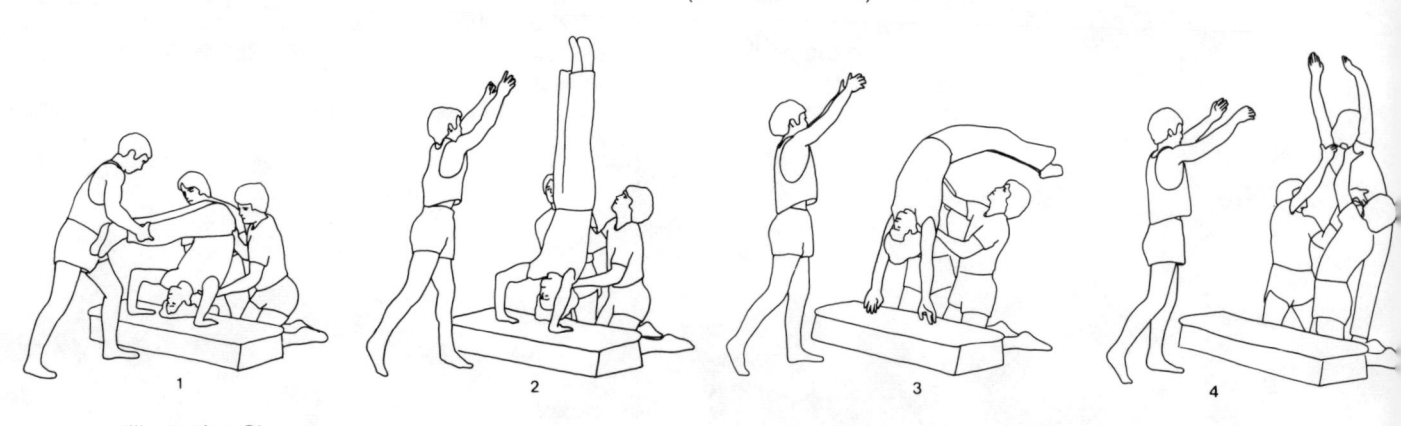

(illustration C)

Headspring Assisted by One or Two Spotters (illustrations D#1-3, E#1-4, and F#3-5).
1. Once the timing of the extension in the headspring is well established, the performer enters the skill without the help of a spotter controlling the leg actions.
2. The spotters assisting on the post-flight side of the box top assist by controlling the performer's body position. This is described below.

Safety and Spotting:
Use mats on the post-flight side of the box top.
Spotting
Fast entry to a Piked Headstand (illustrations A#1-4)
1. The spotter controls and cushions the performer with his thigh as the performer moves forward into the piked headstand. The spotter allows the performer's hips to pass beyond the position of the head and hands.

Piked Headstand to Handstand (illustrations B#1-5)
1. The spotter reaches under the performer's shoulder and around the waist, lifts upward, and pulls the performer toward him during the extension into the handstand.

Headspring Controlled by Three Spotters (illustrations C#1-4)
1. The standing spotter pushes the performer's hips past the line of the head and shoulders. On the count of "three" the spotter throws the performer's legs forward into the headspring.
2. Two spotters kneel on the post-flight side of the box top. One hand supports under the shoulder and the other at the performer's upper seat (illustration C#1).
3. The performer is cradled through the headspring. The landing is controlled and stabilized. The spotters grip strongly at the shoulder and they do not allow the performer to stumble forward in the landing (illustrations C#1-4).

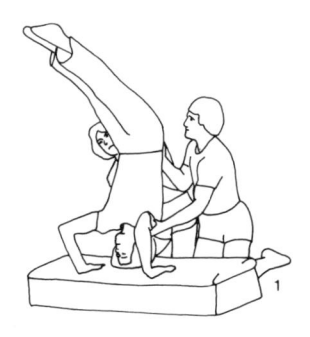

SKILL	TEACHING TECHNIQUES AND OBSERVATION POINTS

Headspring Controlled by Two Spotters (illustrations D#1-3)
1. The spotter controlling the actions of the performer's legs is removed and the performer enters the skill alone. The performer now controls the timing of the extension out of the piked headstand. Spotters support under the shoulder and seat and cradle the performer through to the landing.

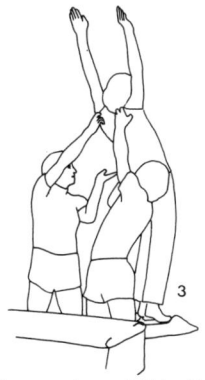

Headspring (2 Spotters)

(illustration D)

Headspring Controlled by Two Spotters (illustrations E#1-4)
This sequence shows an alternative spotting technique that can be used by kneeling spotters.
1. Instead of bending the support arm at the elbow and supporting under the seat (illustration D#2), the spotters cross arms and cradle the performer with their upper arms. Additional support is given as before under the shoulder. The landing is well controlled (illustrations E#1-4).

Headspring (2 Spotters)

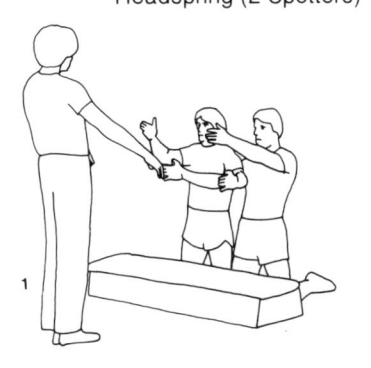

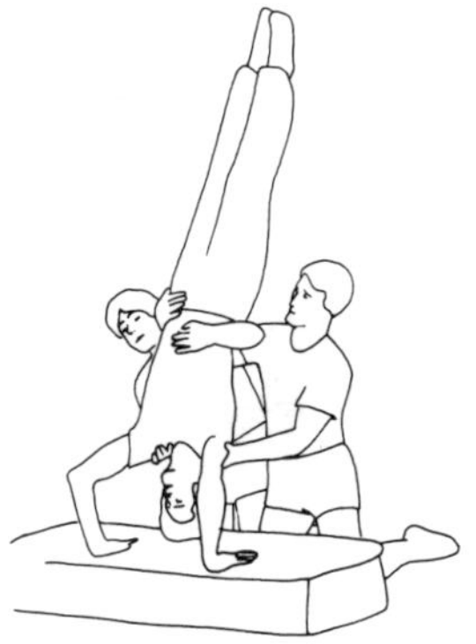

(illustration E)

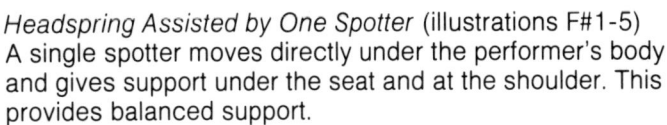

Headspring Assisted by One Spotter (illustrations F#1-5)
A single spotter moves directly under the performer's body and gives support under the seat and at the shoulder. This provides balanced support.

Headspring (One Spotter)

(illustration F)

| SKILL | TEACHING TECHNIQUES AND OBSERVATION POINTS |

Common Errors:
Errors in Performance:
1. Extending out of the piked position before the hips have passed beyond the line of the head and hands. (This is a very common error.) *Correction:* The feet should be kept down and the hips allowed to pass "over" the head and shoulders before the performer extends into the headspring. The spotting technique shown in illustrations E#1-4 is excellent for controlling the body position of the performer, since it allows the spotters to pull him into the correct position for the extension out of the piked headstand.
2. Curving the back and rolling the head under. *Correction:* The forehead must be placed on the box top with the back and neck kept as straight as possible. Spotters can help to place the performer in the correct position.

Errors in Spotting:
1. Assisting at too great a distance from the performer. *Correction:* Stay as close to the performer as possible. The kneeling spotters must resist the temptation to turn sideways and to lean away from the performer.
2. Resisting the performer's efforts to move into a piked headstand position with the hips well ahead of the line of the head and hands. *Correction:* In their eagerness to provide assistance, spotters may lean toward the performer and unknowingly provide a barrier which stops the performer from achieving the correct body positions in this skill. It is essential that the performer's hips move past the line of the head and hands. Spotters should not resist this action in any way.

23. Tucked Press to Handstand (with flexed arms)

This skill leads to:
1. straddle press to handstand (pages 63-64)

Lead-up skills:
1. straddle press to headstand (pages 42-43)
2. jump to tucked handstand (page 33)
3. handstand (pages 55-56)

Tuck Press to Handstand (With Flexed Arms)

Teaching Points for the Skill:
1. With a two-footed take-off, spring lightly onto the hands (illustration #1).
2. Bend the legs (illustrations #1-3).
3. Bend the arms to allow the hips to lift above the shoulders (illustration #2).
4. Straighten the legs into the handstand (illustrations #3-4).

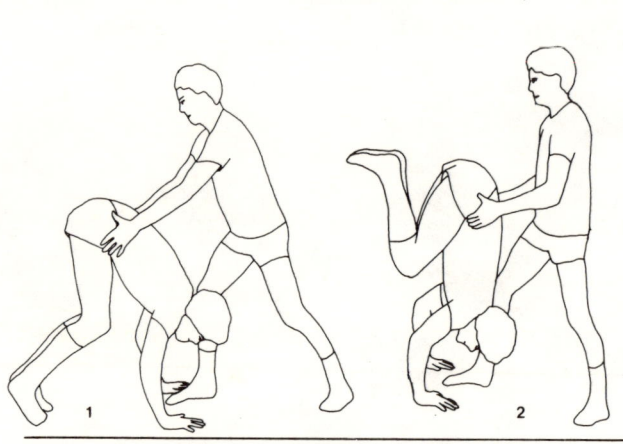

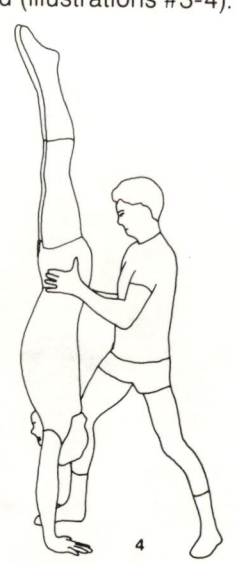

| SKILL | TEACHING TECHNIQUES AND OBSERVATION POINTS |

Safety and Spotting:
The use of a mat is optional. It is usually unnecessary if a spotter assists the performers.
Spotting
1. Grip the performer around the hips and help to control the elevation of the hips and seat (illustrations #1-2).
2. Lift upwards at the hips to assist the performer into the handstand (illustration #3).
3. For additional stabilization shift grip from hips to ankles.

Common Errors:
Errors in Performance:
1. Extending the legs before the hips and seat are above the shoulders. *Correction:* Maintain a tucked position and bend the arms to allow the hips to shift above the shoulders. Then extend the legs upward into the handstand.
2. Collapsing the arms. *Correction:* Keep the arms straighter and "cheat" a little by jumping more vigorously into the skill. This will lift the hips higher. Keep the legs flexed and straighten them only when the hips are above the shoulders.

Level IV Skills

24. Straddle Press to Handstand

This skill leads to:
1. Further advanced balancing skills which combine balance with great power and strength.

Lead-up skills:
1. good flexibility in the wrists
2. tucked press to handstand with flexed arms (pages 62-63)

Teaching Points for the Skill:
1. Assume a straddled position, keeping the seat fairly high. Place the hands on the floor as close to the midpoint between the feet as possible.
2. Lean forward so that the hips shift over the hands
3. Elevate the straddled legs to a handstand (illustrations #2-3).
4. Bring the legs together in the handstand position (illustration #3).

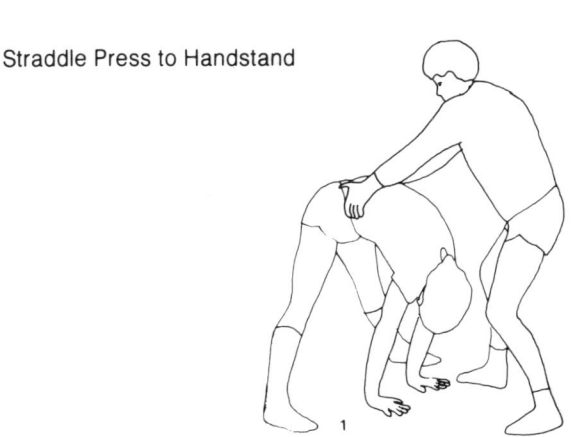

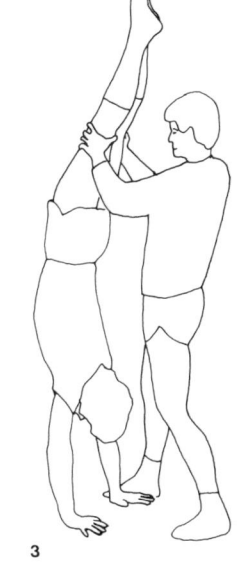

Straddle Press to Handstand

Safety and Spotting:
Spotting
1. Reach over the performer's back and grip around the waist (illustration #1).

SKILL	TEACHING TECHNIQUES AND OBSERVATION POINTS

2. Assist the performer in shifting the hips forward and elevating the legs upward (let the performer do as much of the skill as possible) (illustration #2).
3. Shift the grip to the legs to stabilize the final handstand position (illustration #3).

Common Errors:
Errors in Performance:
1. Placing the hands too far ahead of the midpoint between the feet. *Correction:* Place the hands "in between the feet." Move the hips into a position where they are above and ahead of the shoulders. If necessary cheat a little by lifting up onto tip toes to raise the hips even higher. If this does not help go back to the lead-up skill and practice the skill with flexed arms.
2. Elevating the legs too soon. *Correction:* Hold the flexed position at the hips as long as possible and raise the legs to the final handstand position as the last action performed.

25. L-Support
(3 seconds)

This skill leads to:
1. High V-support (the legs are raised to 45 degrees or more rather than parallel to the floor as in the L-support. The seat is elevated from the floor and the full bodyweight is taken on the hands).

Lead-up skills:
1. V-sit (pages 35-36)
2. L-support and tucked support on the parallel bars (pages   )
3. support in tucked position (illustration #1)

L-Support

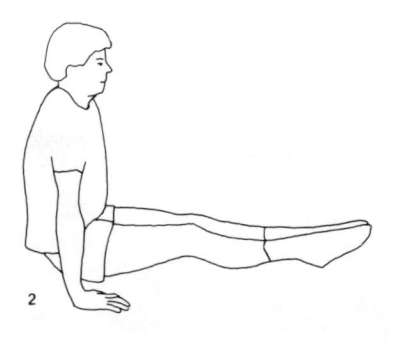

(illustration B)

Teaching Points for the Skill:
Tucked Support
1. In a sitting position draw the knees up close to the chest.
2. Draw the heel in close to the seat. Tighten the stomach muscles.
3. Lift the seat from the floor. Press the shoulders downward and lift the chest high. Hold momentarily (illustration #1).
4. Relax to sitting. Repeat.

Lead-up Tucked Support

(illustration A)

L-Support
1. Begin in sitting position with the legs extended.
2. Tighten the stomach muscles.
3. Press down with the shoulders and lift upward so that the seat and the heels are equidistant from the floor (illustration #2). Hold momentarily. Relax and repeat.

Safety and Spotting:
None necessary. The L-support can be performed on the floor or on mats.

Common Errors:
Errors in Performance:
1. Insufficient strength in the stomach and the upper thighs to maintain the tucked or L-support position. *Correction:* Return to abdominal strengthening exercises (pages 14-16). Practice frequently and work on the tucked and L-support after an increase in strength. Also practice the L-support on the parallel bars, rings and ropes

| SKILL | TEACHING TECHNIQUES AND OBSERVATION POINTS |

26. Headspring on the Floor

This skill leads to:
1. advanced forms of headsprings performed on the floor
2. the headspring as a vault (pages 141-144).
3. necksprings performed on the floor (illustrations B#1-4)
4. the neckspring performed as a vault

Lead-up skills:
1. a headspring from a rolled mat or box top and its associated lead-up skills (pages 59-62)

Headspring on the Floor

(illustration A)

Related Skill Neckspring on Floor

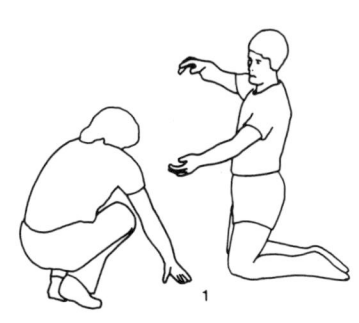

(illustration B)

Teaching Points for the Skill:
When the headspring is performed from the floor (as opposed to a box top), the body positions are more critical. The extension from the piked headstand position must be more vigorous.

Review the teaching sequence for the headspring from a rolled mat or box top.

For the Headspring on the Floor (illustrations A#1-5)
1. Extend from the squatting position into a piked headstand with the feet well below the line of the hips
2. Allow the hips to pass forward and beyond the head and hands (very important).
3. Extend vigorously out of the piked headstand (illustrations A#2-4).
4. Extend upward pressing the hips forward. Leave the arms up and back. Look upward (illustration A#5).

The Neckspring (Related Skill) (illustrations B#1-4)
The neckspring is similar to the headspring with the exception that the extension from the piked position is performed in a lower position (with the head tucked under). A strong extension upward is needed to perform the neckspring at floor level

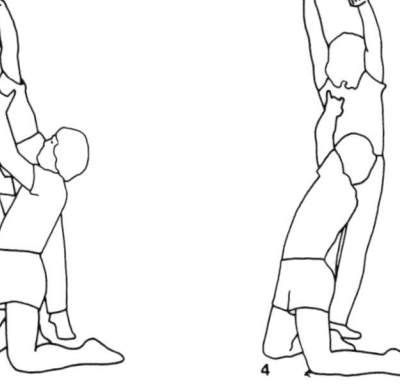

Safety and Spotting:
Perform the headspring and neckspring on mats.
Spotting
1. Spotters support under the shoulder and across the seat. In this manner they cradle the performer through the extension from the piked headstand to the final landing position (illustrations A#2-5).

SKILL	TEACHING TECHNIQUES AND OBSERVATION POINTS

2. A single spotter assists the performer in a headspring (or a neckspring) with one arm across the seat and the other placed under the shoulder. The spotter must get well under the performer's body and support his weight on the *upper arm.* Control must be given in the landing position (illustrations B#1-4).

Common Errors:
Errors in Performance:
1. Extending from the piked position too early. *Correction:* Return to practicing the headspring from a rolled mat or box top. Concentrate on allowing the hips to pass over and beyond the line of the head and hands before extending into the final part of the skill.
2. Insufficient extension and drive from the arms. *Correction:* Return to practicing the headspring from a rolled mat or box top. Concentrate on timing the extension from the hips and the drive from the arms to occur together. If the arms are particularly weak, work on strength exercises (pages 14-18)

Errors in Spotting:
1. Assisting at too great a distance from the performer. *Correction:* Stay as close to the performer as possible without hindering the action of the skill. (See section on spotting errors, pages 23-26).
2. Not allowing the performer to move into the piked headstand position. *Correction:* The spotters must not stop the forward shift of the performer into the piked headstand position. If this occurs the performer is liable to extend directly upward instead of forward into the post-flight section of the skill.

27. Handspring

This skill leads to:
1. variations of the handspring (for example, a handspring with a two-handed entry and a one-footed landing, often called a handspring walk-out)
2. fly-spring (a handspring with a two-footed entry and two-footed landing)

Lead-up skills:
1. handstand (pages 33-35)
2. orientation to complete movement pattern of the handspring (illustrations A#1-5)
3. a fast kick up to the handstand with a single hurdle step approach (illustrations B#1-4)
4. the back arch or bridge position (page 20). This is helpful but not

Teaching Points for the Skill:
Orientation to the Complete Movement Pattern of the Handspring (illustrations A#1-5)
1. Kick to a handstand. (A#1-2)
2. Hold a fully extended position. Maintain this position through to the landing. (A#3-5)

A Fast Kick to a Handstand (illustrations B#1-4)
1. From a two-step approach, take one pace and kick vigorously into a handstand. (B#1)
2. Keep the arms extended throughout with the vision just ahead of the fingertips. Do not allow the shoulders to sag forward.
3. Try to bring the legs together *prior* to the vertical position.
4. Step down and repeat the action.

The Handspring with One or Two Spotters Assisting (illustrations C#1-4, D#1-4, E#1-4, F#1-5, and G#1-3)
In all these sequences the performer carries out the following actions:
1. Approach from no more than three paces.
2. Reach long and low into the take-off. Try to keep the arms and back in a straight line. Do not let the shoulders sag forward ahead of the hand positions on the floor.
3. Kick vigorously from the floor and extend the lead leg. Bring both legs together so that the body is extended as it

SKILL

5. Kicking to a handstand and falling straight bodied into a crash pad. This gives an understanding for body position and body extension.

TEACHING TECHNIQUES AND OBSERVATION POINTS

passes through a handstand position.
4. Have the vision on the floor just ahead of the fingertips.
5. As the legs and hips pass over the hand positions, push away from the floor as vigorously as possible.
6. Hold the extended position through to the landing. Look upward and avoid sitting downward at the landing (illustration D#4).

Safety and Spotting:
Perform the handspring on mats.
Spotting
Orientation to the Complete Movement Pattern of the Handspring (illustrations A#1-5)
1. One spotter supports the performer in the handstand (illustrations A#1-2).
2. Two additional spotters step from the sides to cradle the performer through to the landing. Support is under the shoulder and across the seat (illustration A#3).
3. The single spotter supporting at the ankles leads the performer's feet down to the floor (illustrations A#3-5).
4. The whole action is performed *slowly and with control*. The sole intention of the practice is to give the performer a "feel" for the handspring action.

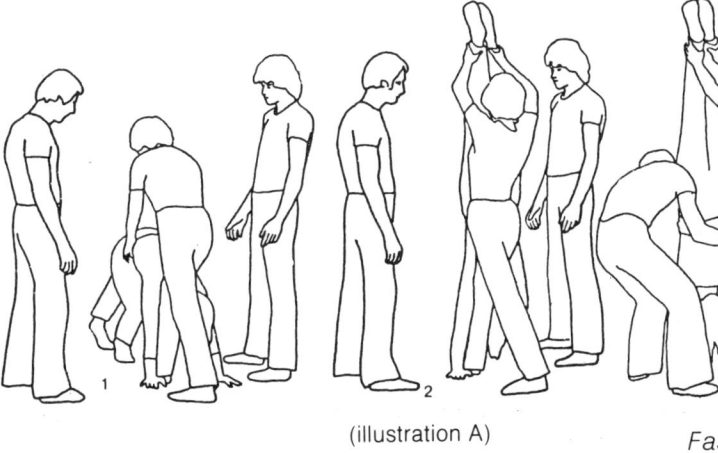

Lead-up Orientation to Handspring Movement Pattern

(illustration A)

Fast Kick to the Handstand (illustrations B#1-4)
1. The spotter stands in a ready position. One foot forward and one foot back. The rear foot is turned to the side for greater stability.
2. The spotter braces himself for the performer's forceful kick into the handstand. He cushions the impact of the performer's thighs against his shoulder (illustration B#4).

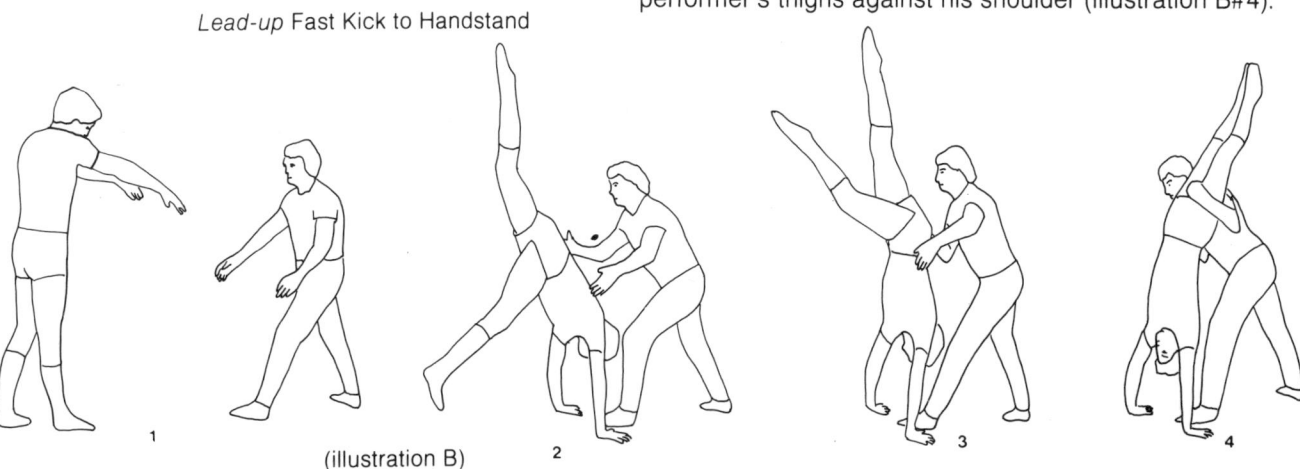

Lead-up Fast Kick to Handstand

(illustration B)

SKILL

Handspring (2 Spotters Standing)

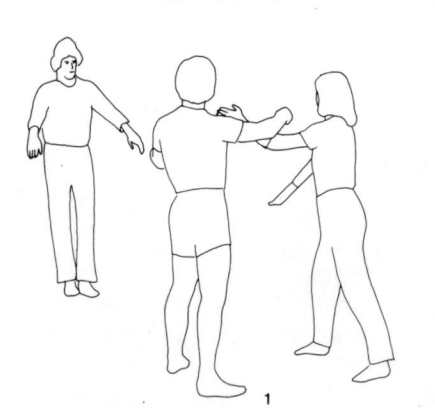

(illustration C)

Handspring (2 Spotters Kneeling)

(illustration D)

TEACHING TECHNIQUES AND OBSERVATION POINTS

The Handspring with Two Spotters Assisting in a Standing Position (illustrations C#1-4)
1. The spotters reach across the seat and support under the shoulder (illustration C#2).
2. The performer is cradled throughout the handspring. The landing is well controlled. The grip at the shoulder stops any further forward motion at the landing (illustration C#4).

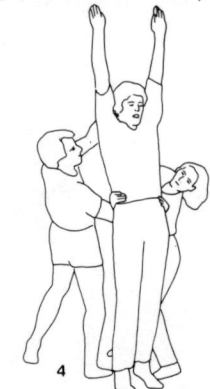

The Handspring with Two Spotters Assisting in a Kneeling Position (illustrations D#1-4)
1. The spotters kneel with the outside knee forward and the inner arms bent at the elbow (illustration D#1).
2. Support is given under the shoulder and under the seat (illustrations D#2-3).
3. The spotters cradle the performer through to the landing and resist any further forward motion with their grip on the shoulder (illustration D#4). This support is less mobile than the standing technique but provides excellent support for beginners.

The Handspring with Two Spotters Assisting in a Kneeling Position (illustrations E#1-4)
1. Spotters give support by reaching well across the performer's body and by gripping under the shoulder (illustration E#1).
2. This support cradles the performer through to the landing. Notice the control of the final landing position (illustration E#4). This support is less mobile than the standing technique but provides excellent support for beginners.

SKILL | TEACHING TECHNIQUES AND OBSERVATION POINTS

Handspring (2 Spotters Kneeling)

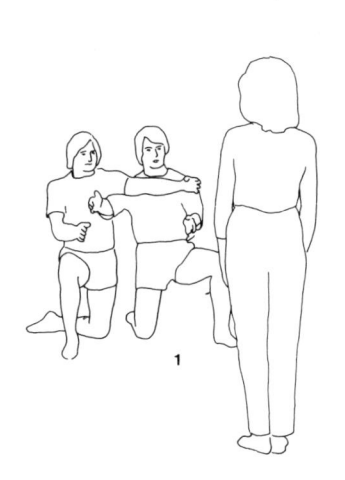

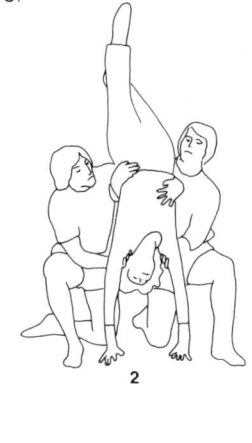

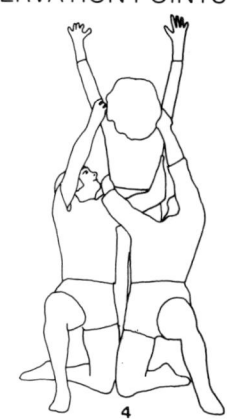

(illustration E)

Handspring (One Spotter Kneeling)

(illustration F)

The Handspring with One Spotter Assisting in a Kneeling Position (illustrations F#1-5)

1. In this spotting technique the single spotter has shifted his bent armed support so that it is in under the center line of the performer's body. The remaining hand (not seen in these illustrations) supports under the shoulder. In this manner stable support is given to a moderate performer.

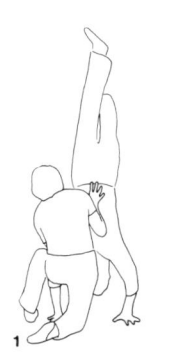

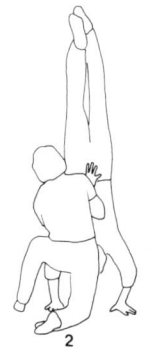

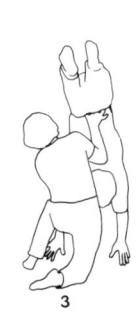

The Handspring with One Spotter Assisting in a Sitting Position (illustrations G#1-3)

1. In this technique the spotter sits straddle-legged and pushes back and upward on the performer's shoulders (illustrations G#2-3).
2. This technique is used to assist performers who have moderate technique but suffer from poor body alignment during the handspring. By pushing back and upward on the shoulders the spotter straightens the performer's body and stops any forward sag of the shoulders.

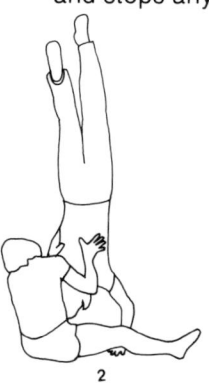

Handspring (One Spotter Sitting)

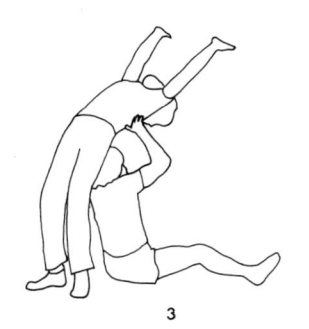

(illustration G)

SKILL		TEACHING TECHNIQUES AND OBSERVATION POINTS

Common Errors:
Errors in Performance:
1. The performer places his hands too close to the leading foot at take off. *Correction:* Reach long and low at the entry to the handspring. Look just ahead of the hands. Do not roll the head under.
2. The body is not extended from the mid-point of the skill through to the landing. *Correction:* Stretch up as the body passes through the handstand position. Try to rotate only around the hands when they are on the floor. Do not let the shoulders sag forward past the hands. The body should be as straight as possible.
3. The leg action is weak and ineffective. *Correction:* Be aggressive in this skill. Kick powerfully from the floor and swing the lead leg upward as strongly as possible. Then make sure that the trailing leg catches up with the lead leg so that they are together in the vertical position.
4. Dropping the hips and sitting at the landing. *Correction:* Hold an extended position and keep the arms and head back. Keep the hips moving forward.

Errors in Spotting:
1. Standing too far away from the performer. *Correction:* Stay as close to the performer as possible without hindering the flow of the skill. Lean the head away, otherwise stay as close as is possible.
2. Giving plenty of support in the first half of the skill and none at the end. *Correction:* Remember that spotting does not cease until the performer is standing motionless at the end of the skill. Cradle the performer through the skill and use the grip above the shoulder to resist any further forward motion after the landing. (See the section on spotting errors, pages 23-26)

28. One-Armed Cartwheel (near arm)

This skill leads to:
1. one-armed cartwheel on the far arm
2. The one-armed cartwheel can be used as a means of changing forward motion into backward motion and as such is often used in gymnastic routines.
3. The one-armed cartwheel can be used as a lead-up to the round-off.

Lead-up skills:
1. the handstand (pages 33-35)
2. a cartwheel using both arms (i.e. elementary cartwheel, pages 47-50).

Teaching Points for the Skill:
1. Begin by practicing the elementary cartwheel.
2. Increase the speed of entry to the elementary cartwheel and get as much lift as possible from the legs.
3. Enter the one-armed cartwheel as though attempting the elementary cartwheel. Use the near arm for support as this is generally considered easier than using the far arm. Try to avoid placing the far arm on the floor. If this occurs, repeat the skill with more lift from the legs and again try to avoid placing the far arm on the floor.
4. Be sure to enter the one-armed cartwheel faster than an elementary cartwheel. Drive up vigorously with the legs to elevate the hips.
5. Push off the single support arm as strongly as possible (illustrations #2-4).

Safety and Spotting:
Perform the one-armed cartwheel on mats.
Spotting
1. If the gymnast is able to perform a technically good cartwheel with both arms there will be no need for spotting the one-armed cartwheel. If the gymnast appears to be collapsing on the single support arm he should return to the

SKILL

One-Armed Cartwheel

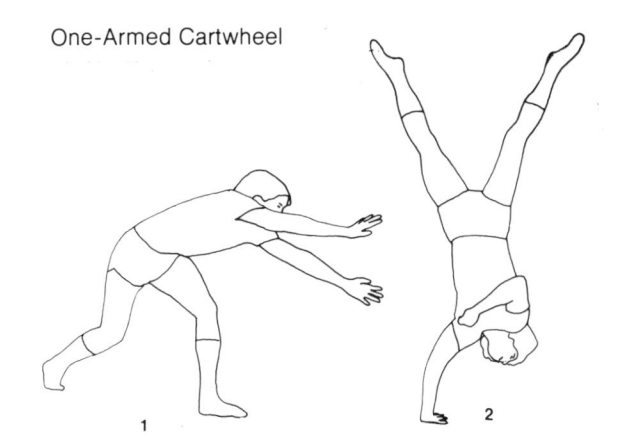

TEACHING TECHNIQUES AND OBSERVATION POINTS

elementary cartwheel and work to obtain more lift from the legs at the entry to the skill.

Common Errors:
Errors in Performance:
1. The one-armed cartwheel is performed too slowly.
   Correction: Remember that there will be no support given by the "far" arm. The body must be moving fast enough and have sufficient elevation to make up for this lack of support. Enter the skill with a powerful upward drive from the legs.
2. The push from the single supporting arm is weak.
   Correction: Work on driving up and over the support arm. Lessen the weight on the support arm by giving strong upward lift from the legs. Avoid flexing the support arm too much. Increase "push power" by triceps extension exercises (pages 14-18)

29. Backhandspring

This skill leads to:
1. advanced variations of the backhandspring, such as the backhandspring walk-out.
2. The backhandspring can be used as a lead-up to the back salto (back somersault).
3. The backhandspring is related in its basic movement pattern to the backwalkover.

Lead-up skills:
1. a good back arch or bridge position (page 20)
2. the handstand (pages 33-35)
3. orientation to the backhandspring (illustrations A#1-5).
4. backhandspring lead-ups (illustrations B#1-2 and illustrations C#1-2).

Teaching Points for the Skill:
Orientation to the Backhandspring
In this practice the performer is carried through the movement pattern of the backhandspring. *There is no attempt to sit back or to drive with the arms and legs into the skill.* Two spotters provide assistance and control through the whole action. The actions in this practice are extremely important. (See Safety and Spotting pages 23-26).
1. Stand erect with the arms extended above the head (illustration A#1).
2. Lie back and allow the spotters to provide a cradling support through to the inverted position (illustration A#2).
3. Keep the arms extended and close to the ears. Look for the mat (illustration A#2).
4. Place the hands on the mat as near to the original starting position as possible (illustration A#3).
5. Pike at the waist and with straight legs bring the feet down to the mat (illustration A#4).
6. After the feet are on the floor stretch up and extend the body (illustration A#5).

Backhandspring Lead-ups (illustrations B#1-2 and C#1-2)
Illustrations B#1-2 and C#1-2 show variations for practicing the starting position to the backhandspring. In both sequences the performer must sit back, keeping the upper body vertical. At the same time he lowers the arms to the sides of the body (illustrations B#2 and C#2).

SKILL	TEACHING TECHNIQUES AND OBSERVATION POINTS

Backhandspring with Two Spotters (illustrations D#1-6, E#1-4, F#1-5 and G#1-5)

Illustrations D#1-6, E#1-4, F#1-5 and G#1-5 show differing spotting techniques—from standing to kneeling, with and without a spotting belt. For the performer the actions are the same irrespective of the spotting technique. The sequence of actions is as follows:

1. Sit back, lowering the arms to the sides of the body. Do not bend forward but keep the body upright.
2. Drive back hard into the backhandspring by forcefully extending the legs. Push back from the floor from the heels, not from the toes. Simultaneously, swing the arms vigorously backward, keeping them extended throughout. Look for the mat (illustrations D#3-4).
3. When the hands make contact, bring the legs down by forcefully piking at the waist (illustrations D#4-5).
4. Push back and away from the floor (illustrations D#4-6).

Safety and Spotting:
Use mats or a crash pad.
Spotting
Orientation to the Backhandspring (illustrations A#1-5)
1. Stand as close to the performer as possible. Reach across the body and grip on either side of his waist. Place the remaining hand to the rear of the thigh just above the knee (A#1).
2. Cradle the performer as he lies backward. Stay close and take his weight on the upper arm (A#2).
3. Rotate his body in order to place him in the handstand position (A#3).
4. Once the performer's hands are placed on the floor, keep his hips and legs moving over and past the hand positions. *This is very important.*
5. Instruct the performer to bring his own legs down from the handstand with a command such as: "Feet to the floor." Be sure that the performer understands that he brings his feet to the floor by piking at the waist and not by bending at the knees.
6. Work through this practice slowly and with control. *Remember there is no sit back and no vigorous drive into the skill. The whole intention of the practice is to get a feel for the movements required in the backhandspring.*

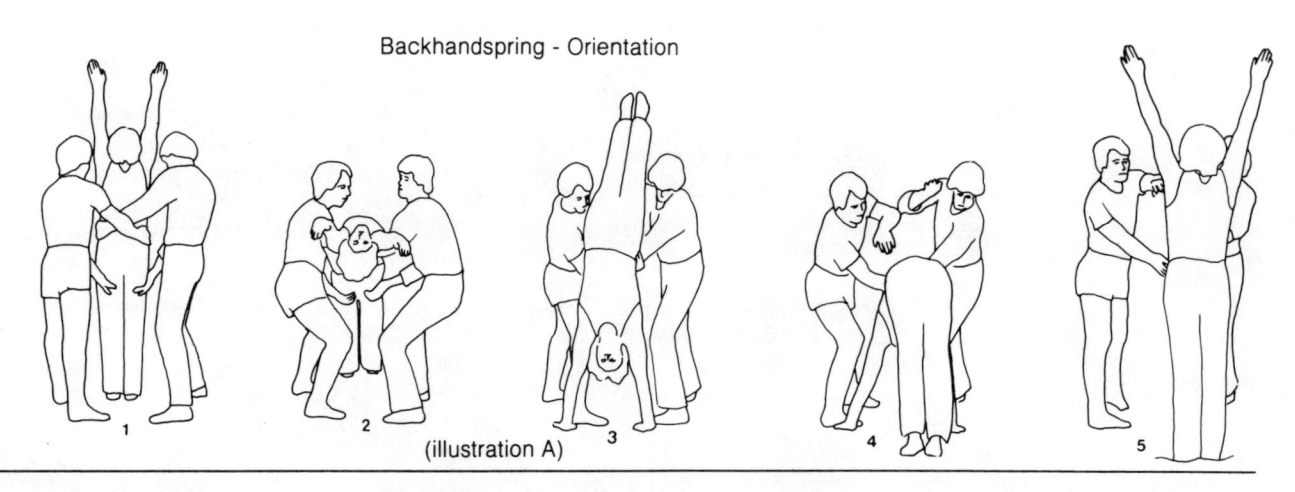

Backhandspring - Orientation

(illustration A)

SKILL

Backhandspring Lead-up

(illustration B)

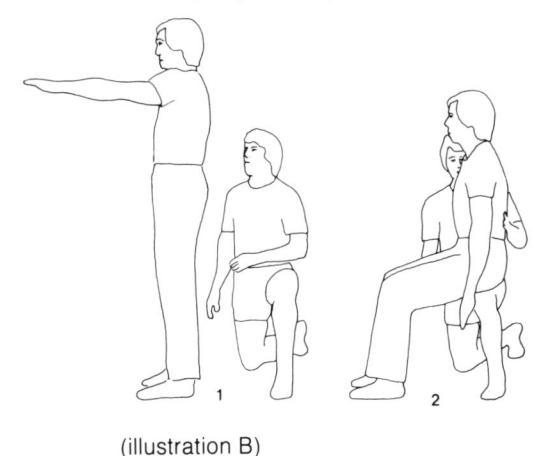

Backhandspring (2 Spotters Standing)

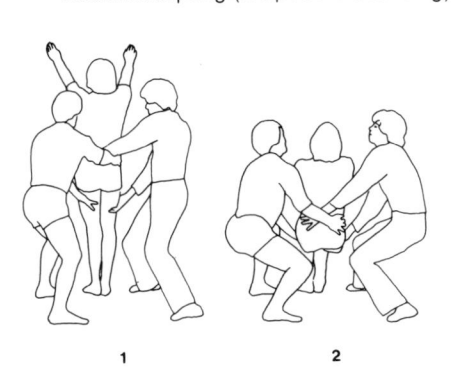

(illustration D)

TEACHING TECHNIQUES AND OBSERVATION POINTS

Backhandspring Lead-ups (illustrations B#1-2 and C#1-2)
Spotting
1. Control the performer's backward sitting action.
2. Ensure that his upper body is vertical in the sitting position and the arms are down to the sides of the body.

Backhandspring Lead-up

(illustration C)

Backhandspring with Two Spotters (illustrations D#1-6)
Spotting
1. Reach across the performer's back and grip around the side of the waist. The other hand supports to the rear of the knee (illustration D#1).
2. Allow the performer to sit backward and lower the arms. *Do not resist this action* (illustration D#2).
3. Cradle the performer through the backhandspring, keeping him moving backward throughout. Additional pressure to the rear of the knee will help in initiating the "snap down" of the legs (illustrations D#3-6)

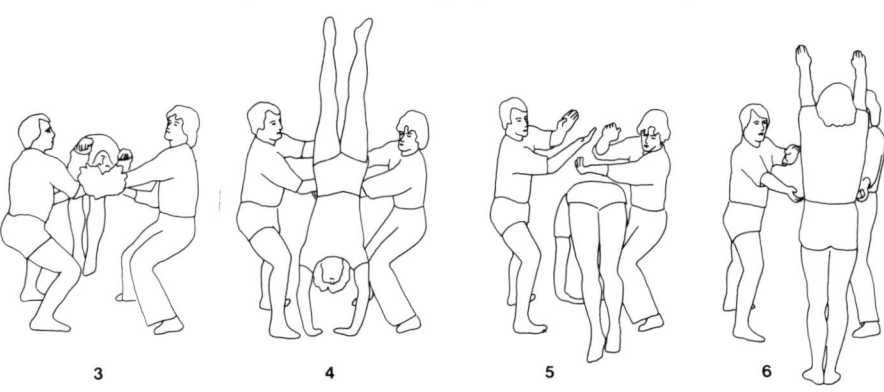

Backhandspring with Two Spotters and the use of a spotting belt (illustrations E#1-4)
Spotting
1. Hold the spotting belt close to the belt pivots and place the other hand to the rear of the knee (illustration E#1).
2. Allow the performer to sit and drive back into the skill. The hand to the rear of the leg then assists in bringing the legs over and past the hand positions (illustration E#2).
3. Keep the performer moving backward and maintain the height of his waist (point of rotation) by holding the belt at an even height throughout (illustrations E#2-4)

73

SKILL

Backhandspring (2 Spotters Standing & Spotting Belt)

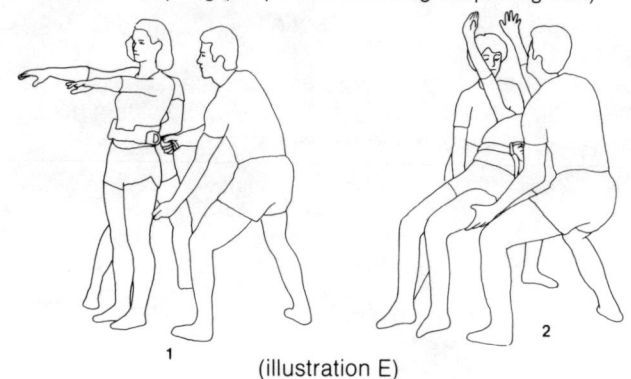

(illustration E)

TEACHING TECHNIQUES AND OBSERVATION POINTS

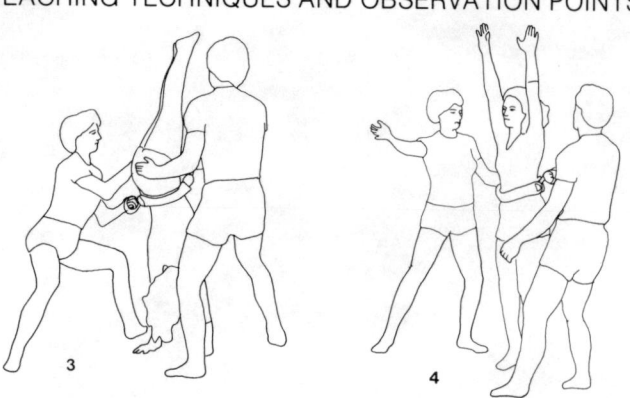

Backhandspring with Two Spotters in Kneeling Position
(illustrations F#1-4 and G#1-5)
Spotting
Kneeling allows the spotters to support more directly under the performer's body. Two methods are shown. Illustrations F#1-4 shows a spotting method where one arm is placed across the body and the other hands supports to the rear of the knee. Illustrations G#1-5 show a "bent" arm support given at the center line of the upper seat and further support given to the rear of the knee. Both techniques offer excellent support particularly in the beginning and mid-phase of the skill.

Spotters should:
1. Turn toward the performer and stay as close as possible without hindering the action of the skill.
2. Allow the backward sitting action to occur without hindrance.
3. Cradle the performer through the backhandspring action.

Backhandspring (2 Spotters Kneeling)

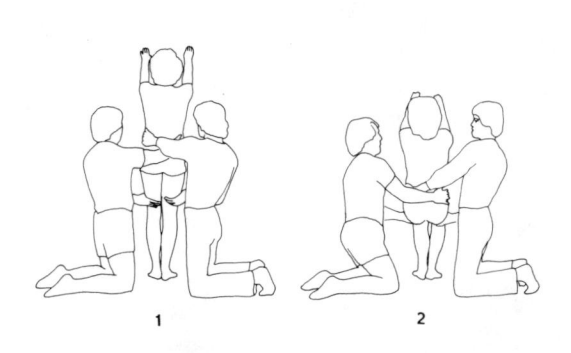

(illustration F)

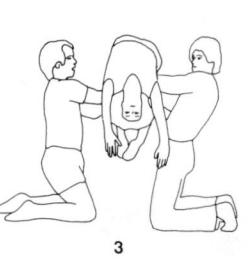

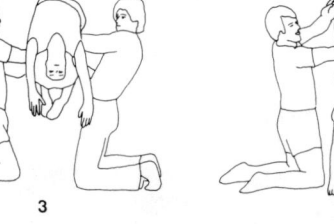

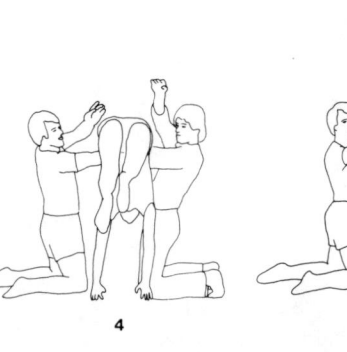

Common Errors:
Errors in Performance:
1. Sitting back in the backhandspring with the upper body leaning forward. *Correction:* Go back to the lead-up practices illustrated in B#1-2 and C#1-2 and practice this action until it is performed correctly.
2. Driving back into the backhandspring from the toes. *Correction:* Extend the legs forcefully and drive into the backhandspring from the *heels* not the toes.
3. Failing to swing the arms backward. *Correction:* Keep the arms extended and swing them past the ears with as

SKILL	TEACHING TECHNIQUES AND OBSERVATION POINTS

much force as possible. Look backward. Do not dive backward as though into a swimming pool.
4. Bringing the legs down to the floor in an over flexed position. *Correction:* After the hands have made contact with the floor, snap the legs down with a powerful piking action from the waist. Keep the legs straight but allow some slight flexion at the knees when the feet contact the floor.
5. No push off from the floor with the hands. *Correction:* As the legs are snapped down push away from the floor as strongly as possible. Keep the backward motion of the backhandspring continuing from feet to hands and from hands to feet.

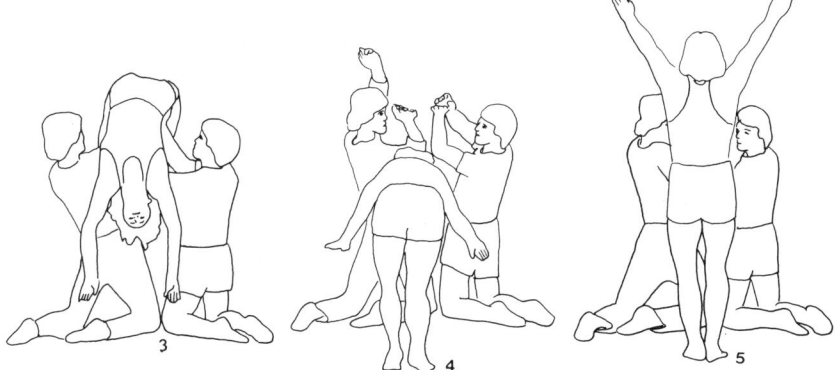

Backhandspring (2 Spotters Kneeling)

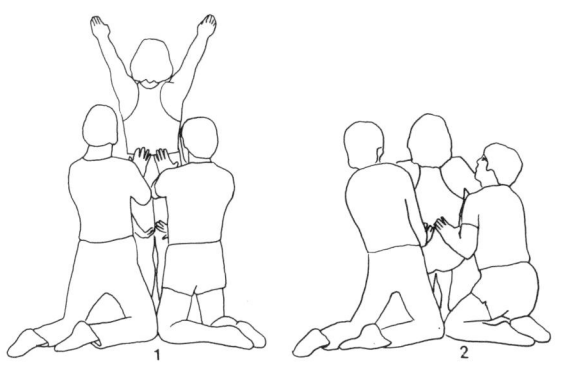

(illustration G)

Errors in Spotting:
1. Failing to stay close to the performer. *Correction:* Do not lean away from the performer. Stay as close to the performer as possible without hindering the flow of the skill.
2. Not letting the performer sit backward at the beginning of the skill. *Correction:* Take up the spotting positions and allow the performer to sit backward without weakening the support.
3. Supporting the performer at too great a height. *Correction:* The line of support through the skill must be equal to the height of the performer's waist. Do not elevate the performer vigorously above this height, or allow his bodyweight to drive the line of support below it.

30. **Handstand Forward Roll in Piked Position (Handstand Piked Forward Roll)**

This skill leads to:
The handstand piked forward roll is complete in itself. It relates to all skills on floor and apparatus where excellent hip flexibility is a requirement.

Lead-up skills:
1. tucked forward roll (pages 37-38)
2. straddled forward roll (pages 51-52)
3. handstand forward roll (pages 45-46)
4. the lead-up to the handstand piked forward roll shown in illustrations A#1-4

Teaching Points for the Skill:
Lead-up to the Handstand Piked Forward Roll (illustrations A#1-4)
1. Roll backward into a shoulder balance. Elevate the hips as high as possible (illustration A#1).
2. Keep the legs straight and roll forward with as much speed as possible (illustration A#2).
3. Pike forward at the hips placing the hands on either side of the body (illustration A#3).
4. As the feet make contact with the floor lean far forward and press the body forward and upward by pushing back at the floor (illustration A#4).
5. Hold the piked position and continue the drive backward with the arms. Elevate to the standing position.

| SKILL | TEACHING TECHNIQUES AND OBSERVATION POINTS |

Lead-up Momentary Shoulder Balance - Piked Forward Roll

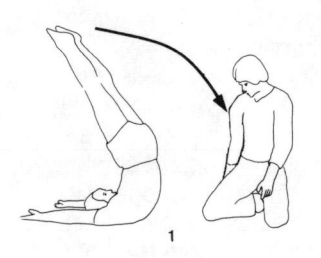

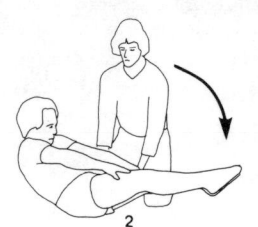

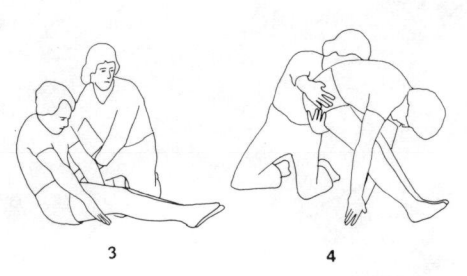

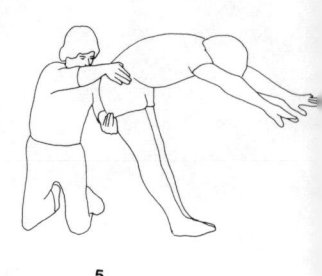

(illustration A)

Handstand Piked Forward Roll (2 Spotters)

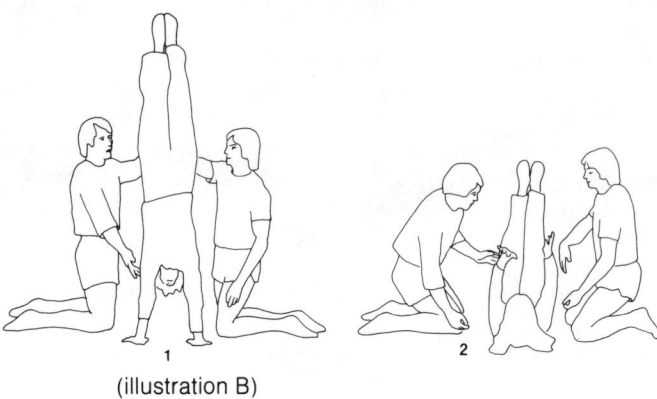

Handstand Piked Forward Roll Assisted by Two Spotters (illustrations B#1-4) *and One Spotter* (illustrations C#1-4)
1. Kick up to a momentary handstand (illustrations B#1 and C#1).
2. Allow the shoulders to "drift ahead" of the hand positions (illustration C#2).
3. Tuck the head under and curve the back.
4. Pike at the waist. Do not bend the legs. Place the hands on either side of the body and press backward with as much power as possible (illustrations B#3 and C#3).
5. Extend the body to complete the skill (illustrations B#4 and C#5).

(illustration B)

Safety and Spotting:
Spotting
1. In all three sequences (illustrations A#1-4, B#1-4 and C#1-5) the object of the spotting is to help the performer move his bodyweight over and past his heels (illustrations A#4-5)
2. As the performer begins the piking action and pushes backward, spotters reach around and under his seat to boost him upward.
3. Illustrations B#1-4 show the spotters stabilizing the handstand prior to assisting the piked forward roll.

Handstand Piked Forward Roll (One Spotter)

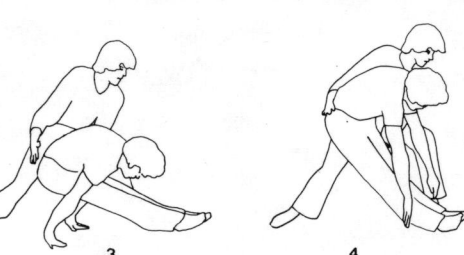

(illustration C)

TEACHING TECHNIQUES AND OBSERVATION POINTS

Common Errors:
Errors in Performance
1. Insufficient pike at the waist *Correction:* This error is usually not a technical problem but one of flexibility. Improve hamstring flexibility (pages 19-20).
2. Insufficient speed entering the piked position. *Correction:* Generate as much forward speed as possible by delaying the pike action at the waist to the last moment. Allow the shoulders to "drift" well beyond the hand positions. This will give considerable speed to the action without causing heavy contact with the floor.
3. Standing up too early out of the piked position. *Correction:* Delay the extension from the piked position as long as possible. Continue pushing backward with the hands. Do not cut this action short.

31. Combinations and Routines

The routines listed in this section are almost exclusively made up of skills taken from Levels I-IV. The instructor should feel free to modify these routines to suit the needs of gymnastics students. Skills not listed in Levels I-IV but with which the instructor is familiar should be included to make routines more attractive. Assistance should be given by spotters where necessary.

Level I

1. Tip-up (hold momentarily) - press to tucked headstand— raise to headstand with straight legs - lower to tucked headstand - return to tip-up—stand.
2. V-sit (hold momentarily) - lower feet to sitting - touch toes - tucked backward roll - stand.
3. Tucked forward roll - tip-up - press to headstand - lower to stand.
4. Tucked forward roll - headstand - lower feet - tucked backward roll - stand.
5. Straddle backward roll - jump - bring feet together - tucked forward roll - stand.
6. Tucked backward roll - pause - tucked forward roll - headstand - lower - stand.
7. Front scale-kick to handstand with assistance - step down -squat - tucked backward roll - pause - tip-up - headstand -lower to stand.
8. Headstand - lower with straddled legs - straddled backward roll - jump - feet together - forward roll with straight legs to sitting - bend forward to touch toes - V-sit - tucked backward roll - stand.
9. Handstand with assistance - step down - front scale - lower to tucked forward roll - headstand - lower feet - tucked backward roll - stand.
10. Forward roll with straight legs to sitting - touch toes - V-sit - tucked backward roll - straddle backward roll - pause - jump - feet together - lower forward to tip-up - press to headstand - lower feet - stand.

Level I and Level II Combined:

1. Momentary handstand - tucked forward roll - pause - tucked backward roll - stand.
2. Straddle backward roll - pause - press to headstand - tucked forward roll - stand.
3. Tucked forward roll - stand - momentary handstand - tucked forward roll to stand - step - cartwheel - stand.
4. Front scale - momentary handstand - tucked forward roll - jump pirouette - stand.
5. V-sit - straddle backward roll - pause - press to headstand - tucked forward roll - stand.

TEACHING TECHNIQUES AND OBSERVATION POINTS

6. Tip-up - press to headstand - tucked forward roll - stand - momentary handstand - tucked forward roll - stand.
7. Momentary handstand - tucked forward roll - forward roll with straight legs to sitting - touch toes - V-sit - lower legs to sitting - touch toes - piked backward roll to stand.
8. Straddle backward roll - pause - press to headstand - tucked forward roll - jump-pirouette - step - front scale - momentary handstand - tucked forward roll - stand.
9. Cartwheel - cartwheel - pause - tucked forward roll -stand - momentary handstand - tucked forward roll - stand.
10. Press to headstand - forward roll with straight legs to sitting - touch toes - V-sit - lower legs to sitting - touch toes - piked backward roll to stand - step - cartwheel - stand.

Levels I, II, and III Combined:

1. Piked backward roll - back extension - pause - standing dive roll - step - handstand - forward roll - stand.
2. Front scale - handstand quarter turn - tucked forward roll - jump pirouette - step - cartwheel - tucked forward roll -stand.
3. Tucked forward roll - straddle forward roll - press to headstand - forward roll - step - round-off - back extension - stand.
4. Cartwheel - round-off - back extension - piked backward roll - jump - half pirouette - standing dive roll - stand.
5. Handstand - tucked forward roll - standing dive roll - straddle forward roll - press to headstand - forward roll -stand.
6. Standing dive roll - jump - full pirouette - standing dive roll - half pirouette - back extension - pause - handstand forward roll - stand.
7. Cartwheel - cartwheel - round-off - back extension -pause - step - handstand - tucked forward roll - step -front scale - handstand - quarter turn - forward roll - stand.
8. Straddle forward roll - press to handstand with flexed arms - tucked forward roll - standing dive roll - stand.
9. Back extension (one footed landing) - kick immediately to handstand - tucked forward roll - straddle forward roll - press to handstand with flexed arms - quarter turn -tucked forward roll - stand.
10. Standing dive roll - jump pirouette - standing dive roll - step - handstand - tucked forward roll - pause - back extension - stand.

Levels I, II, III, and IV Combined:

1. Handspring - step - handstand - tucked forward roll - standing dive roll - pause - backhandspring - stand.
2. Headspring - step - handspring - step - handstand piked forward roll - stand.
3. Press to handstand from straddled position - forward roll - step - handspring - stand.
4. Cartwheel - tucked forward roll - run - handspring - step - handstand piked forward roll - stand.
5. Headspring - step - handstand quarter turn - tucked forward roll - pause - back extension - back handspring -stand.

TEACHING TECHNIQUES AND OBSERVATION POINTS

6. Cartwheel - forward roll with straight legs to sitting - L-support - touch toes - back extension - run - front handspring - stand.
7. Headspring - run - round-off - backhandspring - stand.
8. Handstand - tucked forward roll - handstand - piked forward roll - run - one armed cartwheel - stand.
9. Front scale - handstand-straddled forward roll - press to handstand - forward roll with straight legs to sitting - L-support - back extension - backhandspring - stand.
10. Handstand - piked forward roll - round-off - backhandspring - backhandspring - stand.

B. Pommel Horse (Side Horse)

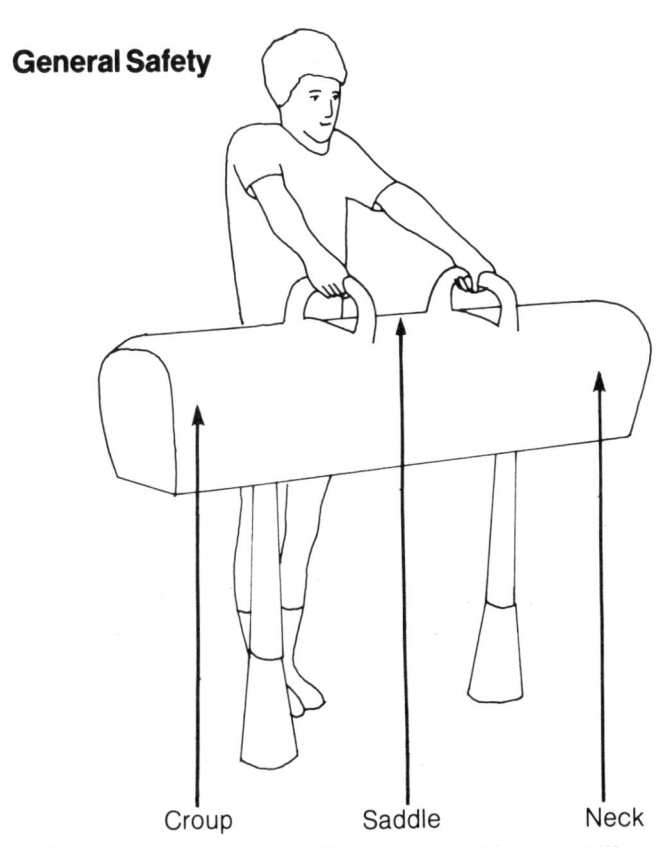

General Safety

Croup   Saddle   Neck

Terminology used for describing pommel horse skills

As the performer faces the horse, the section between the pommels is called the SADDLE
The section of the horse to the performer's left and left of the saddle is called the NECK
The section of the horse to the performer's right and right of the saddle is called the CROUP

Note: the terms-croup-saddle-neck are infrequently used nowadays. The extremities of the pommel horse are usually referred to simply as the "ends." However to assist the reader in differentiating one part of the pommel horse from the other, the terms croup, saddle and neck have been used throughout.

1. Although considered one of the most difficult of all gymnastic events, the pommel horse is also one of the safest. Pommel horse skills are made up of pendular and circular motions and no skill requires the performer to be inverted in the same manner as a headspring or a handspring. Consequently spotting is only occasionally given on the pommel horse. Some skills such as the double leg circle have specialized equipment to help in the learning process. Examples of these are given in the following pages.
2. There are a few safety requirements necessary for the pommel horse. Mats should be placed around all sides of the pommel horse and there should be no gaps, high spots, or overlaps. The pommels should be screwed down securely and have a smooth but non-slippery surface. Wooden pommels seldom wear badly and plastic pommels are also available. Chalk should be used to improve grip and hand positions. Long gymnastic (or track suit) pants are recommended for additional comfort. Volleyball knee pads shifted on the legs to the appropriate position are excellent protection against heavy contact with the pommels and the sides of the horse.
3. The horse should be absolutely stable and not shift during use. At competitive levels a chain tightening device is run from beneath the center of the horse to the floor. This is normally not needed for school use.
4. Continuity and balance are the prime features of the pommel horse and something that the beginner can immediately strive for as he swings from left to right in front support swings. He will also quickly realize how critical balance is on the pommel horse. As he progresses from one skill to the next the need to maintain balance becomes even more exacting and demanding. This in essence is the "fun" of pommel horse. It presents no hazard and yet is one of the most challenging events.

SKILL	TEACHING TECHNIQUES AND OBSERVATION POINTS

Level I Skills

1. Front Support Swings

Front Support Position

(illustration A)

This skill leads to:
1. Further skills such as single leg half circle (pages 84-85) and single leg full circle (pages 86-87)

Lead-up skills:
1. front support (illustration A.)
2. low amplitude front support swings
3. strength exercises for building arm and shoulder strength (pages 13-16)
4. hip flexibility exercises (pages 19-20). The following is a specific exercise for front and rear support swings: hang on a bar or on the rings and swing straddled legs high to the left and to the right (illustrations D#1-3).

Front Support Swings With Assistance

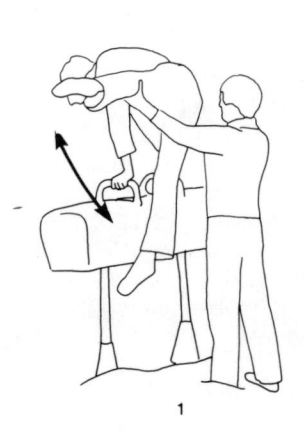

(illustration C)

Teaching Points for the Skill:
1. Jump to front support. Press down with the shoulders. Keep the arms straight. The body is in a slight concave or "dished" position so that the shoulders are above the hands with the legs extended and resting against the side of the horse. The hips are parallel to the long axis of the horse. Look forward (illustration A).
2. Swing the right leg sideways and upward as high as possible. The legs will naturally straddle. Keep the hips parallel to the long axis of the horse. Transfer support to the left arm by leaning the upper body toward the left.
3. The right leg will descend and both legs will be fairly close together at the midpoint of the swings. Use the pendulum swing from right to left to initiate the elevation of the left leg. Raise the left leg as high as possible and transfer support to the right arm by leaning to the right. Develop an even pendular rhythm. Swing the right and left leg down forcefully. This will help in gaining height in each elevation.
4. To develop the amplitude of the swings, push off from the right hand as the right leg is raised and from the left hand as the left leg is raised. This will help to develop a pendular action from the shoulders rather than the legs swinging alone.

Front Support Swings

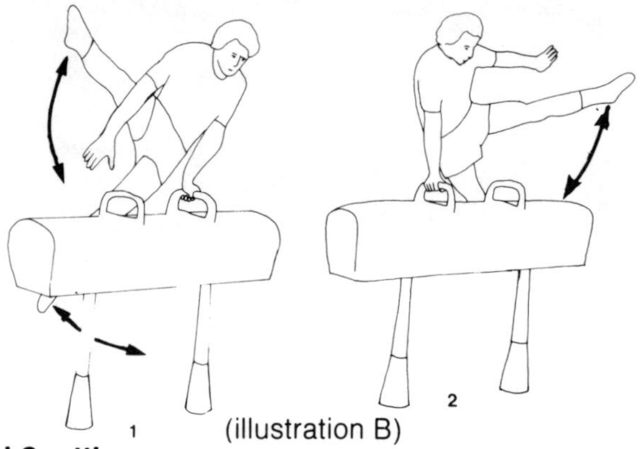

(illustration B)

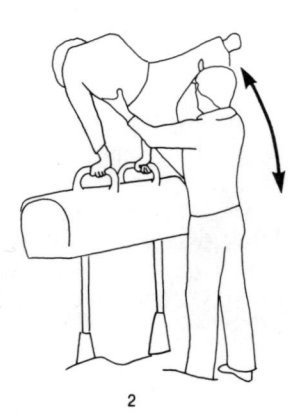

Safety and Spotting:
Surround the base of the pommel horse with mats. Use chalk to improve the grip.
Spotting
1. Some help in developing the rhythm of the front support swings can be given by a spotter standing to the rear of the performer. His duty is to elevate the performer's legs to the right and left. Support is given under the leg and at the hip (illustration C#1-2).

SKILL
Use of the Rings for Developing Pommel Horse Swings

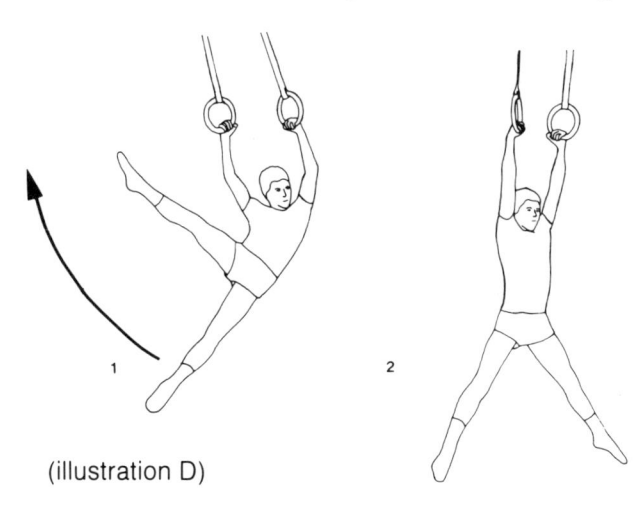

TEACHING TECHNIQUES AND OBSERVATION POINTS

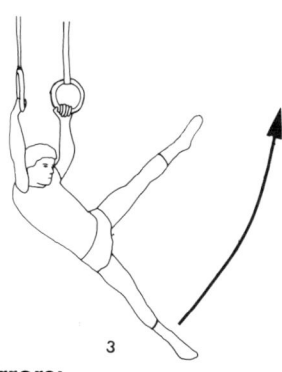

(illustration D)

Common Errors:
Errors in Performance:
1. The body sags between the shoulders and the arms are bent. *Correction:* This is a sign of tiredness and/or physical weakness. Elevate the head and chest and press down with the shoulders. Avoid flexing the arms. Do not practice the skill for long time periods. Get on and off the pommel horse frequently so that each effort is performed with maximum vigor. Improve arm and shoulder strength with complementary exercises (pages 13-16).

2. Rear Support Swings

Rear Support

(illustration A)

Rear Support Swings

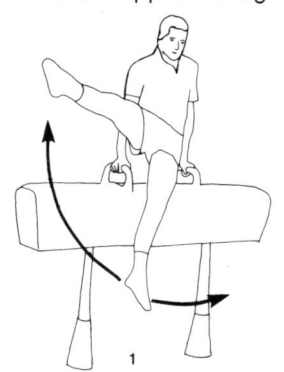

(illustration B)

This skill leads to:
1. Further pommel horse skills, such as single leg half circle (pages 84-85) and single leg full circle (pages 86-87).

Lead-up skills:
1. rear support (illustration A)
2. low amplitude rear support swings
3. strength exercises for building shoulder and arm strength (pages 13-16).

Teaching Points for the Skill:
1. From front support squat through the pommels to rear support (illustration A) or sit between the pommels and elevate the body into rear support. In rear support avoid sitting backward but keep the seat forward so that the body is as straight as possible. Press down with the shoulders. Look forward.
2. Swing the right leg sideways and upward as high as possible. The legs will naturally straddle. Keep the hips parallel to the long axis of the horse. Transfer support to the left arm by leaning the upper body to the left (illustration B#1). Push up with the right arm.
3. The right leg will descend and both legs will be close together at the midpoint of the swings. Use the pendulum swing from right to left to initiate the elevation of the left leg. Raise the left leg as high as possible and transfer support to the right arm. Push up with the left arm. Repeat again to the right. Try to develop an even pendular rhythm. Swing the right and left leg down forcefully. This will help in gaining more height in each elevation.

Safety and Spotting:
Surround the base of the pommel horse with mats. Use chalk to improve the grip. No spotting is necessary.

Common Errors:
Errors in Performance:
1. Piking at the waist and sitting backward. *Correction:* Try to maintain as straight a line as possible from the shoulders through to the feet. Push the seat forward. Swing from the shoulders keeping the hips parallel to the long axis of the horse.

81

SKILL	TEACHING TECHNIQUES AND OBSERVATION POINTS

2. The body sags between the shoulders and the arms are bent. *Correction:* This is a sign of tiredness and/or physical weakness. Elevate the head and chest and press down with the shoulders. Avoid flexing the arms. Do not practice rear support swings for long time periods. Get on and get off the pommel horse frequently so that each effort is performed with maximum vigor. Improve arm and shoulder strength with complementary exercises (pages 13-16).

3. Stride Support Swings

Stride Support

(illustration A)

Stride Support Swings

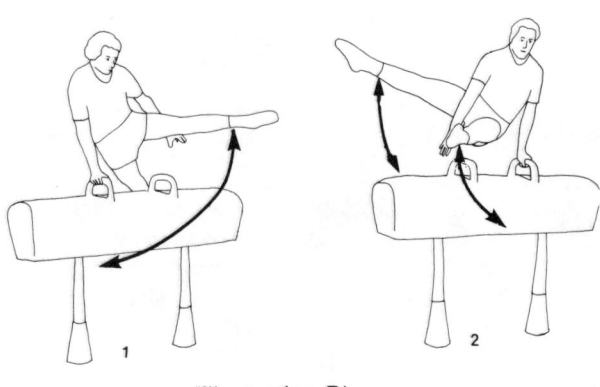

1   2

(illustration B)

This skill leads to:
1. Further pommel horse skills such as single leg half circle (pages 84-85), front scissors (pages 91-92), and back scissors (pages 92-93)

Lead-up skills:
1. front support swings (pages 80-81)
2. rear support swings (pages 81-82)
3. stride support (illustration A).
4. low amplitude stride support swings

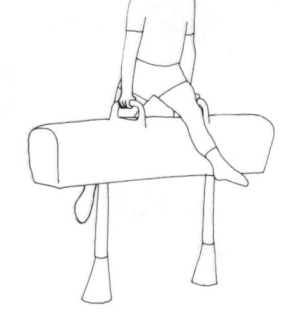

Teaching Points for the Skill:
1. Begin in stride support position (illustration A). Note: The instructor may feel it more appropriate to teach the front support swings and then follow that skill with the single leg half circle (pages 84-85) which brings the performer into the stride support position. From there the performer can then practice the stride support swings.
2. Hold the stride support position as wide as possible. Lift off the horse (do not sit on it), keep the chest high, shoulders pressed down, and arms straight. The legs should not be in contact with the horse and the hips must be at right angles to the long axis of the horse (illustration A).
3. Begin by swinging the hips lightly to the right and left between the arms without elevating the hands from the pommels. Swing from the shoulders and transfer the support to the right when the legs are swung to the left, and vice versa. Maintain a good stride position and keep the legs swinging back and forth at right angles to the long axis of the horse.
4. Increase the amplitude of the swings by elevating both legs higher to each side and by pumping the legs downward forcefully. This will help in elevating the legs upward. Tilt the body more to the right when the legs are being elevated to the left. Push up with the left arm from the pommel to allow for more freedom in the elevation of the legs. Repeat the same on the opposing side. Do not twist sideways but maintain the legs at right angles to the long axis of the horse. The shoulders should also remain parallel to the long axis of the horse throughout the stride support swings. Aim for rhythm and a good pendular swing (illustrations B#1-2). Repeat the skill with right leg forward and then with the left leg forward.

Safety and Spotting:
Surround the base of the pommel horse with mats. Use chalk to improve the grip. No spotting is necessary.

Common Errors:
Errors in Performance:
1. Allowing the straddle position to become smaller with each stride support swing. *Correction:* The legs should stay in a wide straddle and not rub against the side of the horse.
2. Allowing the chest to drop, the arms to bend, and subsequently sitting on the horse. *Correction:* This indicates both fatigue and poor technique. The performer should rest and repeat the skill aiming to lift the chest, keep the arms straight, and elevate the seat up from the

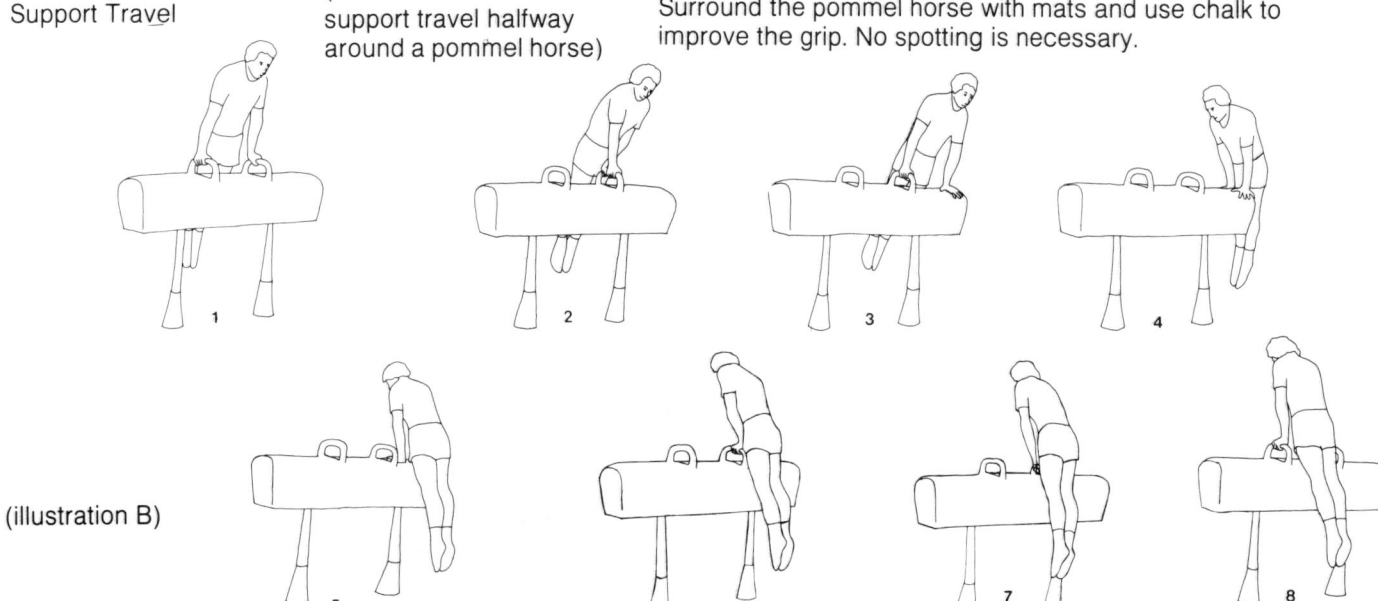

SKILL	TEACHING TECHNIQUES AND OBSERVATION POINTS

saddle of the horse.
3. Allowing the hips to twist or rotate to the right or left. *Correction:* The hips must be parallel to the long axis of the horse with the right leg also at right angles to the long axis. As the swings are developed in amplitude these positions should remain the same.

Level II Skills

4. Support Travel

This skill leads to:
1. improved balance on the pommel horse
2. improved strength in the upper body
3. a firm understanding of "straight arm support" rather than flexed or bent arm support on the pommel horse

Lead-up skills:
1. hop travel on the parallel bars (page 149)
2. sideways travel on a single bar (horizontal, uneven, or parallel bar) (illustrations A#1-4)
3. support travel around a quarter, half, then around a full pommel horse with pommels removed
4. support travel around quarter, half, and then around a full pommel horse with pommels (illustrations B#1-8 show support travel halfway around a pommel horse)

Teaching Points for the Skill:
1. Begin by practicing the travel on a single bar and around a pommel horse with the pommels removed. Keep the head and shoulders above the midline of the horse. *This is particularly important.* Lift the seat slightly so that the legs are "raised" (see illustration B#4). Do not bend the knees or separate the legs.
2. Practice the travel around a pommel horse beginning the action from front support (illustration B#1). Begin by working around a quarter of the pommel horse and then dismounting. Work up to a half circuit of the horse and then progress to a full circuit.

Lead-up Sideways Travel on a Parallel or Horizontal Bar

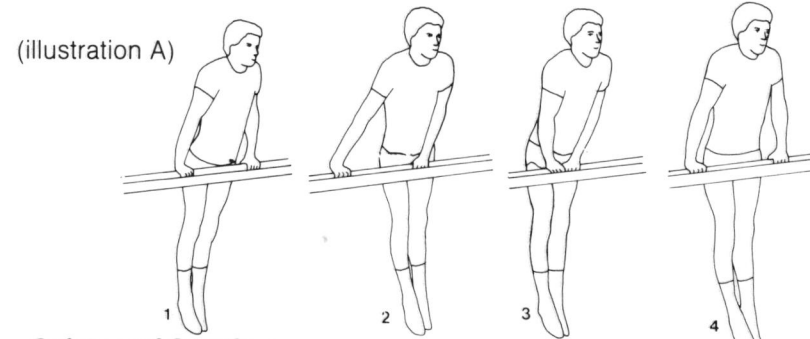

(illustration A)

Safety and Spotting:
Surround the pommel horse with mats and use chalk to improve the grip. No spotting is necessary.

Support Travel

(illustration B)

SKILL	TEACHING TECHNIQUES AND OBSERVATION POINTS

Common Errors:
Errors in Performance:
1. Failing to keep the upper body over the midline of the pommel horse. *Correction:* This error causes the performer to lose balance and to collapse out of the support position. Allow the body to bend a little at the waist so that the legs hang directly downward with the upper body above the horse. This will help in the maintenance of balance.
2. Bending the arms. *Correction:* This error is caused by: a) fatigue, and b) a poor support position. Begin by traveling only a quarter of a circuit around the horse. Keep the arms straight. Press the shoulders down. Concentrate on maintaining the correct body position for the support travel. Work on other suggested lead-up skills for the support travel to improve upper body strength.

5. Single Leg Half Circle

This skill leads to:
1. single leg full circle (pages 86-87)
2. front scissor (pages 91-92)
3. back scissor (pages 92-93)

Lead-up skills:
1. front support swings (pages 80-81)
2. stride support swings (pages 82-83)
3. a single leg half circle practiced on a buck (i.e. a small vaulting horse) with no pommels
4. a single leg half circle practiced on the end of the pommel horse. Support is on one pommel and the end of the horse. The performer attempts the skill with a jump from the floor.
5. a single leg half circle performed in the center of the pommel horse with a jump start rather than beginning from front support.

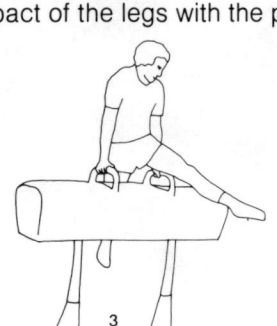

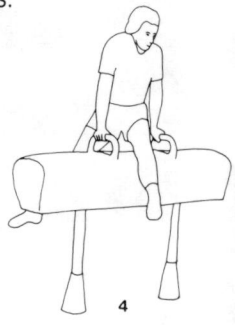

Teaching Points for the Skill:
1. Practice the skills listed in Lead-up skills.
2. After working on the skill from a jump start, attempt the skill from a front support swing.
3. From a front support swing lift the left leg high to the left. Push off with the left arm and transfer support to the right arm. Turn the left hip slightly forward and cut the left leg over the neck of the horse. A high swing to the left makes this action easier to perform (illustration #2).
4. Regrasp the horse with the left arm to arrive in stride support (illustrations #3-4).
5. With an initial stride support swing, the performer can now return the left leg back over the neck of the horse to finish in front support. Again push off from the pommel with the left arm and transfer the bodyweight to the right arm.
6. From front support the performer can also attempt a single leg half circle with the right leg passing over the croup of the horse. From stride support and with an initial stride support swing, the right leg can be returned back to front support position.
7. Depending upon the starting position (front, stride, or rear support) and the direction taken by the right or left leg, numerous variations of the single leg half circle are possible. Practice as many of these as possible before progressing to more difficult skills.

Safety and Spotting:
1. Surround the horse with mats and use chalk to improve grip.
2. Volleyball knee pads can be used on the legs to cushion any impact of the legs with the pommels.

Single Leg Half Circle

SKILL	TEACHING TECHNIQUES AND OBSERVATION POINTS

Spotting
1. When the single leg half circle is attempted from front support, it is possible for a spotter to assist from the rear of the performer. One hand is placed to the side of the performer's body and the other helps to elevate the leg which will be moving through the half circle (see illustrations C#1-2, page 80, front support swings with assistance).

Common Errors:
Errors in Performance:
1. Insufficient height on the swing to bring the leg over the horse from front support to stride support. *Correction:* Re-practice front support swings and learn to elevate the leg high to the side. Transfer the bodyweight from right to left and push off strongly from the pommels to aid in elevating the hips (and legs).
2. Sitting on the saddle of the horse immediately on arriving in the stride support position. *Correction:* Re-catch with the free hand as soon as possible after the leg has been cut over the horse. Keep the arms straight. Lift up with the head and chest and push down with the shoulders so that the seat remains elevated from the saddle of the horse.

6. Flank Dismount

This skill leads to:
1. double leg half circle (pages 87-89)
2. rear pick-up flank both legs to rear support (pages 89-90)
3. double leg circle (pages 95-98)

Lead-up skills:
1. flank vault and its lead-ups (pages 129-130)
2. flank dismount (to the right) performed either:
   a) on the neck of the horse with the right pommel removed
   b) on the croup of the horse.
   Both would be initiated first, by jumping from the floor, and second, from a "feint."
   Illustrations #1 and #2 show the "feint." The "feint" is a preliminary wind-up action performed in one direction which then allows greater momentum to be developed in the opposing direction. In illustration #1 the performer has twisted

Teaching Points for the Skill:
1. Work through the lead-ups listed in #2 and #3 of Lead-up skills. Both lead-ups make it easier for the performer to get his legs over the horse.
2. It will be easier to initiate the flank dismount in the center of the horse from a feint, or from a single leg half circle from stride support leading back through the front support position. Both give momentum into the flank dismount. To attempt a flank dismount from a static front support position is much more difficult.
3. The shoulders must be well over the horse during the mid-phase of the flank dismount (illustration #2).
4. Lean well over the supporting arm to elevate the hips and the legs as they clear the end of the horse.
5. If the flank dismount is performed with a strong rotary motion, it will be necessary to release the final handhold during the landing to avoid twisting the wrist.

Safety and Spotting:
1. Surround the pommel horse with mats and use chalk to improve the grip.
2. For additional comfort and protection, the performer can wear long gymnastic or track pants, and volleyball knee pads.

Spotting
If the lead-ups are well practiced, no spotting will be necessary.

Common Errors:
Errors in Performance:
1. Insufficient elevation of the hips and legs during the flank action. *Correction:* Re-practice front, rear and stride support swings and aim for good hip and leg elevation. Tilt the body well over the support arm. Practice a flank vault

SKILL	TEACHING TECHNIQUES AND OBSERVATION POINTS

his body in a rotary fashion well around to the right. This will then allow him to unwind vigorously in the opposite direction making the flank dismount easier to perform (illustrations #2-5).
3. The flank dismount performed in the center (saddle) of the horse with a jump from the floor.

working for high hip elevation. Transfer this action to the flank dismount on the pommel horse. Be sure that the bodyweight is transferred over the single supporting arm as the legs are flanked over the horse.

Flank Dismount Initiated From a Feint

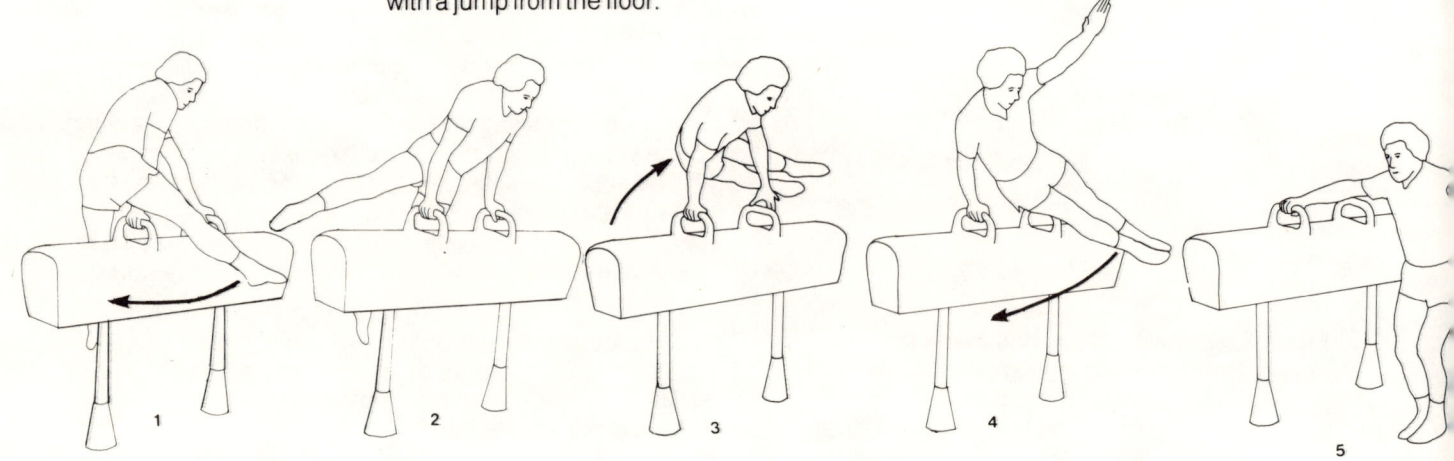

Level III Skills

7. Single Leg Full Circle

This skill leads to:
1. back scissors (pages 92-93)

Lead-up skills:
1. single leg half circle from front support swings (pages 84-85)
2. single leg half circle from stride support swings (illustrations #4-6)

Teaching Points for the Skill:
1. Illustrations #1-4 show a single leg half circle from front support through to stride support. (The teaching points for this skill are on pages 84-85). To add the remaining half of a full circle, the left leg must pass over the croup of the horse and return to front support (illustrations #4-6). This half of the single leg full circle will be more difficult than the first half because the left leg must pass under the right in order to return to front support (illustrations #5-6).
2. To accomplish the final half of the single leg full circle the performer must swing forcefully through stride support (illustrations #2-4). During this action emphasis should be on pushing off the pommel with the right hand and elevating the right or rear leg as high as possible (illustration #5).
3. Beginners can either: a) jump into the skill from the floor, or b) initiate the skill with a front support swing to the right and then follow with a single leg full circle from the left with the left leg.
4. The illustrations show the single leg full circle with the left leg performing the circle. The performer should also learn the single leg full circle with the right leg making the circle.
5. Work for good transference of weight to the support arm and aim for high elevation of the rear leg. Do not "get stuck" in stride support position. Develop a pendulum-like

SKILL	TEACHING TECHNIQUES AND OBSERVATION POINTS

rhythm so that the drop of the leg on one side will help to elevate the leg on the other.

6. The single leg full circle can also be initiated from stride support and rear support. Right or left leg can be made to rotate a full circle in either direction. These variations are more difficult to perform than those begun from front support. The instructor should consider using these variations for those students who are more advanced.

Single Leg Full Circle

Safety and Spotting:
1. Surround the pommel horse with mats and use chalk to improve the grip.
2. For additional comfort the performer should wear long gymnastic or track pants. Volleyball knee pads also give added protection to the legs.

Spotting
1. A single spotter can assist the performer in completing the full circle. The spotter's duty is to stand to the rear of the performer and elevate the rear leg (upper leg in illustration #5) so that the left leg can pass underneath. Support is given under the thigh of the right leg and to the left side of the body in the same manner as when assistance is given in front support swings (page 80).

Common Errors:
Errors in Performance:
1. For errors occurring in the first half of the single leg full circle, see single leg half circle, (pages 84-85)
2. Failing to elevate the rear leg sufficiently to allow the forward leg to pass underneath it. *Correction:* Work on stride support swings, concentrating on pushing off the pommel, tilting the body well over the support arm and elevating the rear leg as high as possible. Practice the single leg full circle and aim for high elevation of the hips at both ends of the horse.

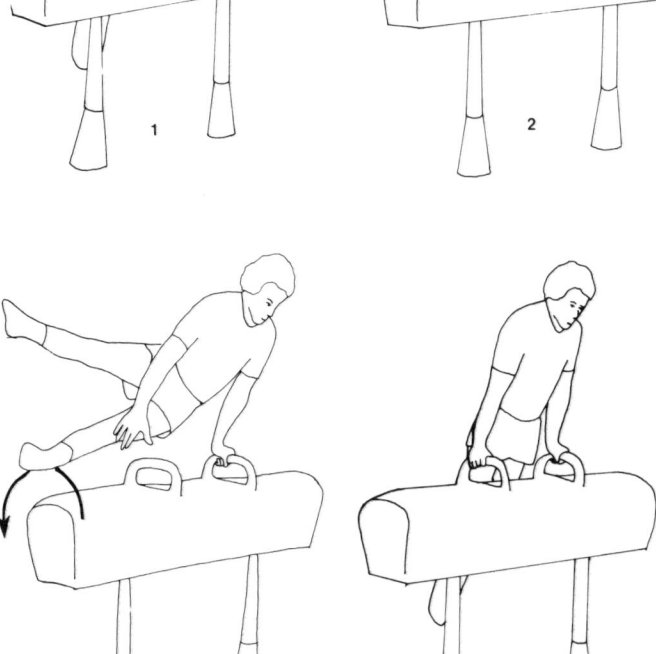

8. Double Leg Half Circle

This skill leads to:
1. rear pick up flank both legs to rear support (pages 89-90)
2. double leg circle (pages 95-98)

Teaching Points for the Skill:
1. Work through as many of the lead-ups listed above as possible. Begin the double leg half circle from a standing start (illustrations A#1-3). Then attempt the skill from a feint (illustrations B#1-5). The feint will generate a strong circular

| SKILL | TEACHING TECHNIQUES AND OBSERVATION POINTS |

Lead-up Double Leg Half Circle From a Jump Start

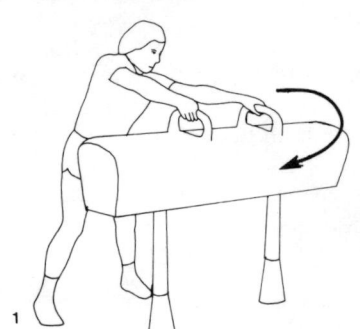

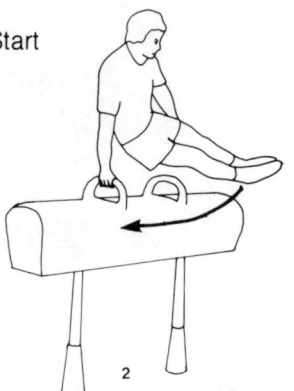

(illustration A)

Lead-up Skills:
1. flank vault (pages 129-130)
2. flank dismount (pages 85-86)
3. single leg half circle (pages 84-85)
4. double leg half circle from a jump start performed on a buck (no pommels)
5. a double leg half circle to the left from a jump start on the end of the pommel horse. To do this the performer would shift to the neck of the horse. The right hand would grasp the left pommel and the left hand would be placed on the end of the horse. This allows the legs to be brought around the outside of the horse to rear support with minimum elevation. The same skill can be practiced in the opposite direction on the croup of the horse.

drive into the double leg half circle.
2. To begin the feint, hold the legs in a straddle position and rotate the legs and hips as far around to the right as possible (illustration B#1).
3. Unwind in a circular fashion to the left. Swing the right leg in a circular fashion around to the left. As the body rotates to the left assist the action by using the pommels to generate torque.
4. As the body passes to the front of the horse re-catch with the free arm (left). Keep the arms straight and the shoulders above the midline of the horse.
5. Try to hold the rear support position. Note: The stronger the circular action produced by the feint, the more difficult it will be to hold the rear support. It is a good practice to have a spotter catch the performer in an extended rear support position with the body held well out from the horse. (The spotter cradles under the legs and hips). This practice develops confidence for subsequent attempts at the double leg circle.

Safety and Spotting:
1. Surround the pommel horse with mats and use chalk to improve the grip.
2. For additional comfort the performer should wear long gymnastic or track pants. Volleyball knee pads also give added protection to the legs.

Double Leg Half Circle From a Feint (illustration B)

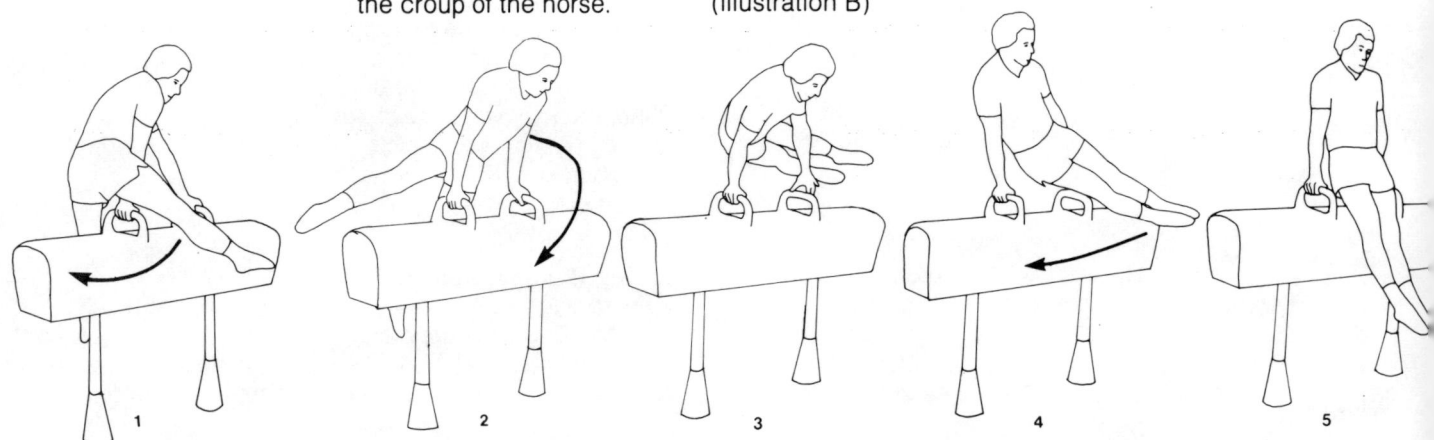

SKILL	TEACHING TECHNIQUES AND OBSERVATION POINTS

Common Errors:
Errors in Performance:
1. Insufficient height in the elevation of the legs to allow them to pass over the end of the horse. *Correction:* If the performer is jumping from the floor, he must jump vigorously, elevating the hips to the side so that there is room for the legs to pass over the free pommel. This action is the same as a flank vault. If the double leg half circle is initiated from a feint, there must be sufficient drive around in a circular fashion to raise the legs upward and outward. The body must be well tilted over the support arm. If this arm is the right, push off strongly with the left from the pommel.
2. Collapsing in the rear support position and sitting on or falling off the horse. *Correction:* The shoulders must remain over the center of the horse and the movement of the hips into the rear support position must be counteracted by the upper body leaning back.

9. Rear Pick-Up Flank both legs to Rear Support

This skill leads to:
1. back scissors (pages 92-93)
2. double leg circle (pages 95-98)

Lead-up skills:
1. single leg half circle (pages 84-85)
2. double leg half circle (pages 87-89)

Rear Pick-up Flank Both Legs to Rear Support

Teaching Points for the Skill:
1. Begin by practicing a) front support to stride support, and b) stride support back to front support (illustrations #1-3).
2. Develop a high elevation of the right leg over the croup of the horse. The body must be well tilted to the left with support fully on the left arm. Push off strongly with the right arm to achieve this position (illustration #2).
3. The right leg should then be pumped downward in a strong pendular action in order to obtain sufficient lift of both legs to the left for the remaining double leg half circle.
4. The stronger the pendular action from stride support through the front support position (illustrations #1-3) the easier it is to perform the double leg half circle.

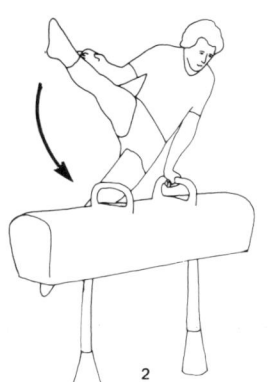

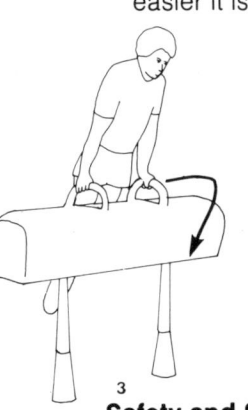

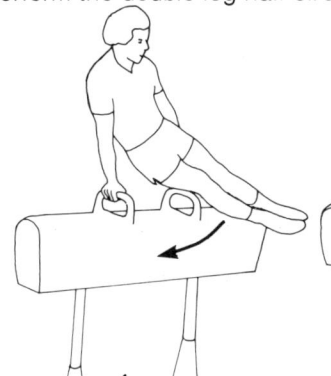

Safety and Spotting:
1. Surround the base of the pommel horse with mats and use chalk to improve the grip.
2. For additional comfort the performer should wear long gymnastic or track pants. Volleyball knee pads also give added protection to the legs.

Common Errors:
Errors in Performance:
1. Inability to move through front support into the double leg half circle. *Correction:* The performer must elevate the hips

SKILL	TEACHING TECHNIQUES AND OBSERVATION POINTS

sufficiently to the right and then drive them down and through front support. This generates a strong pendular swing which makes the completion of the double leg half circle much easier. A strong push off with the right arm (illustration #2), followed by the same from the left arm will accentuate the pendular swing and raise the hips even higher. The shoulders must remain over the center line of the horse and the performer should resist piking, or sitting backward, particularly as he re-grasps for the rear support position.

Level IV Skills

10. Front Pick-Up Flank both legs to Front Support

This skill leads to:
1. back scissors (pages 92-93)
2. double leg circles (pages 95-98)

Lead-up skills:
1. single leg half circle (pages 84-85)
2. double leg half circle (pages 87-89)

Teaching Points for the Skill:
1. Begin by practicing a) front support to stride support, and b) stride support to rear support (illustrations #1-3).
2. Aim for a high elevation of the left leg over the neck of the horse with the body well supported on the right arm and the hips elevated to the left (illustration #2). Push off the pommel with the left arm.
3. The left leg must be pumped downward in a strong pendular action to develop good elevation to the right in the double leg half circle.
4. The body is then tilted over the left arm and both legs are lifted to the right for the double leg half circle ending in front support (illustrations #3-5). Push off vigorously with the right arm.
5. The double leg half circle will be easier to complete if it is initiated from a single leg half circle which has good hip lift and high leg action.
6. A stride support swing to the right and left will help this initial pick-up of the left leg over the neck of the horse. The improved pendular action then helps to complete the double leg half circle.
7. The illustrations show the performer with the right leg forward in stride support. The skill can also be completed with the left leg forward in stride support. The single leg half circle is then made over the croup of the horse and the double leg half circle performed to the left over the neck of the horse.

Front Pick-up Flank Both Legs to Front Support

1   2   3   4   5

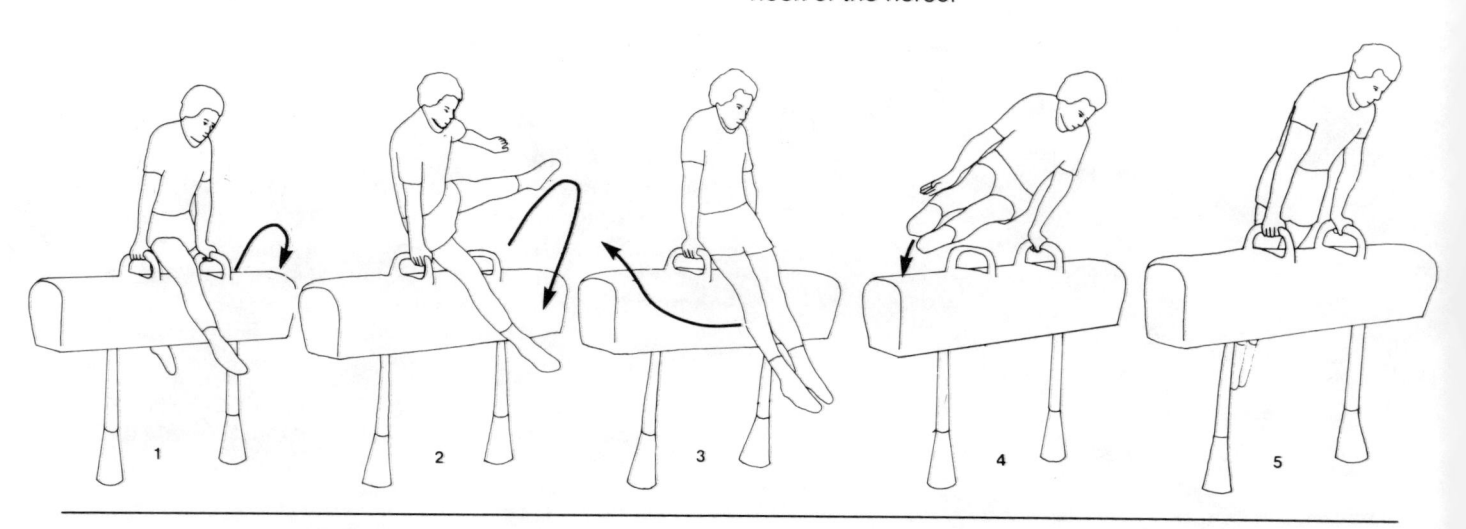

SKILL	TEACHING TECHNIQUES AND OBSERVATION POINTS
	Safety and Spotting: 1. Surround the base of the pommel horse with mats and use chalk to improve the grip. 2. For additional comfort the performer should wear long gymnastic or track pants. Volleyball knee pads also provide added protection to the legs. **Common Errors:** *Errors in Performance:* 1. Inability to move from rear support through the double leg half circle to front support. *Correction:* This indicates that the stride support swing into rear support is poor. Practice stride support swings. Aim to lift the hips and legs as high as possible and drive down through the rear support position with as much pendular swing as possible. This pendular action will make the completion of the double leg half circle much easier. Keep the hips forward; avoid piking at the waist and sitting on the horse. Remember that a strong push off each pommel helps to tilt the body to the right and left, and that this generates a good pendular action.
11. Front Scissors (also known as Forward Scissors) **This skill leads to:** 1. The ability to perform the scissor action (both front and back, pages 92-93) is a pre-requisite for advanced pommel horse skills. It is a skill that should be mastered as soon as possible by students interested in competitive gymnastics. **Lead-up skills:** 1. front support swings (pages 80-81) 2. stride support swings (pages 82-83) 3. single leg circles (pages 86-87) 4. good flexibility in the hip area is also important in the front scissors. 5. Practice the scissor action with the horse placed under the parallel bars. The performer is in underarm support (illustrations B#1-2).	**Teaching Points for the Skill:** 1. The front scissors can be initiated from stride support or from a single leg half circle leading from front support through stride support, and directly into the front scissors. 2. The stride support swing is performed strongly to the left with the left or rear leg elevated as high as possible (illustration A#3). Simultaneously the left hand pushes hard off the pommel. The weight of the body is placed well over the right arm (illustrations A#3-5). 3. The performer now executes a slight turn of the hips. This enables the left leg to be brought forward and the right leg to be taken under and backward (illustration A#4). 4. The pommel is re-grasped as quickly as possible with the left arm, and the performer returns to stride support position (illustrations A#5-6). 5. The normal sequel to the scissors over the neck of the horse is to continue through stride support and execute the same form of scissors over the croup. **Safety and Spotting:** 1. Surround the horse with mats and use chalk to improve the grip. 2. For comfort the gymnast should wear long gymnastic or track pants. Volleyball knee pads are recommended for protection of the knee area. *Spotting:* 1. Some assistance can be provided by a spotter standing to the rear of the performer. 2. As the performer enters the single scissor forward, the spotter raises the rear leg as high as possible giving the performer some support and additional time to execute the scissors action.

SKILL	TEACHING TECHNIQUES AND OBSERVATION POINTS

Front Scissors

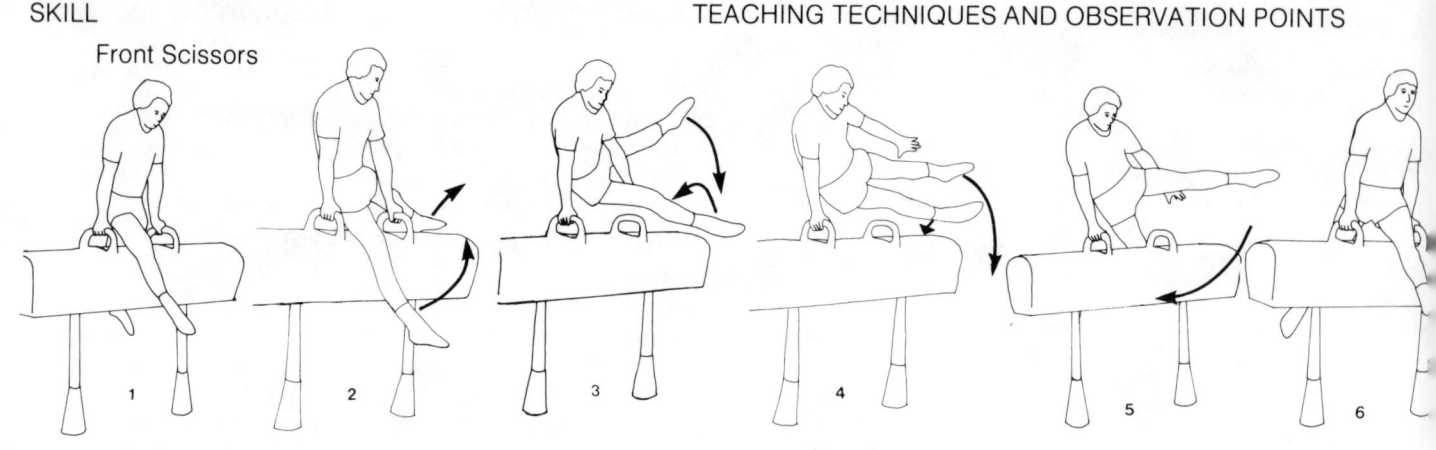

(illustration A)

Use of the Parallel Bars to Learn Front and Back Scissors

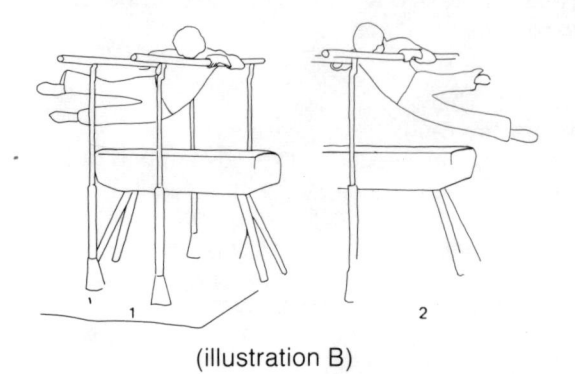

(illustration B)

Common Errors:
Errors in Performance:
1. The elevation of the hips and legs to the side is poor. *Correction:* This usually indicates that the stride support swings are inadequate and should be re-practiced. It may also mean that the push off the pommels is insufficient. A strong drive upward with the left arm will lift the body upward on the left side and give more room for the scissor action to be executed.
2. The hips stay to the rear of the horse so that when the scissor action is attempted the performer falls backward and ends up sitting in stride support. *Correction:* The hips must be made to stay over the center line of the horse and rotated forward during the scissor action. This facilitates the forward and backward action of the legs and makes it easier for the performer to achieve the stride support position.
3. The re-grasp is too slow. *Correction:* This error will also cause the performer to fall into a stride sitting position on the horse. The re-grasp should occur the instant the leg scissors have been completed.

12. Back Scissors (also known as Reverse or Backward Scissors)

This skill leads to:
1. The ability to perform an excellent scissor action (both front and back) is a pre-requisite for advanced pommel horse skills. It is a skill that should be mastered as soon as possible by anyone interested in competitive gymnastics.

Lead-up skills:
1. front support swings (pages 80-81)
2. stride support swings (pages 82-83)

Teaching Points for the Skill:
1. The performer can begin in stride support position initiating the backward scissor with a preliminary stride support swing.
2. An alternative is to lead into the stride support with a single leg half circle from front support. In this case the performer could make a single leg half circle forward with the right leg into stride support and using the pendular action swing to the left; and then on the return swing to the right, initiate the back scissors. If the performer follows this sequence of actions the right leg must be lifted high backward and upward. Simultaneously the right hand pushes off the pommel. The weight of the body is placed onto the left arm (illustrations #1-2).
3. With the body tilted to the left a scissor action is made with the left leg being brought under the right leg. The hips which are initially to the rear of the horse shift forward over the center line of the horse (illustration #2-3).

SKILL

Back Scissors

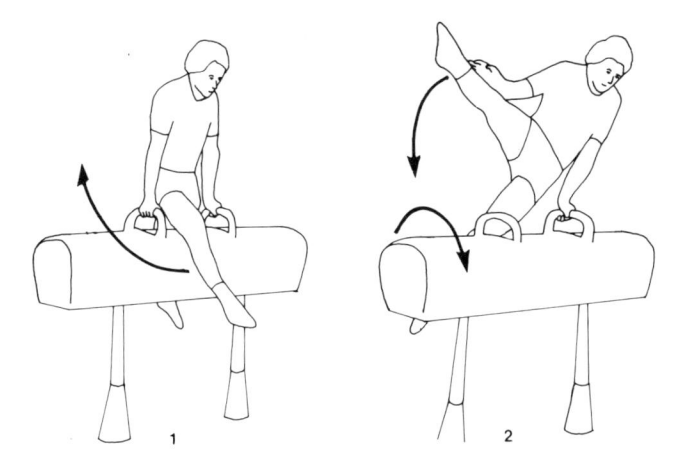

TEACHING TECHNIQUES AND OBSERVATION POINTS

4. The performer re-grasps the pommel with the right hand as soon as possible (illustrations #4-5).
5. A common sequel to a back scissors performed over the croup of the horse is to continue the pendular action to the left and perform the back scissors action again over the neck.

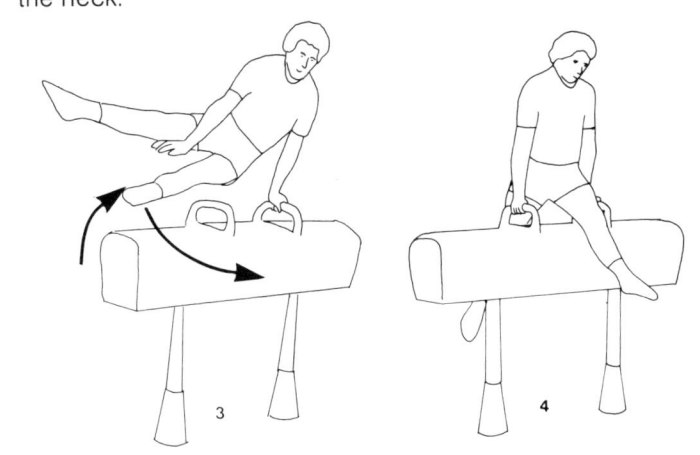

Safety and Spotting:
1. Surround the horse with mats and use chalk to improve the grip.
2. For greater comfort the performer should wear long gymnastic or track pants. Volleyball knee pads are recommended for protection of the knee area.

Common Errors:
Errors in Performance:
1. The elevation of the hips and legs to the side is poor. *Correction:* This indicates that the stride support swings are poor. These should be re-practiced. It also indicates that the push off the pommel is insufficient. A strong drive upward with the right arm will lift the body on the right side and give more room for the scissor action to be executed.
2. The hips stay to the rear of the horse so that when the scissor action is made the performer falls backward or cannot achieve the stride support position. *Correction:* The hips (which will be to the rear of the horse during the initial upward and backward swing of the right leg, (illustrations #1-2) must shift forward with the action of the left leg. This brings the performer into the correct position for the stride support position.
3. The re-grasp is too slow. *Correction:* This error usually means that the performer ends sitting in a stride position. The re-grasp should occur the instant the back leg has been brought forward.

| SKILL | TEACHING TECHNIQUES AND OBSERVATION POINTS |

13. Rear Dismount

This skill leads to:
1. double leg circles (pages 95-98)

Lead-up skills:
1. front support to rear support performed on the floor (page 96)
2. single leg half circles (particularly from stride support to front support, (pages 84-85)
3. single leg full circles (pages 86-87)
4. double leg half circles using either a front or rear pick-up (pages 89-90)
5. a rear dismount using a jump from the floor, performed on any of the following: a) a buck without pommels, b) a pommel wheel or pommel dome (page 98)
6. a rear dismount performed on a pommel horse without pommels
7. a rear dismount performed on the neck of the pommel horse with the right pommel removed or on the croup of the pommel horse with the left pommel removed. Initiate these lead-ups with a jump from the floor (see illustrations A#1-5)

Teaching Points for the Skill:
The rear dismount is in essence a double leg circle dismount (see illustrations B#1-6). It is made easier than a double leg circle because the dismount eliminates any problem of the re-catch of the pommels and continuation into another skill.
1. Work through as many of the lead-ups listed above as possible.
2. To make the rear dismount easier to perform, begin each attempt with either a jump start from the floor, or a "feint." Each of these actions will generate a strong rotary entry into the rear dismount.
3. For a rear dismount circling to the left (illustrations B#1-6) the performer drives his legs and hips outward and above the neck of the horse (illustrations B#1-3). The body must be in a slightly piked position. The left arm is pushed off the horse and the shoulders leaned to the right and slightly forward. The hips are elevated and rotated as the body moves forward toward rear support. The bodyweight is well over the right arm.
4. As the performer rotates to the front of the horse, the body is stretched out and the shoulders leaned backward.
5. The left hand is quickly replaced on the horse and the bodyweight transferred over the left arm. The performer now pikes at the waist and the final part of the dismount is performed with support fully on the left arm. The legs are carried over the right pommel and extended to the floor for the landing.

The latter part of the rear dismount is the part that differs considerably from the double leg circle. The hips are allowed to drop downward and the upper body shifts from its position above the horse (illustrations B#5-6). This action "kills" any further circular motion around the horse. The body rotates around the left arm and the legs to its final dismount position.

Lead-up Rear Dismount on Horse With One Pommel Removed

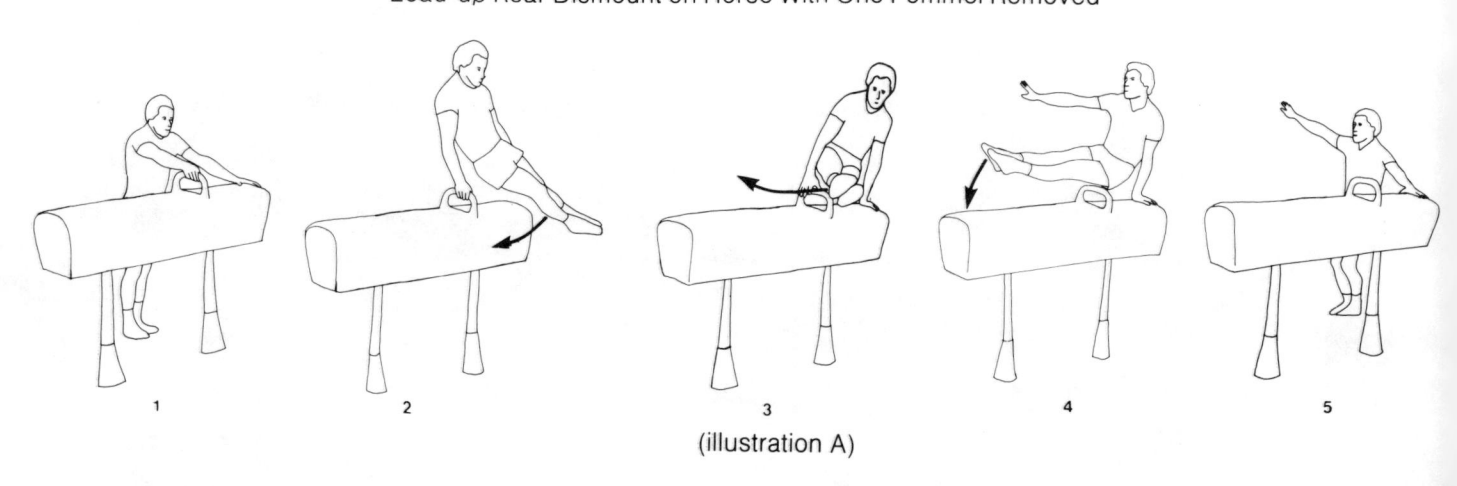

1 2 3 4 5

(illustration A)

SKILL

Rear Dismount Initiated With a Feint

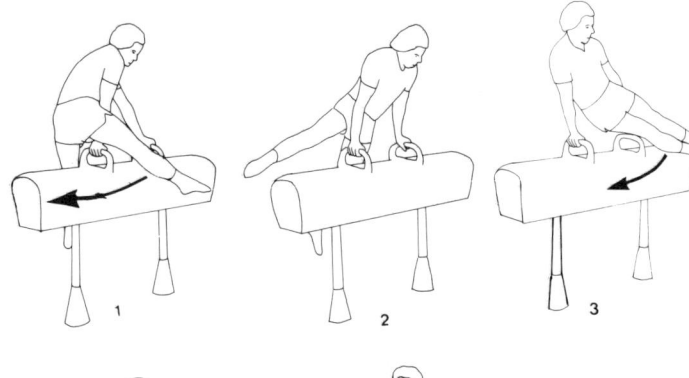

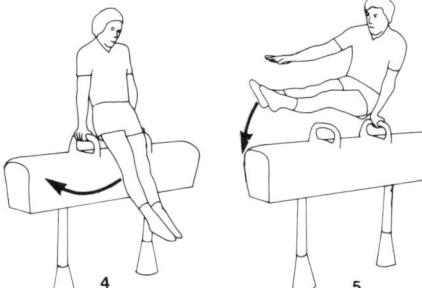

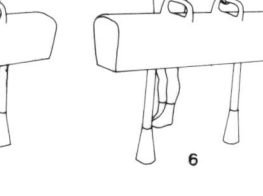

(illustration B)

TEACHING TECHNIQUES AND OBSERVATION POINTS

Safety and Spotting:
1. Surround the base of the pommel horse with mats and use chalk to improve the grip.
2. For additional comfort the performer should wear long gymnastic or track pants. Volleyball knee pads can also be worn as protection for the knee area and the inner part of the leg.

Spotting:
Physical assistance in the performance of the rear dismount will be more hindrance than help. If the lead-up skills are well practiced, the rear dismount is a safe skill and will cause few problems.

Common Errors:
Errors in Performance:
1. The arms and legs are bent through the first half of the rear dismount. *Correction:* The performer must keep his upper body well over the horse and keep his arms and legs straight at all times. This is particularly important during the phases of one-armed support. With the exception of those parts of the skill where a piking action occurs, the performer should stretch his body out and avoid collapsing his arms or bending the legs.
2. The performer pikes too early in anticipation of the final phase of the dismount. *Correction:* The first half of the rear dismount is similar to the double leg circle. The performer must concentrate on passing through rear support with the body well stretched out and with no pike at the waist. Thereafter he pivots on the left arm and pikes strongly for the final dismount. This is begun after the left arm has been replaced on the pommel.
3. The re-grasp of the pommels is made too late. *Correction:* The illustrations show how important the action of the left arm is in providing support for the final half of the dismount. It not only gives support but provides a pivotal point around which the body rotates. The earlier the re-grasp of the left hand on the pommel the greater the stability and control (illustrations B#4-6).

14. Double Leg Circle

This skill leads to:
1. All further pommel horse skills. The double leg circle is one of the most important intermediate pommel horse skills. With leg scissors it forms the basis of advanced pommel horse routines.

Lead-up skills:
1. front support to rear support performed on the floor (illustrations A#1-4)

Teaching Points for the Skill:
1. Work through as many of the lead-ups listed above as possible.
2. To make the double leg circle easier to initiate on the pommel horse, the performer can begin with a jump start from the floor (illustrations B#1-6), or from stride support (illustrations E#1-7). In the latter case a single leg half circle backward with the right leg from stride support would provide impetus for a double leg circle to the left. The double leg circle can also be initiated from the support position using a "feint" to the right for a double leg circle to the left and vice versa for a double leg circle to the right (see illustrations D#1-5).

| SKILL | TEACHING TECHNIQUES AND OBSERVATION POINTS |

Lead-up Front Support to Rear Support Performed on the Floor

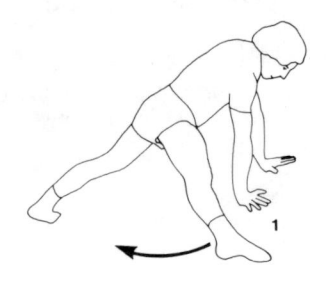

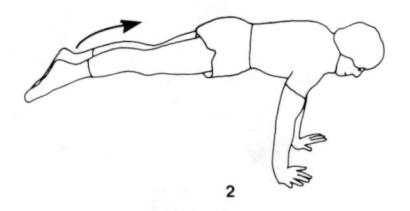

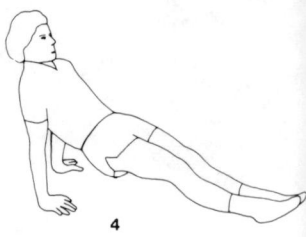

(illustration A)

Double Leg Circle Initiated From a Jump Start

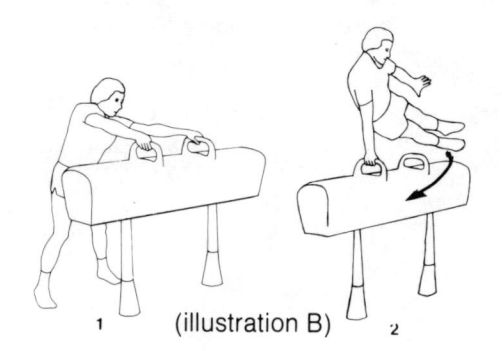

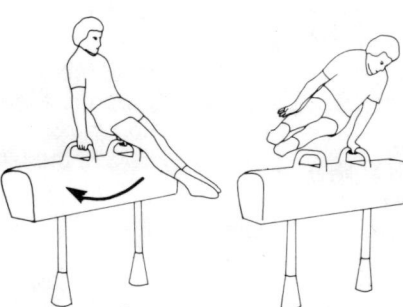

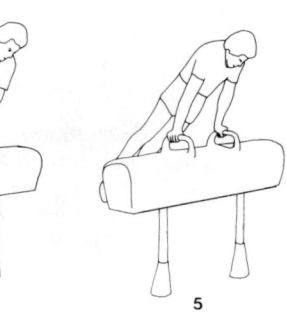

2. single leg half circles (particularly those from stride support to front support, (pages 84-85)
3. single leg full circles (pages 86-87)
4. double leg half circles using either a front or rear pick-up (pages 89-90)
5. double leg circles performed on any of the following: a) a buck without pommels, b) a pommel wheel (illustration F#2), c) a pommel dome (illustration F#3), or d) floor pommels (illustration F#4)
6. double leg circles performed on the neck of the pommel horse with the right pommel removed or double leg circles performed on the croup of the pommel horse with the left pommel removed (illustrations C#1-5)

3. For a double leg circle to the left the performer drives his legs in a circular action above the neck of the horse (illustrations B#1-2). The body must be in a slightly piked position. The left arm is pushed off the horse and the shoulders leaned to the right and slightly forward. The hips are elevated and rotated as the body moves forward toward rear support. The weight is on the right arm (illustration B#2).
4. As the performer rotates to the front of the horse, the body is stretched out and the shoulders leaned backward. The left hand is quickly replaced so that the performer passes through a phase of double arm support (illustration B#3). At the midpoint of the double leg circle the performer's body is equally balanced between both arms.
5. As the performer circles toward the right side of the horse, he pikes his body slightly, leans toward the left and transfers his bodyweight onto the left arm. The right arm pushes off the horse so that the left arm is providing total support (illustration B#4). The hips rotate again in preparation for front support (illustration B#4-5).
6. The right arm re-grasps the pommel and the performer returns through the front support position. The circular momentum developed at this point holds the legs away from the horse and the performer will dismount or continue into another skill.

(illustration B)

SKILL

TEACHING TECHNIQUES AND OBSERVATION POINTS

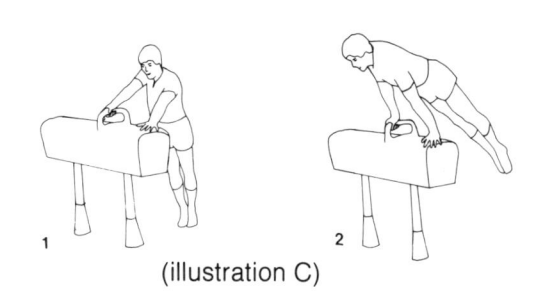

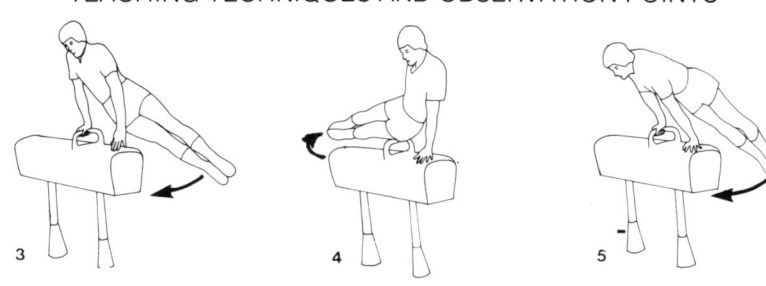

(illustration C)

Lead-up Double Leg Circles
Performed on the Horse With One Pommel Removed

Double Leg Circle Initiated From a Feint

(illustration D)

Safety and Spotting:
1. Surround the base of the pommel horse with mats and use chalk to improve the grip.
2. For additional comfort the performer should wear long gymnastic or track pants. Volleyball knee pads can also be worn as protection for the knee area and the inner part of the leg.
3. The double leg circle is a safe skill to practice. However it is important for the performer to work progressively through the lead-up skills suggested above. Many other lead-up methods are available.
4. Illustrations F#1-4 give examples of teaching devices for learning the double leg circles. Illustration F#1 shows the performer supported in a spotting belt. This method is more successful if a trampoline twisting belt or a bucket is substituted for the belt. The performer's feet or legs can then rotate within the belt or bucket as the circle is being completed. The pommel wheel or dome (illustrations F#2 and F#3) allow the performer's legs to rotate through the double leg circle at a height lower than on a regular pommel horse. A buck can also be used in the same manner as the dome or the wheel. Illustration F#4 shows floor pommels and a small platform set on castors. This also allows the performer to practice the double leg circles.

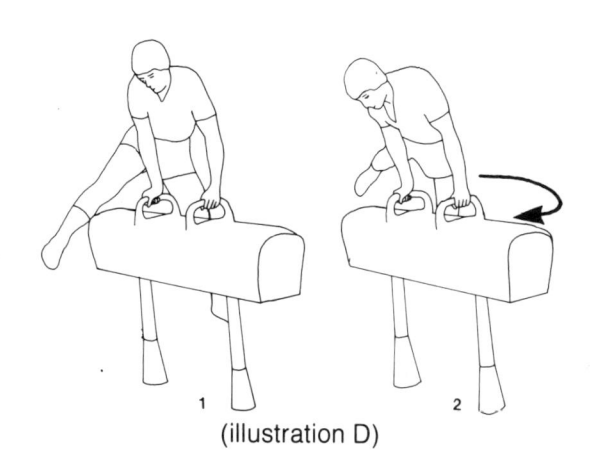

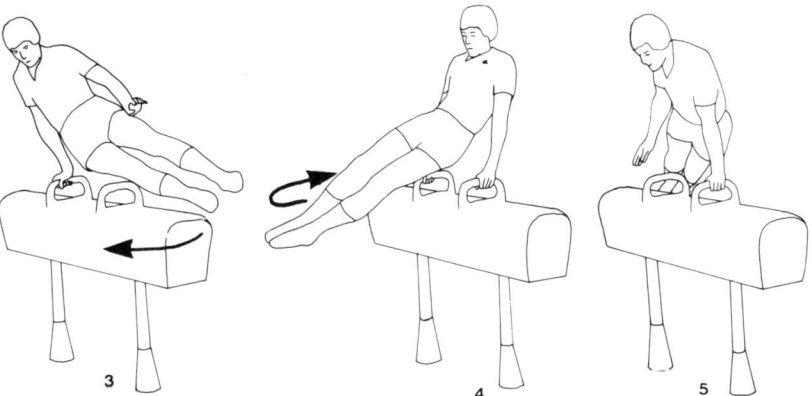

Common Errors:
Errors in Performance:
1. The arms and legs are bent throughout the circle.
   Correction: It is important that the athlete attempt to keep the arms and legs straight at all times. This is particularly important during the phases of one-armed support. With the exception of those parts of the double leg circle where a slight piking action occurs, the performer should attempt to stretch his body out as much as possible, avoiding bending the legs (illustrations B#3 and D#4).

SKILL   TEACHING TECHNIQUES AND OBSERVATION POINTS

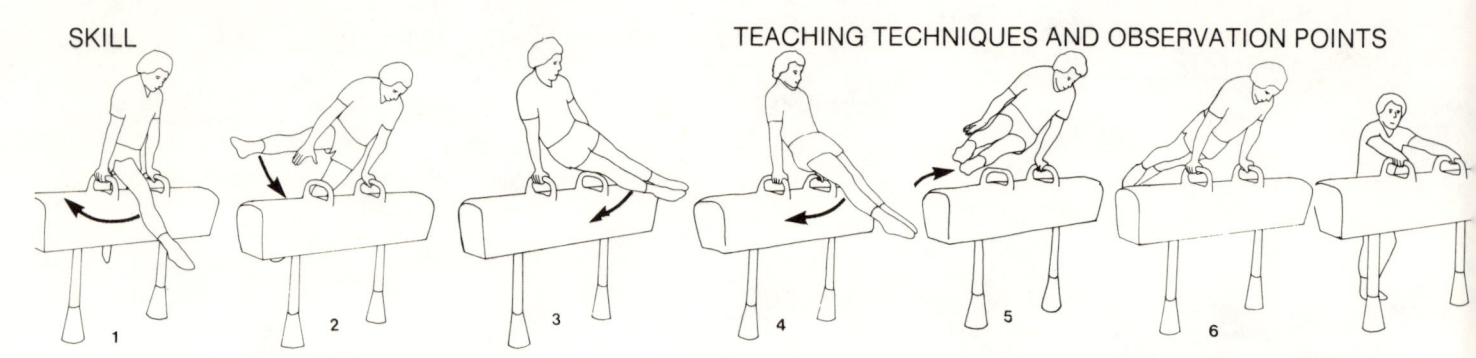

(illustration E)
Double Leg Circle
Initiated From Single Leg Half Circle Backward

2. The bodyweight is not leaned or tilted sufficiently in opposition to the movement of the legs. *Correction:* When the hips and legs are on one side of the horse the upper body must lean in the opposite direction. This continuous circular shift of balance is one of the most important technical aspects of the double leg circle.
3. The re-grasp of the hands on the pommels is made too late. *Correction:* Greater control and support is provided when both hands are in contact with the pommels than when the performer is in single arm support. The re-grasp of the pommels should be made the instant the body has passed over the pommel.

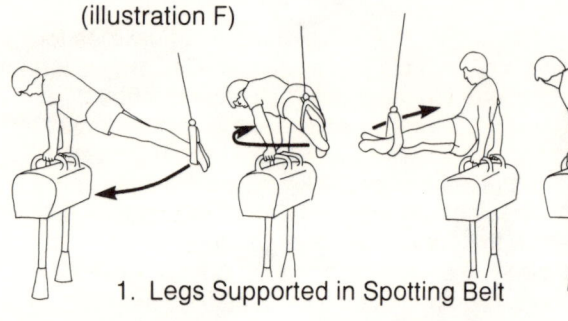

Teaching Devices for Double Leg Circles
(illustration F)

1. Legs Supported in Spotting Belt
2. Pommel Wheel
3. Pommel Dome
4. Floor Pommels Platform on Casters

15. Combinations and Routines

The routines listed in this section are almost exclusively made up of skills taken from Levels I-IV. The instructor should feel free to modify these routines to suit the needs of gymnastics students. Skills not listed in Levels I-IV but with which the instructor is familiar should be included to make the routines more attractive.

Level I Skills:

1. Jump into front support swings and repeat the swings three times to each side-stop-dismount.
2. From sitting between the pommels-lift to rear support and perform rear support swings three times to each side-stop-dismount.
3. Jump to front support-lift one leg through to stride support and perform stride support swings three times to each side-stop-return to front support-dismount.
4. Jump into front support swings and repeat the swings two times to each side-stop-squat through to rear support and perform rear support swings two times to each side-stop--dismount.
5. Jump into front support swings and repeat the swings two times to each side-stop-step through the pommels to stride support and perform stride support swings two times to each side-stop-return to front support and then squat through to rear support—rear support swings two times to each side-stop-dismount.

Level I and Level II Combined:

1. Jump into front support swings and repeat the swings two times to each side-single leg half circle-stride support swings two times to each side-single leg half circle back to front support-stop-dismount.

TEACHING TECHNIQUES AND OBSERVATION POINTS

2. Jump into front support swings and repeat the swings two times to each side-single leg half circle to stride support (right leg)-single leg half circle return to front support (right leg)-front support swing-single leg half circle to stride support (left leg)-single leg half circle return to front support (left leg)-stop-dismount.
3. Jump to front support at any end of the horse-support travel from the end of the horse to front support-front support swings (once each direction)-single leg half circle to stride support (right leg)-single leg half circle return to front support (right leg)-stop-dismount.
4. Jump to front support (on pommels)-support travel around half of the horse to front support on the pommels-single leg half circle to stride support (right leg)-single leg half circle to rear support (left leg)-stop-dismount.
5. Jump to single leg half circle to stride support (right leg)-single leg half circle to rear support (left leg)-single leg half circle back to stride support (right leg)-single leg half circle back to front support (left leg)-shift to feint position-flank dismount.

Levels I, II, and III Combined:

1. Jump to single leg half circle to stride support (left leg)-rear pick up (left leg)-flank both legs to right to flank dismount.
2. Jump into front support swings and repeat the swings two times in either direction-single leg full circle to front support (right leg)-stop-dismount.
3. From a jump start-double leg half circle to rear support-single leg half circle to stride support (left leg)-single leg half circle to front support (right leg)-stop-dismount.
4. Jump to single leg full circle (with favoured leg)-shift to feint position-flank dismount.
5. Jump to single leg full circle (right leg)-front support swings-single leg half circle to stride support (left leg)-rear pick up (left leg)-flank both legs to right to flank dismount.

Level I, II, III, and IV Combined:

1. Jump to single leg half circle (right leg) to stride support-front pick up (left leg) flank both legs to front support-single leg half circle (left leg)-rear pick up (left leg)-flank both legs to right for flank dismount.
2. Jump to single leg half circle to stride support (right leg)-front scissors (left side)-single leg half circle (left leg) through front support to flank dismount.
3. Jump to single leg half circle to stride support (left leg)-front pick up (right leg) flank both legs to front support-shift to feint position-rear dismount.
4. Jump into single leg full circle (right leg)-single leg half circle (right leg)-stride support swing-back scissors-(right side)-stride support swing-back scissors (left side)-single leg half circle through front support to flank dismount.
5. Jump to front support-shift to feint position-double leg circle-dismount.

C. Rings
General Safety

TEACHING TECHNIQUES AND OBSERVATION POINTS

1. As a lead-up and to complement activities on the rings, the instructor should develop the strength and coordination of students in related skills on the parallel bars, horizontal bar and ropes. Simple travels, supports, climbing, hanging, and moving from rope to rope all develop upper body strength which is so necessary for the rings. Many of the basic positions and skills listed in Levels I and II can be duplicated in this manner. Ropes have the added advantage of requiring no height adjustment and students can work in stream quickly and efficiently.
2. In the school gymnastics class, it is particularly important that the rings adjust in height in order to accommodate both the learner and the specific requirements of the skill. Adjustable rings are usually constructed with cables that run over pulleys to a chain attachment set on the wall. The rings are then raised and lowered easily and efficiently.
3. **Beginners should not attempt skills in rings set at competitive height since they have insufficient strength or coordination. This is particularly the case with those skills that require movement above the rings.**
4. The gymnastics instructor must also be aware that changes in the cable length of adjustable rings alter the motion of the performer as he swings or moves within the rings. Each adjustment in length means variation in timing and control. For elementary skills this rarely presents a problem. However, for the moderate to advanced performer the cables should be the correct length.
5. Because of the tremendous forces exerted on ring equipment it is essential that each section of the equipment be examined frequently for wear and fatigue. The rings should also be equipped with swivels. These allow the cables to rotate and adjust to variations in tension.
6. At all times chalk should be used. This is as important for the beginner as for the advanced performer. Handgrips are also recommended although they are not absolutely essential for elementary skills.
7. Mats or crash pads should cover a wide area beneath the rings (and ropes). There should also be sufficient space between rings, ropes and other apparatus.
8. Since the rings are essentially "unstable" and can shift suddenly in any direction, the beginner will have greater control problems than on the parallel bars or the horizontal bar where the apparatus is fixed. For this reason it is important that spotters follow the actions of the performer with great care. In the majority of cases the duties of the spotters are simple and uncomplicated. They lift, cradle and stabilize the performer. With the rings set low spotters are able to assist easily and accurately.
9. Because of the demands placed on the upper body, fatigue will occur quickly. Beginners should exercise for small bouts of time, allowing for recovery after each effort. There are many simple skills to maintain interest. Routines should be kept to three or four skills in succession as a maximum number.

Rope Activities as Lead-Ups to the Rings

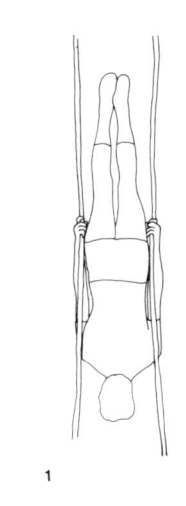

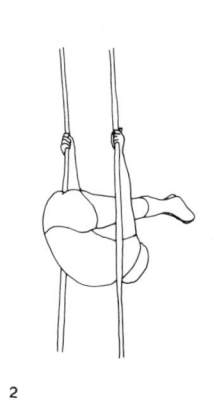

1 Straight Inverted Hang

2 Piked Inverted Hang

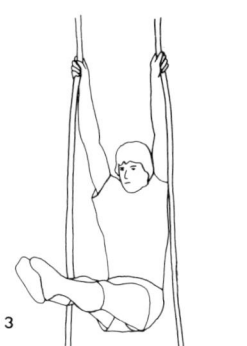

3 L-Hang In Two Ropes

4 Rope Climb - Hands & Feet

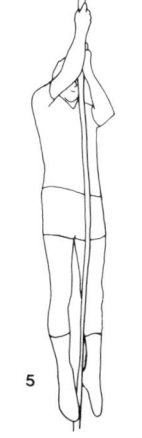

5 Rope Climb - No Feet

6 Rope Climb - 2 Ropes in 'L' Position

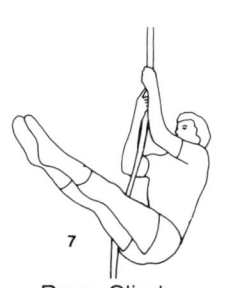

7 Rope Climb - One Rope in 'L' Position

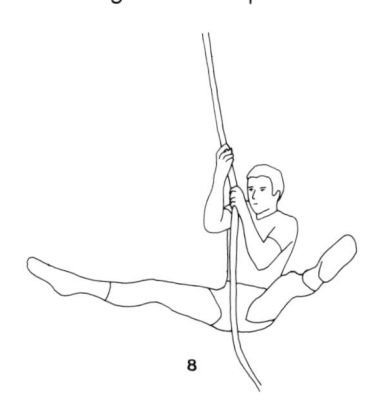

8 Rope Climb - One Rope in Straddle Sit Position

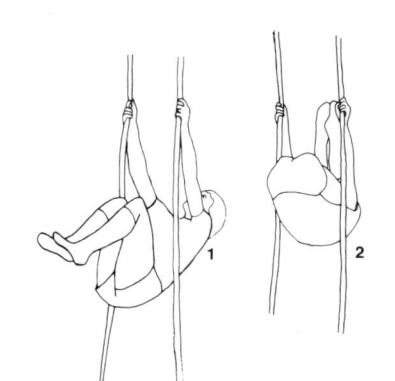

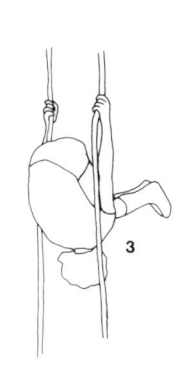

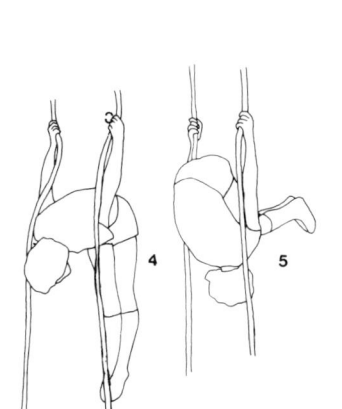

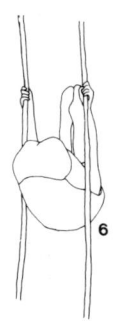

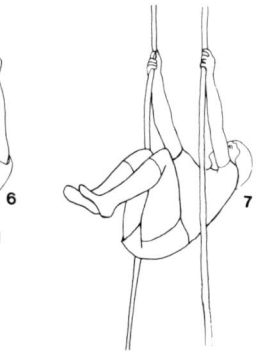

Skin the Cat

| SKILL | TEACHING TECHNIQUES AND OBSERVATION POINTS |

Level I Skills

1. Straight Inverted Hang

This skill leads to:
1. All further ring skills. The straight inverted hang is a fundamental position on the rings.

Lead-up skills:
1. tucked inverted hang and straight inverted hang on parallel bars.
2. tucked inverted hang on the rings (illustration #1).

Lead-up
Tucked Inverted Hang

Straight Inverted Hang On Low Rings

Straight Inverted Hang On Full Height Rings

Teaching Points for the Skill:
1. Begin on low rings.
2. Kick to tucked inverted hang (illustration #1). Slowly raise the legs to straight inverted hang (illustrations #2). Hollow the chest and use the muscles of the shoulders and back to maintain stability. Look downward and use the vision for orientation.
3. Lower legs to tucked inverted hang. Dismount.

Safety and Spotting:
1. Use mats, chalk, and low rings (illustrations #1 and 2).
2. With practice raise the height of the rings (illustration #3).

Spotting
Tucked inverted hang
Support under the shoulder and to the rear of the lower back and assist the performer in maintaining the tucked inverted hang (illustration #1).

Straight inverted hang (low rings)
As the performer shifts from tucked inverted hang to straight inverted hang, move support and control to the legs. Illustration #2 shows one spotter aligning the performer's body.

Straight inverted hang (medium to full height rings)
Stabilize the performer with a squeeze grip on either side of the chest (illustration #3).

Common Errors:
Errors in Performance:
1. Piking at the waist and allowing the legs to collapse downward. *Correction:* Tighten the muscles of the stomach and back and use vision to give an idea of body position. Tighten the muscles of the shoulders to help in controlling body position.

2. Piked Inverted Hang

This skill leads to:
1. further ring skills. A large number of ring skills pass through or begin with the piked inverted hang position, e.g. inlocate (pages 116-118) and back straddle dismount (pages 113-114)

Lead-up skills:
1. tucked inverted hang on the rings, (page 102), and also on the horizontal bar and parallel bars
2. piked inverted hang on parallel bars and low horizontal bar (page 148)

Teaching Points for the Skill:
1. Begin on low rings or on ropes (see page 101).
2. Kick up to a tucked inverted hang (allow spotters to stabilize and adjust the body position).
3. Slowly straighten the legs to the piked inverted hang (illustration #1).
4. Return to tucked inverted hang. Lower legs and dismount.
5. With practice raise height of rings (illustration #2).

Safety and Spotting:
Use mats below low rings and chalk to improve the grip.

Spotting
1. Either support under the shoulders and back and allow the performer to control the piked position (illustration #1), *or* support under the back and control the position of the performer's legs (illustration #2).

SKILL

Piked Inverted Hang On Low Rings

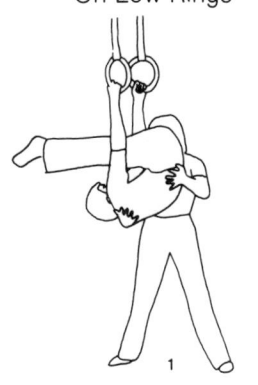

Piked Inverted Hang On Full Height Rings

TEACHING TECHNIQUES AND OBSERVATION POINTS

Common Errors:

Errors in Performance:
1. Failure to maintain the piked position. *Correction:* Look toward the feet or thighs and try to hold the thighs in a horizontal position. Use the shoulders and upper body to control the position of the seat. The spotter can assist initially in aligning the performer's body position.

3. Cross Support (3 seconds)

This skill leads to:
1. further ring skills. The cross support is a fundamental position on the rings.

Lead-up skills:
1. bent arm support and cross support on the parallel bars (page 148)
2. bent arm support on the rings (illustration #1)

Teaching Points for the Skill:
1. Use low rings so that the performer can attempt the bent armed support by either simply bending the legs, or by jumping lightly and easily into the bent arm support position.
2. Grasp the rings in bent arm support. (Have a spotter assist and stabilize the performer from the rear where necessary.)
3. Pull the rings in tight against the body. Hold for 3 seconds. Dismount.
4. For cross support set the rings *lower* than for bent arm support (approximately hip height).
5. Grasp the rings in cross support. Pull the rings in tight against the body. Press the shoulders downward and keep the arms straight. Look forward. Bend or raise the legs so that cross support is achieved. Hold for 3 seconds. Dismount and repeat.
6. Raise the rings a little higher. With spotting assistance (from the rear of the performer) jump into cross support. The legs are now extended throughout. Hold for 3 seconds. Dismount, rest and repeat.

Safety and Spotting:
1. Use a mat also chalk to improve the grip.
2. Set the rings as low as possible. *Do not make a beginner perform this skill on full height rings.*

Spotting:
Spotting is usually unnecessary when the rings are low and the performer enters the bent arm or cross support position by bending the legs. When the rings are set higher, a spotter should stabilize the performer by standing behind and gripping on either side of the waist.

Common Errors:

Errors in Performance:
1. Chest dropping between the shoulders—bending the arms—rings moving away from the body. *Correction:* All these problems indicate a lack of upper body strength. Increase strength with complementary strength exercises and work on related activities on the parallel bars and

Lead-up Bent-Arm Support

Cross Support

Cross Support With a Spotter Stabilizing the Performer

SKILL	TEACHING TECHNIQUES AND OBSERVATION POINTS

horizontal bar. When working on the rings, hold the required position momentarily, dismount, rest and repeat. Perform the support position at low height and gradually increase the height of the rings as strength and control improves.

4. Skin the Cat

This skill leads to:
1. all backward rotational skills on the rings, notably backward tuck dismount (pages 107-108), backward straddle dismount (pages 113-114), flyaway (pages 112-113).

Lead-up skills:
1. for orientation to the backward rotation, any backward roll skills on the floor (pages 38-39)
2. tucked inverted hang on ropes, the rings (page 102), or on the parallel bars
3. piked inverted hang on ropes (page 101) rings, (page 102) on parallel bars (page 148) or on a low horizontal bar (page 173)
4. straight inverted hang on ropes (page 101), rings (page 102), on the parallel bars or on a low horizontal bar (page 148)

Teaching Points for the Skill:
1. Use rings set just above head height (illustration #1), or use ropes (page 101). The arms should be in flexed position (illustration #1).
2. Bend at the waist and knees, put the head back and lift or jump into a tucked inverted hang (illustration #2-3).
3. Lower backward to the mat. The rings must be set low enough to allow a comfortable standing position at this stage in the skill (see illustration #4).
4. Pull hard and lift the seat. If this is too difficult, initiate this action by jumping upward. Return to the tucked inverted hang position (illustration #5-6).
5. Lower through to the original starting position (illustration #6-7).
6. Repeat with less support from the spotters.

Safety and Spotting:
Use mats below the rings. Set the rings low enough to allow the performer to comfortably place his feet on the floor at the midpoint of the skill (see illustration #4). Use chalk to improve the grip.

Spotting
1. Cradle the performer around the waist and to the rear of the knees (illustration #1).
2. Help to elevate him into a tucked inverted hang (illustration #2).
3. Shift support to the lower thigh (illustration #3).
4. Maintain this grip and control the lowering of the performer's legs to a standing position (illustration #4).
5. Lift the performer's legs back to the tucked inverted hang (illustration #4-5).
6. Shift the hands to a cradling support (illustration #6).
7. Allow the performer to lower out of the tucked inverted hang (illustration #6-7).

Common Errors:
Errors in Performance:
1. The performer attempts the skill with straight legs. *Correction:* In the early stages make the skill as easy as possible. Set the rings low, jump upward, and tuck as tightly as possible. To make the skill more difficult raise the rings to full height and attempt it from a full hang with straight legs. As a challenge to the better performers see who can perform the most repetitions of skin the cat.
2. Inability to lift into the tucked-inverted hang without the help of spotters. *Correction:* This indicates lack of upper body and abdominal strength. Continue to practice the skill with assistance and from a jump start. In the meanwhile improve pulling power and abdominal strength (see pages 14-15).

SKILL	TEACHING TECHNIQUES AND OBSERVATION POINTS

Errors in Spotting:
1. Confusion in assuming hand positions. *Correction:* Work with the rings set low. If the spotters initially make an error, there is no discomfort to the performer. Practice is necessary for the shift of hand positions from lifting in the first half of the skill to cradling the descent and vice versa.

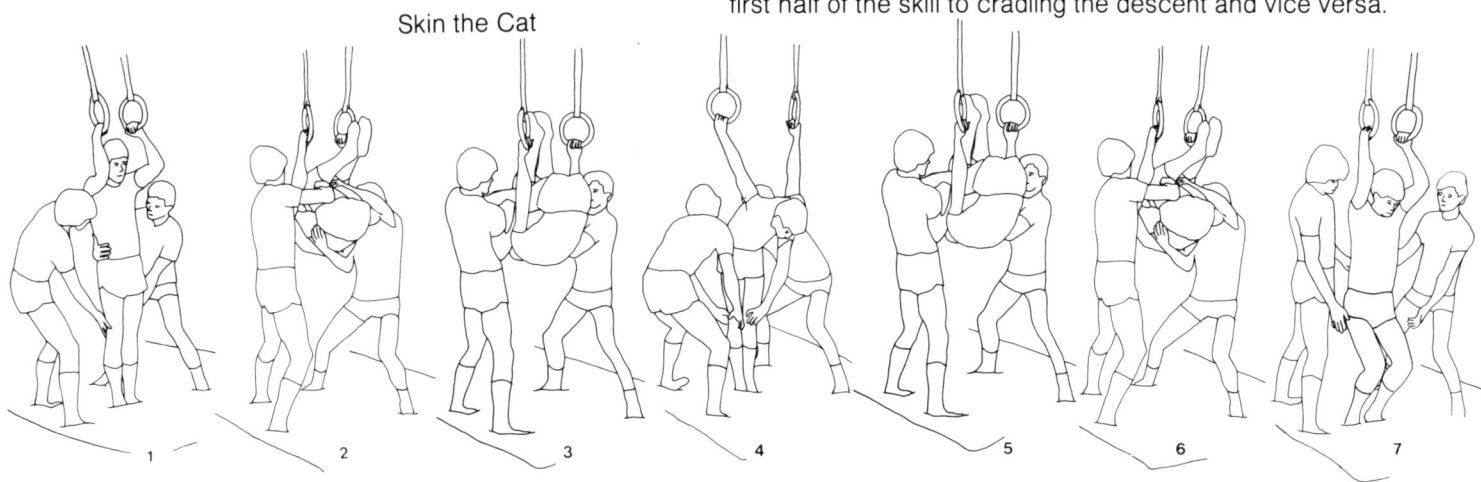

Skin the Cat

5. Swings

This skill leads to:
1. all further ring skills. Swings are fundamental to good performance on the rings. Good swings make it much easier to accomplish skills that demand that the gymnast move from below to above the rings.

Lead-up skills:
1. swings on the horizontal bar set at a height that allows the body to swing back and forth in hang position.
2. swings on the parallel bars in cross support (pages 149-150).

Teaching Points for the Skill:
1. Practice swings on the rings with one spotter standing either side of the performer. Work at low amplitude and do not rush. Good swings take plenty of practice.
2. To start a front swing, pull with the arms as though performing a pull-up. At the same time pike slightly at the waist.
3. After pulling up a short way and flexing at the waist, extend forward. This motion will start the swings and the body will swing to its furthest point backward (illustration A#6). The front swing now begins.

Front swing
1. The body will have a slight arch (illustration A#6). Keep the arms straight and hold them slightly more than shoulder width apart. The head is in its normal position.
2. As the swing downward begins, hold the body straight and extend as much as possible (illustrations A#5-4).
3. As the body passes through the vertical hang position, it is flexed slightly at the hips (illustrations A#4-3). This will cause the body to accelerate through the final part of the front swing.
4. At the end of the front swing, pull outward with the arms to lift the body higher (illustration A#1).

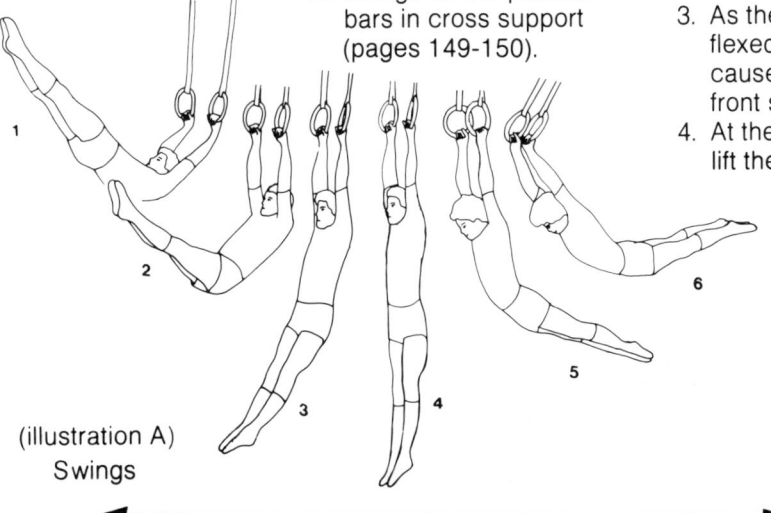

(illustration A) Swings

| SKILL | TEACHING TECHNIQUES AND OBSERVATION POINTS |

Swings (With Assistance)

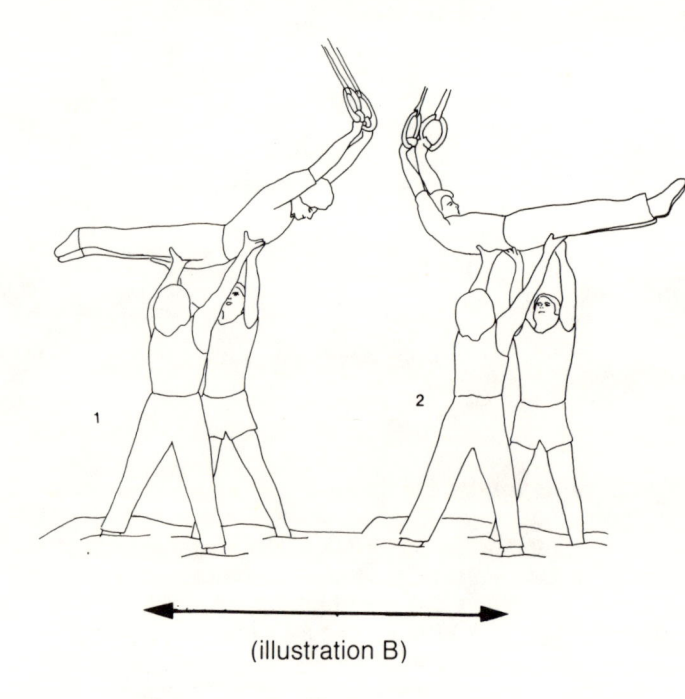

(illustration B)

Back swing (Beginning from the furthest point forwards)
1. In preparation for the backswing, flex the hips slightly (illustration A#2). The arms are more than shoulder width apart and the elbows slightly flexed.
2. Aim to pass through the vertical position with a smooth pendular action (illustration A#4).
3. As the body passes through the vertical position, arch slightly (illustration A#5).
4. Allow the legs to swing back and up and at the same time press the rings forward, down, and slightly to the side (illustration A#6).

Safety and Spotting:
Set the rings at a height where the performer's feet are just above the mat. Use chalk to improve the grip.

Spotting
1. Elevate under the chest and thighs to help the performer achieve the correct position on the back swing (illustration B#1).
2. Elevate under the back and the rear of the thighs to help the performer achieve the correct position on the front swing (illustration B#2).

Common Errors:
Errors in Performance:
1. The body arches too much throughout, particularly on the backswing.
2. The arms bend at the back of the backswing causing the body to jerk at the bottom of the swing.
3. The body bends too much at the waist (piking action) during the front swing.
Corrections: Practice the action on the horizontal bar before using the rings. Practice also on the parallel bars in cross support and in under arm support position. Return to the rings and practice the swings. Spotters adjust the body position. When working on the rings swing gently at first, concentrating on the correct action.

Errors in Spotting:
1. The performer is made to torque or twist during the swings.
Correction: The spotters must make sure that their support is balanced and that one spotter does not lift the performer more than the other.

Level II Skills

6. Tucked Support
(3 seconds)

This skill leads to:
1. L-support (3 seconds)

Lead-up skills:
1. cross support for 3 seconds (page 103)
2. stomach strengthening exercises (pages 14-15)

Teaching Points for the Skill:
1. Jump to cross support.
2. Hold the arms in the extended position and keep the rings close to the sides of the body.
3. Lift the knees to a tucked position. Hold for 3 seconds. Lower the legs to cross support.
4. Dismount.

Safety and Spotting:
Lower the rings so that the performer's feet are 15 centimeters (6") from the mat in the cross support position. Use chalk to improve the grip.

SKILL

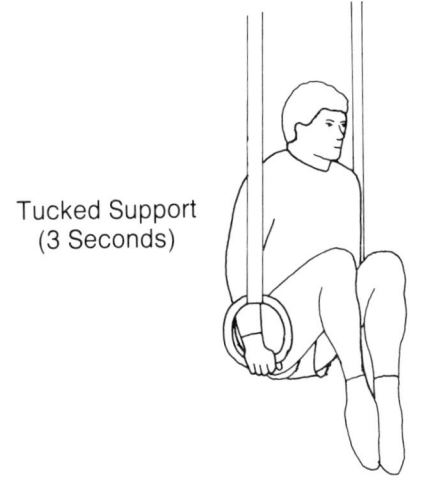

Tucked Support (3 Seconds)

TEACHING TECHNIQUES AND OBSERVATION POINTS

Spotting
Generally, spotting is not necessary. If spotting is used, stabilize the performer in cross support and tucked support by standing to the rear of the performer and supporting around the waist. (See illustration #3, page 103).

Common Errors:
Errors in Performance:
1. Allowing the rings to swing away from the body.
   Correction: Keep the arms straight and hold the rings close to the sides of the body.
2. Allowing the chest to sink between the shoulders.
   Correction: Press down with the shoulders and lift the chest upward.
3. Inability to hold the legs in position for 3 seconds
   Correction: This weakness can be corrected by abdominal exercises. (See pages 14-15).

7. Backward Tuck Dismount (from hang)

This skill leads to:
1. backward straddle dismount (pages 113-114)
2. flyaway (pages 112-113)

Lead-up skills:
1. skin the cat on ropes and on the rings (pages 104-105)
2. backward tuck dismount from standing (on low rings)

Backward Tuck Dismount

Teaching Points for the Skill:
1. Practice skin the cat on low rings and on ropes.
2. Practice the backward tuck dismount from a hang position on the rings (with the feet touching the mat).
3. Raise the rings so that the performer is in hang position with the feet just clearing the mats.
4. From the hang position pull through and past the tucked inverted hang (illustrations #1-3) with a strong upward lift. Keep the rotation of the skill continuous. Look for the mat.
5. As the seat passes between the arms - let go. Hold the tuck through to the landing. Use the vision throughout for orientation (illustration #4-6).

Safety and Spotting:
1. Use mats; also chalk to improve the grip.
2. Work through the skin the cat skill several times. This will indicate at what point the rings are to be released.

SKILL	TEACHING TECHNIQUES AND OBSERVATION POINTS

Spotting
1. Support around the performer's back and to the rear of the knee (illustration #1).
2. Help the performer through the tucked inverted hang position (illustration #2)
3. Shift the supporting grip to the arms (illustration #4). Maintain this grip through to the landing (illustrations #4-6).

Common Errors:
Errors in Performance:
1. Not letting go of the rings at the correct time. *Correction:* Practice the release of the rings on the skin the cat skill with the rings set low. Raise the rings and attempt the back tuck dismount with good support from the spotters.
2. Insufficient rotational speed through the skill. *Correction:* Good biceps and abdominal strength will increase the speed of body lift into the back tuck dismount. Work on complementary exercises to improve this strength (see pages 14-18). The performer can also jump into the skill (on low rings). This will give the skill some initial speed. Use spotters.

Errors in Spotting:
1. Confusion in shifting hands and establishing new hand positions. *Correction:* Practice the hand shift on the skin the cat skill with the rings set low. Raise the rings after the correct sequence is well established.

Level III Skills

8. Muscle-Up

This skill leads to:
1. The muscle-up is an indication of upper body strength. It shows that the gymnast has the power to work on more advanced ring skills.

Lead-up skills:
1. cross support in the rings (page 103)
2. pull-ups (chin-ups) on the horizontal bar (page 14)
3. dips in the parallel bars (page 16)
4. knowledge of the "high" grip (illustration B)

Teaching Points for the Skill:
1. Begin with the rings set low and practice the push phase of the muscle-up (A#1-3). Keep the rings close to the body and push directly downward.
2. Practice the "high" grip (illustration B). Use plenty of chalk and make sure that the rings rest diagonally across the hands (see illustration B). Notice that the lowest part of the ring is under the base of the hand).
3. Raise the rings to head height and place the hands in the "high" grip position (illustration C#1). The elbows point directly forward. Pull directly downward. Do not allow the rings to move out from the body. Have a spotter assist if necessary (see illustrations #D1-5). Turn the hands and press downward (illustration C#3). This will be the most difficult part of the action. Keep the rings in to the sides of the body and press down so that the body finishes in cross support (illustrations C#3-5).
4. Raise the rings to full height and attempt the skill from a hang position. A spotter can help the performer to obtain the "high" grip and also elevate him upward (illustrations D#1-5).

Common Errors:
Errors in Performance:
1. Sliding out of the "high" grip position. *Correction:* Use plenty of chalk and make sure that the correct position is

SKILL

Lead-up Push Phase Only in Low Rings

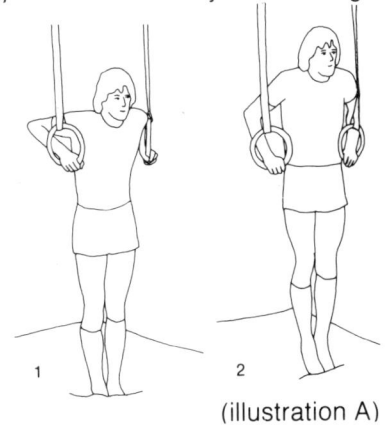

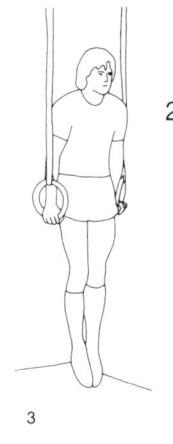

(illustration A)

Pull & Push in Moderate Height Rings

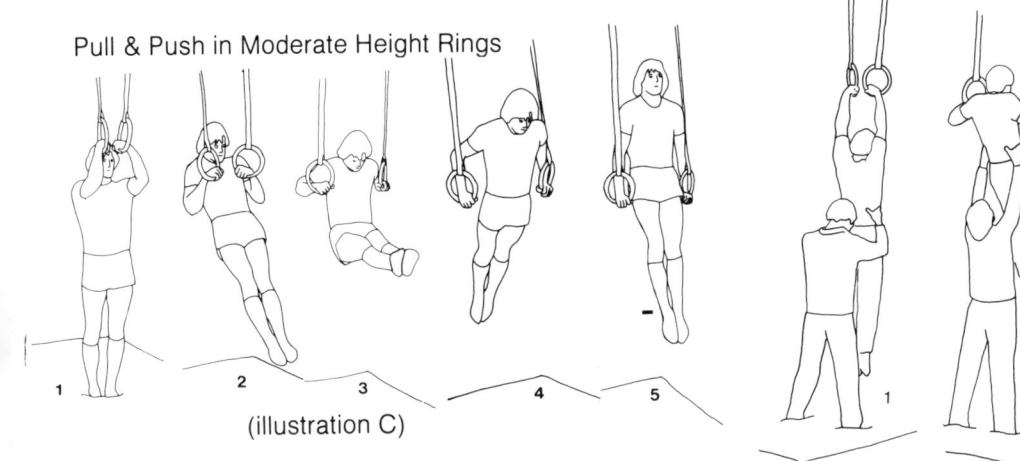

(illustration C)

9. L-Support

(3 seconds)

This skill leads to:
1. more advanced ring skills. The L-support shows that the performer has good upper body and abdominal strength. This is a pre-requisite for many ring skills.

Lead-up skills:
1. cross support in the parallel bars (page 148) and on the rings (page 103).

TEACHING TECHNIQUES AND OBSERVATION POINTS

obtained before pulling downward. (See illustration B for the "high" grip position).
2. Pulling the rings away from the body. *Correction:* The pull and push of the muscle-up must be in a straight line directly downward. Do not allow the rings to shift away from the body.

Preparatory High Grip for Pull Phase

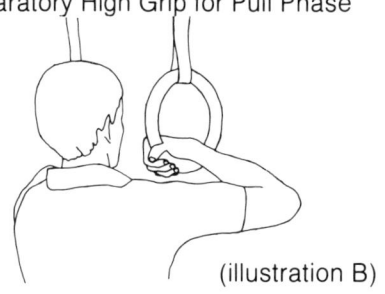

(illustration B)

Errors in Spotting:
1. Not in lifting directly upward. *Correction:* The spotter must lift directly upward and not push the performer off to one side.

Muscle-up in Full Height Rings

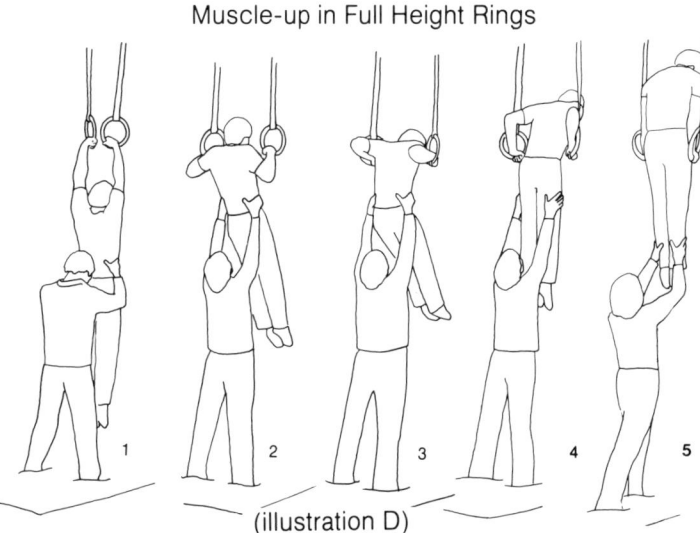

(illustration D)

Teaching Points for the Skill:
1. In low rings begin in cross support.
2. Lift the legs to tucked support.
3. Extend the legs and point the toes. Return to tucked support.
4. Repeat frequently. Hold the L-support for as long as possible (3 seconds or more).

Safety and Spotting:
Use a mat; also chalk to improve the grip.

Spotting
1. The spotter assists by placing one hand under the performer's legs and other on the lower back. This helps the performer to maintain the correct position.

SKILL

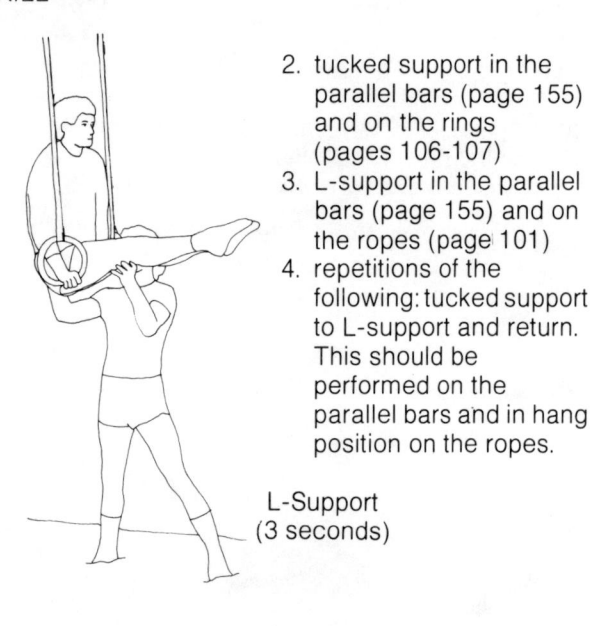

L-Support
(3 seconds)

2. tucked support in the parallel bars (page 155) and on the rings (pages 106-107)
3. L-support in the parallel bars (page 155) and on the ropes (page 101)
4. repetitions of the following: tucked support to L-support and return. This should be performed on the parallel bars and in hang position on the ropes.

10. Tucked Shoulder Balance
(3 seconds)

This skill leads to:
1. shoulder balance with straight legs (pages 115-116)

Lead-up skills:
1. tucked shoulder balance on the parallel bars (pages 155-157)
2. shoulder balance with straight legs on the parallel bars (pages 155-157)

Tucked Shoulder Balance (3 seconds)

TEACHING TECHNIQUES AND OBSERVATION POINTS

Common Errors:
Errors in Performance:
1. The legs are held too low. *Correction:* This is caused through lack of flexibility and abdominal strength. This can be improved through complementary activities (see pages 14-20). Work on the lead-ups suggested above, particularly tucked support to L-support and return.
2. The chest is allowed to sink downward. *Correction:* This is caused through lack of upper body strength. Press down as hard as possible with the shoulders and hold the head high. Work on complementary strength exercises for the upper body (pages 14-16).
3. The performer falls backward out of the L-support position. *Correction:* This is caused through lack of abdominal strength, flexibility, and upper body strength. Work on complementary exercises for improving strength and flexibility (pages 14-20). Hold the L-support momentarily and then quickly return to tucked support. Practice this action on the parallel bars until it is improved and then return to the rings.

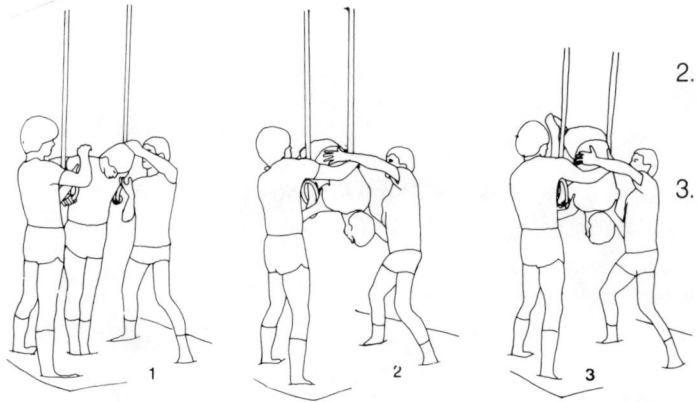

Teaching Points for the Skill:
1. Attempt the skill in low rings.
2. Begin in bent arm support (illustration #1).
3. Jump upward from the floor raising the hips above the shoulders. Keep the legs bent (illustrations #2-3).
4. Maintain balance with the arms and the shoulders. Keep the rings in against the shoulders and look downward (illustration #3).

Safety and Spotting:
Use a mat; also chalk to improve the grip.

Spotting
1. Spotters support under the shoulders and across the back. This prevents the performer from over-balancing and also gives upward support.

Common Errors:
Errors in Performance:
1. The rings are held in too close to the chest and stop the arms and shoulders from controlling balance. *Correction:* Hold the rings in close to the shoulders. This position is shown in illustration #3.
2. The legs are extended before the tucked shoulder balance is obtained. *Correction:* Hold the tuck throughout. If the legs are extended, the performer will fall back to the starting position or over-balance.
3. The head is tucked under causing the performer to over-balance. *Correction:* Look downward and use vision as a means of maintaining balance.

| SKILL | | TEACHING TECHNIQUES AND OBSERVATION POINTS |

11. From Cross Support-Half Backward Roll to Piked Inverted Hang

This skill leads to:
1. more advanced ring skills. Each part of this skill (that is, cross support, piked backward roll, and piked inverted hang) is fundamental to ring activities.

Lead-up skills:
1. cross support on the rings (page 103) and on the parallel bars (page 148)
2. piked inverted hang on the rings (page 103) and on the parallel bars (page 148)
3. skin the cat on the rings (pages 104-105) and on the ropes (page 101)
4. back tuck dismount (pages 107-108)

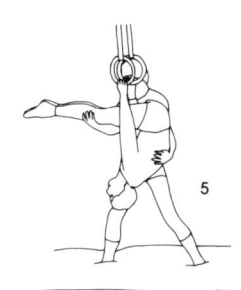

Teaching Points for the Skill:
1. Practice kicking into the piked inverted hang from standing. The arms should be flexed. Use a spotter to control the final piked inverted hang.
2. On low rings begin in cross support position (illustration #1).
3. With spotter(s) assisting, pike at the waist, lean backward and lower to the piked inverted hang (illustration #2-5). Press down hard with the arms to control the backward rotation (illustration #2). For initial attempts bend the legs.
4. Lower the legs into the final piked inverted hang position (illustrations #3-5).

Safety and Spotting:
1. Start with low rings and raise the rings as the performer improves.
2. Place a mat below the rings and use chalk to improve the grip.

Spotting
1. The spotters play an important part in this skill since they help considerably in controlling backward rotation and the movement of the performer's body into the piked inverted hang.
2. Support is given under the performer's back (illustration #2). The free hand controls the lowering of the performer's legs into the piked inverted hang (illustration #3-5).
3. Two spotters provide balanced and strong support and should be used for beginners.

From Cross Support
- Half Backward Roll to Piked Inverted Hang

Common Errors:
Errors in Performance:
1. Falling backward heavily into the piked inverted hang. *Correction:* Press down on the rings as the body is lowered backward. Complementary strength exercises may be needed (see pages 14-18). Spotters should help to control the speed of this action.
2. Inability to perform the skill with straight legs. *Correction:* This indicates that the performer has insufficient abdominal strength. Begin the skill from tucked cross support. Complementary exercises should be practiced to improve abdominal and quadriceps strength (see pages 14-18)

Errors in Spotting:
1. Insufficient support under the performer's back as he lowers into the piked inverted hang. *Correction:* The spotters must give strong support to the performer as he attempts the skill for the first time. Once orientation to the skill has been gained support can be reduced.

| SKILL | TEACHING TECHNIQUES AND OBSERVATION POINTS |

12. Flyaway (Backward Dismount with Straight Body)

This skill leads to:
1. back straddle dismount (pages 113-114
2. advanced back salto dismounts on the rings

Lead-up skills:
1. swings (pages 105-106)
2. skin the cat (pages 104-105)
3. back tuck dismount (pages 107-108)

Teaching Points for the Skill:
1. Practice swings and increase their amplitude (see pages 105-106).
2. Practice the back tuck dismount (pages 107-108). With each attempt at the back tuck dismount, perform the skill with greater forward swing and with less tuck.
3. When the flyaway is attempted begin with a good backswing (illustration #1) and on the forward swing elevate the body through a straight inverted hang position (illustration #3-4).
4. Use vision to give orientation (illustration #4-6).
5. Drive the body in an extended position between the rings and release the rings when the legs have passed through and beyond the straps (illustrations #4-5).
6. Note: Good swings *are* essential in the performance of the flyaway.

Safety and Spotting:
Use mats; also chalk to provide a good grip on the rings.

Spotting
1. For the sake of clarity, the illustrations show only one spotter. Two spotters give stronger and more balanced support. One spotter can be removed when the performer is showing moderately good form.
2. The spotter(s) follow the action of the swings, watching the motion of the performer's shoulders, because their grip will eventually be around the upper arm (illustration #7).
3. When the performer reaches the midpoint of the skill, the spotter(s) initially support under the chest and then shift their grip to the performer's upper arm.
4. Through this grip they maintain the height of the performer's upper body and allow his lower body to rotate down toward the floor.

Common Errors:
Errors in Performance:
1. Poor swings forcing the performer to tuck the body during the flyaway. *Correction:* Practice the swings, aiming for greater elevation of the body at both ends of the swing (front and back swing). Once the swings are improved, the body can be extended more and more.
2. Poor timing in the release of the rings. *Correction:* The position of the head is essential for orientation in this skill. The head leads the body and it should not be tucked into the chest. The performer must "look for the mats."

SKILL	TEACHING TECHNIQUES AND OBSERVATION POINTS

Errors in Spotting:
1. Poor timing in obtaining spotting handholds. *Correction:* Practice obtaining the correct hand positions on a back tuck dismount (pages 107-108). Transfer this action to the flyaway.

13. Backward Straddle Dismount

This skill leads to:
1. backward straddle dismount from high amplitude swings
2. advanced back rotational dismounts

Lead-up skills:
1. straight inverted hang (pages 101-102)
2. skin the cat (pages 104-105)
3. back tuck dismount (pages 107-108)
4. flyaway (pages 112-113)

Teaching Points for the Skill:
1. Begin in hang position (illustration #1).
2. Pull vigorously to straddle inverted hang, releasing the rings when the thighs contact the arms (illustrations #2-4).
3. Look for the mats to give visual orientation through the skill (important).
4. Once the rings have been released, bring the legs together for the landing (illustrations #4-5).
5. Practice the skill using an easy swing to initiate the action.

Safety and Spotting:
Use mats beneath the rings and chalk to improve grip.

Backward Straddle Dismount

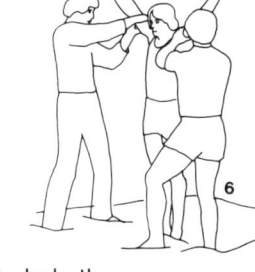

Spotting
1. Spotters press upward under the seat to help the performer move up and through the straddle inverted hang position (illustrations #1-3).
2. Support under the shoulder prevents the performer from falling downward at the midpoint of the skill (illustrations #3-4).
3. The spotters' hands are shifted to a "squeeze" grip on the performer's upper arm in the final half of the skill (illustrations #4-6).

Common Errors:
Errors in Performance:
1. Elevation to the straddle inverted hang is too slow. *Correction:* A faster swing will help in elevating the body to the inverted position. If the problem is caused through lack of strength, the performer should go back to simpler skills (such as back tuck dismount) and complementary activities which will build up shoulder and abdominal strength (see pages 14-15).
2. Poor timing in the release of the rings. *Correction:* Use the vision to give orientation during the backward rotation. Like the flyaway, the head should lead the action with vision "looking for the mat."

| SKILL | TEACHING TECHNIQUES AND OBSERVATION POINTS |

Errors in Spotting:
1. Spotters are too slow in shifting from their initial support positions to the "squeeze" grip around the upper arms. *Correction:* The back straddle dismount does not have to be performed with great speed. Initially the performer should lift to the straddle inverted hang and then back to hang position. In this way, the spotters can practice their hand shift for when the skill is performed in its entirety.

Level IV Skills

14. From Cross Support-Half-Forward Roll to Piked Inverted Hang

This skill leads to:
1. skills using forward rotation (forward roll)
2. skills initiated from a piked inverted hang position (dislocate and other advanced skills).

Lead-up skills:
1. cross support (page 103)
2. piked inverted hang (page 103)
3. forward roll from front support on the horizontal bar (pages 174-175). This lead-up would be performed in a piked position. The movement should be slow and with great control.
4. forward roll in the rings (see shoulder balance forward roll dismount, pages 115-116)

Teaching Points for the Skill:
1. Begin in cross support position (illustration #1).
2. Pike at the waist and lower the upper body forward, flexing at the elbows (illustration #2).
3. Slowly extend the arms until they are fully extended (illustration #3).

Safety and Spotting:
1. Use mats; also use chalk to improve grip.
2. Use low rings.

Spotting
1. Two spotters can be used to provide balanced support. A single spotter is shown for greater clarity.
2. The spotter(s) support under the back and legs and control the lowering of the performer's body into the piked inverted hang.
3. The support hand under the legs holds the legs in a horizontal position.

Common Errors:
Errors in Performance:
1. Falling forward heavily and jerking into the piked inverted hang position. *Correction:* Control of the body through the half-forward roll depends to a great degree on upper body strength. It may be necessary to develop this strength through complementary exercises (see pages 14-16).
2. Inability to raise the hips into the half-forward roll. *Correction:* This may be a problem of lack of strength, or it may be that the shoulders are not being lowered sufficiently in order to elevate the hips. Enter the half-forward roll with bent legs and extend them immediately the rolling action begins.

From Cross Support - Half Forward Roll to Piked Inverted Hang

115

| SKILL | TEACHING TECHNIQUES AND OBSERVATION POINTS |

15. Shoulder Balance
(3 seconds)

This skill leads to:
1. advanced balances in the rings e.g. handstand

Lead-up skills:
1. shoulder balance in tucked and extended position on the parallel bars (pages 155-157)
2. tucked shoulder balance on the rings (page 110)

Shoulder Balance (3 seconds)
Forward Roll Dismount

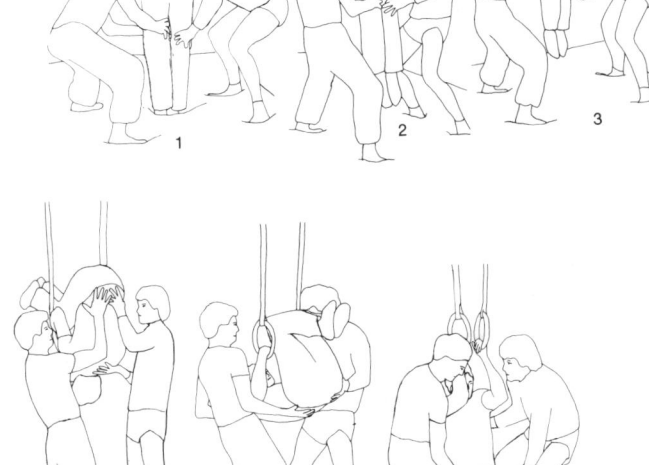

(illustration A)

Teaching Points for the Skill:
1. Begin by practicing the shoulder balance (and forward roll dismount) on the parallel bars (pages 157-158).
2. Illustrations A#1-9, B and C#1-3 show various approaches to learning the shoulder balance. The forward roll dismount should be familiar to the performer for each method.
3. Illustrations A#1-9. In low rings, lower forward into the shoulder balance, keeping the rings tight against the shoulders (illustration #1-3). Look downward to maintain orientation during the balance. Elevate the hips (this can be made easier by raising bent legs rather than straight legs throughout). Use the shoulders and arms to maintain balance (illustration #6). Lower the legs into a tucked position in order to roll out of the balance (illustrations #7-9).
4. Illustrations B, and C#1-3. These illustrations show the performer kicking from a box which is used to elevate the hips. A spotter can assist in stabilizing the shoulder balance (illustration B) and two further spotters control the movement of the rings. The performer must be knowledgeable with a tucked forward roll dismount out of the shoulder balance.

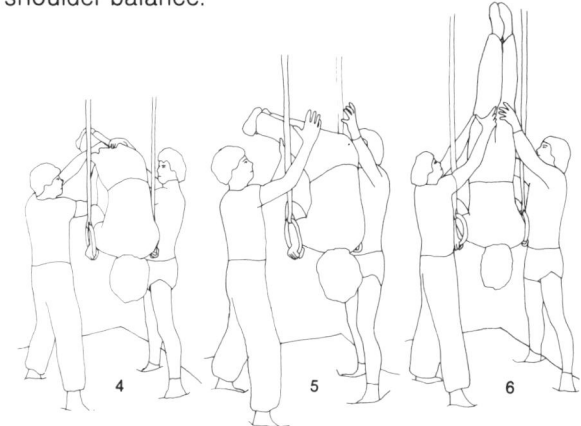

Safety and Spotting
Use chalk and a mat for cushioning the forward roll dismount.

Spotting
1. Spotters grip around the performer's legs to help elevate him into the shoulder balance (#1-6). Notice that the spotters shift their hand positions so that they grip the performer's legs on either side of the ring straps (illustration #6). Spotters shift their grip once again to cushion the descent in the forward roll (illustrations #7-9).
2. In illustrations B and C#1-3 the performer kicks into the shoulder balance from a vaulting horse or box top. The rings are stabilized by two spotters. An additional spotter can be

SKILL

(illustration B)

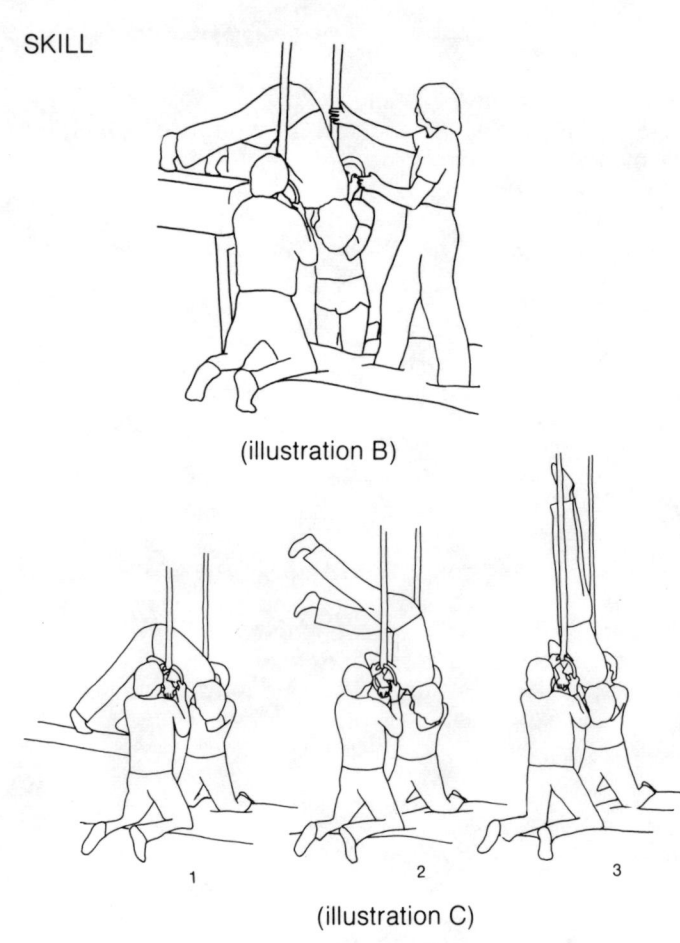

1 2 3
(illustration C)

16. Inlocate

This skill leads to:
1. advanced ring skills. The inlocate action is used frequently in intermediate and advanced ring routines.

Lead-up and Orientation
Inlocate on Low Rings With Assistance
(illustration A)

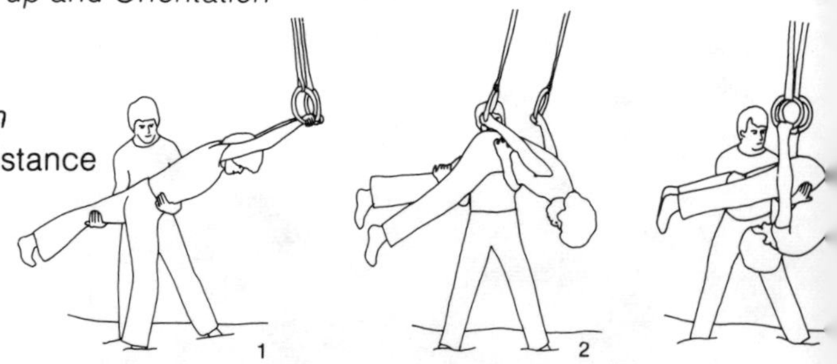

Lead-up skills:
1. good swings with high amplitude (pages 105-106)
2. mastery of the inlocate action on low rings (illustrations A#1-3).

TEACHING TECHNIQUES AND OBSERVATION POINTS

used to help control balance. Stabilizing the rings in this fashion can be used when the performer is transferring from the parallel bars to the rings. The amount of stability provided by the spotters is progressively reduced. Kicking up from a box or vaulting horse makes it easier for the performer to elevate the hips into the shoulder balance. The teaching points for the shoulder balance are the same as in illustrations A #1-9.

Common Errors:
Errors in Performance:
1. The rings are held too close to the chest, preventing the performer from controlling the shoulder balance. *Correction:* Hold the rings against the shoulders. Do not let the rings shift out, or conversely, pull the rings in too far towards the chest (see A#3-6).
2. The legs are extended before the hips are above the shoulders. *Correction:* Maintain a tucked or piked position until the hips are above the shoulders and then extend the legs upward (illustration A#3-6).
3. The head is tucked under with the chin on the chest. *Correction:* Look downward and keep the vision on the mats directly below the rings. This will help in maintaining balance (illustrations A#3-6).

Errors in Spotting:
1. Spotting (illustrations B and C#1-3) is simple and gives no problem. Confusion about the shifting of hand positions may occur in illustrations A#1-9. Spotters should work through their hand positions without the performer so that they understand what they have to do when they provide support.

Teaching Points for the Skill:
Orientation to the inlocate on low rings (illustrations A#1-3)
1. With the assistance from a spotter, jump upward, flexing at the hips and forcing the rings out to the side to inlocate forward

Lead-up and Orientation

The inlocate with assistance from tall spotters (illustrations B#1-4) *or with spotters standing on spotting blocks* (illustrations C#1-5)
1. The inlocate can be initiated either from a piked inverted hang (which gives added impulse to the backswing) or from a series of forward and back swings. Aim for a high horizontal position on the backswing (very important). Pull the arms from the overhead position outward and downward.

SKILL	TEACHING TECHNIQUES AND OBSERVATION POINTS

Place the chin on the chest and flex vigorously at the hips. The combination of the above actions forces the body to inlocate and assume the final piked inverted hang position

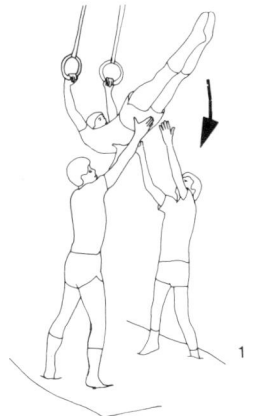

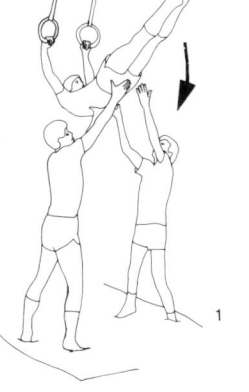

Inlocate

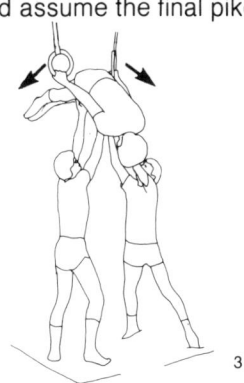

(illustration B)

Inlocate

(illustration C)

Safety and Spotting:
Use mats also chalk for a good grip on the rings.

Spotting
1. The inlocate must initially be practiced on low rings with the help of a spotter. This is extremely important. The spotter's grip around the waist and leg elevates the performer upward and allows the performer to practice the arm action easily.
2. Two spotters should be used when the inlocate is to be attempted from a swing. Illustrations B#1-4 and C#1-5 show the inlocate initiated from a swing. Two spotters provide good balanced support lifting upward on the backswing and lessening the performer's bodyweight on his arms. This is well shown in illustration C#3. Lift is provided under the thigh and under the chest (illustrations B#2 and C#2-3). Spotting *must* be balanced and accurately performed.

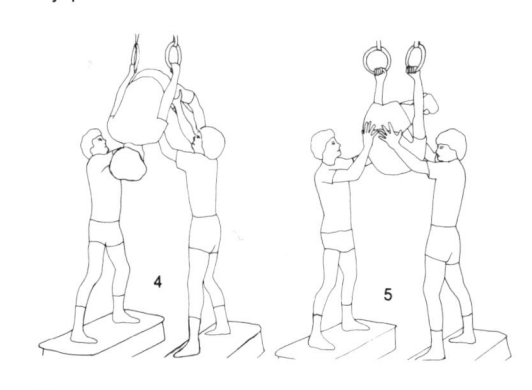

Common Errors:
Errors in Performance:
1. Poor swings. *Correction:* Practice swinging aiming to increase the amplitude of the swings on both the forward and the backward swing.
2. The inlocate is attempted at the midpoint of the backswing. *Correction:* The inlocate should be attempted at the *high point* of the backswing when the body has ceased to move upwards.

SKILL	TEACHING TECHNIQUES AND OBSERVATION POINTS

3. The head is extended away from the body. *Correction:* The head should be pushed forward and downward with the chin on the chest. This occurs at the initiation of the inlocate and helps to drive the body toward the piked inverted hang position.
4. The arms are bent during the inlocate. *Correction:* This problem is caused mainly through poor swings and insufficient lift backward and upward. The backswing should reach the horizontal position with the hips at least parallel to the floor. Use spotters until the technique is improved.

Errors in Spotting:
1. Insufficient speed in shifting from one hand position to the next. *Correction:* Spotters must first drive the performer upward on the back swing and then quickly shift to support the piked inverted hang position.
2. Insufficient support during the backswing. *Correction:* This is the most important phase of the support. The stronger the lift, the greater the ease with which the inlocate is performed. Spotting should be balanced and not twist the performer to one side. Reduction of spotting should occur only when the performer has improved in technique.

17. Back Uprise

This skill leads to:
1. advanced ring skills

Lead-up skills:
1. good swings on the rings (pages 105-106)(high amplitude forward and backward.
2. muscle-up (pages 108-109) particularly power in downward-pulling actions.
3. see exercises for strength and power (pages 14-20).

Teaching Points for the Skill:
1. Good swings are absolutely essential for this skill. Practice the swings until the body is lifting high on both forward and backswing.
2. On the backswing drive the hips and legs forcefully upward.
3. At the highest point in the swing, push sideways and downward with the rings toward the sides of the body (illustration #3). Hold the rings tightly against the sides of the body in the final cross support position. During initial attempts at the uprise, the arms can be flexed at the elbows.

Safety and Spotting:
Use mats and chalk for a good grip on the rings.

Back Uprise

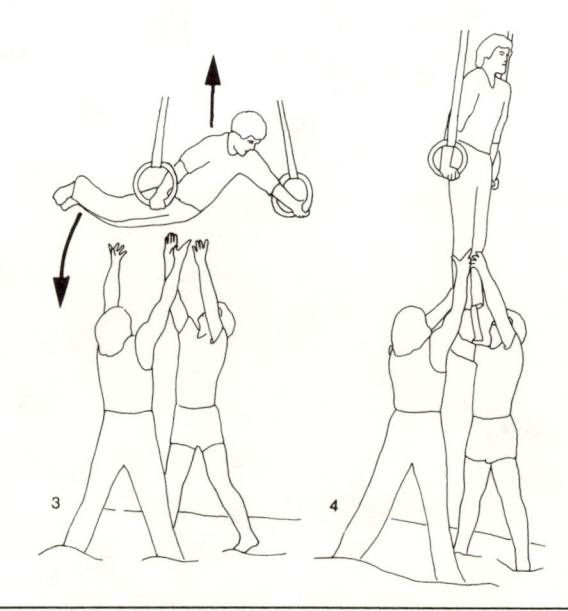

SKILL	TEACHING TECHNIQUES AND OBSERVATION POINTS

Spotting
1. Experienced spotters should be used to help the performer in this skill.
2. Spotters must first drive the performer upward on the backswing, and then quickly shift to a stabilizing position once the cross support position is reached. This latter action is extremely important.
3. Two spotters provide balanced support. Because the skill is performed with the rings set at full height, it is recommended that tall spotters are used, or that the spotters stand on spotting blocks (see inlocate on full height rings pages 116-118).
5. Spotters elevate the performer under the chest and the thigh. This lessens the load on the performer's arms as he pulls downward to the side of the body (illustration #2). The grip around the legs controls any swinging action which occurs at the end of the skill. Quick reactions on the part of the spotter are essential.

Common Errors:

Errors in Performance:
1. Poor swings. *Correction:* Return to practicing swings. At the same time, continue to increase downward pulling power of the body with complementary activities (see pages 14-20).
2. The arms are badly bent during the downward pull. *Correction:* This is an indication of lack of power or a poor swing. Increase this strength with exercises on weight machines, pulleys and similar complementary activities. Practice swinging in the rings.
3. The legs are not lifted sufficiently during the backswing. *Correction:* Practice elevating the legs from a high back swing without trying to complete the uprise. Let go of the rings and dismount before reaching support position. Use spotter assistance.
4. The back is arched too much during the backswing. *Correction:* Drive the legs up in the backswing but do not allow the body to arch. Lift the hips. Keep the body relatively straight during the backswing. Do not allow the legs to flex at the knees.

Errors in Spotting:
1. Lack of balance in spotting and spotting actions are too slow. *Correction:* The back uprise is performed fairly quickly. Spotters must equalize their support so that they do not cause the performer to torque during the lift upward. Once the spotters have completed their upward lift, they must shift quickly to the performer's legs and control the forward swing which will occur at the end of the skill.

SKILL	TEACHING TECHNIQUES AND OBSERVATION POINTS

18. Combinations and Routines

The combinations and routines listed in this section are made up almost exclusively of skills taken from Levels I-IV. The instructor should feel free to adjust and modify these routines to the needs of gymnastics students. Skills not listed in Levels I-IV, but with which the instructor is familiar, should be included to make routines more attractive. Assistance should be given by spotters where necessary.

Level I Skills (With the exception of #2 rings are chest height throughout)

1. Kick up to straight inverted hang-lower to piked inverted hang-return to straight inverted hang-lower to stand.
2. Swing (gently back and forth)-pull to straight inverted hang-lower to piked inverted hang-lower to standing. (Rings are raised to allow swinging to occur)
3. Jump to cross support (3 seconds)-dismount and using the floor for impulse immediately pull through skin the cat and return-jump to cross support (3 seconds)-dismount.
4. Skin the cat and return-pull to straight inverted hang-lower to piked inverted hang-lower back to skin the cat and return to standing.

Level I and II Combined (Rings from chest height to hang position)

1. Jump to cross support (3 seconds)-tucked support (3 seconds)-dismount.
2. Pull to straight inverted hang-lower to piked inverted hang-lower forward to hang-back tuck dismount.
3. Jump to cross support-tuck support (3 seconds)-lower to cross support-dismount and immediately pull to piked inverted hang-lower forward-and using floor for impulse-backward tuck dismount.
4. Swing (moderate amplitude)-pull to piked inverted hang-lower forward to hang—swing—pull to piked inverted hang—lower forward—dismount.

Level I, II and III Combined (Rings vary from shoulder to full height)

1. Jump to cross support-tucked support-momentary L-support-lower to standing and using the floor for impulse-backward tuck dismount.
2. Muscle-up with impulse from the floor—cross support—half-backward roll to piked inverted hang-lower forward-and using the floor for impulse-backward tuck dismount.
3. Muscle-up with impulse from the floor-cross support-tucked shoulder balance (3 seconds)-forward roll dismount-and using the floor for impulse-backward tuck dismount.
4. Muscle-up-L-support (3 seconds)—half-backward roll to piked inverted hang—lower forward to hang-swing-flyaway.
5. Muscle-up from hang-L-support (3 seconds)—tucked support—tucked shoulder balance (3 seconds)—forward roll to hang-swing-flyaway.

Level I, II, III and IV Combined (Rings at full height)

1. Muscle-up—L-support (3 seconds)—half-forward roll to piked inverted hang—lower forward-swing—backward tuck dismount.
2. Swing—back uprise—shoulder balance—forward roll—swing—flyaway.
3. Swing-inlocate-lower forward-swing back uprise-half-backward roll to piked inverted hang-lower forward-swing-back straddle dismount.

TEACHING TECHNIQUES AND OBSERVATION POINTS

4. Muscle-up-L-support (3 seconds)-shoulder balance (3 seconds)—forward roll to hang-swing-flyaway.
5. Swing—back uprise—shoulder balance (3 seconds)—forward roll to hang—swing—inlocate—lower forward—swing—backward tuck dismount.

D. Vault

General Safety

1. All jewelry should be removed. Gymnastic slippers are the best footwear for vaulting. Socks may slip, and bare feet are not recommended because of the possibility of stubbing and catching toes. Jogging shoes should not be worn since they do not provide either a secure take off or a secure landing.
2. All vaulting apparatus should be set as low as will comfortably accomodate the height of the performer and the type of vault being performed. Excessively high equipment causes difficulties for both performers and spotters.
3. As with other areas of gymnastics, a thorough warm-up is absolutely essential for vaulting. This should be performed systematically and carefully prior to attempting even simple vaults.
4. Vaulting can be taught using a variety of apparatus. As an example, the beam can be used for vaulting and because of its length, it is an excellent piece of apparatus for teaching the whole class elementary vaults such as the squat and straddle vault. The more common vaulting apparatus ranges from the vaulting horse (or pommel horse with the pommels removed) to the slope-sided vaulting box. Each of these items has its own characteristics which should be well known to the instructor.

Characteristics of Vaulting Apparatus

i The slope-sided vaulting box

1. This piece of apparatus varies in height according to the number of sections used. As sections are added, floor skills such as the squat, straddle, and headspring become vaults. Increasing the height of the box requires much greater ability and confidence. At full height, the vaulting box's sloping sides tend to keep spotters away from the performer, and can cause problems in providing support quickly and accurately. (This is not the case with the vaulting horse where spotters are able to step between its legs, and so get closer to the performer.) Used for side-box vaulting, a sectional vaulting box can come apart if hit hard horizontally. The pegs which hold each section together often become worn and should be replaced so that each section fits tightly into the other.
2. Occasionally a vaulting box is used as a spotting block on which the instructor stands to assist a performer. In this case, the sloping sides become a hindrance, particularly in spotting swinging skills on the parallel bars and horizontal bar. Straight-sided vaulting boxes, which are more popular in Europe, do not have this disadvantage, although they are also unstable for side-box vaulting.

TEACHING TECHNIQUES AND OBSERVATION POINTS

ii The Vaulting Horse

1. A vaulting horse may have no pommel attachments or it may double as a pommel horse and have plugs which fill the holes when the pommels have been removed. To avoid injury the vaulting horse should never be used with the pommel holes unplugged or taped over.
2. Its four legs allow spotters to stand close to the performer, but its lowest height is usually the full height of a vaulting box and so the vaulting horse is limited in height reduction. Both horse and box can cause difficulties when they are transported, particularly if they do not have castors. Some vaulting horses have a pair of wheels attached to one set of legs. This adds greatly to their mobility. Delays in class organization frequently occur because the adjustable legs on the vaulting horse refuse to extend or retract easily. These adjustments must be checked and oiled periodically. Three of the legs have holes for height adjustments. The fourth leg is used for minor adjustments and often causes more problems than the other three. It should adjust easily and then hold its position. When a vaulting horse is set up for side or long horse vaulting this fourth leg should be one of the pair on the near or pre-flight side of the vaulting horse.

iii Take-Off Apparatus

1. Take-off apparatus for vaulting varies from beat boards to springboards and trampettes. Each has advantages and disadvantages. Their individual use depends upon the preference of the instructor and the objectives of the gymnastic program. Many instructors teach vaulting using only the beat board. Others vary their choice. Springboards, beat boards, and trampettes can all be used to teach vaulting safely *providing* the instructor is well aware of the limitations of each piece of apparatus, and makes adjustments accordingly. Illustrations in this handbook show each piece of take-off apparatus in use, both in lead-ups and in the final vault.

iv Beat boards

1. A beat board is the take-off apparatus used for competitive vaulting. It normally requires a long and aggressive run-up, and in order to convert horizontal speed into vertical lift, a specific body position at take off. Many performers fail to achieve the correct body position at take off and they can enter a vault with exaggerated horizontal speed and little upward lift. This causes problems for spotters who panic and become confused in their attempts to establish handholds and spotting positions quickly.
2. Because of eagerness to get on to actual vaulting, an instructor will often limit the time spent in learning to use the beat board. This produces the fairly common sight of performers attempting to vault with insufficient lift at take off. Difficulties are then compounded by the use of a vaulting horse which cannot be lowered any further because of limitations in its adjustments. A partial solution to this problem is to place one beat board on top of another. This gives additional lift at take off and also reduces the need for a long run up.

TEACHING TECHNIQUES AND OBSERVATION POINTS

v Springboards

1. Springboards often have a long, protruding base which supports a ramp-like board section producing the spring. The base can become a hindrance to spotters on the pre-flight side of a horse. If used with a slope-sided vaulting box a springboard requires a take off some distance from the box, and it is almost impossible for spotters to obtain an early grip on the performer. This problem does not occur when a springboard is used with a vaulting horse since both pieces of apparatus can be placed close together.
2. The main advantage of springboards (and trampettes) is that neither demands the aggressive attack at take off required by a beat board nor the same length of run-up. This can be a great help in teaching elementary vaulting.

vi Trampettes

1. Trampettes are often used as a means of providing the take off impulse for vaulting. However, they are deceptive in the ease with which they produce lift and this aspect must always be well controlled. Too much lift is as much a problem to the vaulter as too much horizontal speed. Novices using a trampette for the first time should work on accustoming themselves to stepping onto and taking off from a trampette, landing onto a mat without any vault being included. The angle at which a trampette is sloped to a large degree determines the amount of lift produced and for beginners this angle should not be extreme. If trampettes are sloped down and toward the horse, the approach run can be eliminated. Spotters then have no problem in grasping the performer both in the pre-and post-flight stages of the vault. When they are sloped away from the vaulting horse, there is no need to use a fast or long run-up, and three to four paces is quite sufficient as an approach for all but advanced vaults.
2. Trampettes used in this manner are beneficial to the instructor who is interested strictly in recreational vaulting and is limited by time and gymnasium space. It is also possible to progress from trampette vaulting to beat board vaulting by using an intermediate stage of two beat boards placed one on top of the other. Later, when a single beat board is used, take off and run-up are adjusted accordingly.

vii The Run-up and Landing area

1. For all forms of vaulting, the run-up should be clear of obstructions, and there should be no possibility of other students moving into the path of the approaching vaulter. Mats should cover a large area so that there is plenty of cushioning, particularly for poorly performed vaults. Mats and crash pads should be placed close together so that there is an even surface throughout, one which is adequate for the performer to land on, and for the spotters to move around on without tripping. Care should be taken that the mats do not shift on the gym floor as the vaulter completes a landing. Trampettes, beat boards, and springboards should not slide on take off, and as with other apparatus, should be checked periodically for broken springs and other forms of equipment fatigue.

Suggestions On How To Teach Vaulting

All vaulting incorporates the following action:
a) run-up (or approach)
b) take off (i.e. take off from a beatboard, springboard, or trampette)
c) pre-flight (i.e., the movement through the air from the take-off apparatus to the box or horse)
d) action on the apparatus (i.e., the push-off from the apparatus)
e) post-flight (i.e., the movement through the air from the apparatus to the landing)
f) landing

Vaulting is performed on a horse or box, lengthwise or sideways. In competitive vaulting men use the horse lengthwise and women use the horse sideways.

TEACHING TECHNIQUES AND OBSERVATION POINTS

It is recommended that vaulting is introduced to a gymnastic class in the following manner:

1. Introduce all actions performed above the vaulting horse as floor skills. Squatting, straddling, stooping, headsprings and handsprings should all be taught initially as floor skills. Body positions in the flank, front, and other vaults can also be taught on the floor.
2. Introduce the take-off apparatus as a separate activity apart from vaulting. Performers are required to jump from the take-off apparatus onto mats using a short run-up of two to three paces. In this way they familiarize themselves with the hurdle step onto the take-off apparatus and the two-footed take off from the apparatus onto the mats. This activity can be made more interesting by requiring them to perform a tuck, straddle, stride, or pirouette in the air prior to landing.
3. The next stage is to become familiar with the vaulting horse or box. Begin by teaching side horse or side box vaulting. This is much easier. After the class is familiar with this type of vaulting, males can then progress to long horse vaulting.
4. Develop vaulting in the following manner:
   a) Teach the post-flight and landing. Eliminate the run-up, pre-flight, and the push off. Performers step onto the take-off apparatus and from there climb onto the vaulting horse. Once on the horse, they then dismount using a variety of actions in the air (tuck, straddle, pirouettes, and so on).
   b) Add the pre-flight to post-flight and landing. (There is no run-up). With assistance the performer squats from the take-off apparatus onto the horse, stands up and dismounts performing a prescribed action in the air. The instructor progresses to more advanced mounts onto the horse such as the straddle and stoop. All are performed without a run-up. The same method can be used for the front and flank vaults.
   c) The pause on the box is now eliminated. With spotting assistance the performer squats or straddles fully over the horse. There is still no run-up.
   d) A run-up is added. Initially this is no more than two or three paces and it is more of a walk-up than a run-up.
   e) The run-up is progressively lengthened and the speed of approach increased. More pre-flight is added to the vault.

Orientation to Vaulting

1. Illustrations #1-7 show a teaching progression for vaulting in which performers begin by climbing on and climbing off the horse and work up to vaulting using a single beat board. In this sequence the instructor systematically adds run-up and requires the performer to provide more and more of his own take-off lift. The format of this teaching progression is as follows:
   a) The instructor begins with a trampette sloping down toward the horse. No run-up is used.
   b) The trampette is turned around and slopes away from the horse. A short run-up is used of two to three paces.

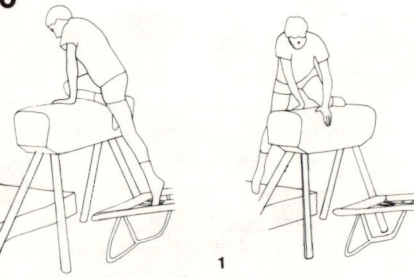

Climb on—climb off

Climb on—jump off with a tuck-straddle or half turn

Squat on—stand up and dismount using a tuck, straddle, or stride jump

Straddle on—bring the legs together and dismount using one of the variations mentioned in illustrations #2-3

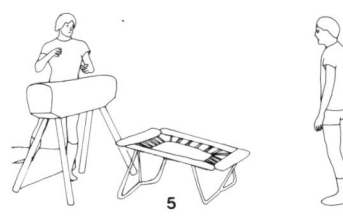

The trampette is turned around and the vaulter approaches with a two to three pace run-up

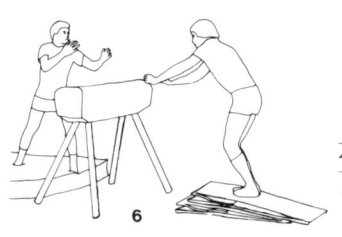

Two beatboards placed one on top of the other are substituted for the trampette. A longer run-up is used.

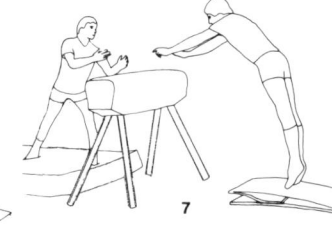

The vaulter progresses to using one beatboard and a full length run-up

Use of the Beat-Board For Vaulting

TEACHING TECHNIQUES AND OBSERVATION POINTS

   c) Two beat boards, one placed on top of the other are substituted for the trampette. A three to four pace run-up is used.

   d) A single beat board is used and the run-up is progressively increased in length.

2. When the trampette is sloping down toward the horse, the performer simply steps onto it from the side, places his hands on the horse, and performs the required actions to get on top of the horse. When the trampette is turned around, the performer approaches with a one to three pace run-up (again this is a walk-up rather than a run-up). During these two stages, spotters learn their handholds and support positions.

3. The instructor who expects to progress to vaulting using a single beat board should have an intermediate stage between the trampette (or springboard) and a single beat board. Two beat boards placed one on top of the other is a good idea. These give a little more height and spring at take off than a single beat board. The transition to the single beat board is then less of a problem to the performer.

4. If a springboard is used instead of a trampette, the following sequence could be employed:

   a) The springboard is placed close to the horse (no run-up is used).

   b) The springboard is shifted a short distance back from the horse (a two to three pace run-up is used).

   c) Two beat boards are placed one on top of the other (a three to four pace run-up is used).

   d) A single beat board (the run-up is progressively increased in length).

Many instructors may not progress beyond using a springboard in their classes. This apparatus provides quite adequate take off for elementary vaulting. However the limitations of it should be well known. The same applies to the trampette (see page 123). The instructor who uses a single beat board throughout must realize that the take off from this apparatus needs special attention and considerable practice.

1. The correct use of the beat board takes careful development over a long period of time. The gymnast's leg power must be developed through specific exercises and the technique of take off practiced so that maximum lift from the beat board is obtained. This is particularly important for those vaults that require maximum hip lift at the take off. Vaults which can be successfully completed with a low hip position do not require such a refined take off technique from the beat board.

2. Those instructors who will be using a beat board in their gymnastics classes should concentrate on the following major points of technique. (More detailed explanations of beat board technique are available in *Olympic Gymnastics for Men and Women*, by Taylor, Bajin, and Zivic, or in the C.G.F. Coaching Certification Manual, Level II). (See Appendix I)

TEACHING TECHNIQUES AND OBSERVATION POINTS

The Run-up
1. The approach run is similar to that used by the long jumper in track and field. The gymnast starts slowly, increases speed, and reaches maximum speed three to four paces prior to performing the hurdle step and landing on the beat board.
2. Competitive vaulting uses a run-up of anywhere from 13-25 meters in length. In a school gymnastic class this run-up will be reduced in length and involves less speed.
3. Accuracy of run-up is extremely important and the pacing of the run-up should be measured back from the board in the same way that the long jumper measures his run-up.

The Hurdle
1. A simple description of the hurdle is stepping or jumping off one foot and then placing both feet together on the beat board for the take off. This kind of action occurs elsewhere in gymnastics—for example, in the front salto (somersault). To practice the hurdle, the vaulting horse should be removed. The gymnast begins with a walk, thereafter from a short run-up of a few paces. Using the hurdle, he jumps from the beat board onto the mats. During a vault the hurdle occurs after the gymnast has reached the maximum speed in the run-up. When he lands on the board, both feet will be placed together approximately a foot from the far end of the board. This means that he will be landing on the most flexible and springy part of the board (see illustration #2).
2. The body position (when both feet are placed on the board) is by far the most important factor in the take off. The gymnast's body should be leaning back at about 30 degrees to the vertical with the hips to the rear of the feet. By obtaining this position, forward speed is translated into upward lift (see illustrations #1 and 2). As the take off occurs the upper part of the body rotates forward over the feet.

Take off
1. The take off in many ways resembles that of the volleyball player jumping for a spike. It must be both explosive and powerful. At the completion of the hurdle the gymnast's arms are swung forward vigorously to a horizontal position and then arrested suddenly at that level. This action helps in providing lift (illustrations #1 and 2).
2. The arm action is coordinated with an upward drive from the legs.

Common Errors:
1. The gymnast slows down just before hurdling onto the board. *Correction:* Using the beat board and landing mat, place large visible marks on the run-up to ensure the pacing is correct and to indicate where maximum speed should be reached. With a short run-up, practice increasing the tempo of the approach run. With each successive practice session, increase the approach speed and the length of the run-up.

Use of the Beat Board for Vaulting

SKILL	TEACHING TECHNIQUES AND OBSERVATION POINTS

2. The hurdle is performed with a large leap upward and down onto the board. *Correction:* Step low and forward, pushing the hips ahead of the upper body.
3. The upper body is leaning forward at the moment the feet are placed on the beat board. *Correction:* Reach forward with the feet, allowing the shoulders to rotate backward. Practice this action freely on the gymnasium floor. The same motion occurs in high jump, long jump and the approach in the volleyball spike.

Level I Skills

1. Front Vault (Side Horse)

This skill leads to:
1. The front vault performed with the hips and legs passing low over the horse (illustrations B#1-4) leads to the more advanced form of front vault in which the legs pass vertically above the hand position at the mid-phase of the vault (illustrations C#1-5). The advanced front vault is related to the cartwheel vault.
2. The front vault can also be used as a dismount from the parallel bars (pages 154-155).

Lead-up skills:
1. see suggestions on how to teach Vaulting and Orientation to Vaulting (page 124)
2. see Lead-up (illustrations A#1-5)

Teaching Points for the Skill:
1. With no run-up, vault or jump (with bent legs) onto the horse (illustrations A#1-3). Place the hands at one end of the horse and jump up so that the feet are placed at the other end. Keep the arms straight and the chest square to the long axis of the horse.
2. Bend the legs slightly and push off the horse, using the arm on the pre-flight side of the horse for support (illustrations A#4-5).
3. Practice the front vault from a short approach run. Elevate the hips as high as possible and push off the horse as strongly as possible with the support arm to elevate the upper body for the landing.
4. With each vault, work to raise the hips as high as possible. Illustrations C#1-5 show an advanced form of front vault in which the hips are elevated vertically above the hand positions. This type of front vault would be placed in Level III-IV.

Safety and Spotting:
1. Use a mat on the post-flight of the horse. Set the horse (or box) at the performer's waist height.
2. If a trampette is used, slant it downward toward the horse (illustration A#1). If a springboard is used, place it close enough to the horse so that the vault can be taught without a run-up. With practice, the take-off apparatus can be moved back.

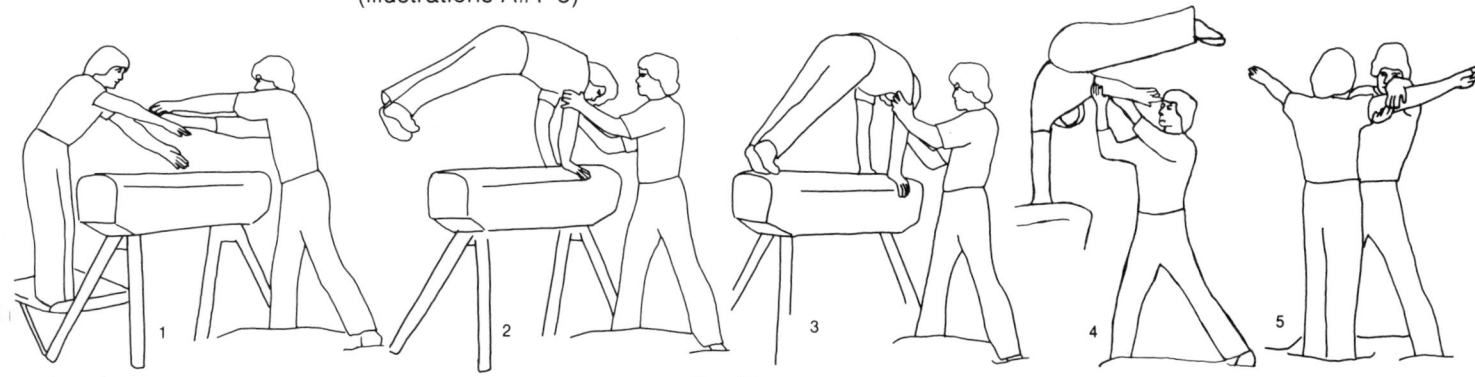

Lead-up
Front Vault onto the horse
-Jump off (illustration A)

Spotting
1. The spotter grips around the performer's upper arm on the post-flight side of the horse. During lead-ups, stabilize the performer on the horse. Maintain the height of the

SKILL

Front Vault (Side Horse)
(Side View)

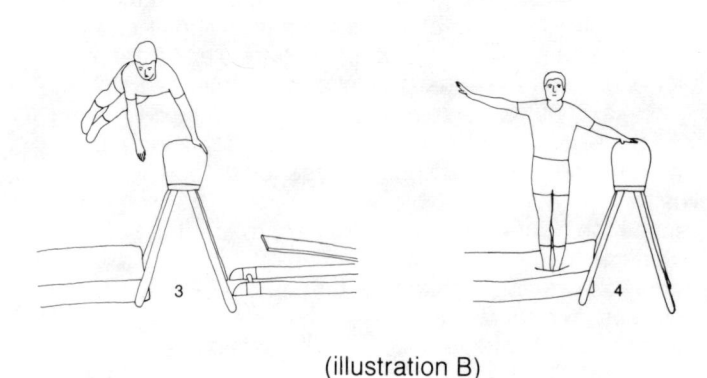

(illustration B)

Advanced Front Vault (Side Horse)
(Legs Vertically Above Hand Positions At Mid-point of Vault)

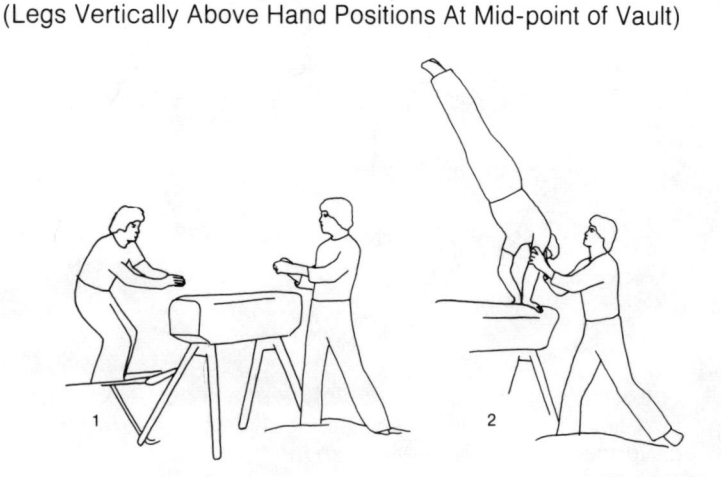

(illustration C)

TEACHING TECHNIQUES AND OBSERVATION POINTS

performer's upper body during the dismount from the horse. Obtain the grip around the performer's upper arm *as early as possible.*

2. The same actions are used when the performer is approaching with a run-up. An early grip on the upper arm is absolutely essential. Step with the flight of the performer on the post-flight of the vault. Maintain the height of the upper body.

Common Errors:
Errors in Performance:

1. Releasing the wrong hand from the horse on the post-flight part of the vault. *Correction:* Rather than vaulting onto the horse, climb on and assume the mid-phase of the vault (see illustration A#3). Concentrate on jumping off the horse, facing toward the side, and maintaining contact on the horse with the arm on the pre-flight side. Repeat until the action becomes established. Use a spotter for assistance.
2. Insufficient upward push with the arms. *Correction:* Raise the head and drive upward with the arms. This lifts the head and shoulders and helps to achieve the upright stance in the landing.
3. Too much speed in the run-up. *Correction:* A two to three pace run-up is all that is necessary for this vault. *Do not run quickly. This makes the vault more difficult.*

Errors in Spotting:

1. Gripping too low on the support arm. *Correction:* A "squeeze grip" must be assumed at the highest part of the arm.
2. Not stepping with the performer on the post-flight of the vault. *Correction:* The faster the approach, the larger the post-flight of the vault. Make allowance for the flight of the performer by stepping with him as he descends in the latter part of the vault.
3. Insufficient upward support on the post-flight of the vault. *Correction:* Aim to keep the performer's shoulders and head up during the post-flight of the vault. If the performer catches his feet on the horse, good upward support on the part of the spotter will be necessary to stop the head and shoulders from falling downward.

| SKILL | TEACHING TECHNIQUES AND OBSERVATION POINTS |

2. Flank Vault (Side Horse)

This skill leads to:
1. flank vaults in which the hips and legs are elevated above the height of the shoulders at the midpoint of the vault.
2. flank vault dismounts on other apparatus—for example, a flank vault dismount on the pommel horse or the horizontal, uneven and parallel bars

Lead-up skills:
1. flank actions performed over a box, beam, or horizontal bar set lower than the minimal height of the vaulting horse.

Teaching Points for the Skill:
1. Using a trampette, springboard, or beat boards, begin by teaching the vault without a run-up (illustrations A#1-3). With good support from the spotter, vault lightly onto the horse so that the body stops in a flank position (illustration #2). Do not let the hips sag downward. Push away from the horse into the landing position (illustration #3).
2. Without a run-up, vault directly over the horse (no pause on top of the horse).
3. Add a short run-up and repeat the same vaulting actions as were used in #2 above. Raise the hips and legs as high as possible, making sure that the side of the body passes over the horse (illustrations B#1-4). Push away from the horse strongly with the support arm (illustration B#3). *This vault will not need a fast run-up.*

Safety and Spotting:
Use mats or a crash pad for the landing

Spotting
1. A single spotter is used to aid the performer in this vault. Grip the performer with both hands on the upper arm as soon as the performer places his hands on the horse (illustrations A#1 and B#1).
2. Maintain the height of the performer's upper body and step with him to the landing on the post-flight of the vault (illustrations B#3-4).

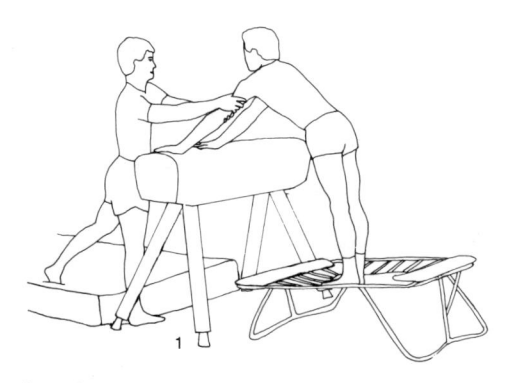

Lead-up Flank Vault onto the horse - dismount in Flank Position.

(illustration A)

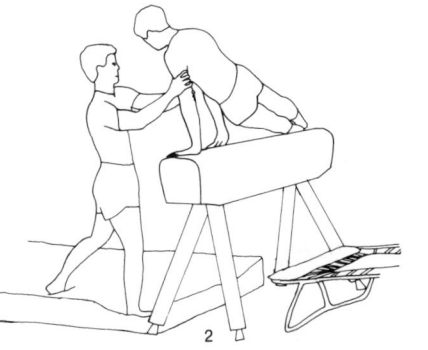

Common Errors:
Errors in Performance:
1. Inability to push away from the horse with the support arm. *Correction:* This problem is a combination of lack of arm strength and poor technique. The support arm must be slightly flexed at the midpoint of the vault so that it can be extended and drive the shoulders upward to their final position in the landing. Poor extension strength in the arms (triceps) will make this action difficult to perform (see page 16 for complementary exercises).
2. Insufficient height of the legs and hips at the midpoint of the vault. *Correction:* The hips must be driven both upward and to the side at the take off. This action should be well practiced without using a run-up. Aim to raise the hips and legs so that they are parallel to the long axis of the horse.

SKILL

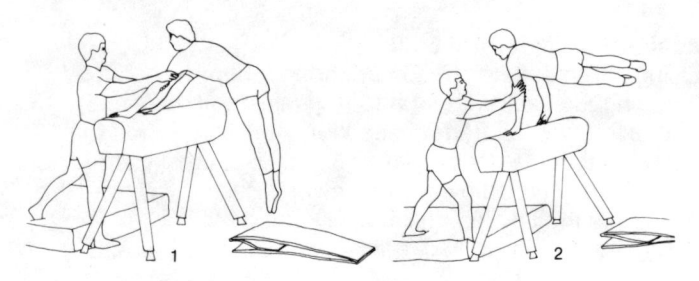

Flank Vault (Side Horse)

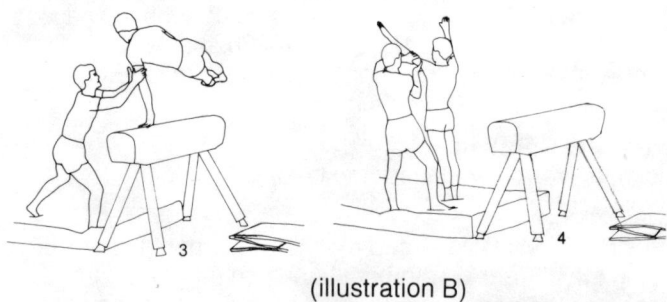

(illustration B)

Level II Skills

3. Rear Vault (Side Horse)

This skill leads to:
1. more advanced types of rear vault, for example, rear vaults with quarter and half turns inward toward the horse.
2. The rear vault action relates to the rear dismount on the pommel horse (pages 94-95).

Lead-up "Sit on—Slide off"

Lead-up skills:
1. Without a run-up, climb on the horse and assume a sitting position with the hands

TEACHING TECHNIQUES AND OBSERVATION POINTS

3. Too much speed in the run-up. *Correction:* This vault can be performed adequately with little or no run-up. Reduce the speed of the approach to a minimum. *Do not run quickly. This makes the vault seem more difficult.*
4. Piking the body at the hips at the midpoint of the vault. *Correction:* Beginners will commonly pike at the hips in an effort to bring their legs over the horse. With practice they should attempt to keep the legs and upper body in a straight line as they pass over the horse. The body rotates over the horse around the supporting arm.

Errors in Spotting:
1. Insufficient upward lift on the performer's support arm during the post-flight of the vault. *Correction:* The spotter must step with the performer on the post-flight of the vault and with a "squeeze grip" on the upper arm, lift upward, or at least maintain the height of the performer's shoulders. The push off the horse will be the most difficult part of the flank vault to perform. Beginners will find that they get caught with the support arm trailing behind. The spotter can help in the completion of this part of the vault with an upward lift on the performer's upper arm.

Teaching Points for the Skill:
1. Without a run-up and with the spotter assisting, attempt the complete rear vault action. Elevate the hips and legs sideways and work the hand change quickly.
2. Attempt the skill without the aid of a spotter (illustrations C#1-4). Again, no run-up is used.
3. Using a *short, slow run-up*, attempt the rear vault with a spotter assisting. Do not run quickly. When the technique is well established, perform the skill without a spotter.

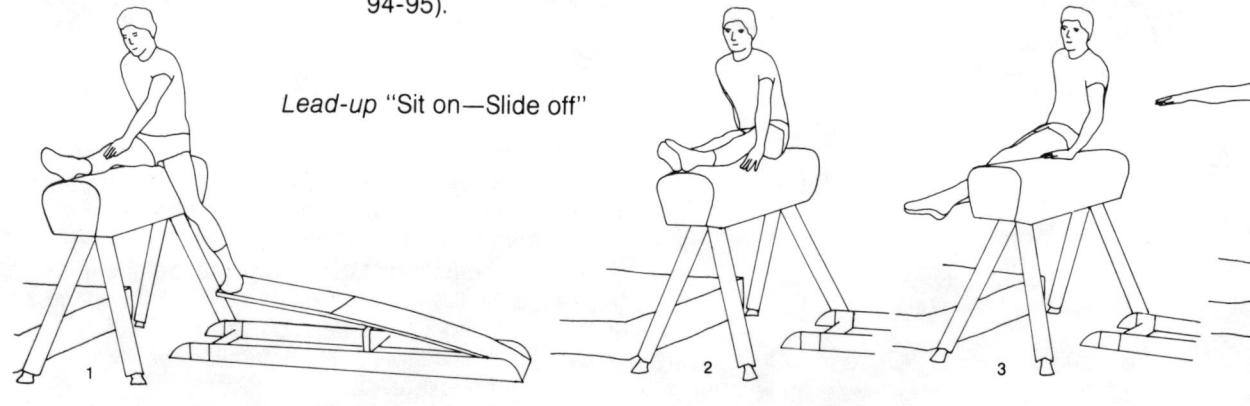

(illustration A)

Safety and Spotting:
1. Use a mat for landing.
2. Set the horse low (performer's waist height).

SKILL	TEACHING TECHNIQUES AND OBSERVATION POINTS

on the horse to the rear of the body (illustrations A#1-4). Slide off the horse to a standing position. The hand on the post-flight side of the horse will be removed and the hand on the pre-flight side will remain on the horse to provide support (illustrations A#3-4). Repeat this action until it becomes familiar. A spotter can provide assistance in the manner shown in illustrations B#1-5.

Spotting
1. The spotter supports the performer in a "squeeze grip" around the upper arm (illustrations B#2-5).
2. Step with the performer on the post-flight of the vault. Maintain the height and stability of his shoulders.

Common Errors:
Errors in Performance:
1. Confusion in the shift and change of the support arm. *Correction:* Return to the lead-up stage of climbing onto the horse in a sitting position and sliding off. This will allow the performer to concentrate on the arm action. Repeat until it becomes familiar.
2. Insufficient rotation of the body during the vault. *Correction:* The vaulter must rotate a full quarter turn from the start of the vault to the landing. This rotation must be well learned during the lead-up phases of the vault.
3. Too much speed in the run-up. *Correction:* For beginners, this vault is performed more easily when the approach run is slow and controlled. *Do not run quickly.*

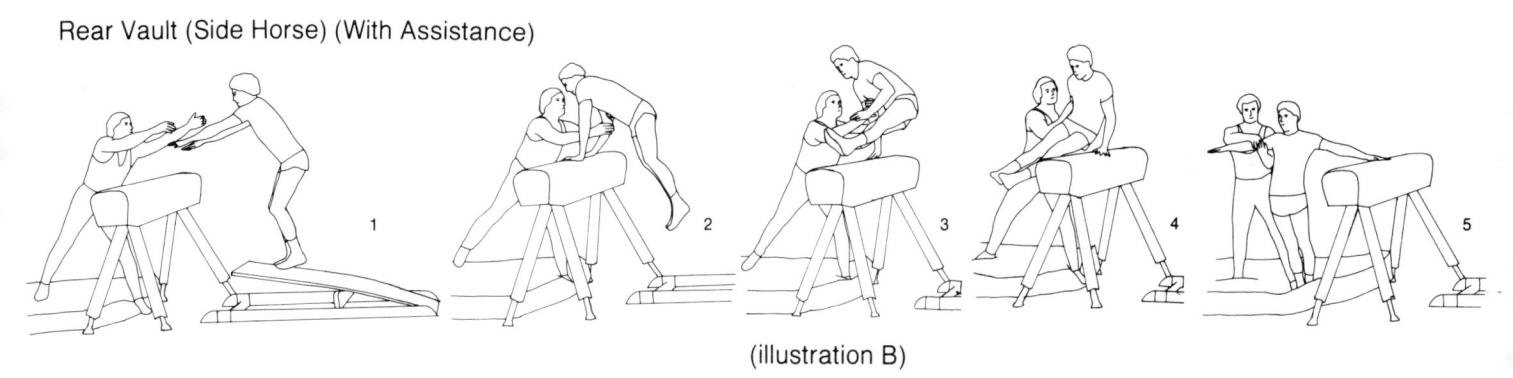

Rear Vault (Side Horse) (With Assistance)

(illustration B)

Errors in Spotting:
1. Anticipating the post-flight of the vault before the vaulter has completed his actions above the horse. *Correction:* Allow for the time taken by the vaulter to change support positions above the horse. When the final support arm is placed on the horse, step with the performer on the post-flight of the vault. *Do not drag the support arm off the horse.*

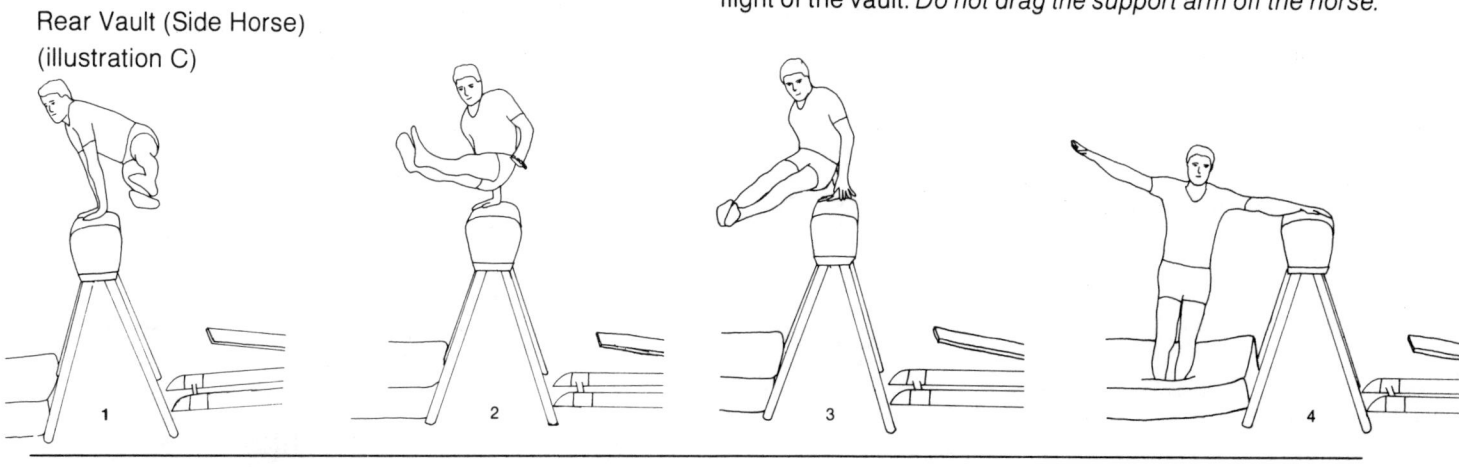

Rear Vault (Side Horse) (illustration C)

SKILL		TEACHING TECHNIQUES AND OBSERVATION POINTS

4. Squat Vault (Side Horse)

This skill leads to:
1. more advanced forms of squat vault on the side horse, that is, a squat vault performed with the hips well above the shoulders on the pre-flight of the vault.
2. stoop vault on the side horse (pages 136-138).
3. elementary and advanced forms of the squat vault on the long horse (pages 138-141).
4. squat mounts and dismounts on other apparatus, such as horizontal bar, parallel bars, uneven bars, and beam.

Lead-up Squat on Jump off

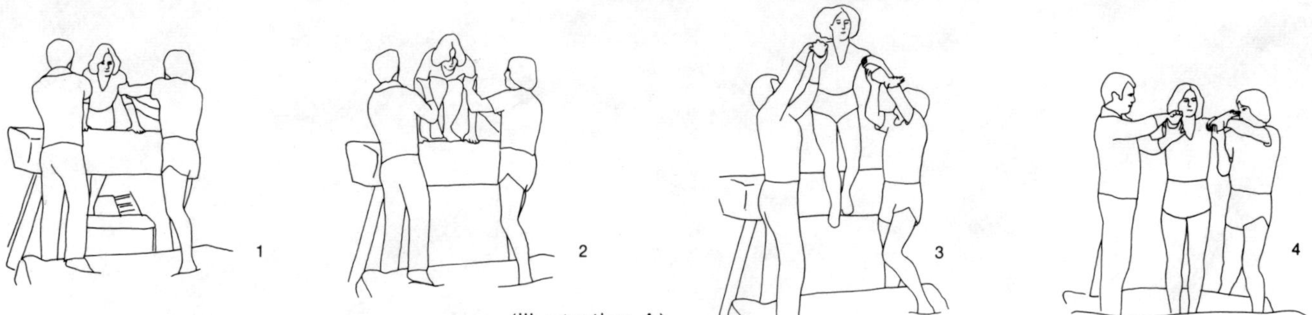

Teaching Points for the Skill:
1. With the horse set at waist height and with the assistance of two spotters, squat onto the horse and jump off. No run-up is used (illustrations A#1-2).
2. With a run-up of two or three paces, squat over the horse. Place the hands flat on the horse. Elevate the hips as much as possible during the pre-flight of the vault and push off as strongly as possible on the post-flight. Lift the head and elevate the shoulders (illustrations B#1-4). Use two spotters for assistance.

Safety and Spotting:
Use a mat for landing, a slow approach run, and two spotters for maximum spotting.

Spotting
1. Spotters grip the performer in a "squeeze grip" around the upper arm. This grip is obtained as early as possible, preferably while the performer is still on the pre-flight side of the horse.
2. Elevate the performer's shoulders and step with the performer on the pre-flight portion of the vault.

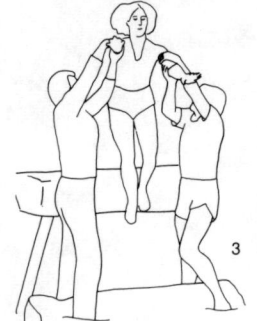

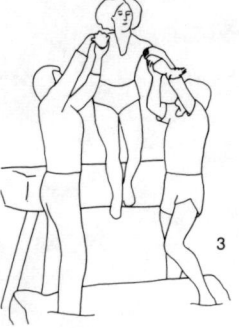

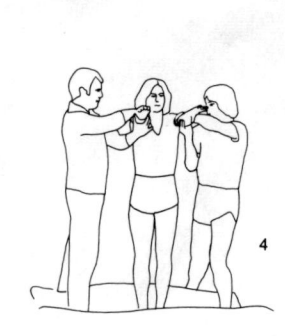

(illustration A)

Squat Vault

Lead-up skills:
1. squat jumps and momentary tucked handstands performed on the floor (page 33)
2. the lead-ups discussed in teaching points for the skill and illustrated in A#1-4.

Common Errors:
Errors in Performance:
1. Allowing the hips to remain well below the line of the shoulders during the vault. *Correction:* Practice the tucked handstand on the floor and learn to raise the hips at least to the level of the shoulders. Incorporate this action in the squat vault.
2. Dropping the head down and not pushing off the horse. *Correction:* A strong drive up from the horse will raise the shoulders in the post-flight of the vault.

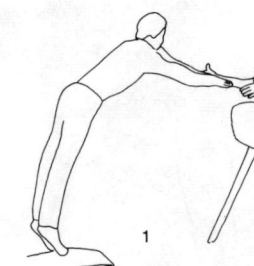

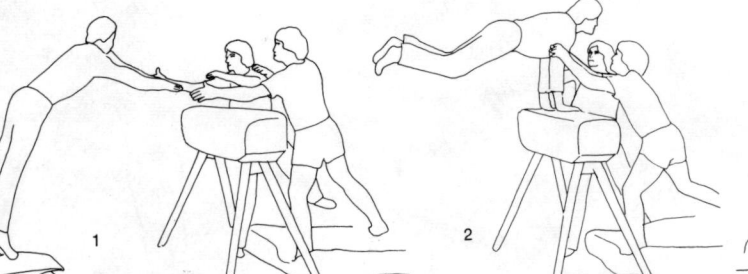

(illustration B)

SKILL	TEACHING TECHNIQUES AND OBSERVATION POINTS

Errors in Spotting:
1. Failing to obtain the "squeeze grip" early enough on the upper arm. *Correction:* Spotters must reach over the horse and obtain their grip on the performer's arms while he is still on the pre-flight side of the horse.
2. Standing at the ends of the horse instead of on the post-flight side of the apparatus. *Correction:* Spotters must stand as close together as possible on the post-flight side of the horse, allowing just sufficient room for the performer to pass between them.
3. Failing to step with the performer on the post-flight side of the vault. *Correction:* Spotters must grip the performer quickly on the upper arm and then move with him during the post-flight of the vault.
4. Failing to elevate the performer's shoulders on the post-flight of the vault. *Correction:* Spotters must grip the performer in a "squeeze" grip and then lift upward on the post-flight of the vault. This is well shown in the lead-up sequence, illustration A #3.

Level III Skills

5. Straddle Vault (Side Horse)

This skill leads to:
1. more advanced forms of straddle vault on the side horse (high elevation of the hips on the pre-flight side of the horse)
2. straddle vault on the long horse (elementary and advanced forms)
3. straddle vault as a mount and dismount on other apparatus such as horizontal and parallel bars.

Teaching Points for the Skill:
1. Without a run-up and with the assistance of a spotter, straddle onto a low horse. The hips must be raised to at least the level of the shoulders in the straddle action. The legs can be bent for this initial practice. Stand up, bring the legs together and jump off.
2. Repeat but attempt to straighten the legs in the straddle action. Bring the legs together and jump off.
3. Without a run-up and with the assistance of the spotter, straddle completely over the horse. There is no pause in the middle of the vault.
4. With the assistance of the spotter, use a short run-up of three to four paces and attempt the full vault. *Do not run quickly.*

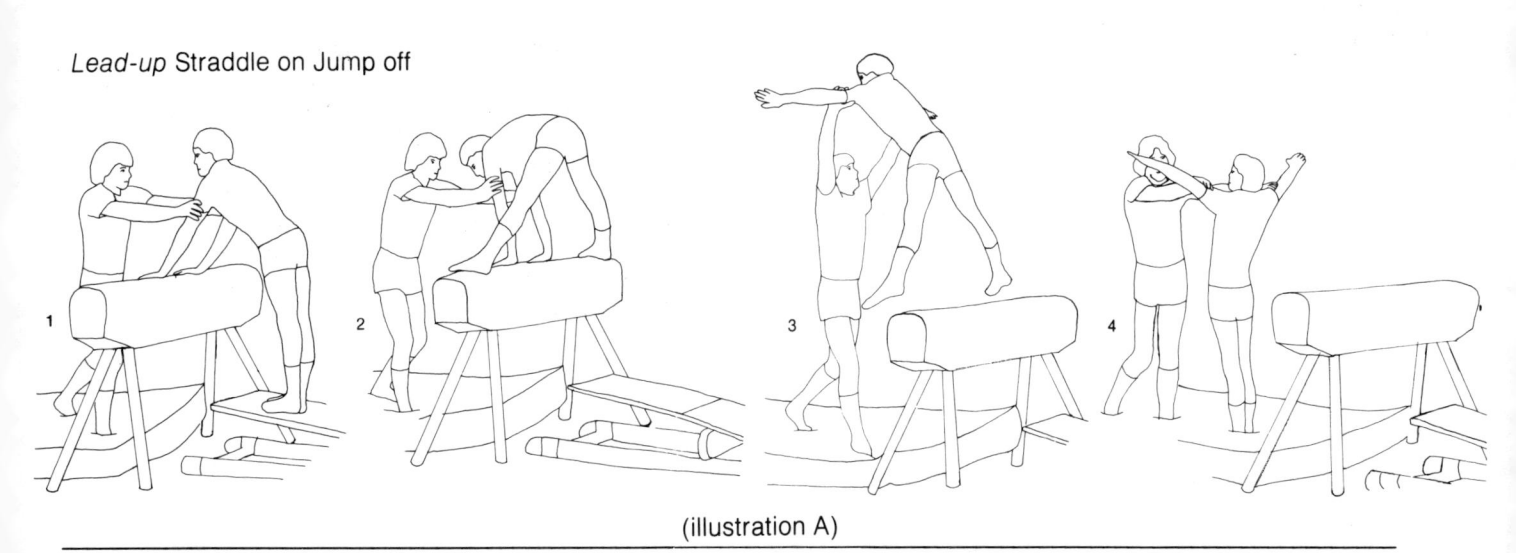

Lead-up Straddle on Jump off

(illustration A)

| SKILL | TEACHING TECHNIQUES AND OBSERVATION POINTS |

Lead-up skills:
1. straddle actions performed on the floor and flexibility exercises to improve the straddle (pages 19-20).
2. straddle mounts onto low apparatus, e.g. a bench, beam, and a low vaulting box
3. straddle on-jump off lead-up illustrated in A#1-4

Safety and Spotting:
Use a mat for landing and set the horse at just above the performer's waist height. Make sure that the spotter can step back easily on the landing mat.

Spotting
1. The spotter grips the performer on the upper arms (not on the wrist). As the performer passes over the horse and enters the post-flight of the vault the spotter steps backward with arms raised. This elevates the performer's shoulders. The speed with which this is performed depends on the speed with which the performer is attempting the vault. For good spotting, the vault should be performed slowly.

Common Errors:
Errors in Performance:
1. The performer has a poor straddle position above the horse. *Correction:* Practicing squat to straddle actions on the floor, and straddle on and jump off on the horse (illustration A#1-4). Increase straddle flexibility with complementary exercises (pages 19-20)
2. The performer's hips are not elevated sufficiently on the pre-flight side of the horse. *Correction:* Practice momentary tucked handstands on the floor and work more on a squat vault aiming to get good hip lift at take-off. The improvement in technique will transfer to the straddle vault.
3. Failure to bring the legs together during the post-flight of the vault. *Correction:* Practice bringing the legs together from a straddle position on the floor and from a straddle position standing on the horse. This error is relatively easy to correct with a little practice.

Straddle Vault (Side Horse)

(illustration B)

Errors in Spotting:
1. Gripping the performer around the wrists instead of the upper arms. *Correction:* Instruct the spotter in the correct grip. The spotter must understand that if the performer catches his feet on the horse, a grip around the wrists will not hold up the head and shoulders.
2. Failing to obtain an early grip around the performer's upper arms. *Correction:* The grip on the performer's upper arms must be obtained prior to, or the moment the performer sets his hands on the horse. This demands quick actions from the spotter and a slow approach from the vaulter. The performer must not use a fast run-up in the early stages of learning this vault.
3. Failing to step back quickly enough on the post-flight of the vault. *Correction:* Reduce the vaulter's approach speed (if necessary remove the run-up totally). Increase the tempo of the run-up only when the performer and spotter show that they have correctly learned their respective techniques.

SKILL

6. Straddle Vault (Long Horse)

This skill leads to:
1. advanced straddle vaults on the long horse (high hip position during the pre-flight)

Lead-up skills:
1. straddle vault on the buck (illustration A) straddle vault on the long horse, beginning in a squat position, initially from halfway then progressively working back along the horse (illustrations B#1-2).
3. all lead-ups and straddle actions on the side horse (illustrations A#1-4 and B#1-3, pages 133-134).
Note: Some students may find the straddle vault on the long horse easier to perform than on the side-horse because of the minimal straddle action necessary to complete the vault.

Lead-up Straddle Vault Over a Buck (illustration A)

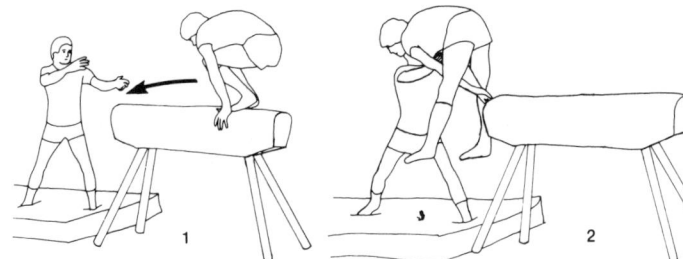

Squat on—Straddle off on the Long Horse (illustration B)

TEACHING TECHNIQUES AND OBSERVATION POINTS

Teaching Points for the Skill:
1. If a buck is available, practice the straddle vault using a short run-up of two to three paces.
2. For a straddle vault on the long horse, begin by climbing on the horse, assuming a squatting position halfway down the horse and straddling off (illustrations B#1-2). Progress to two-thirds back from the post-flight end of the horse. *To make this easier, raise the post-flight end of the horse.* (see squat vault on the long horse, pages 132-133).
3. Using two spotters and a fairly quick run-up, straddle over the full length of the horse. Elevate the hips as much as possible at take off and push off hard from the horse. This will lift the shoulders for the post-flight of the vault.

Safety and Spotting:
Use mats for landing and set the horse at approximately waist height for the performer.

Spotting
1. To spot the straddle vault over the buck, the spotter can either:
   a) assist in the same manner as for side horse vaulting (see page 134).
   b) assist from the side in the same manner as for a squat vault (illustrations C#1-5).
2. For a straddle vault on the long horse, spotting must be given from the side in the same manner used for the squat vault on the side horse. An upper arm "squeeze grip" is taken by each spotter. This should occur at the moment the performer places his hands on the end of the horse. Because of the greater speed of this vault, spotters must step quickly with the motion of the vault on the post-flight.
3. Illustration C#4 shows the performer raising his arms for the landing stance. Spotters will have to rotate their grip on the upper arm to allow for this action (illustration #4). In the learning stages for this vault, it is recommended that the performer leave his arms down or only raise them forward. This makes spotting easier.

Common Errors:
Errors in Performance:
1. Insufficient speed entering the vault. *Correction:* Before attempting the full vault work on the lead-ups shown in illustrations A and B#1-2. If the performer should slow at take off but still commit himself to the vault, the spotters must grip the performer on the upper arm and vigorously assist him in clearing the end of the horse. It is recommended that the instructor be one of the two spotters for initial attempts at this vault.
2. Insufficient push off from the end of the horse. *Correction:* The performer must drive upward from the end of the horse in order to elevate the shoulders for the landing. If there is any problem with this part of the technique, return to lead-ups and re-practice this part of the vault. Practice the push off the horse using a squat vault on the side horse.
3. The hips are extremely low during the vault. *Correction:* This is a common fault with beginners. Hip elevation must be practiced on the floor with momentary tucked handstands

SKILL	TEACHING TECHNIQUES AND OBSERVATION POINTS

Straddle Vault (Long Horse) (illustration C)

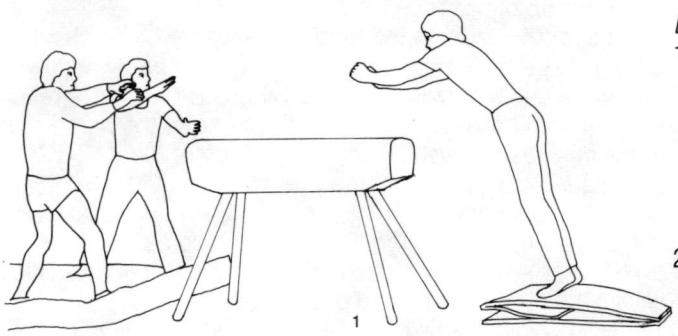

(pages 33-35) or with the squat and straddle vaults on the side horse (pages 132-133).

Errors in Spotting:
1. Insufficient speed throughout the whole spotting sequence. *Correction:* Spotters must first practice their spotting techniques on the side horse before attempting to spot on the long horse. On the side horse the grip on the performer can be obtained earlier and the performer will not be moving as fast as is necessary for long horse vaulting.
2. Not allowing sufficient distance for the post-flight part of the vault. *Correction:* Because the performer is moving fast, he will travel further during the post-flight part of the vault. Spotters must make allowance for this fact and step far enough along the mat to be either side of the performer during the landing.

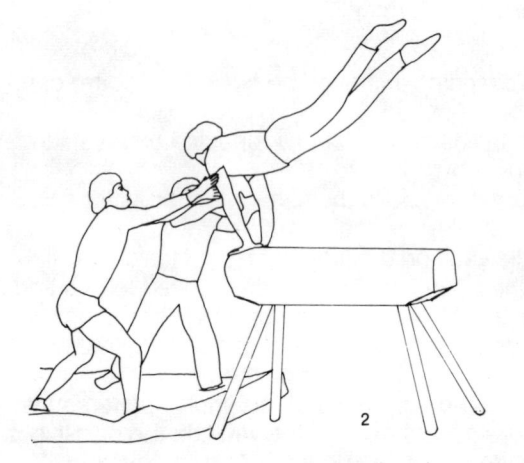

7. Stoop Vault (Side Horse)

This skill leads to:
1. stoop vault on the long horse performed on the far end of the horse (pages 140-141).
2. stoop vault mounts and dismounts on other apparatus, e.g. horizontal bar

Lead-up skills:
1. flexibility activities performed on the floor (illustrations pages 11-12).
2. squat vault performed on the side horse.
3. lead-up activities for the stoop vault (illustrations A#1-6).

Teaching Points for the Skill:
1. Using a trampette, springboard, or two beat boards placed one on top of the other, practice stooping onto the horse without a run-up (illustrations A#1-6). Set the horse at waist height. Begin this practice by squatting onto the horse, and with each attempt increasingly straighten the legs. Elevate the hips as high as possible. A spotter is essential for this practice. After stooping onto the horse, jump off (illustrations A#5-6).
2. Practice the full stoop vault without pausing on the top of the horse. Do not use a run-up. Take-off apparatus which gives more lift than a single beat board is essential for this practice. Two spotters should be used. The horse should remain at waist height.
3. In order to progress to the stoop vault using a run-up, it is recommended that a trampette, springboard or two beat boards (placed one on top of the other) be used. The performer approaches from a *slow two to three* pace run-up. The hips are driven up at take off. This is performed partly from leg drive and partly from strong flexion at the waist. A powerful push upward from the horse then elevates the upper body for the post-flight and landing. Spotters must assist strongly by raising the performer's shoulders during the post-flight.

| SKILL | TEACHING TECHNIQUES AND OBSERVATION POINTS |

Lead-up Stoop Vault (Side Horse)

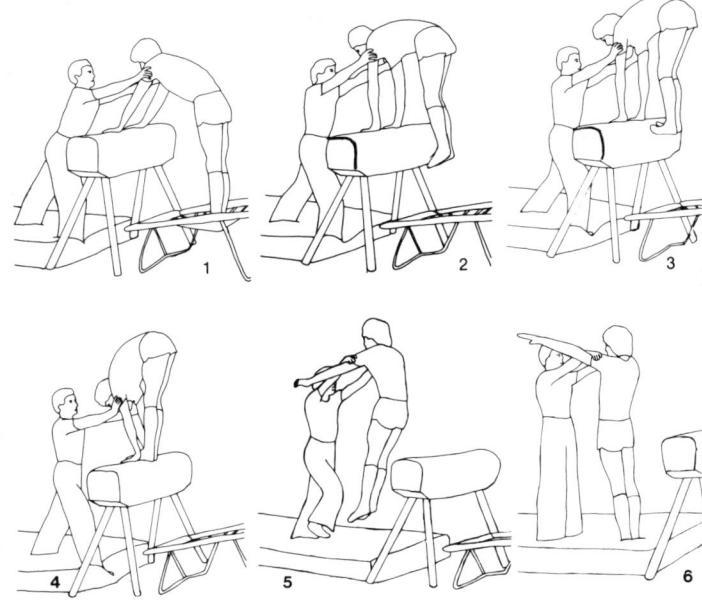

(illustration A)

4. Illustrations B#1-6 show the performer attempting the skill using a single beat board. This necessitates a good take off and correct technique above the horse. Notice the strong upward lift provided by spotters (illustration B#4).

Safety and Spotting
Spotting
1. Two types of spotting are shown in illustrations A#1-6 and B#1-6. The spotting technique used in illustrations B#1-6 can also be used for the lead-up in which the performer stoops onto the horse and then jumps off. The objective of the spotting in illustrations A#1-6 is to prevent the performer from pitching forward and falling off the horse. The spotter assumes an upper arm grip, steadies the performer in his "toe-touch" position on top of the horse and then steps backward to allow the performer to jump forward off the horse (illustrations A#4-6).
2. For those performers who find it particularly difficult to steady themselves on top of the horse, it is recommended that two spotters use the method shown in illustrations B#1-6. For a stoop vault using a run-up, spotters must concentrate on elevating the performer's shoulders on the post-flight side of the horse. This is an important action since it helps the performer to rotate the shoulders upward and the hips downward prior to the landing (illustrations B#3-4). Spotters then step with the performer through the post-flight of the vault and stabilize the landing position (illustrations B#4-6).

Common Errors:
Errors in Performance:
1. Insufficient elevation of the hips above the horse. *Correction:* This problem may be due to lack of flexibility (hip flexion) or poor technique. It is recommended that the performer improve hip flexion through flexibility exercises (pages 11-12) and return to the lead-up practices aiming for better hip elevation and hip flexion above the horse.
2. Not raising the shoulders in the post-flight. *Correction:* The stoop vault is a combination of vigorous hip flexion followed by hip extension (in other words a strong pike at the waist followed immediately by a vigorous straightening of the body). The performer must drive the hips upward on the pre-flight of the vault and follow that action by a strong push off the horse. This is coupled with elevation of the head and straightening of the back. Spotters can help the performer to become oriented to this action.

Errors in Spotting:
1. Insufficient lift on the performer's shoulders on the post-flight side of the horse. *Correction:* Spotting for the stoop vault is easy to perform. Spotters must remember that they lift upward on the performer's shoulders during the post-flight.

| SKILL | TEACHING TECHNIQUES AND OBSERVATION POINTS |

Stoop Vault (Side Horse)

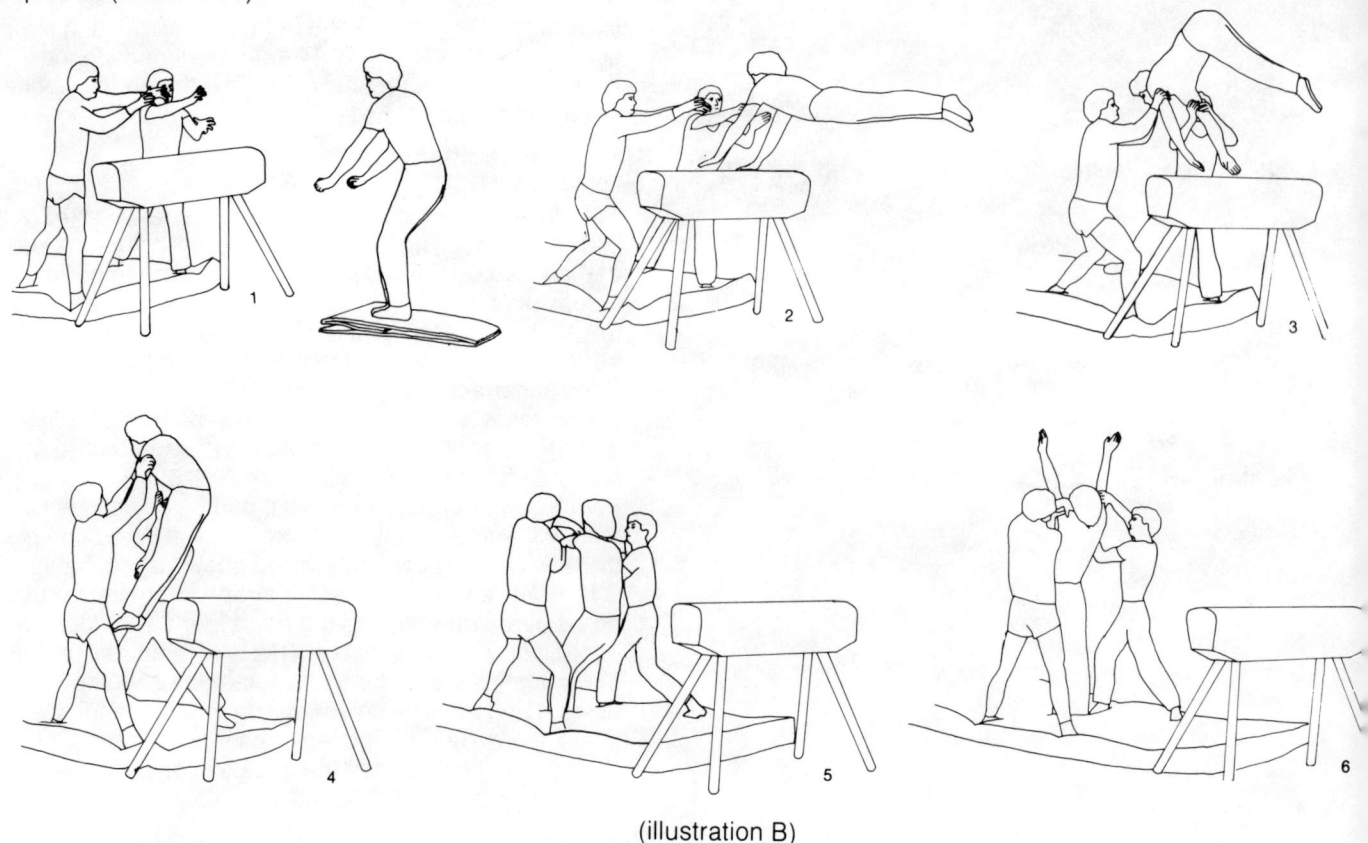

(illustration B)

Level IV Skills

8. Squat Vault (Long Horse)

This skill leads to:
1. squat vault on the long horse with the hands placed on the near (pre-flight) end of the horse
2. stoop vault on the long horse (pages 140-141)

Lead-up skills:
1. squat vault on the side horse (page 132)
2. squat vault on a tilted long horse (see illustrations, A#1-4 and B#1-5

Teaching Points for the Skill:
1. Begin by practicing the squat vault on the side horse. Work for good hip elevation.
2. Turn the horse lengthwise and lower the pre-flight end of the horse 6" lower than the post-flight end. With two spotters, squat off the far end of the horse. Begin in a crouch position at the midpoint of the horse. Work back toward the pre-flight end of the horse. By lowering the pre-flight or near end of the horse, the squat action is easier to learn. (For clarity a single spotter has been shown in illustrations A#1-4 and B#1-5)
3. With the end of the horse lowered, practice the full vault with two spotters assisting. Aim for hip elevation during the pre-flight and a strong push off from the horse.
4. Progressively raise the near end of the horse until it is level. Continue to work for good hip elevation and a strong push off the horse.

Safety and Spotting:
1. Work through the lead-ups illustrated in A#1-4 and B#1-5. This will develop confidence and prepare the performer for a squat vault with the horse horizontal.

SKILL

Lead-up Squat Vault from halfway along a horse set lengthwise. Pre-flight end of horse is lower than post flight.

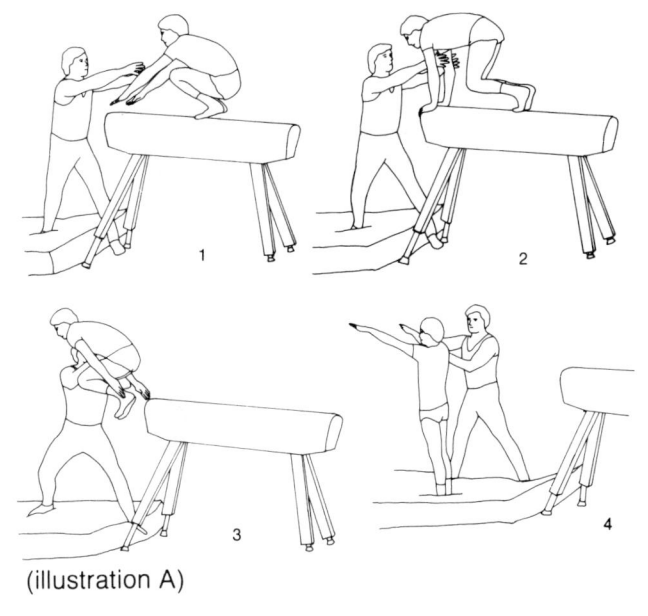

(illustration A)

Lead-up Squat Vault on a horse set lengthwise. Pre-flight end of horse is lower than post-flight.

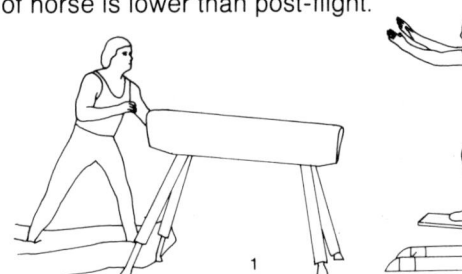

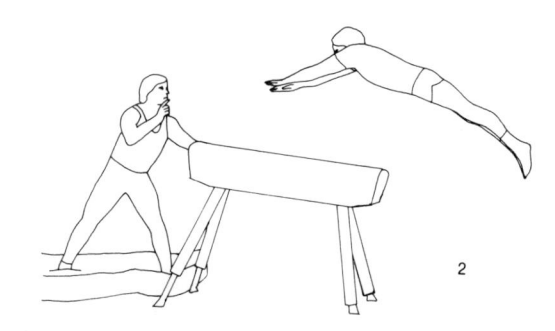

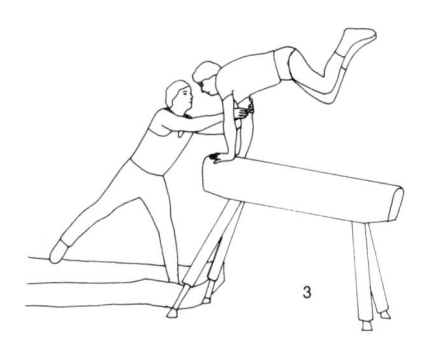

(illustration B)

TEACHING TECHNIQUES AND OBSERVATION POINTS

Spotting
1. Spotters use the familiar "squeeze grip" on the upper arm. Then elevate the performer's head and shoulders during the post-flight.
2. When the performer is attempting the squat vault with a run-up, spotters must be prepared to step with the performer through the post-flight. This is shown in illustrations C#1-5.
3. Because of the speed of the vault, spotters must be prepared to act quickly and accurately.

Common Errors:
Errors in Performance:
1. Insufficient hip elevation during the pre-flight. *Correction:* Return to the side horse and practice hip elevation during the pre-flight of the squat, straddle, and stoop vaults. Apply the same practice to the lead-ups of the squat vault on the long horse (illustrations A#1-4 and B#1-5).
2. Insufficient elevation of the head and shoulders in the post-flight of the vault. *Correction:* The performer must block the forward motion of the body over the horse with his arms and push strongly upward off the horse. This will elevate the head and shoulders. Spotters can also help by elevating the performer's head and shoulders.

Errors in Spotting:
1. Failing to move with the performer during the post-flight of the vault. *Correction:* A squat vault over the long horse demands a fairly fast run-up. Spotters must make allowance for the performer's speed of movement and shift equally as fast during the post-flight of the vault.

SKILL
Squat Vault (Long Horse)

TEACHING TECHNIQUES AND OBSERVATION POINTS

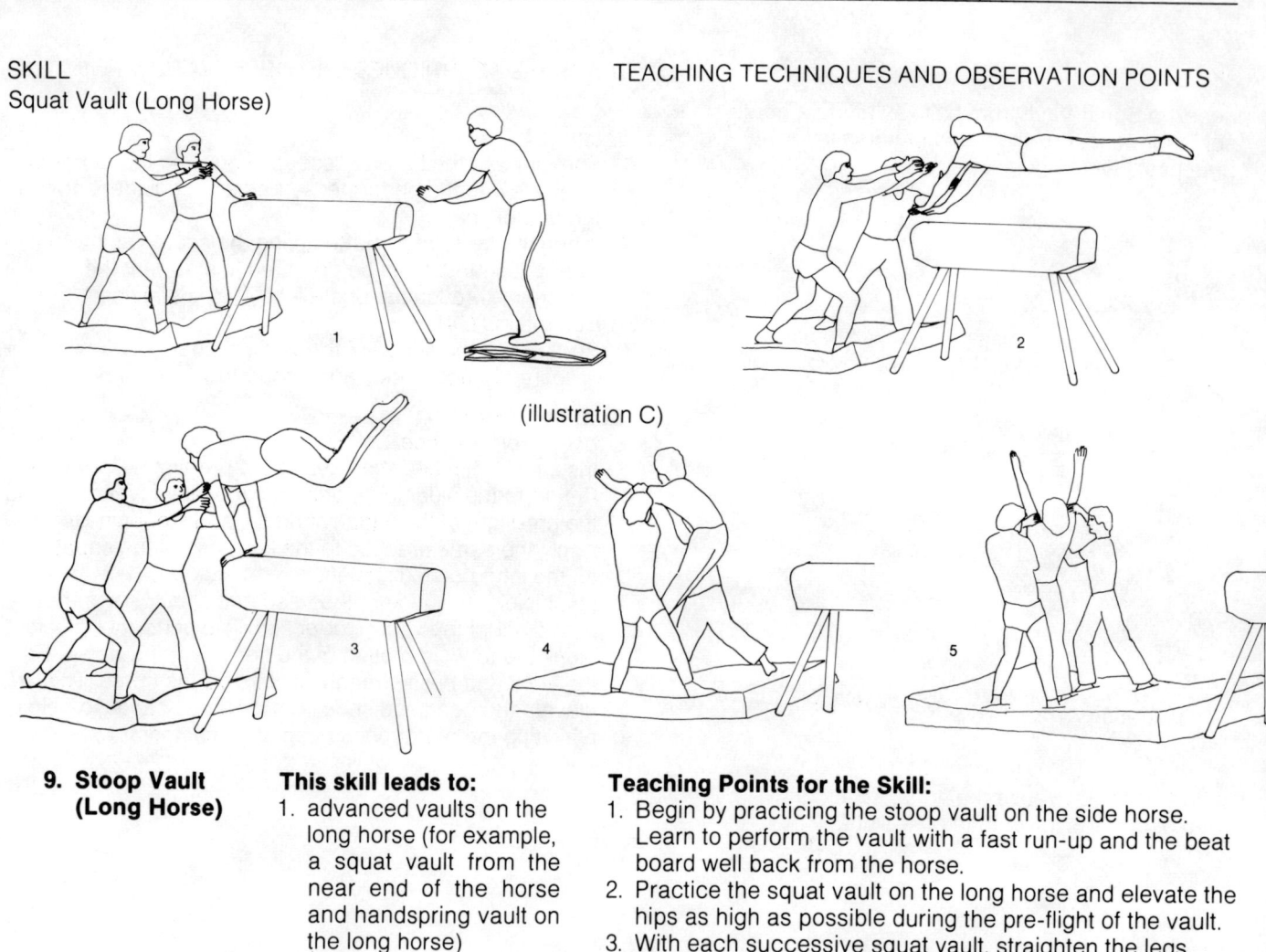

(illustration C)

9. Stoop Vault (Long Horse)

This skill leads to:
1. advanced vaults on the long horse (for example, a squat vault from the near end of the horse and handspring vault on the long horse)

Lead-up skills:
1. stoop vault on the side horse (pages 136-138)
2. squat vault on the long horse (pages 138-139)

Teaching Points for the Skill:
1. Begin by practicing the stoop vault on the side horse. Learn to perform the vault with a fast run-up and the beat board well back from the horse.
2. Practice the squat vault on the long horse and elevate the hips as high as possible during the pre-flight of the vault.
3. With each successive squat vault, straighten the legs during the pre-flight. Elevate the hips and pike vigorously. Push off from the horse with as much power as possible. Use two spotters during the early stages of learning the vault (see illustrations #1-5).

Stoop Vault (Long Horse)

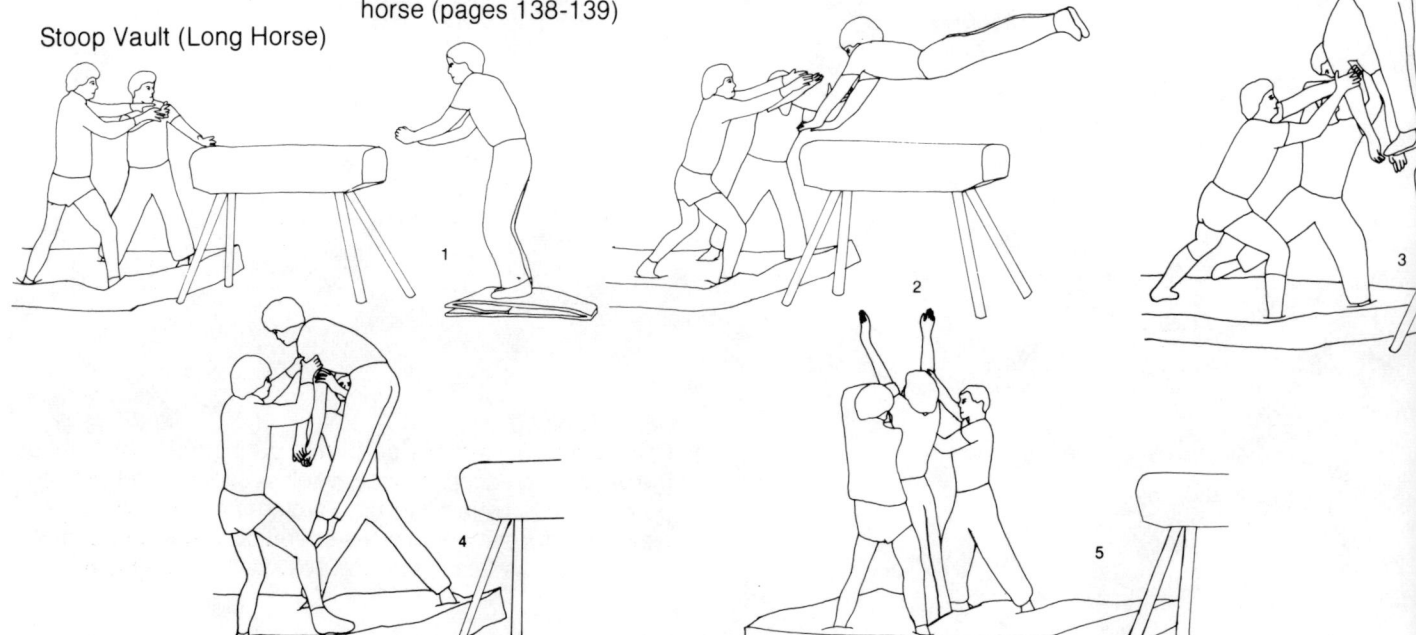

SKILL	TEACHING TECHNIQUES AND OBSERVATION POINTS

Safety and Spotting:
1. Spotting for the stoop vault is the same as for the squat vault. An upper arm grip is obtained as early as possible. The spotters then lift upward so that the performer's head and shoulders are elevated during the post-flight of the vault. The spotters cannot assist the performer in his effort to elevate the hips and bring the legs through (without bending at the knee). If the performer should catch his feet on the end of the horse, it is the spotter's duty to maintain the height of his head and shoulders. Spotters must be ready to act fast during this vault.

Common Errors:
Errors in Performance:
1. Insufficient elevation of the hips. *Correction:* This is a common error and means that the stoop action cannot be successfully performed. The performer should return to working on the stoop vault on the side horse, or buck, concentrating on hip elevation coupled with a vigorous pike at the waist. The take-off apparatus is then progressively shifted away from the horse until it is far enough back to accommodate the length of the long horse. The long horse is then substituted for the side horse.
2. Insufficient push off the horse. *Correction:* Elevation of the hips must be followed immediately by a vigorous and powerful drive off the horse. This lifts the head and shoulders upward. The performer must push off the horse and at the same time lift the head and shoulders and straighten the back. These actions must be powerful and vigorous. Spotters can help the performer become accustomed to this action by lifting strongly at the shoulders.

Errors in Spotting:
1. Insufficient lift at the performer's shoulders during the post-flight. *Correction:* Spotters should grip the performer around the upper arms as early as possible and then lift upward. This action is coupled with a fast shift along the mat. This allows for the distance traveled by the performer during the post-flight of the vault.

---

10. Headspring Vault (Side Horse)

This skill leads to:
1. neckspring vault (side horse)
2. short arm vault (side horse)
3. handspring vault (side horse)(pages 144-146)

Lead-up skills:
1. headspring performed on the floor (pages 65-66)
2. headspring performed on a low box (pages 59-62)
3. lead-ups described below and shown in illustrations A#1-4, B#1-5, and C#1-4.

Teaching Points for the Skill:
1. Begin with the post-flight of the vault (illustrations A#1-4). Two horses or boxes are placed together in the form of a "T" (illustration A#1). With the legs held straight, the performer "walks forward" using his feet only *until the hips are well past the line of the head and shoulders* (illustration A#1). He then extends into the post-flight of the vault in the same manner as when performing the headspring from a low box. Because of the additional height of the horse, there is less vigor and drive into the post-flight.
2. Using a springboard, trampette (sloped down toward the horse), or two beat boards place one on top of the other, the performer now adds the pre-flight portion of the vault *but without a run-up* (illustrations B#1-5). The body position above the horse is controlled by one (or two

SKILL	TEACHING TECHNIQUES AND OBSERVATION POINTS

spotters) who grasp the performer around the knees (illustration B#1). Using a count of "one-two-three" the performer jumps into the piked headstand on top of the box (illustrations B#2-3). The spotter holds the performer's knees and presses his hips forward into the correct position before allowing any extension to occur (illustration #3). With practice the whole action is made more fluid, with minimal pause on top of the horse.

3. Illustrations C#1-4 show the performer now entering the vault without a spotter controlling the pre-flight of the vault. In this stage a trampette sloping down toward the horse is used. There is no run-up. Spotters on the post-flight side of the horse control the extension, flight, and landing (illustrations C#2-4).
4. Illustration D shows the performer using two beat boards to provide additional lift into the vault. Spotters are progressively removed according to the ability of the performer.

Lead-up Headspring Vault (post-flight only)

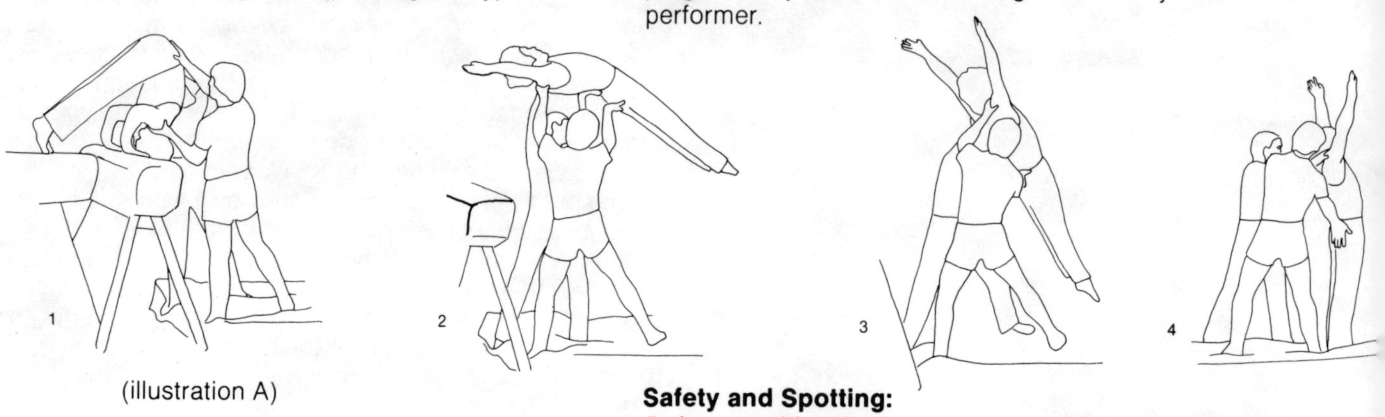

(illustration A)

Safety and Spotting:
*Before teaching the headspring as a vault, the correct actions **must** be firmly established with practice first on the floor and then from a low box. The biggest problem that exists in the headspring vault is the likelihood of the performer extending into the post-flight of the vault before the hips (or center of gravity) have passed well beyond the line of the head and hands. If the correct body positions are established on the floor the headspring is then performed safely as a vault.*

Lead-up Headspring Vault (controlled throughout by spotters)

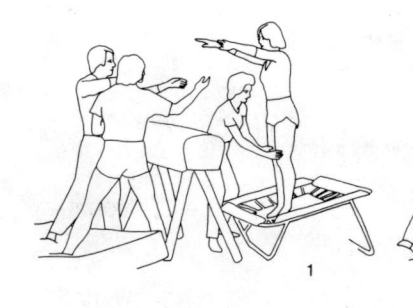

(illustration B)

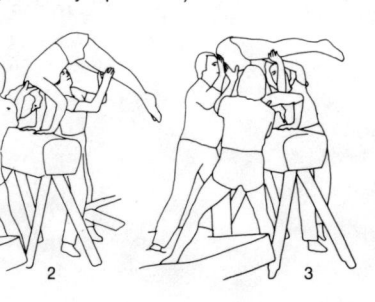

Spotting
Spotting for the headspring vault can vary.
1. Illustrations A#1-4 show the spotters on the post-flight of the vault cradling the performer to the landing. Support is

| SKILL | TEACHING TECHNIQUES AND OBSERVATION POINTS |

given under the shoulder and under the seat (not in the lower back). As the performer extends into the vault, the spotters step with him providing a cradling support through to the landing. The grip above the shoulder prevents the performer from moving forward. The same support is given on the post-flight side of the horse in illustrations B#1-5. One or two spotters on the pre-flight side of the horse control the position of the performer's hips which are pushed forward. The angle of the performer legs is at horizontal or below (illustration B#3).

2. Illustrations C#1-4 show a different method of support on the post-flight side of the horse. Spotters support under the shoulder, and instead of using a bent armed support under the seat (illustration A#2), they reach across the performer's seat to provide a strong cradling support. *The advantage of this method is that the spotters are able to grip the performer by the hips and pull him forward into the correct position for the post-flight of the vault. This is particularly helpful when there are no spotters controlling the pre-flight part of the vault.*

3. Illustration D# shows a single spotter preparing to support under the shoulder and with a bent arm under the seat. Spotters are first removed from the pre-flight side of the horse and then one at a time from the post-flight side. A single spotter must move directly under the performer's weight to provide balanced support.

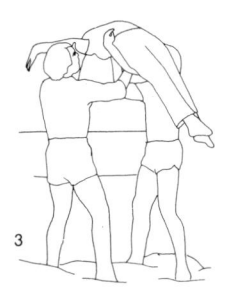

Lead-up Headspring Vault (no run-up)
(illustration C)

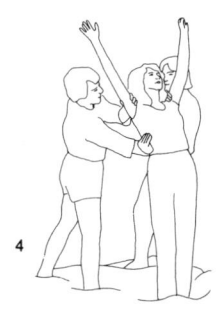

Headspring Vault (Side Horse)
(illustration D)

Common Errors:

Errors in Performance:

1. Insufficient lift of the hips on the pre-flight side of the horse (i.e. failure to reach the piked headstand position above the horse). *Correction:* a) Lower the box or horse. b) Use spotting assistance on the pre-flight side of the horse to reach the correct position.
2. Extending into the post-flight of the vault before the hips have passed over the head and hands. *Correction:* This error indicates that the lead-ups have not been well taught. The headsprings on the floor and from a low box should be re-practiced to establish the correct pattern.
3. Failing to maintain an extended position in the landing. *Correction:* Frequently the performer will land on the mat and then allow the head and shoulders to rotate forward. This causes movement to continue along the mat. Students must be taught to push away from the horse with an extension of the arms, and then leave the arms extended, with the head back.

| SKILL | TEACHING TECHNIQUES AND OBSERVATION POINTS |

Errors in Spotting:
1. Resisting the forward motion of the performer's hips above the horse. *Correction:* Spotters on the post-flight side of the horse, in their eagerness to provide support, will often lean into the performer and stop him from obtaining the correct hip positions. Spotters must allow the performer's hips to "slide" forward into the piked headstand. Thereafter they provide a strong "cradling" support through to the landing

11. Handspring Vault (Side Horse)

This skill leads to:
1. more advanced rotational vaults on the side and long horse—for example, cartwheel vault.
2. handspring dismount on other apparatus, notably the horizontal bar and the parallel bars.

Lead-up skills:
1. handspring on the floor (pages 66-70)
2. handspring over a one-section box
3. lead-ups shown in illustrations A#1-5, B#1-5, and C#1-4.

Teaching Points for the Skill:
1. Begin by teaching the post-flight of the vault only (illustrations A#1-5). Two horses or boxes are placed together in the form of a "T." The performer places his hands on the side horse and kicks through a handstand. Spotters cradle the performer through to the landing. The performer *must* hold a straight body position through the post-flight. This makes spotting much easier.
2. Illustrations B#1-5 show the addition of pre-flight. Using a trampette sloping down to the box and with one preliminary bounce, the performer is elevated into a handstand position on the box by one (or two) spotters. (A single spotter is shown for clarity.) Spotters on the post-flight side of the box then cradle the performer through to the landing.
3. The performer now enters the skill with a short run-up (illustrations C#1-4). In this sequence a trampette is used. (Two beat boards placed one on top of the other can be used also.) If a springboard is used, care must be taken to ensure that the spotter on the pre-flight side of the horse can carry out his spotting duties and is not hindered by the leg extensions of the springboard. The performer drives up into the handstand position. The spotter reaches around the waist (or upper thighs) and pushes the performer up into the handstand (illustration C#2). The performer maintains this handstand position in order to be cradled through to the landing by spotters on the post-flight side of the horse (illustrations C#3-4).

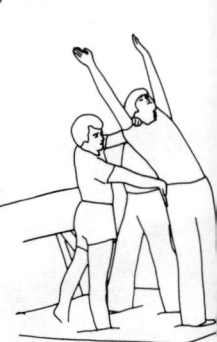

Lead-up Handspring Vault (post-flight only)

1   2   3   4

(illustration A)

Safety and Spotting:
The handspring action must be well established on the floor, and then over one or two sections of a box, before it is attempted on higher apparatus.

SKILL	TEACHING TECHNIQUES AND OBSERVATION POINTS

Spotting
1. Spotting on the post-flight side of the horse is similar in each stage of the teaching progressions. One hand is placed under the shoulder and the other supports under the seat (not in the lower back). This provides a strong cradling support.
2. The grip above the shoulder controls the landing and resists any further forward motion of the performer (see illustration A#5).
3. The single spotter on the pre-flight side of the box makes sure that he does not obscure the horse from the performer. His upward lift on the performer's thighs helps to elevate him into the handstand position. A trampette is an excellent device for teaching the preliminary stages of the handspring vault (illustrations B#1-5 and C#1-4). Illustrations C#1-4 show the trampette being used with a run-up of no more than four paces. A long and fast run-up using this apparatus is not necessary. Two beat boards placed one on top of the other can be substituted for the trampette and following that, a single beat board. Correct use of the beat board must be established prior to using it for the handspring vault. (See the discussion on the use of the beat board, pages 122, 125-127).

Lead-up Handspring Vault (controlled throughout by spotters)

(illustration B)

Common Errors:
Errors in Performance:
1. Ducking the head and piking (or bending) at the waist on the post-flight section of the vault. *Correction:* The performer must maintain an extended body in the handstand with the vision just ahead of the hands (or between the hands). The head must not be tucked under. Do not attempt a handspring vault until these body positions are correctly performed on the floor and from one or two sections of a box.

SKILL	TEACHING TECHNIQUES AND OBSERVATION POINTS

2. Failing to elevate the hips on the pre-flight side of the vault. *Correction:* Practice good elevation of the hips in non-rotational vaults such as the squat and stoop vault on the side horse. Practice momentary tucked handstands on the floor. Slant the trampette down toward two sections of a box. Place the hands on the box and bounce back and forth using the lift from the trampette to elevate the hips above the shoulders. Use spotters on the post-flight side of the box in the same manner as for the handspring vault.
3. Piking (or bending) at the hips excessively on the pre-flight. *Correction:* Beginners will find that piking at the hips makes it easier to raise the body above the hand positions on the horse. However, this action also increases the speed of forward rotation through the vault. This is undesirable since the performer is, in effect, turning the vault into a front salto (front somersault). The performer must try to achieve an extended (straight) body position prior to placing the hands on the horse.

Lead-up Handspring Vault (Side Horse)

(illustration C)

Errors in Spotting:
1. Insufficient lift on the pre-flight side of the horse. *Correction:* Use one (or two) spotters on the pre-flight side of the horse and make sure that they are tall enough to be able to drive the performer's hips into the handstand position.

E. Parallel Bars

General Safety

1. Parallel bars vary in design, both in the way they adjust and in the manner in which they are moved as a unit. Some have castors, others use differing types of transporters. In all cases this apparatus is usually heavy and great care should be taken when shifting it from storage into the gymnasium. Feet must be kept well clear when the bars are being lowered and set in place on the floor.
2. Some parallel bars also adjust into uneven bars, and these are adequate for elementary work on the uneven bars. However, they have two disadvantages: first, the bars become unstable for uneven bar skills where the performer is pulling out and away from the bar, particularly in gliding and casting actions; and second, the lower bar usually bends out of shape when dual purpose parallel bars are used constantly for uneven bar work. This causes

SKILL	TEACHING TECHNIQUES AND OBSERVATION POINTS

Lead-up to All Skills Performed in Cross-Support
Quarter-turn Dismount Between the Bars

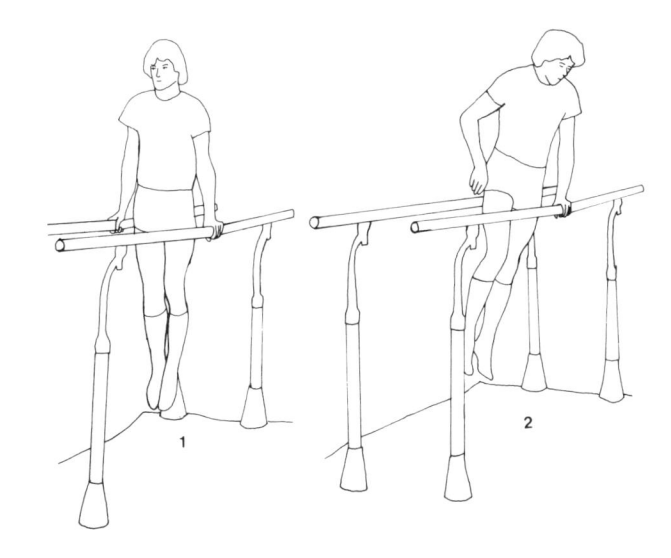

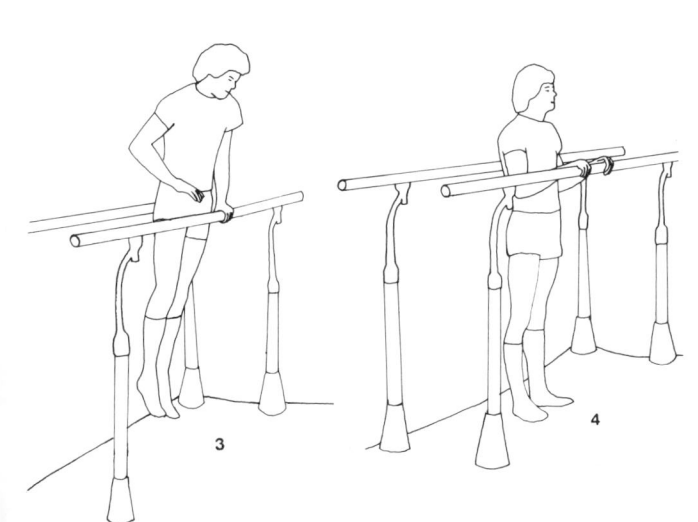

problems if the bars are then used for parallel bar competitions. For this reason many instructors prefer to have separate sets of parallel and uneven bars.

3. Parallel bars should never have a glossy, smooth finish. If this occurs, they should be sanded so that the gloss is removed. Chalk should always be used but never allowed to build up in lumps on the bars. Hand grips are a preferred item although not absolutely necessary for elementary work.

4. All locking devices for controlling the height of the bars should be periodically checked to ensure that they open and close easily and stay locked when required. Bars should not pop out of the supports when skills are performed at one end.

5. Mats should cover the base of the bars and an area well out from the sides of the supports. No gaps or high edges should exist. Mats fitted to the design of the base of the bars are best for this purpose. Some gymnasiums also use inclined glide boards at either end of the bars in place of matting. The object of these boards is to prevent toes from hitting the metal base of the bars during skills where the feet sweep or glide forward and backward between the supports.

6. Parallel bars should always be set as low as will accommodate both the performer and the skill. The width of the bars must also be adjusted to individual requirements. As a general rule the performer should be as close to the floor as possible without hindering the requirements of the skill.

7. When the bars are set between chest and shoulder height, a simple, quarter turn dismount must be one of the first skills taught to beginners. This safety measure prevents the bars from hitting the performer under the arms when dismounting from cross support (see illustrations #1-4, opposite).

8. Sponge wrapped around the bars, or in some cases the use of small mats, adds cushioning and comfort to skills, which, in their learning stages, cause abrasions. Volleyball knee pads can be used as a protection for the upper arm during practice of underarm skills.

9. So much of parallel bar work, like that on the rings, is based on swinging actions occurring above the bar, in underarm support, and in hang position below the bar. This places unaccustomed demands on the grip and upper body strength of the performer. Most beginners find this kind of activity difficult and soon become exhausted. With this in mind, the instructor must make sure that the performers work for small periods of time, repeating either single skills or small routines which include momentary rest pauses. This not only improves learning but is an important safety feature.

10. The parallel bars should be positioned in such a way that dismounts in any direction do not project the performer into other students or into other apparatus. At the same time, activity on other apparatus should not throw the performer into the end of one of the bars. Consequently, careful layout of the apparatus must occur before

TEACHING TECHNIQUES AND OBSERVATION POINTS

beginning instruction.
11. Control must also be exercised in storing the parallel bars at the end of the lesson. Time restrictions, tiredness, or a relaxation in discipline can cause an uncontrolled situation to develop which can be potentially hazardous.

Examples of Basic Positions on the Parallel Bars

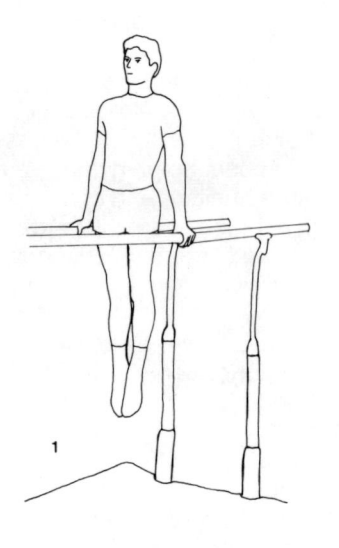

1. Cross Support
2. Bent-Arm Support 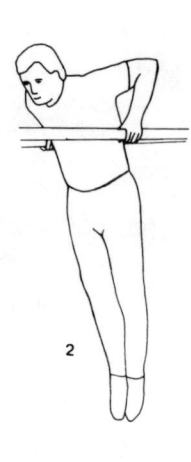
3. Under Arm Support 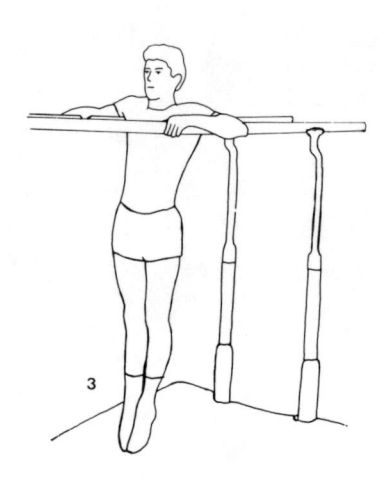
4. Piked Inverted Hang 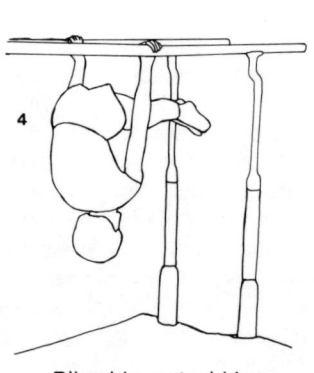
5. Piked Inverted Support 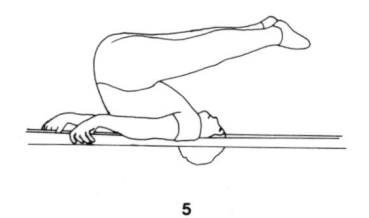
6. Piked Hang Position

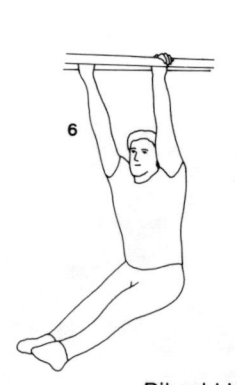

| SKILL | TEACHING TECHNIQUES AND OBSERVATION POINTS |

Level I Skills

1. Cross Support-Hop travel

This skill leads to:
1. general upper body strength necessary for further parallel bar work.

Lead-up skills:
1. from standing-push up from a bent arm position to cross support on:
   a) low bars,
   b) bars set at a height so that the performer must lift on tip-toes to enter bent-arm support
This develops arm and shoulder strength.

Cross-Support Hop Travel

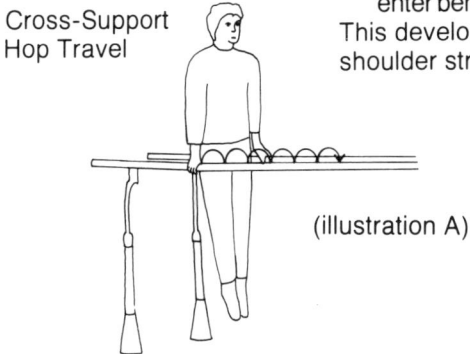

(illustration A)

Teaching Points for the Skill:
1. Set the bars low so that the performer's feet in cross support just clear the mats.
2. Jump or press to cross support.
3. Drive down with the shoulders and quickly shift the grip forward six to ten centimeters (illustration A). Do not bend the arms. Travel for half the length of the bars. Turn between the bars to dismount.
4. Repeat adding a slight swing. Perform the hop-shift on each of the *forward* swings.

Safety and Spotting:
1. Set the bars at chest height for each performer.
2. Place a mat between the bars. Use chalk to improve the grip.

Spotting
No spotting is necessary

Common Errors:
Errors in Performance:
1. Collapsing between the bars or being unable to shift forward. *Correction:* This is due to lack of strength. Increase triceps and shoulder strength (see pages 14-18). Repeat the lead-ups listed above.

2. Cross Support Swings

This skill leads to:
1. All further parallel bar skills, particularly those performed above the bars. Swinging is a fundamental skill on the parallel bars.

Lead-up skills:
1. Sufficient strength to maintain a cross support position and swing with low amplitude.
2. Cross support-hop travel half the length of the parallel bars (illustration #1-3 page 149)

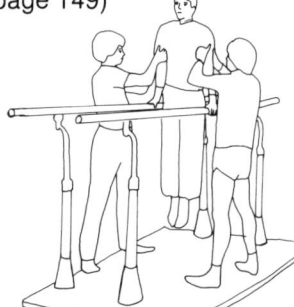

Cross Support
(illustration A)

Teaching Points for the Skill:
1. Begin in a cross support position (illustration A)
2. Begin the swings by piking slightly at the waist and then extending the hips forward.
3. Maintain an extended body on the back swing.
4. Work the swings from the shoulders and not from the hips.
5. Increase the amplitude of the swings over a period of time (several practice sessions). Illustrations B#1-2 show the swings performed with high amplitude. Do not copy this action until thoroughly familiar with swings at a low amplitude. Progress slowly.

Safety and Spotting:
1. Set the bars low. The performer's feet should just clear the mat between the bars.
2. Adjust the width of the bars so that they approximate the performer's shoulder width.
3. Use chalk to improve the grip.

Spotting
1. Spotters can assist with a squeeze grip on the upper arm.
2. They should not hinder the swinging action but provide a safety measure if the performer should lurch forward or backward.

Common Errors:
Errors in Performance:
1. Swinging too much from the waist. *Correction:* A slight pike action will help to initiate the swings. From then

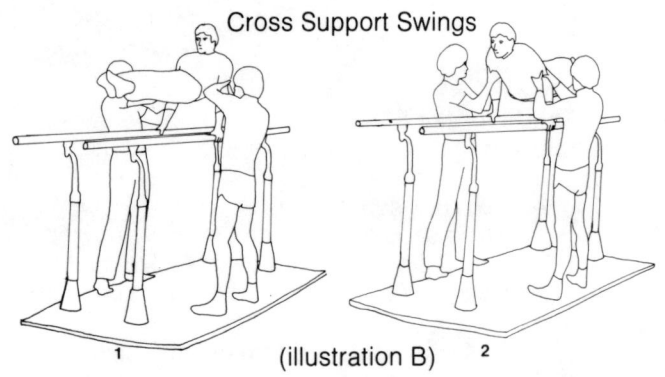

| SKILL | TEACHING TECHNIQUES AND OBSERVATION POINTS |

Cross Support Swings

(illustration B)

onward the swings are worked solely from the shoulders.

Errors in Spotting:
1. Overspotting. *Correction:* Do not spot the performer so much that it hinders the action of the swings. Maintain a fairly loose grip and provide strong assistance only if the performer falls forward or backward.

3. Dismount From a Forward Swing (often called a Rear Vault Dismount)

This skill leads to:
1. dismount from a forward swing with quarter and half turns in toward the bars.

Lead-up skills:
1. cross support swings (page 149).
2. the lead-ups discussed in Teaching Points for the Skill

Teaching Points for the Skill:
1. Begin in cross support position and without swinging, hook the legs forward over the outside of the bar on the dismount side. Sit on the bar and slide off to standing. Practice the hand change for the dismount (see illustrations #4 and #5).
2. Add in the cross support swings. Swing forward, then backward and on the next forward swing, swing the legs outward and push to the side for the dismount.

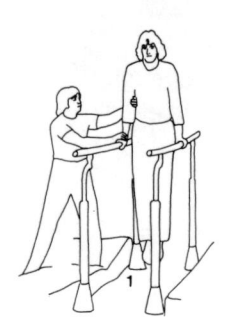

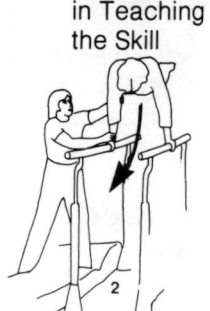

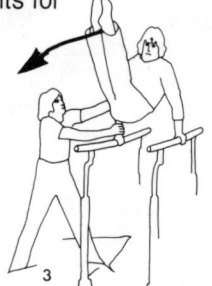

Dismount From a Forward Swing
(Rear Vault Dismount)

Safety and Spotting:
1. Set the bars as low as possible. The performer's feet should just clear the mat between the bars. Use chalk to improve the grip.
2. Place a mat on the dismount side of the bars.
3. The dismount can be performed easily with low amplitude swings. There is no need to swing high.

Spotting:
1. A single spotter grips the performer around the wrist and the upper arm. His duty is to help the performer clear the bar for the dismount (illustrations #3-5).

Common Errors:
Errors in Performance:
1. Insufficient drive sideways during the bar clearance. *Correction:* The performer must push sideways strongly with both arms to effect the bar clearance. The forward swing must be both upward and outward to assist this action.

SKILL

TEACHING TECHNIQUES AND OBSERVATION POINTS

Errors in Spotting:
1. Insufficient shift sideways with the motion of the performer. *Correction:* The spotter must support strongly at the performer's shoulder and step quickly sideways to guarantee that the performer's seat clears the bar. The timing of spotting assistance must be accurate. Do not pull the performer prematurely away from the bar.

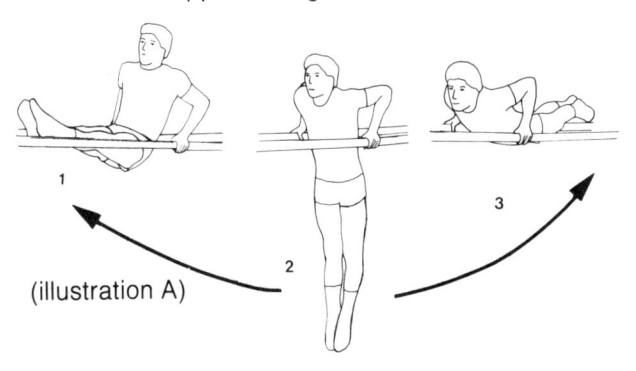

4. Underarm Support Swings

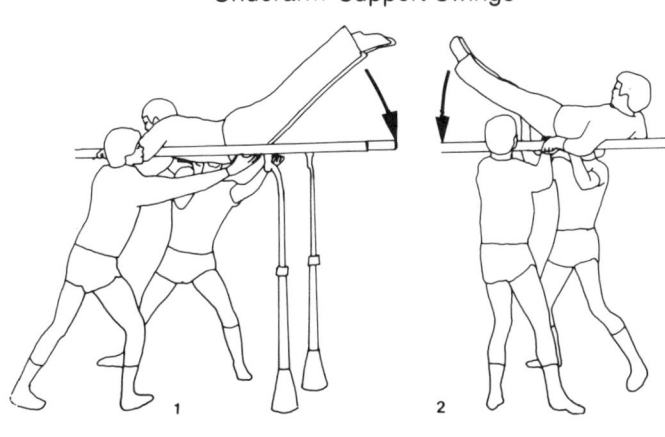

This skill leads to:
1. parallel bar skills, initiated from or passing through underarm support, for example, underarm kip (pages 159-161), shoulder balance-forward roll (pages 157-158)

Lead-up skills:
1. cross support swings (pages 149-150)
2. bent arm support swings (illustration A#1-3).

Teaching Points for the Skill:
1. Practice bent-arm support swings (illustration A#1-3) then shift to underarm support (illustration B).
2. Commence swinging by piking slightly at the waist and thrusting the hips forward at the end of the front swing.
3. Extend the body and continue the swings by working from the shoulders and not from the waist. Aim initially for low amplitude swings.
4. With practice increase the amplitude and elevate the hips as much as possible at either end of the swing. Try to maintain a fairly straight body throughout. Press down with with the elbows to maintain the support position.
5. Perform 3-4 swings, rest and repeat.

lead-up
Bent Arm Support Swings

(illustration A)

Underarm Support

(illustration B)

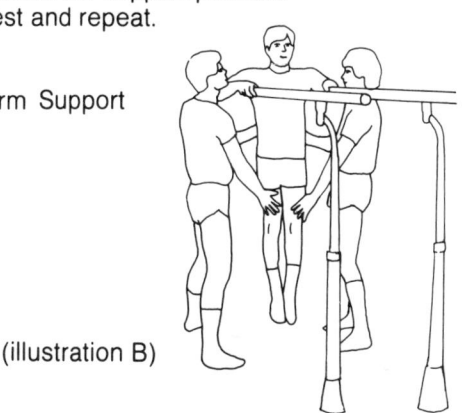

Safety and Spotting:
1. Set the bars as low as possible. Use chalk to improve the grip.
2. Adjust width of bars for each individual.
3. Use volleyball knee pads or wear a thick sweater for additional comfort on the upper arms.

Spotting
1. Spotters elevate under the seat and thigh on the front swing and under the chest and hips on the back swing (illustration C#1-2).

Common Errors:
Errors in Performance:
1. Too much pike at the waist on the front swing and too much flexion at the knees on the backswing. *Correction:* With the exception of the small pike at the waist to initiate the swings, keep the swings going by working from the shoulders. Spotters can assist in maintaining the correct body position. Aim initially for low amplitude and increase this amplitude of the swings with each attempt.
2. Insufficient strength in the shoulders. The body tends to drop down between the bars. *Correction:* Press down on the bars with the arms during the swings. Increase shoulder strength with complementary exercises (pages 14-18).

Underarm Support Swings

(illustration C)

SKILL

5. Glide Swing and Return

This skill leads to:
1. glide swing to piked inverted hang (pages 153-154)
2. glide kip (pages 163-165)
3. further advanced skills that incorporate a glide action below the bars

Lead-up skills:
1. run out to full extension and run back (performed on the horizontal bar, page 182)
2. walk out to full extension and walk back, performed on the parallel bars
3. run out to full extension and run back, performed on the parallel bars (illustrations A#1-9)
4. abdominal strengthening exercises (pages 14-18)

Lead-up
Run Out to an Extended Position-Run Back

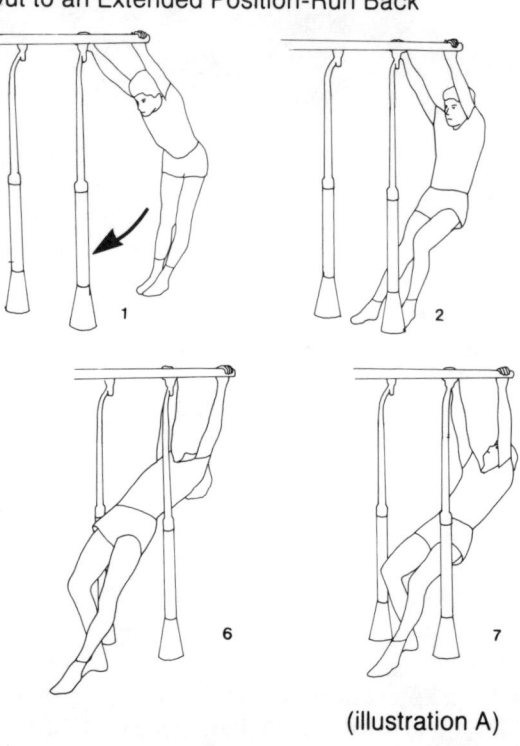

(illustration A)

TEACHING TECHNIQUES AND OBSERVATION POINTS

Teaching Points for the Skill:
1. Practice the lead-ups listed in Lead-up Skills.
2. For the glide swing and return, begin with the upper body and arms extended and with the seat pushed back (see illustration A#1 for this position)
3. Jump upward, simultaneously piking forward at the waist (illustrations B#1-2).
4. Swing forward, keep the legs straight and hold the feet just above floor level (illustration B#2).
5. Extend the body and reach forward with the feet as far as possible (illustration B#3).
6. Pike at the waist and return to the starting position (illustrations B#4-5).

Safety and Spotting:
1. Set the bars at head height. This should allow the glide action to be completed without too much pike at the waist.
2. As the performer improves, lower the bars. This will make the performer pike more at the waist and challenge him to hold the feet off the ground throughout the skill.
3. A thin mat covering the supports of the bars is necessary.

Spotting
No spotting is needed.

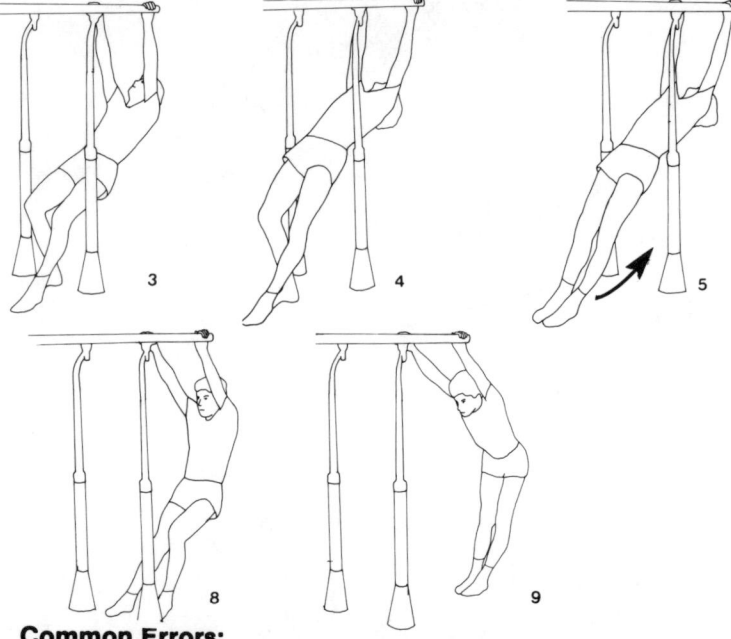

Common Errors:
Errors in Performance:
1. Insufficient elevation of the hips back and upward at the start of the glide. *Correction:* The performer must bend the legs and jump strongly up and backward before piking at the waist. This gives some impetus to the whole action.
2. Inability to pike at the waist (illustrations B#2 and B#4). *Correction:* This indicates inadequate abdominal strength. Return to the lead-ups of walking and running into the extended position, using the horizontal bar and parallel bars. Develop abdominal strength (see pages 14-18).

| SKILL | TEACHING TECHNIQUES AND OBSERVATION POINTS |

Glide Swing and Return

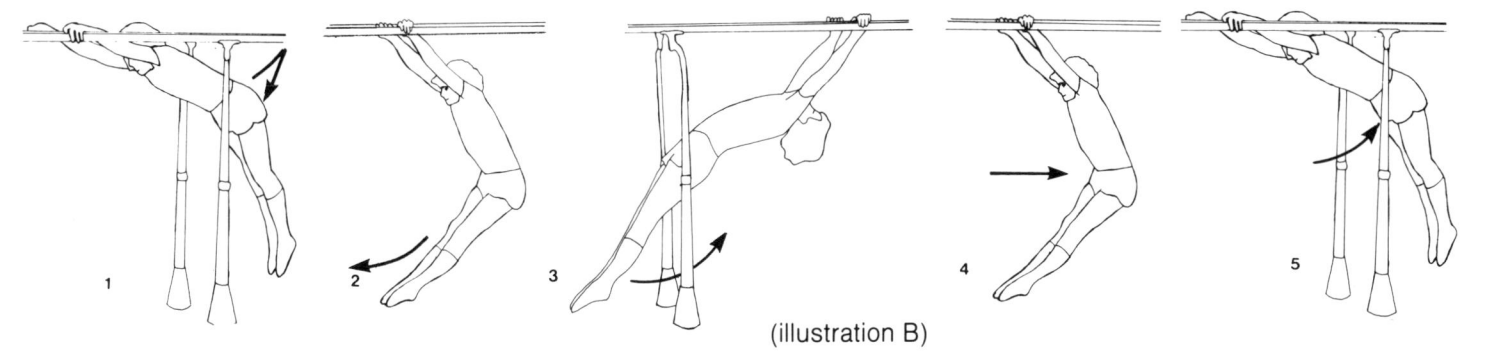

(illustration B)

Level II Skills

6. Glide Swing to Piked Inverted Hang

This skill leads to:
1. glide kip (pages 163-165) and other intermediate and advanced parallel bar skills.

Lead-up skills:
1. piked inverted hang as a static position (illustration A#5)
2. swinging back and forth in piked inverted hang position. Use a spotter for assistance. Practice piked inverted swings on the horizontal bar (page 187)
3. glide swing and return (page 152).

Teaching Points for the Skill:
1. Practice the glide swing and return.
2. With assistance, glide out to full extension and lift the legs into the piked inverted hang position. Begin by performing the shift from the extension of the glide to the piked inverted hang with bent legs. If necessary, kick off the floor to get into the piked inverted hang.
3. Attempt the full action with straight legs throughout. Use spotter assistance (illustration A#1-5).
4. Try the skill alone. Use a spotter to follow the action and to assist only if necessary. The shift from the extension to the piked inverted hang will be a strong challenge to the stomach muscles.

Safety and Spotting:
1. Set the bars at head height or just above. Use chalk to improve the grip.

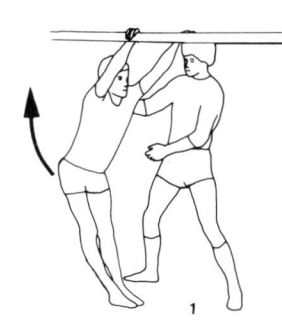

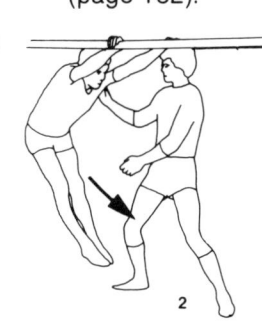

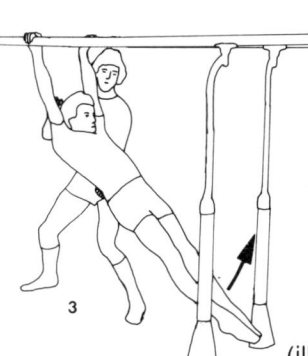

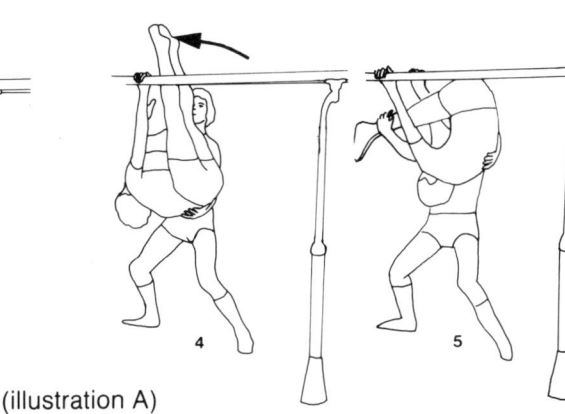

Lead-up
Glide Swing to Piked Inverted Hang (With Assistance)

(illustration A)

Spotting
1. The spotter(s) follow the flow of the glide and stabilize the performer in the piked inverted hang with one hand under the back and the other positioning the legs. It may be necessary for spotters to assist in elevating the performer's legs into the piked inverted hang position.

SKILL	TEACHING TECHNIQUES AND OBSERVATION POINTS

Common Errors:
Errors in Performance:
1. Inability to raise the legs into the piked inverted hang.
   Correction: Go back to the lead-ups, walk out between the bars and kick into the piked inverted hang. Then run out to the extension and lift bent legs into the piked inverted hang. With each attempt straighten the legs, both in the glide and in the shift to the piked inverted hang.

Glide Swing to Piked Inverted Hang

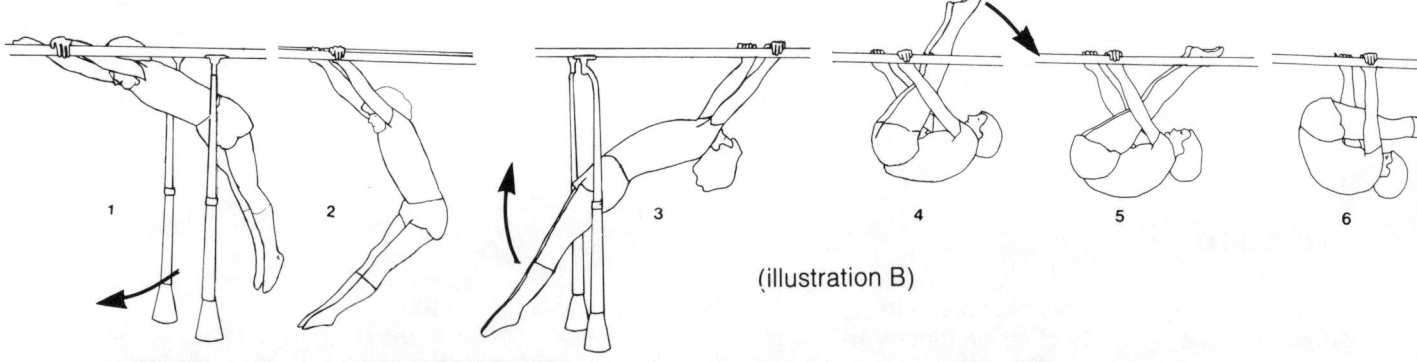

(illustration B)

7. Dismount from the Backswing (often called a Front Vault Dismount)

This skill leads to:
1. dismount from backswing with a quarter turn in toward the bars.

Lead-up skills:
1. cross support swings (page 149).
2. the lead-ups to the dismount from backswing outlined below.

Teaching Points for the Skill:
1. Begin without swinging. Hook the feet backward to the outside of the bar and slide off for the dismount. This will give the performer an orientation to the correct action.
2. With assistance swing forward and backward elevating the hips and legs higher than the bars on the backswing (illustrations #1-3).
3. Push with the arms to the side of the bars for the dismount. Transfer the grip on the bars (illustrations #3-5).

Dismount From a Backswing
(Front Vault Dismount)

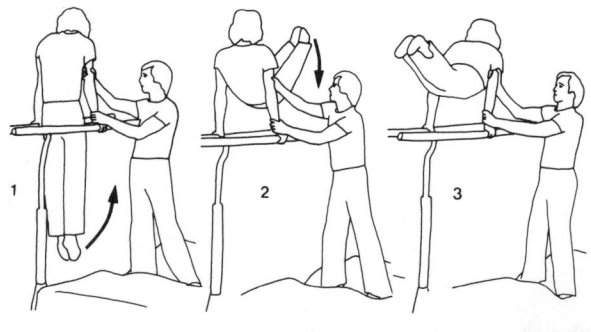

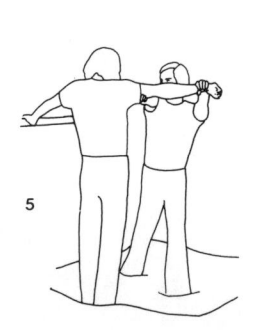

Safety and Spotting:
1. Set the bars low enough to accommodate the swings without the performer's feet hitting the mat between the bars. Use chalk to improve grip and adjust the bars for width.
2. *Extremely* high swings are not necessary in this skill.

Spotting
1. The spotter grips on the wrist and upper arm and helps to shift the performer to the side of the bars for the dismount. Stabilization is given to the performer while in a one armed support position (illustration #4).

SKILL		TEACHING TECHNIQUES AND OBSERVATION POINTS

Common Errors:
Errors in Performance:
1. Insufficient elevation of the legs on the backswing and insufficient drive sideways in the dismount. *Correction:* Return to practicing swings, aiming for higher amplitude. Re-practice the lead-up by climbing off sideways. Attempt the full skill with strong spotting assistance.

8. L-Support
(3 seconds)

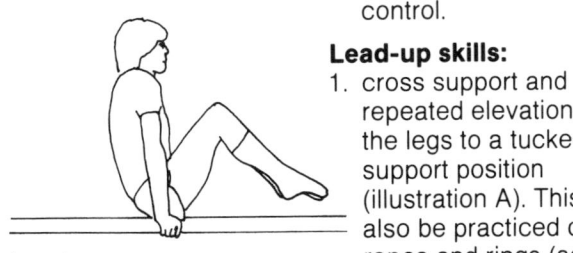

This skill leads to:
1. V-support on parallel bars. The L-support displays abdominal strength and body control.

Lead-up skills:
1. cross support and repeated elevation of the legs to a tucked support position (illustration A). This can also be practiced on the ropes and rings (see page 101).
2. all abdominal strengthening exercises (see examples on pages 5-10).

Teaching Points for the Skill:
1. Begin by elevating the legs to a tucked support position (with spotter assistance).
2. Extend the legs momentarily to the L-support. Hold and return to tucked support. Repeat.
3. Begin in cross support. Maintain straight legs throughout the lift to L-support. Tilt the upper body slightly backward. Hold for a count of three seconds and then lower. Rest and repeat. *Caution:* Do not lean too far backward in an effort to raise the legs higher than bar level.

Safety and Spotting:
1. Set the bars at their lowest position. Adjust for width and use chalk to improve the grip.
2. A mat can be set between the bars as an additional safety precaution.

Spotting:
1. The spotter supports under the legs around the back (illustration B).

Common Errors:
Errors in Performance:
1. Inability to raise the legs to the horizontal position. *Correction:* Return to repetitions of the tucked support (illustration A). Complementary abdominal strengthening exercises should be practiced (see pages 5-10).

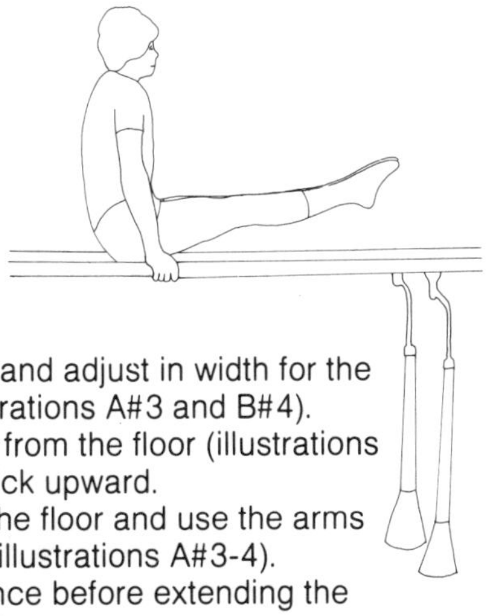

Lead-up
Tucked 'L' Support
(illustration A)

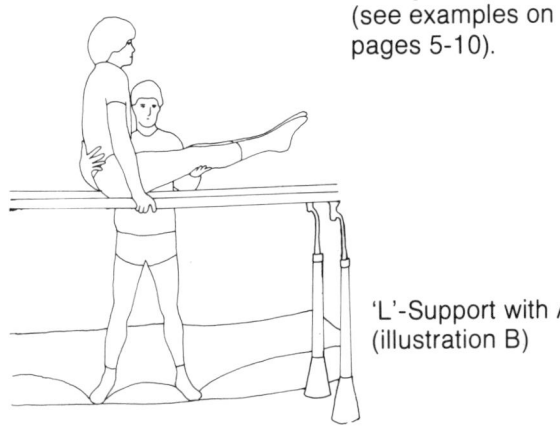

'L'-Support with Assistance
(illustration B)

'L'-Support
(illustration C)

Level III Skills

9. Shoulder Balance
(3 seconds)

This skill leads to:
1. more advanced balances on the parallel bars, such as the handstand.
2. the shoulder balance can be incorporated as part of more advanced skills (for example, L-support elevate with control to a shoulder balance).

Teaching Points for the Skill:
1. Set the bars as low as possible, and adjust in width for the performer's shoulders (see illustrations A#3 and B#4). Enter the skill, either by jumping from the floor (illustrations A#1-2) or by using the bars to kick upward.
2. Press the elbows down toward the floor and use the arms and vision to maintain balance (illustrations A#3-4). Attempt a tucked shoulder balance before extending the legs for the straight shoulder balance.
3. Illustrations B#1-4 show the shoulder balance initiated from cross support position. This is more difficult. Enter the balance in a tucked position and then elevate the legs.

SKILL	TEACHING TECHNIQUES AND OBSERVATION POINTS

Lead-up skills:
1. tucked, piked, and straight headstands on the floor (pages 31-32)
2. underarm support swings (pages 151-152).

4. To dismount from a straight shoulder balance, lower to tucked position and, with spotting assistance, lower to standing or cross support.
5. A forward roll dismount from a shoulder balance is shown on pages 157-158.

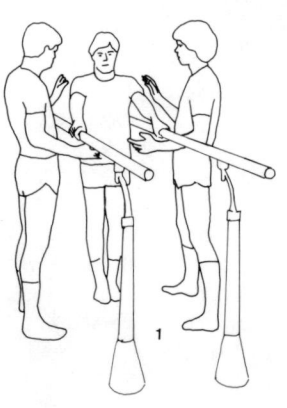

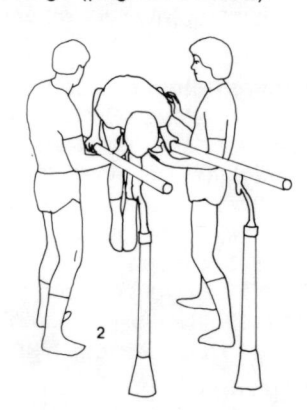

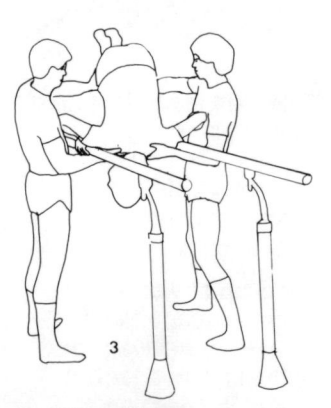

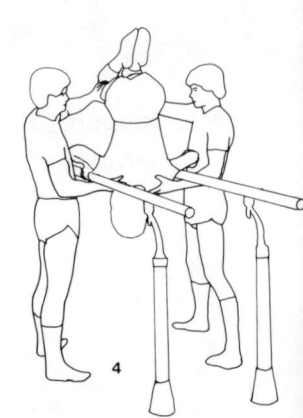

Lead-up Tucked Shoulder Balance (illustration A)

Safety and Spotting:
1. Set the parallel bars as low as possible. Adjust the width to support comfortably under the performer's shoulders. It is preferable to wear a sweater or padding on the upper arms for initial attempts.

Spotting:
1. Spotters support under the performer's shoulder (illustrations A#3 and B#3) and if the performer is well in control of his arm positions on the bars, they then can shift their support to the legs (illustration B#4).

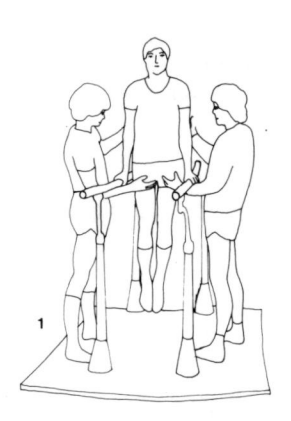

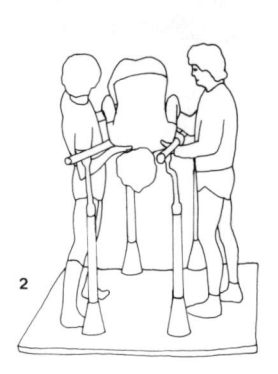

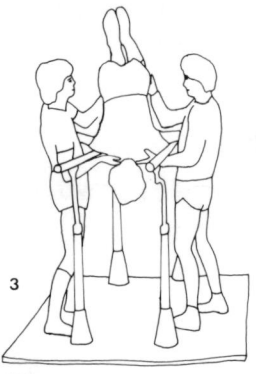

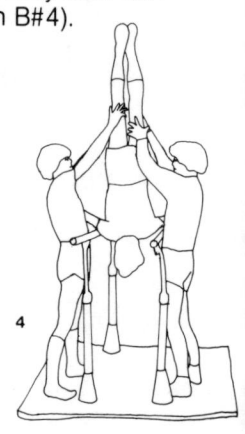

Tucked Shoulder Balance to Straight-Legged Shoulder Balance (illustration B)

Common Errors:
Errors in Performance:
1. Elevation of the legs into the straight shoulder balance before the hips are above the shoulders. *Correction:* Maintain a tucked position until the hips are vertically above the shoulders. Then raise the legs. Use spotter assistance.
2. Failing to press out and down with the elbows. *Correction:* The performer must press the elbows down toward the floor. If this is not done he is liable to slide between the bars.
3. Tucking the head under. *Correction:* Vision should be toward the floor. If the head is tucked under the performer may lose balance and roll forward.

| SKILL | TEACHING TECHNIQUES AND OBSERVATION POINTS |

Errors in Spotting:
1. Insufficient support under the performer's shoulders. *Correction:* Beginners must be given strong support under the shoulders during initial attempts. This prevents any possibility of falling between the bars. Spotters should also carefully control the descent from the balance back to standing or cross support.

10. Forward Roll from a Momentary Shoulder Balance

This skill leads to:
1. more advanced parallel bar skills leading into or following the shoulder balance and forward roll. Examples are: forward roll (no shoulder balance at the midpoint of the roll), back uprise to cross support.

Lead-up skills:
1. tucked, piked and straight-bodied headstands on the floor (pages 31-32).
2. underarm support swings (pages 151-152)
3. tucked and straight-bodied shoulder balance on the parallel bars without a forward roll (pages 155-157)

Teaching Points for the Skill:
1. With the bars set as low as possible and adjusted for the performer's shoulder width, jump into or kick from the bars into a tucked shoulder balance.
2. Extend the legs into a straight-bodied shoulder balance (illustration A#1), then lower again to a tucked shoulder balance. Keep the elbows splayed outward during the balance. Work hard with the grip on the bars to maintain balance.
3. With assistance from spotters, roll out forward onto the mat draped across the bars (illustrations A#1-3). Keep the elbows turned out and with the support of the mat learn to shift the hands forward to their final support position.
4. Without the use of the mat, and with one or two spotters, lift into a tucked shoulder balance. Elevate the legs into the extended shoulder balance position (illustration B#1). The elbows are out and the vision is downward toward the floor.
5. To lower out of the shoulder balance, pike at the waist and tuck the head into the chest. Roll slowly on the upper arms. Re-grasp as quickly as possible and lower into underarm support (illustrations B#1-4).

Safety and Spotting:
1. Set the bars as low as possible and adjust to the width of the performer's shoulders.
2. The performer should initially wear a sweater, or some additional padding on the upper arms (volleyball knee pads).
3. A mat placed across the bars supports the performer in his first efforts at the forward roll.

Spotting:
1. Spotters reach under the bar with one hand and support under the performer's shoulders. The other hand is above the bars and helps to maintain balance. When the forward roll is performed the spotter(s) must have both support arms under the bars. When the bars are elevated the spotter(s) can support with both arms reaching up from below the bars (illustration B#1).

Common Errors:
Errors in Performance:
1. Raising the legs into the straight shoulder balance before the hips are above the shoulders. *Correction:* Hold the tucked position until the hips are above the shoulders and then raise the legs.
2. Failing to keep the elbows turned outward. *Correction:* The performer must press the elbows downward toward the floor while in the shoulder balance. If this is not done his body will slip between the bars.

Lead-up
Forward Roll From Momentary Shoulder Balance into a Mat

(illustration A)

SKILL

Forward Roll From Momentary Shoulder Balance to Under Arm Support

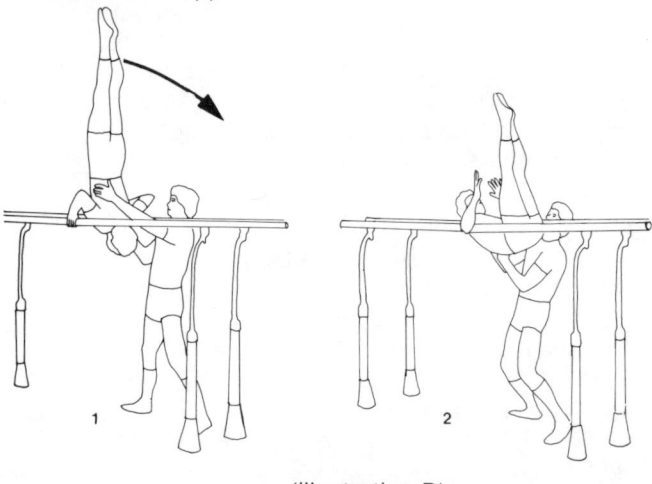

(illustration B)

TEACHING TECHNIQUES AND OBSERVATION POINTS

3. Failing to pike prior to initiating the forward roll. *Correction:* An extended body generates great speed during the roll and should be avoided by beginners. By piking at the waist the speed of the roll is reduced.

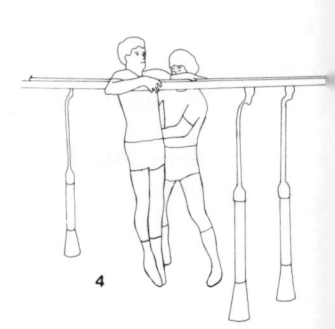

Errors in Spotting:
1. Failing to remove the support arm above the bars when the performer attempts the forward roll. *Correction:* The spotters must quickly remove their arms and shift to support from under the bars. This error occurs most frequently when the bars are set low.
2. Failing to provide sufficient support under the performer's shoulder during the shoulder balance. *Correction:* Beginners attempting the shoulder balance may fail to press their arms downward with sufficient force. Spotters should have one hand under the bars supporting the performer's shoulder (see illustration B#1).

11. Back Uprise

This skill leads to:
1. skills in which the back uprise leads to more advanced support positions, such as back uprise to shoulder balance, or more advanced, back uprise straddle the legs above the bars to L-support.

Lead-up skills:
1. underarm support swings (pages 151-152)
2. back uprise from bent arm swings (illustrations A#1-4)
3. strength exercises for developing triceps extension (pages 14-18)

Teaching Points for the Skill:
1. Work through the lead-up skills illustrated in A#1-4.
2. Practice the underarm swings, lifting the hips as high as possible at both ends of the swing. Elevate the hips higher than the bar on the backswing.
3. At the highest point of the backswing straighten the arms vigorously and elevate the body to cross support position. Do not bend at the knees.

Safety and Spotting:
1. Adjust the height and width of the bars for the performer. Do not raise the bars any higher than necessary. Place a mat under the bars.
2. For comfort the performer can wear a sweater, or volleyball knee pads on the upper arms. Use chalk to improve the grip.

Spotting
1. Spotters can help to initiate the first backswing (illustration B#1) (one spotter shown for clarity).
2. Following a forward swing, the spotter(s) place one hand on the performer's chest and the other on the thigh. With this support they help to lift the performer upward (illustrations B#3-4). Immediately following this action spotters must quickly stabilize the performer in cross support position. This is important since the performer's legs will swing downward with some force after the back uprise.

| SKILL | TEACHING TECHNIQUES AND OBSERVATION POINTS |

Lead-up
Back Uprise from Bent Arm Swings

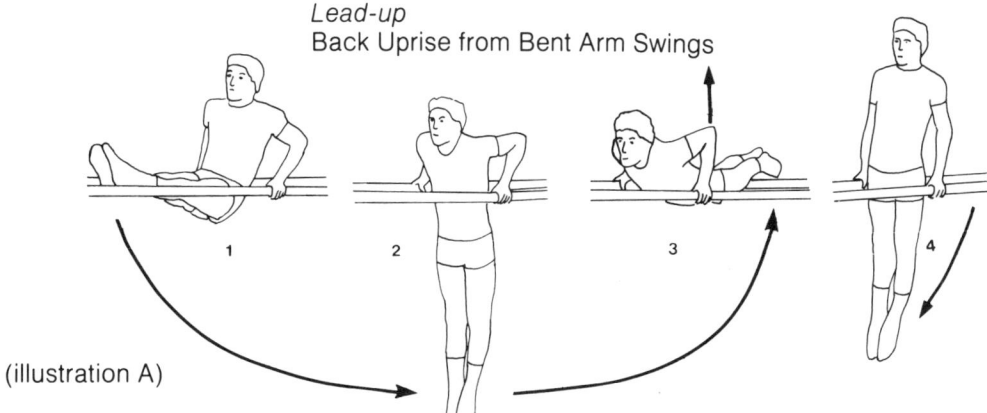

(illustration A)

Back Uprise

(illustration B)

Common Errors:
Errors in Performance:
1. The backswing is too low. *Correction:* Improve the quality of the underarm swings until the hips are rising above the bars. Do not hyperextend the back or bend the legs.
2. The hands are placed on the bars too far ahead of the shoulders in the underarm support position. *Correction:* Bring the hands in close to the shoulders. This makes the arm extension easier.
3. The hands slide along the bars as the body rises upward. *Correction:* This is a common error. Improve the swings so that the backswing actually lifts the body upward rather than backward.
4. The shoulders drop between the bars during the underarm support swings. *Correction:* Press down with the arms on the bars to keep the shoulders above the bars throughout the action.

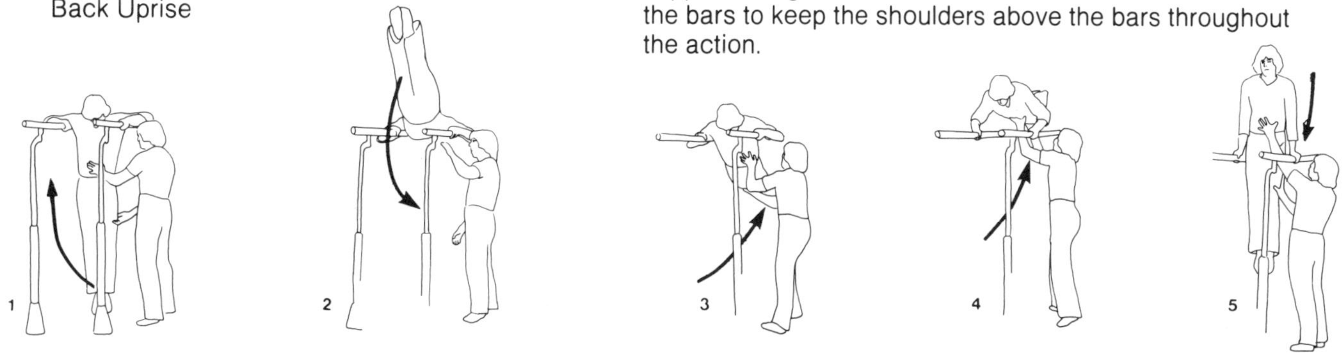

Errors in Spotting:
1. The spotters throw the performer backward during the execution of the back uprise. *Correction:* The spotters must lift directly upward so that the performer finishes the skill with his bodyweight above his hands rather than to the rear of them. Spotters should lift upward and stabilize the performer immediately afterward in the cross support position.

12. Underarm Kip to Cross Support

This skill leads to:
1. all skills in which a kipping action occurs, such as glide kip, drop kip (see pages 163-166)

Teaching Points for the Skill:
1. Begin by practicing the underarm support swing to piked inverted support. Make sure that the hips are well elevated and the feet brought back past the head (illustration B#2).
2. Begin with a forward swing followed by a backswing.
3. On the next forward swing, carry the legs up and roll back

| SKILL | TEACHING TECHNIQUES AND OBSERVATION POINTS |

Lead-up skill:
1. underarm support swings (page 151)
2. underarm support swings to piked inverted support (illustrations A#1-2 and illustrations B#1-2,
3. any other skills in which a vigorous extension at the hips occurs such as a headspring or neckspring (pages 65-66)

into a tight piked inverted support position (illustrations A#2 and B#2).
4. With as much vigor as possible, drive the legs up and forward so that the body is partially extended at the hips. *Do not extend completely* (see illustration B#3). The thrust up and forward of the legs is then "arrested" which will cause the upper body to rise. This action is complemented by an upward thrust from the arms. Spotters assist by lifting under the back (illustrations B#3-5).
5. After the upper body has risen sufficiently, lower the legs into the cross support position (illustrations B#4-5).

Safety and Spotting:
1. Set the bars no higher than is necessary for underarm swings. Adjust the width of the bars.
2. Place a mat between the bars. Use chalk to improve the grip.

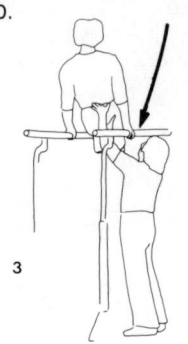

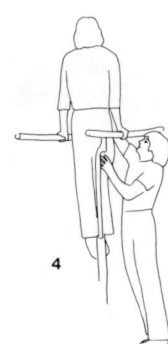

Under Arm Kip to Cross Support
Seen From Behind

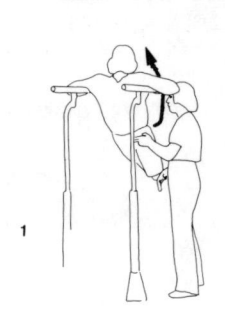

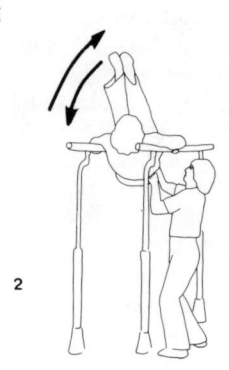

(illustration A)

Spotting
1. Spotters assist the action of the forward swing into the piked inverted position (illustrations B#1-2). They then allow the performer to cast forward with the legs (illustrations B#2-3) (one spotter is shown for clarity).
2. One hand stops the performer's legs from being lowered completely and the other elevates under the back (illustration B#3).
3. When the performer's upper body has risen sufficiently, the spotters lower the performer's legs and quickly shift to a stabilizing position (illustrations B#4-5).

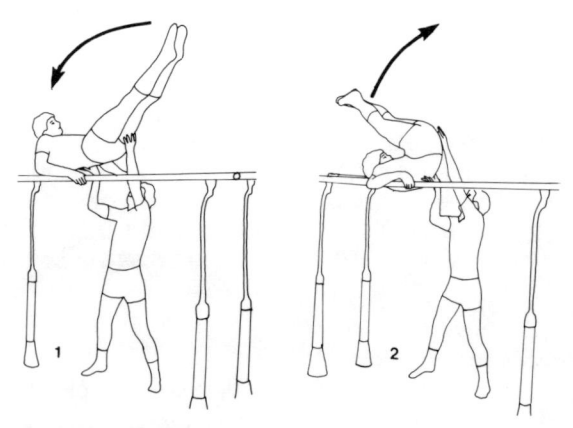

Under Arm Kip to Cross Support
Seen From the Side
(illustration B)

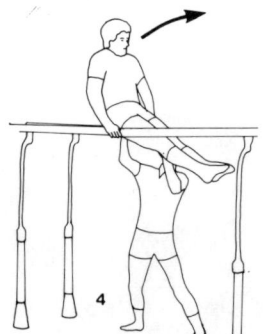

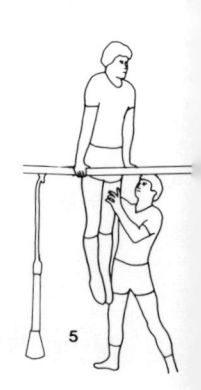

Common Errors:
Errors in Performance:
1. Insufficient flexion at the hips in the piked inverted support. *Correction:* This action should be practiced

SKILL	TEACHING TECHNIQUES AND OBSERVATION POINTS

without the addition of a kip, Swing forward vigorously and allow the legs to carry the body back into a tight pike. Elevate the hips so that they are well above the line of the shoulders (illustration B#2). Keep the legs straight. Use spotters.

2. There is no "arresting" action of the legs in the kip. *Correction:* Learn to cast vigorously with the legs to a point some 30 degrees past the vertical (see the leg position in illustration B#3). By casting to this point and immediately locking the stomach muscles the upper body will be made to rise upward. Have spotters assist in this action. Practice this action on the floor.

Errors in Spotting:

1. Assistance is badly timed. *Correction:* The spotters must follow the swing to the piked inverted support. They then time their "boost" under the back to coincide with the cast forward of the performer's legs. This timing is critical.
2. Not allowing the performer's legs to be lowered at the end of the kip action. *Correction:* Poor spotting in this skill can make it almost impossible for the performer to rise into a cross support position. Spotters must help to "arrest" the forward cast of the performer's legs and then quickly allow them to lower so that the upper body can rise. If the legs are held up in the air it will be almost impossible for the performer to elevate his upper body to the cross support position.

Level IV Skills

13. Front Uprise

This skill leads to:
1. advanced parallel bar skills. The technique of the front uprise is particularly important and should be well executed before more advanced parallel bar skills are attempted.

Teaching Points for the Skill:
1. Practice the front uprise from bent arm swings (illustrations A#1-4).
2. Practice underarm support swings. Straddle the legs over the bar on a front swing and press up to the extended arm position (illustrations B#1-5).
3. Perform the complete front uprise with two spotters assisting. Elevate the hips forward and upward without piking too much at the hips. At the highest point of hip elevation extend the arms to cross support position.

Lead-up
Uprise From a Bent Arm Swing

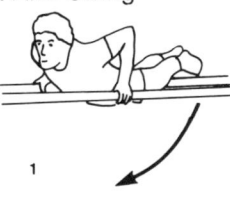

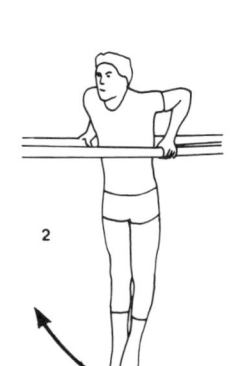

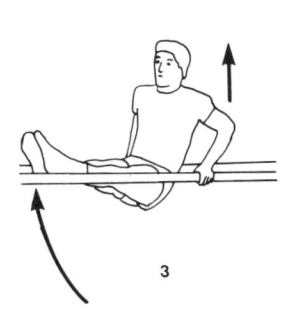

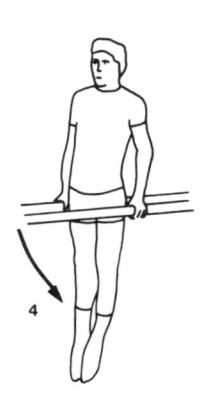

(illustration A)

SKILL	TEACHING TECHNIQUES AND OBSERVATION POINTS

Lead-up skills:
1. underarm support swings (pages 151-152)
2. front uprise from bent arm swings (illustrations A#1-4)
3. front uprise from straddled legged support (illustrations B#1-5)

Safety and Spotting:
1. Set the bars at a height that will just allow the underarm swings to be performed.
2. Adjust the width to accommodate the performer comfortably. Wear a sweater or volleyball knee pads around the upper arm. Use chalk to improve the grip.

Spotting (illustrations C#1-5)
1. Support under the thighs and seat and elevate the performer to the cross support position.
2. Control the lowering of the performer's legs to the final cross support position. Do not allow them to drop quickly.

Lead-up
Front Uprise to Straddle-Legged Sitting Support

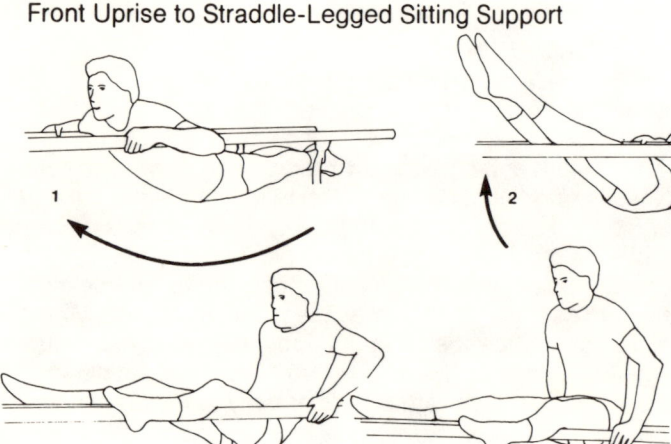

(illustration B)

Common Errors:
Errors in Performance:
1. The shoulders are allowed to drop downward between the bars during the underarm support swings. *Correction:* Press downward with the arms (elbows) to maintain the height of the shoulders.
2. There is too much pike during the uprise which causes the performer to fall backward. *Correction:* Make sure that the hips are lifting high during the underarm support swings. Combine the rise of the hips with the upward drive of the arms. Do not dissipate the lift of the hips by piking at the waist.
3. The arm extension is weak. *Correction:* Check to see whether this is due to lack of strength or poor underarm swings. If the performer is too weak, return to strength exercises, and leave the uprise until later. If the underarm swings are poor, correct them by concentrating on hip lift (particularly on the forward swing).

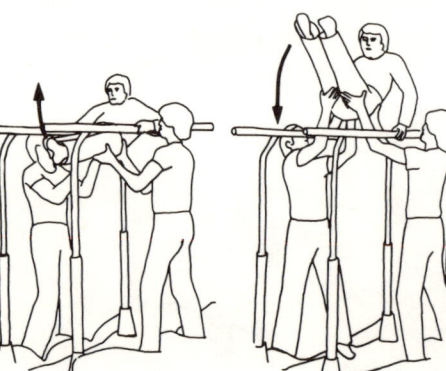

Front Uprise

(illustration C)

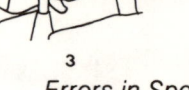

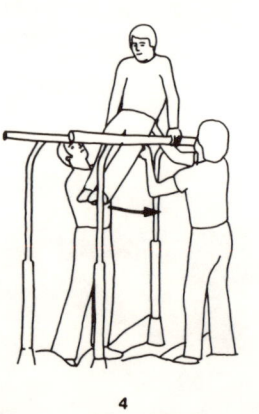

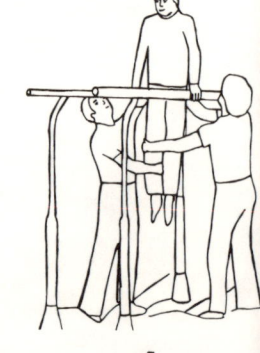

Errors in Spotting:
1. Throwing the performer forward during the uprise. *Correction:* Spotters must be sure that their lift under the performer's thighs and seat is directly upward and that it complements his arm extension rather than counteracts it.

SKILL	TEACHING TECHNIQUES AND OBSERVATION POINTS

14. Glide Kip

This skill leads to:
1. more advanced kip actions on the parallel bars, such as drop kip (pages 165-166)

Lead-up skills:
1. On a chest height horizontal bar:
   - i glide swing and return (pages 152-153)
   - ii a kip initiated by a run under the bar and supported by two spotters (page 163)
2. On the parallel bars:
   - i glide swing and return (pages 152-153)
   - ii glide swing to piked inverted hang (pages 153-154)
   - iii underarm kip to cross support and its associated lead-ups (pages 159-160)

Teaching Points for the Skill:
1. Teach the kip from a run and from a glide on the chest height horizontal bar. Use spotters
2. Then teach the skill in the middle of the parallel bars. Spotting is easier in the middle of the bars (see illustrations A#1-7 and B#1-5).
3. Run out to full extension and bring the legs back to a piked inverted hang position (illustration A#3).
4. After returning to the piked inverted hang, extend vigorously at the hips. As this action occurs, press down on the bars with the arms to elevate the body upward (illus. A#5-7).
5. Lower the legs to cross support position (illustrations A#5-7).
6. Allow the spotters to provide strong support through the whole motion during initial attempts.
7. Instead of running out to the extended position under the bars, glide out (illustrations B#1-5).
8. When the glide kip is performed from the end of the bars, the performer must be able to glide and return to a piked inverted position without the assistance of the spotters. They provide their support after the performer's legs have been brought back to the piked position. (The parallel bar supports stop spotters following the glide to its full extension.)

Safety and Spotting:
1. The performer should be able to run under or glide under the bars without being hindered by thick matting between the bars. A thin resilite mat is preferable.
2. The bars should be set at head height and adjusted for width. Chalk should be used to improve the grip.

Lead-up Kip Using a Running Entry Rather than Glide

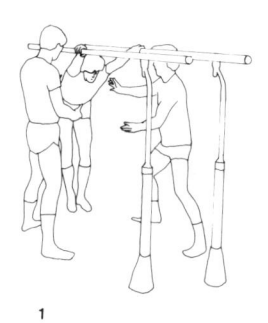

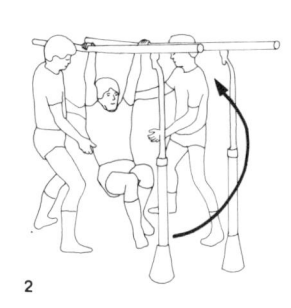

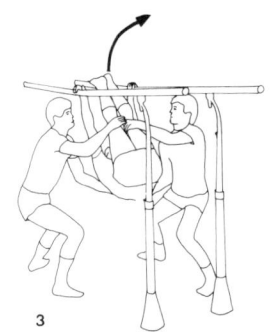

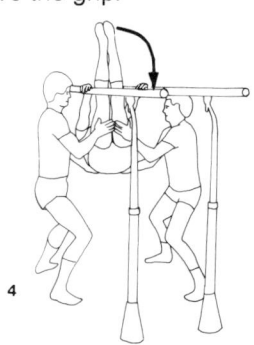

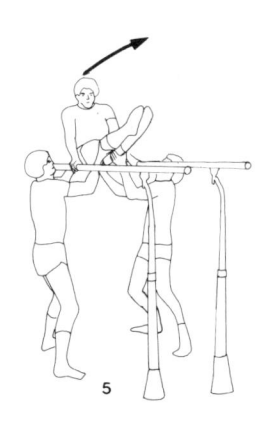

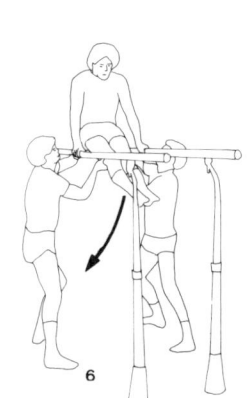

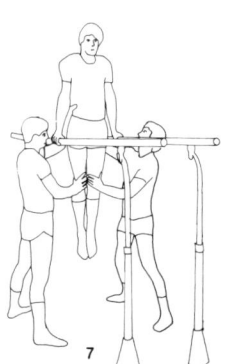

(illustration A)

SKILL	TEACHING TECHNIQUES AND OBSERVATION POINTS

Spotting:
1. Good spotting is instrumental in helping the performer become familiar with the glide kip. When the glide kip is performed between the bars, the spotters can "press" the performer out into the extension and then bring his legs back into a piked inverted position (see B#1-3). Support under the thighs and the seat then boosts the performer up to the final cross support position (illustrations B#4-5).
2. When working at the end of the bars, the spotters wait for the performer to return from the glide and then elevate the performer into cross support. Stabilization of the final cross support position is very important (illustration C#5).

Glide Kip in Middle of Bars

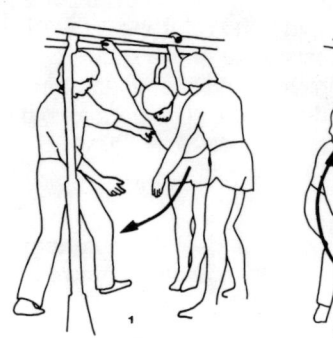

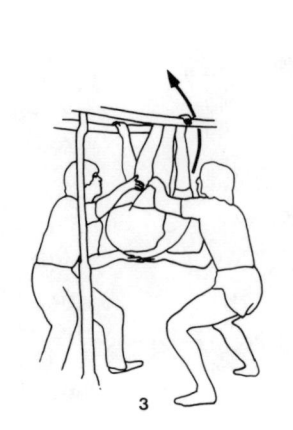

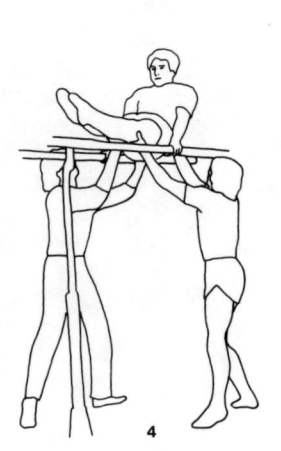

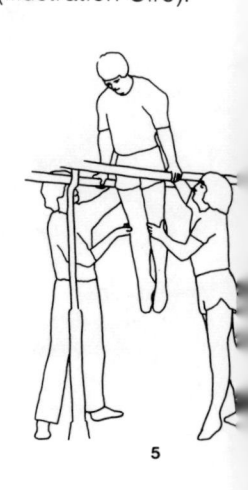

(illustration B)

Common Errors:
Errors in Performance:
1. The extension at the end of the glide is poor. *Correction:* Practice glide swings aiming to reach full extension at the end of the glide.
2. The pike at the waist is performed too late, with the body already into the backswing. *Correction:* Perform the piking action at the end of the extension. Have spotters assist in orientation to this action.
3. The timing of the kip is wrong (either performed too early or too late). *Correction:* Extend the legs upward and then downward the moment the pike action is complete (see illustrations A#3-7).
4. The arms bend during the kip. *Correction:* The performer must learn to swing from the hands. The timing of both the glide and the kip is very important and the performer should not attempt to "bully" his way up to cross support. Use spotters until timing becomes more refined.

Errors in Spotting:
1. Anticipating the elevation upward in the kip. *Correction:* Spotters must time their assistance to coincide with the performer's glide and kip. They must have a feel for glide—return—and lift. Elevating the performer too early will break down the pattern of action and its timing.

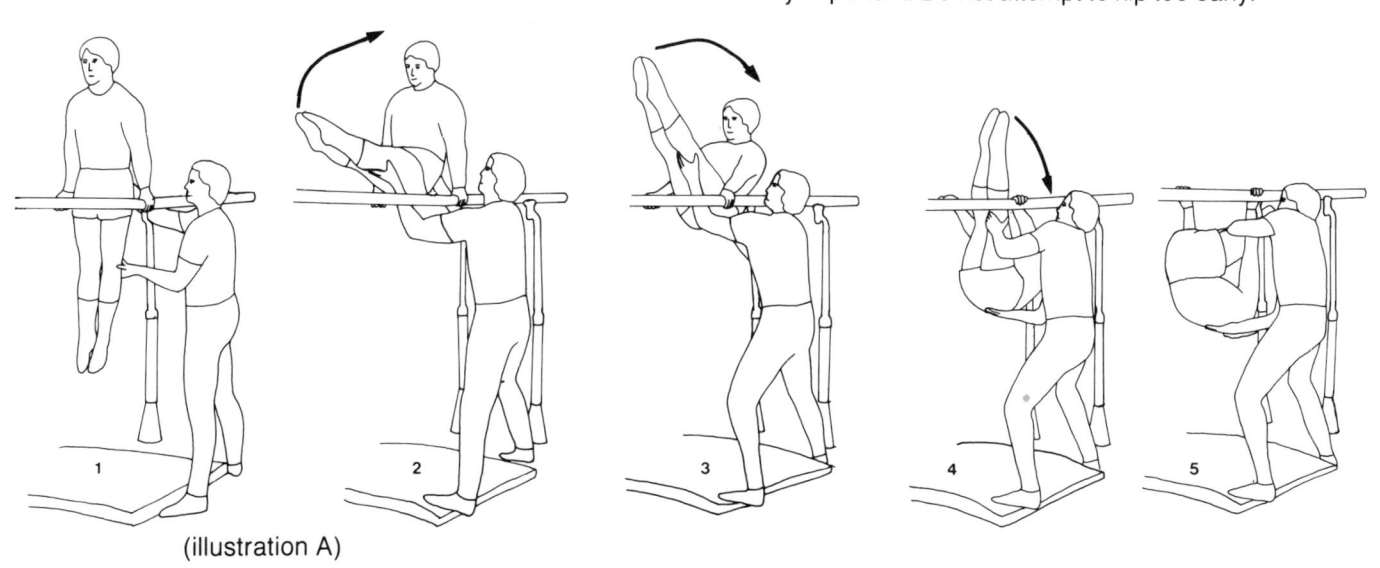

| SKILL | TEACHING TECHNIQUES AND OBSERVATION POINTS |

Glide Kip From End of Bars

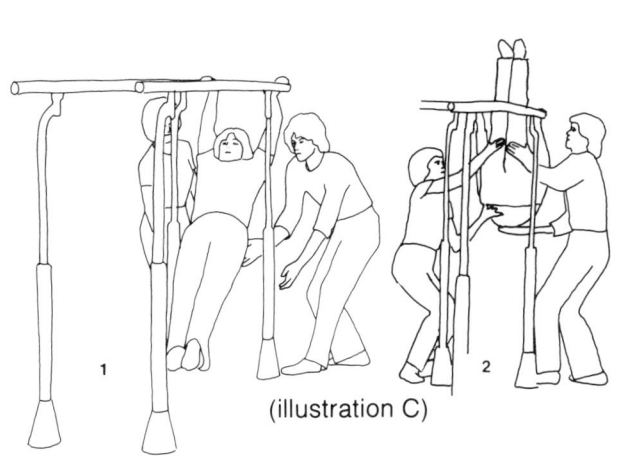

(illustration C)

15. Drop Kip at End of Bars

This skill leads to:
1. advanced kip actions on the parallel bars and the horizontal bar.

Lead-up skills:
1. the glide kip performed in the middle and at the end of the parallel bars (pages 164-165)
2. dropping back from cross support to piked inverted hang (illustrations A#1-5)

Teaching Points for the Skill:
1. Begin by practicing the glide kip at the end of the bars (pages 163-165).
2. Attempt the drop kip from standing before attempting it from cross support position (illustrations B#1-7). (For the drop kip from cross support see illustrations C#1-6).
3. The difference between the drop kip from standing and the glide kip is the lack of a glide entry on the drop kip. Practice jumping into a piked inverted hang position (illustrations B#1-4).
4. Jump into the piked inverted hang, wait momentarily for the backswing and kip strongly upward. With the exception of the entry into the piked inverted hang this action is exactly the same as for the glide kip.
5. For the drop kip from cross support, use spotter assistance to drop backward into the piked inverted hang position. Maintain extended arms, and pike at the waist during the drop backward (illustrations C#1-3). Wait momentarily for the return swing and kip strongly upward. Timing is extremely important. Do not attempt to kip too early.

Lead-up From Cross Support to Piked Inverted Hang

(illustration A)

SKILL	TEACHING TECHNIQUES AND OBSERVATION POINTS

Safety and Spotting:
1. Adjust the bars and use chalk to improve the grip.
2. Grip the bars at the extreme end and place thumb and fingers together.

Drop Kip From Standing

(illustration B)

Common Errors:
Errors in Performance:
1. Bending the legs and the arms. *Correction:* The arms and legs must be kept straight throughout. If the drop kip is performed from cross support, the spotters can give strong support so that the performer has no trouble in keeping the arms and legs straight.
2. Kipping upward too soon. *Correction:* The timing on this action is critical. The performer must allow his hips to swing forward between the bars and then begin the return swing before the kip action is initiated.

Drop Kip From Cross Support

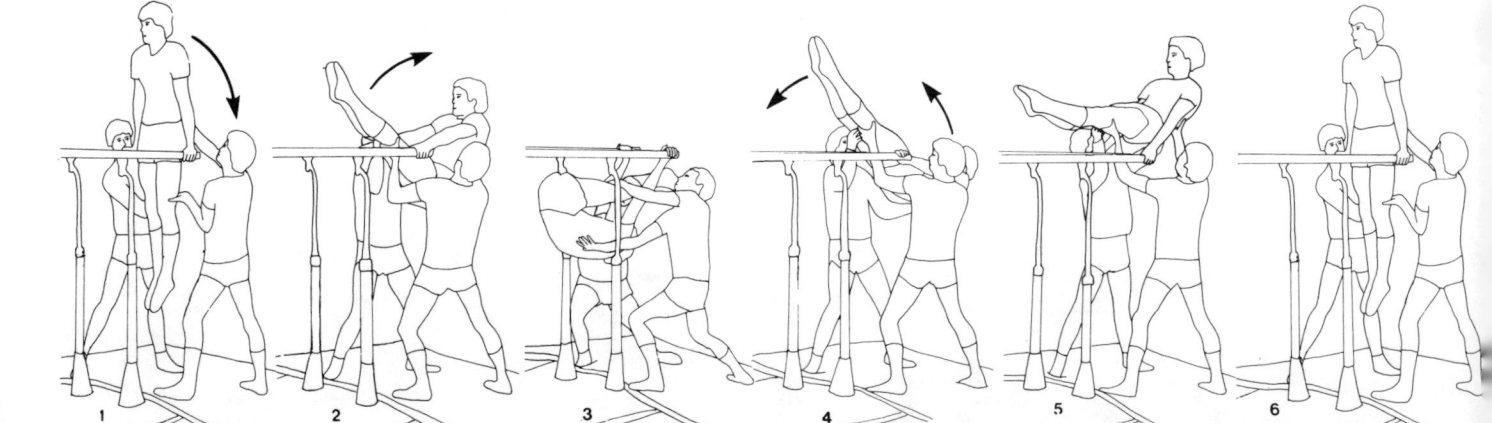

(illustration C)

Errors in Spotting:
1. Over-anticipation of the kip. *Correction:* Spotters must time their upward lift to coincide with the performer's vigorous extension at the hips. They must resist pushing upward too soon.

| SKILL | TEACHING TECHNIQUES AND OBSERVATION POINTS |

16. Momentary Handstand Quarter Turn Dismount at the End of the Parallel Bars

This skill leads to:
1. handstand in the center of the parallel bars

Lead-up skills:
1. handstand on the floor (three seconds) (pages 55-56)
2. handstand quarter turn dismount in the low parallettes (illustrations A#1-4)
3. swings on the low parallel bars (high amplitude-good technique (pages 149-150)

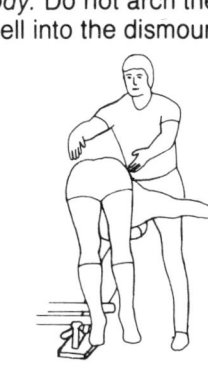

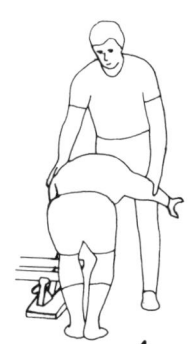

Lead-up
Handstand Quarter turn Dismount on Parallettes (illustration A)

Teaching Points for the Skill:
1. Practice the handstand quarter turn dismount on the low parallettes. The method of dismount must be well learned.
2. Practice high amplitude swings on low parallel bars. Work for a good pendulum swing from the shoulders. Do not pike at the waist on the front swing. Do not hyperextend the back or bend the legs on the back swing.
3. With one or two spotters assisting (see illustrations B#1-3), swing to a momentary handstand. Extend the body and make the handstand as straight as possible. Perform a quarter turn dismount.
4. Repeat the skill and try to hold the handstand for one or two seconds. Make sure the quarter turn is *around the long axis of the body.* Do not arch the back. Do not bend the knees until well into the dismount.

Safety and Spotting:
1. Set the parallel bars as low as possible. Stand on a spotting block or box.
2. Surround the end of the parallel bars with mats.

Spotting
1. Follow the swing and stabilize the performer in the momentary handstand (illustrations B#1-3).
2. Rotate his legs into the quarter turn dismount (illustration B#4).
3. Two spotters will control the performer much better than a single spotter.

Common Errors:
Errors in Performance:
1. Swinging wildly through the handstand position. No control. *Correction:* Re-practice the cross support swings. Correct the technique aiming for a pendulum swing from the shoulders and control throughout. There must be no whip-like action of the lower legs.
2. Allowing the shoulders to fall forward as the body rises toward the handstand. *Correction:* Re-practice cross support swings. Re-practice kicking into the handstand on the low parallettes. Press the shoulders back and stretch up into a straight-bodied handstand.
3. Piking on the front swing and arching the back and bending the legs on the backswing. *Correction:* Re-practice cross support swings. Re-practice kicking into the handstand on the low parallettes. Do not attempt the swing into the momentary handstand on parallel bars until the swing technique has improved.

| SKILL | TEACHING TECHNIQUES AND OBSERVATION POINTS |

Momentary Handstand
Quarter Turn at the End of the Parallel Bars

(illustration B)

17. Combinations and Routines

The combinations and routines listed in this section are almost exclusively made up of skills taken from Levels I-IV. The instructor should feel free to adjust and modify these routines to the needs of students. Skills not listed in Levels I-IV, but with which the instructor is familiar, should be included to make routines more attractive. Assistance should be given by spotters where necessary.

Level I Skills:

(Parallel bars vary in height to allow cross support swings or underarm support swings as required)

1. Jump to cross support at the end of the bars—straddle travel to the center of the bars—cross support swings (twice-forward and backward)—dismount from a forward swing.
2. Jump to cross support at the end of the bars—hop travel (twice without a swing)—hop travel (twice-incorporating a shift on the forward swing each time)—swing—dismount on the forward swing.
3. Jump to cross support in the center of the bars—swing (twice-forward and backward) lower to bent arm position—swing—(twice-forward and backward)—lift to cross support from bent arm support on back swing-swing-dismount on forward swing.
4. Glide swing and return (at end of the bars)—jump to cross support—hop travel with shift on forward swing (twice)—swing -(four times forward and backward)—stop—quarter turn dismount between the bars.
5. (for this combination adjust the bars so that the performer can lower to standing from underarm support without discomfort)—Glide swing and return (at the end of the bars)—jump to bent arm support-swing-raise to cross support on front swing—straddle travel (twice)—lower legs to cross support—swing (forward and backward)—stop—

TEACHING TECHNIQUES AND OBSERVATION POINTS

quarter turn dismount between the bars—remount in under arm support—under arm support swings (forward and backward twice)—raise arms to dismount.

Level I and Level II Combined:

(Parallel bars set low but with sufficient height for cross support swings.)
1. Cross support—hop travel from end to center of bars—swing—dismount from forward swing
2. Jump to cross support in the center of the bars—L-support—swing dismount from backswing
3. L-support (at end of bars)—cross support—swing—jump down to standing—glide swing and return—stand
4. Jump to cross support at end of bars—swing—dismount from backswing
5. Glide swing to piked inverted hang (at end of bars)—stand—jump up to cross support—hop travel—L-support—swing—dismount from forward swing

Levels I, II, and III Combined:

(Parallel bars set high enough to accommodate under arm support swing.)
1. Under arm support swings—piked inverted under arm support-kip to cross support—swing—dismount from front swing (rear vault dismount).
2. Under arm support swings—back uprise—cross support swing—dismount from backward swing
3. Cross support (in center of bars)—momentary shoulder balance—forward roll—back uprise—swing—dismount from forward swing
4. Cross support (in center of bars)—L-support—shoulder balance (3 seconds)—forward roll—underarm support swing to piked inverted under arm support—kip to cross support—dismount from backward swing
5. Under arm support swings to piked inverted under arm support—under arm kip to cross support—L-support—shoulder balance—forward roll—back uprise—dismount from forward swing

Level I, II, III and IV Combined:

(Parallel bars set high enough to allow under arm support swings)
1. Under arm support swings—front uprise—shoulder balance—forward roll-back uprise—swing-dismount from forward swing
2. Glide kip (in center of the bars)—L-support—shoulder balance—forward roll—back uprise—cross support swings-momentary handstand quarter turn dismount at end of bars. (If necessary add a straddle travel in order to shift to the end of the bars for the dismount)
3. Drop kip from standing—momentary shoulder balance—forward roll—swing—front uprise—swing—dismount from front swing (for variation add a quarter turn inward toward the bar on the dismount)

TEACHING TECHNIQUES AND OBSERVATION POINTS

4. Under arm support swings—under arm kip to cross support—L-support—lift with control into a shoulder balance (hold for 3 seconds)—forward roll-back uprise—momentary handstand—quarter turn dismount at end of bars. (Shift the starting position for this routine so that the dismount occurs at the end of the bars without additional adjustment)
5. Glide kip (at end of bars)—drop kip from cross support—L-support (3 seconds)—shoulder balance (3 seconds) forward roll-under arm support swings—under arm kip to cross support—dismount on back swing.

F. Horizontal Bar

General Safety

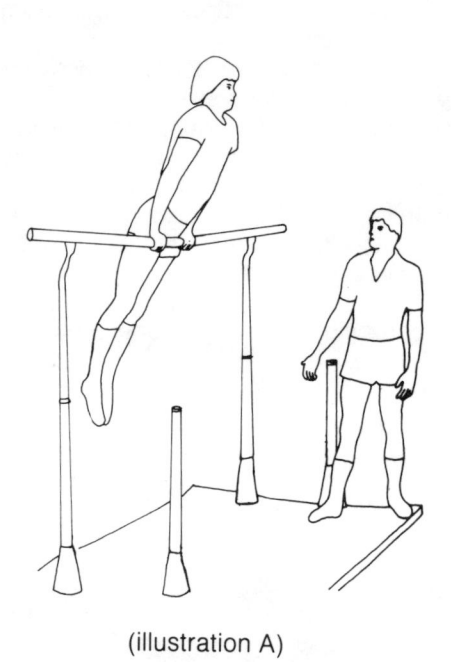

(illustration A)

The majority of horizontal bar skills listed in Levels I-IV can be performed on a single parallel bar providing that adequate stabilization is given to the base of the bars. The weight of two spotters is sufficient to hold the bars stable or (depending on the type of the bars) they can be locked to the gymnasium floor. One performer should work at a time and all skills should be attempted in the center of the bars.

1. An introduction to the horizontal bar should be made on a bar set at about chest height. Many fundamental skills for the horizontal bar can also be practiced on the lower of two uneven bars or on a single parallel bar (the other bar being completely removed) (illustration A).
2. An excellent piece of apparatus for school use is the wall-mounted adjustable horizontal bar. This bar swings out from the wall and is quickly locked into place. When not needed, it is easily folded back against the wall (illustration B, C, and D).
3. In a gymnastic class there will be no need to use a horizontal bar set at full height. The basic skills on the horizontal bar are learned on a low bar and it is highly unlikely that any performer would progress beyond this level in the regular class. Once the fundamentals are mastered, performers can "graduate" to the high bar as part of the after-school gymnastic club. Safety and spotting are also easier on low equipment, and much of it is similar to that required on the parallel bars.
4. Mats should cover the area below the bars without any overlap or gaps in the surface. Fitted mats which will remain with the apparatus are preferred. Place crash pads in position according to the requirements of the skill and make allowance for distances covered in dismounts.
5. Wooden rails in uneven and parallel bars are now made to withstand tremendous stress, but even so they should be inspected periodically to ensure that they remain in good condition. They should be replaced if they are splintering or if the laminations are coming apart.
6. Sweat should always be wiped off all rails after each participant has used them. Use hand grips and chalk to reduce the problem of blisters and torn skin. The instructor must also adjust demands on the student, both in the amount of time spent on the bar and the type of skill being practiced. A certain amount of chalk build-up is necessary on both wooden and steel bars to help the gymnast to grip the bar. However, chalk should not be allowed to build up excessively, nor should any type of bar be sanded so that it is over-smooth.

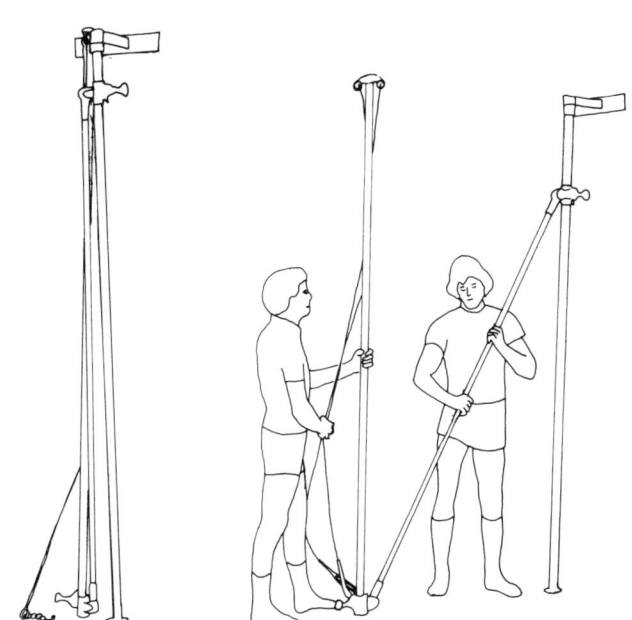

Wall-mounted Horizontal Bar Stacked Prior to Use (illustration B)

Wall-mounted Horizontal Bar Being Set Out For Use (illustration C)

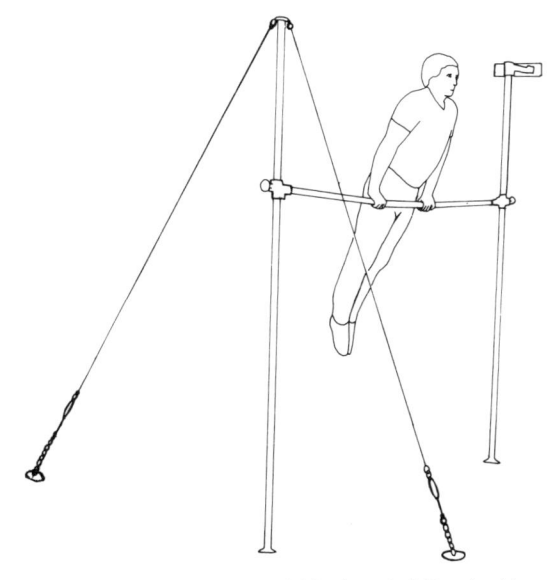

Wall-mounted Horizontal Bar In Use (illustration D)

The wall-mounted horizontal bar is very easy to set up and can be put in place in less than a minute. An additional feature is the ease with which the height of the horizontal bar can be changed to suit the needs of each individual. Its only disadvantage is that it is not adequate apparatus for higher levels of competitive gymnastics.

TEACHING TECHNIQUES AND OBSERVATION POINTS

7. Cables and turnbuckles used to stabilize bar apparatus must be inspected before each class to ensure that there is sufficient bite on threads and that cables are not frayed and twisted. The bar should adjust easily for each performer and not cause serious delays during instruction. Careful grouping of gymnasts according to height can minimize this delay.

8. In small gymnasiums cables angling out from supports may cause tripping and will present a liability unless well sighted and protected. Rubber tubing, brightly painted, and slit so that it fits over the cables will minimize this problem. Sponge rubber can also be wrapped around bars to lessen the impact of hips and stomach. This rubber wrapping can be permanently attached and slid to the side of the bar when not in use.

9. Spotting techniques are fairly simple and quickly learned providing the instructor does not rush from one skill to another. Spotting for mounts and dismounts on the horizontal bar frequently resemble the support given on vaulting and tends to be less complex than for circular or rotational skills. Many techniques reinforce principles taught during floor exercises and tumbling, which makes the task of teaching spotting for bar skills a great deal easier.

10. For some of the circle skills, spotting techniques take more time to learn and the spotter must always know whether support hands and arms should be placed over or under the bar. Quick movements and fast shifting of hand positions are also required which may initially confuse the spotter. Many skills can be spotted adequately with spotters standing either in front or to the rear of the bar. Both methods work well and the final choice ultimately depends upon personal preference. Instructors can teach one method and introduce variations later.

11. Skills performed by males on the low horizontal bar duplicate those used by females on the uneven bars. This is an important feature for the instructor who has a mixed class and who is considering the best way to set up groups working on apparatus. Males and females can work together on the lower of the uneven bars or on a low horizontal bar. Several illustrations in this chapter show them practicing together in this manner.

Examples of Basic Positions on the Horizontal Bar

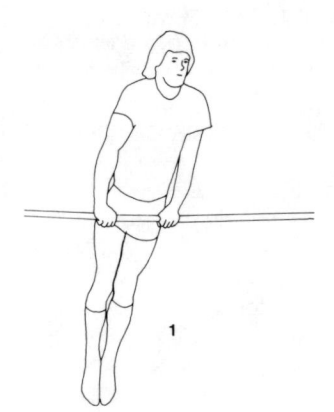

1. Front Support (Overgrip)
2. Front Support (Undergrip) 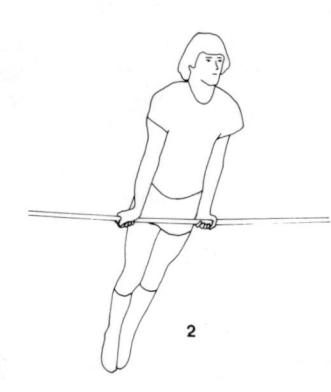
3. Front Support (Mixed Grip) 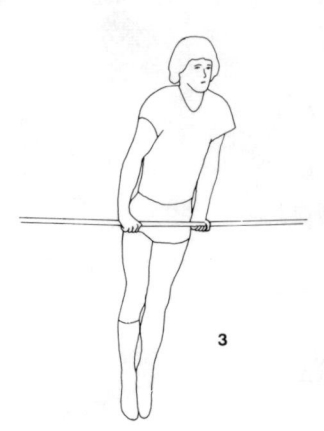
4. Rear Support (Overgrip) 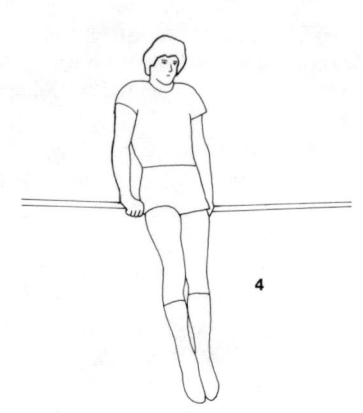
5. Rear Support (Undergrip) 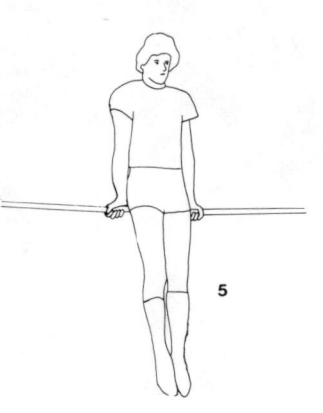
6. Straight Inverted Hang 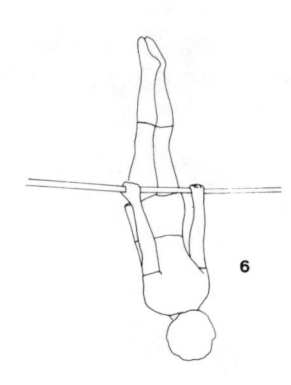
7. Single Knee Hang 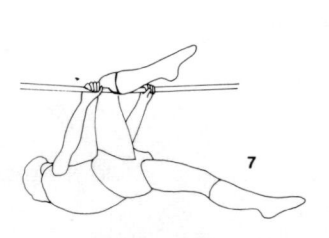
8. Stride Inverted Hang

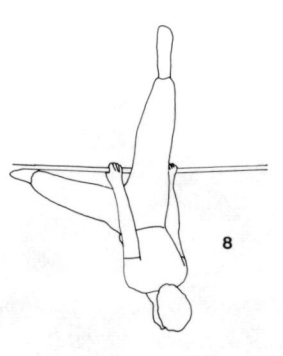

| SKILL | TEACHING TECHNIQUES AND OBSERVATION POINTS |

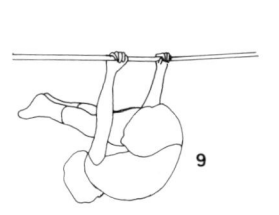

Piked Inverted Hang

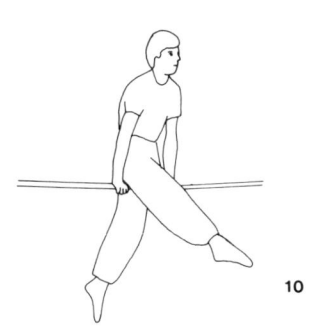

Stride Support

Level I Skills

1. Front Support Swings (also called a Simple Cast)

This skill leads to:
1. further horizontal bar skills. The front support swings and cast are preliminary actions leading into rotational skills such as backward hip circle (pages 179-180)

Lead-up skills:
1. front support (overgrip) (page 172)

Teaching Points for the Skill:
1. Jump to front support and hold the bar in overgrip (illustration #1).
2. Pike slightly at the waist (illustration #2).
3. Extend backward from the bar. Keep the arms straight, the chest high, and look forward (illustration #3).
4. Cushion the return to the bar by piking slightly the instant the body contacts the bar (illustration #4).

Safety and Spotting:
1. Set the bar at chest height. Use chalk to improve the grip. Handgrips are optional.
2. If available, use rubber cushioning around the bar. This lessens the impact of the hip bones and the stomach against the bar.

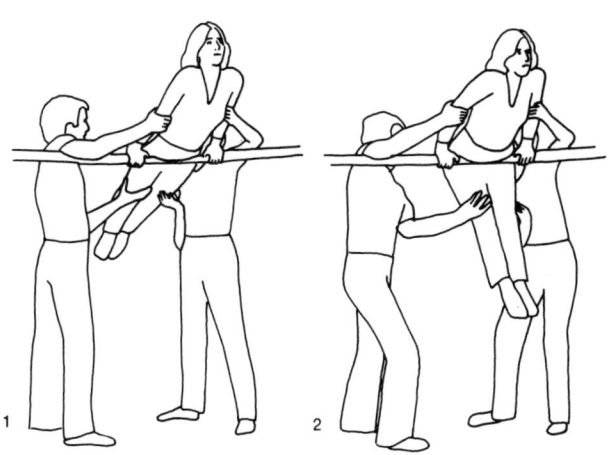

Front Support Swings or Simple Cast

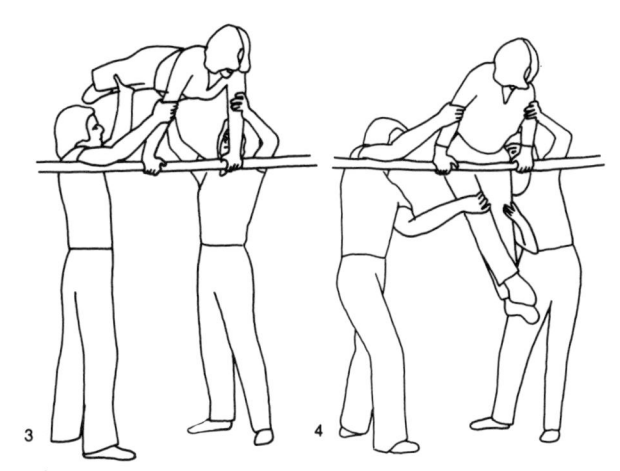

Spotting
1. Spotters support under the arm and the thigh. They elevate the performer during the cast or swing action and cushion the return to the bar.

Common Errors:
Errors in Performance:
1. Bending the arms. *Correction:* The performer should elevate the body, keeping arms extended throughout. If this problem

SKILL	TEACHING TECHNIQUES AND OBSERVATION POINTS

is caused through lack of strength, attempt one or two swings, dismount, and repeat. Work on complementary strength activities (pages 14-18).
2. Piking prior to the return to the bar. *Correction:* The body must remain extended until the moment the body contacts the bar on the return. The pike action at the waist then occurs.
3. Arching the back or bending the legs during the cast. *Correction:* The cast action is initiated by piking and extending from the waist. Once the extension is complete, the arms assist in lifting the body away from the bar. There is no flexion at the knees or hyperextension in the lower back.

2. Front Support-Forward Roll Dismount

This skill leads to:
1. orientation to advanced rotational skills, such as the forward hip circle (pages 185-186)

Lead-up skills:
1. front support (overgrip) (page 132)
2. tucked forward roll on the floor (pages 37-38)

Teaching Points for the Skill:
1. Jump up to front support. Hold the bar in an overgrip.
2. Stretch up so that the arms are extended and the upper body is high above the bar (illustration #1).
3. Pike at the waist, lowering the upper body downward. Rotate the grip around the bar. The legs can remain straight or bent.
4. As the lower body descends, control the speed of action by using the stomach muscles. Try to rotate as slowly as possible. Vary this action by holding the legs in stride position.

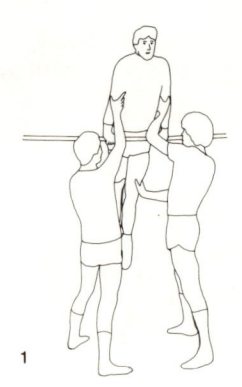

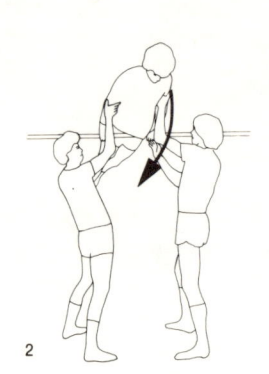

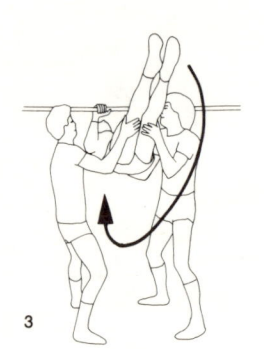

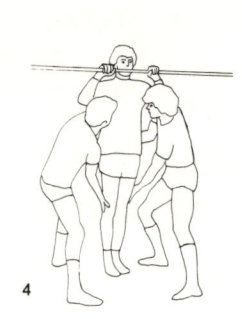

Front Support—Forward Roll Dismount

Safety and Spotting:
1. Use mats; and chalk to improve the grip.
2. Handgrips are optional.

Spotting
1. This skill is quite safe and spotters are optional. If they are used, their duty is to control the performer's rotation.

Common Errors:
Errors in Performance:
1. Lowering the upper body and then being unable to rotate further. *Correction:* Lift the body as high as possible in the

SKILL	TEACHING TECHNIQUES AND OBSERVATION POINTS

support position. Extend the arms and raise the shoulders. Push the bar as low as possible.
2. Inability to control the speed of rotation. *Correction:* This is usually caused by poor stomach and arm strength. This error can be corrected by working on strength and power exercises (pages 14-18)

3. Front Support to Stride Support

This skill leads to:
1. This skill is used as a preparatory move to enter the forward stride circle (pages 184-185)

Lead-up skills:
1. front support (page 172)
2. flexibility exercises (pages 19-20)

Teaching Points for the Skill:
1. This skill can be performed either from standing, or from front support (illustration #1). It is usually easier in front support.
2. Jump to front support (illustration #1). Hold the bar in an overgrip.
3. If the active leg is performer's right leg, lean slightly to the left so that more bodyweight is on left arm than the right.
4. Kick the right leg directly to the right. Do not bend either leg. Point the toes (illustration #2).
5. Bring the right leg forward over the bar allowing support for that instant to be totally on the left arm. Re-grasp the bar (illustrations #3-4). If a forward stride circle follows this action, *the grip must be changed to undergrip.*
6. The faster the action, the easier it becomes.

Front Support to Stride Support

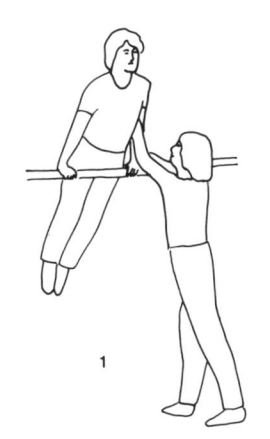

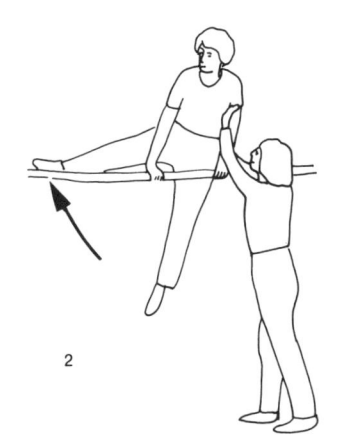

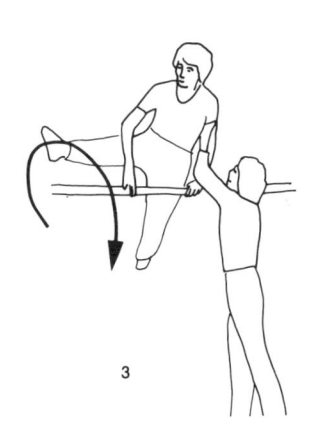

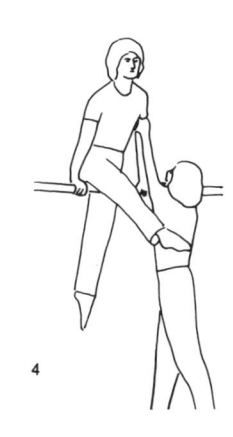

Safety and Spotting:
1. Place a mat below the bar and use chalk to improve the grip.
2. Rubber cushioning can be placed around the bar beneath the performer's legs.

Spotting
1. A single spotter supports the performer with a grip under the upper arm. (An optional form of support is to grip around the upper arm with both hands.)
2. Maximum support should be given during the phase where the performer rests on one arm.

Common Errors:
Errors in Performance:
1. Failing to point the toes. Bending the active leg. *Correction:* The toes must be pointed and the leg kicked directly to the side. If this is not done, the performer will kick the bar.

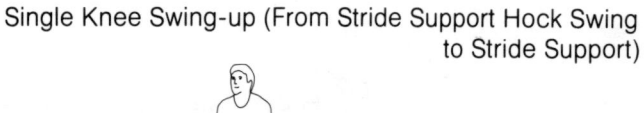

SKILL	TEACHING TECHNIQUES AND OBSERVATION POINTS

2. Failing to release the bar so that the leg can be brought over. *Correction:* If the spotter provides strong support and the performer attempts the action quickly, this problem is soon overcome. Leaning to the left makes it easier to release the right hand, and vice versa. Its cause is mainly fear of sitting heavily on the bar or kicking the bar with the toes.

4. Single Knee Swing-Up (From Stride Support Single Knee Swing to Stride Support)

This skill leads to:
1. orientation to the forward and backward stride circles (pages 184-185)
2. advanced skills on the horizontal bar where one or both legs are brought between the hands such as:
   a) glide-stride inverted swing to stride support pages 187-188 and
   b) glide-piked inverted swing to rear support (pages 191-193)

Lead-up skills:
1. front support to stride support (pages 175-176)
2. single knee hang (page 176)
3. swings in the single knee hang position

Teaching Points for the Skill:
1. Transfer from front support to stride support. Remain in overgrip.
2. Lean backward, bringing the bar to the rear of the flexed leading leg (illustration #2).
3. Keep the arms straight and maintain the extension of the free leg (illustrations #2-3).
4. Allow a good swing under the bar to occur (illustration #3).
5. Drive the free leg down toward the floor. Press down with the arms toward the waist. Rotate the grip from below to above the bars. Return to a stride position (illustrations #3-6).

Safety and Spotting:
1. Set the bar low. Use chalk to improve the grip and place rubber cushioning under the performer's legs (and knee) to make the action more comfortable.

Spotting
1. Spotters stand on the forward side of the bar. They reach under the bar and place one hand behind the performer's back and the other on the knee (illustration #1).
2. Spotters cushion the performer's backward rotation with their support under the back and their resistance against the extended leg (illustrations #2-3).
3. Once under the bar, the spotters "pump" the performer back up to the stride position by pressing down on the free leg (illustrations #3-6).
4. Good stabilization is provided in stride support (illustration #6).

Common Errors:
Errors in Performance:
1. Bending the arms and piking badly at the waist during the descent at the back of the bar. *Correction:* Beginners commit this error because they fear they will fall off the bar as they rotate backward. Spotters can initially control the backward rotation until the performer becomes

Single Knee Swing-up (From Stride Support Hock Swing to Stride Support)

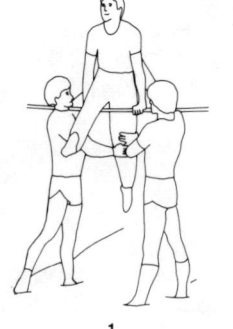

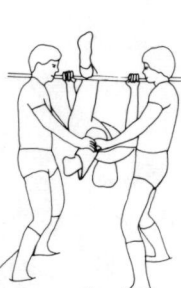

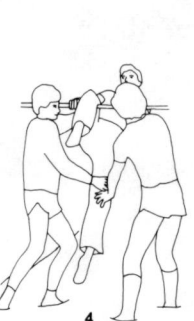

SKILL	TEACHING TECHNIQUES AND OBSERVATION POINTS

comfortable with the action. The performer should push away from the bar so that the arms and upper body remain straight.
2. Failing to use a downward swing of the free leg to provide upward lift. *Correction:* The drive down with the free leg gives much of the lift back to stride support. The performer must time this action so that it occurs at the right instant and provides the necessary upward lift. He must wait until the swing under the bar has ceased and the backswing is about to begin before initiating this action.
3. Bending the arms in order to get up at the back of the bar. *Correction:* This is a common error and occurs because the free leg is not being used sufficiently or the timing is poor. The performer then struggles with the arms to rise with the stride position. Concentrate on using the swing under the bar and generating a strong impulse with the free leg.

Errors in Spotting:
1. Failing to press downward on the performer's free leg in order to elevate him upward. *Correction:* Spotting is relatively simple in this skill. Cradle the descent at the back of the bar, allow for the swing under the bar and then press down on the free leg. This will elevate the performer upward. Do not support *under* the free leg.

Level II Skills

5. Pullover Mount

This skill leads to:
1. more advanced mounts and circles on the horizontal bar, such as back hip circle (pages 179-180)

Lead-up skills:
1. backward roll skills performed on the floor (pages 38-41)
2. skin the cat on the rings or ropes (pages 104-108)
3. strength activities to develop biceps and abdominal strength (pages 14-18)

Teaching Points for the Skill:
1. The pullover can be made easy or difficult depending on the manner the skill is performed.
2. The easiest way is to kick either from the floor or from a box top placed just ahead of the performer. It is recommended that beginners use overgrip rather than undergrip since the final front support position is more comfortable.
3. To perform the skill, stay close to the bar, keeping the arms flexed. Kick upward and backward over the bar. Drop the head backward and pull with the arms when the hips are passing over the bar (illustrations A#1-4).
4. Illustrations B#1-5 show a more difficult way of performing the back hip pullover. The performer must be able to support himself with flexed arms, pike at the waist and pull his lower body over the bar. This takes considerable bicep and stomach strength. The supreme test is to perform the Pullover Mount in overgrip from a hanging position.

Safety and Spotting:
1. A mat should be placed below the bar and chalk used to improve the grip.
2. Rubber cushioning can also be placed around the bar to lessen the impact of the hips and stomach with the bar.

Spotting
1. One or two spotters can be used depending on the performer's ability.

SKILL

TEACHING TECHNIQUES AND OBSERVATION POINTS

2. Spotters cradle to the rear of the knee and behind the performer's back. They lift the performer up and over the bar and then stabilize the final front support position (illustrations B#1-5).

Pullover Mount

(illustration A)

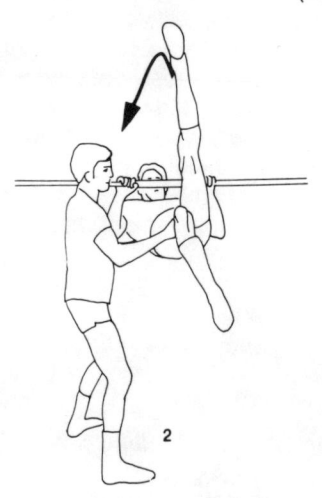

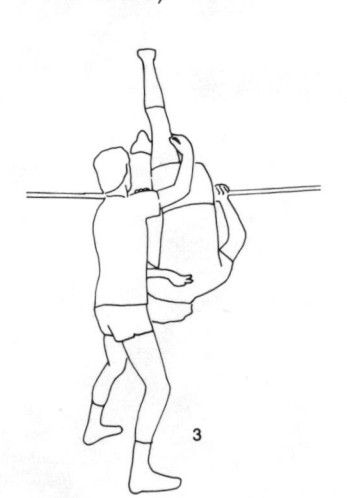

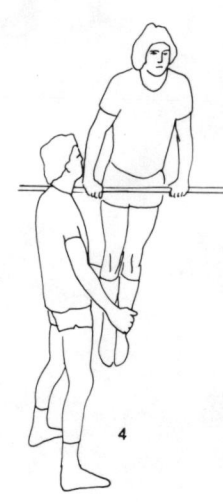

Common Errors:
Errors in Performance:
1. Kicking forward instead of back over the bar. *Correction:* Beginners often make it more difficult for themselves by kicking forward and away from the bar. The legs should be lifted only upward and backward.
2. Straightening the arms and lowering the body. *Correction:* This often occurs because the performer does not have the strength either to maintain a flexed arm position, or to pull with the arms when the hips are shifting over the bars. Use spotter assistance to improve the technique and work to increase bicep strength (pages 14-18).
3. Inability to straighten up once the hips are above the bar. *Correction:* This error occurs because the hips are still not far enough over the bar. The performer must pull harder with the arms to lift the hips higher.

Pullover Mount Both Legs Straight and Together

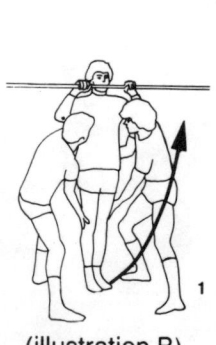

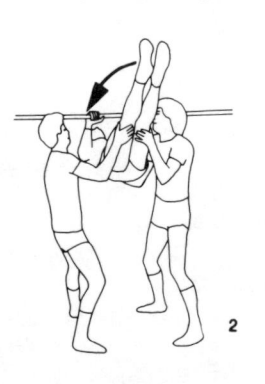

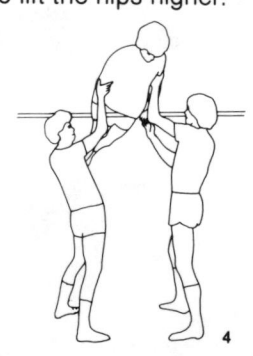

(illustration B)

Errors in Spotting:
1. Confusion in hand actions. *Correction:* There are two phases for providing support:
    a) elevation of the performer over the bar
    b) stabilization of the final front support position. This is best given on the upper arm.

SKILL	TEACHING TECHNIQUES AND OBSERVATION POINTS

6. Backward Hip Circle (Back Hip Circle)

This skill leads to:
1. advanced back hip circle (for example, the free hip circle backward, where the body makes no contact with the bar)
2. orientation for other advanced rotational skills

Lead-up skills:
1. Pullover Mount (pages 177-178)
2. front support swings and cast (pages 173-174)

Teaching Points for the Skill:
1. Begin in front support on the bar using an overgrip (illustration #1).
2. Swing the legs back from the hips and lift from the bar in a cast position (illustration #2).
3. Hold an extended position as the body returns to the bar.
4. Drop the shoulders backward when the hips contact the bar. Pike slightly and allow the legs to swing forward and upward. This will cause the body to rotate around the bar. Hold the thighs against the bar.
5. Straighten the body to slow down rotation and to control the front support position.

Safety and Spotting:
1. Use chalk to improve the grip. Place a mat below the bars. Set the bar at chest height, and if available, use rubber cushioning around the bar.

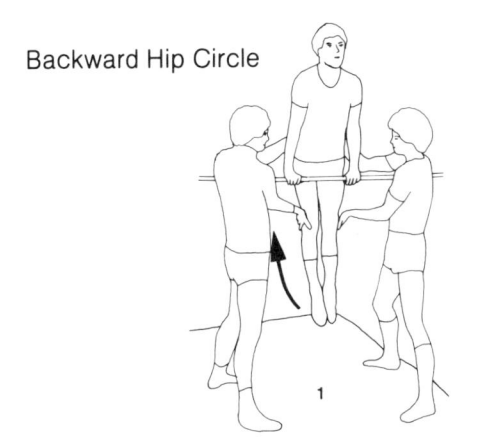

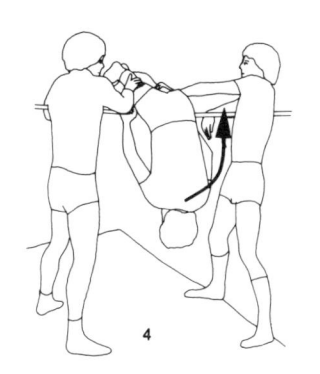

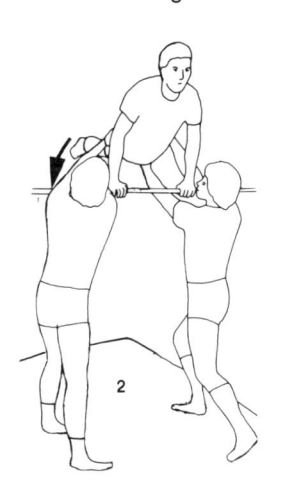

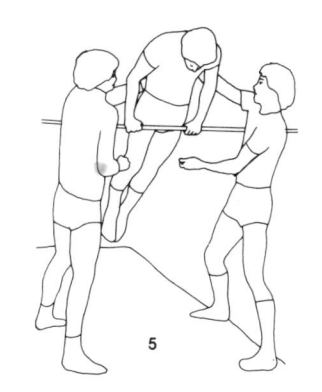

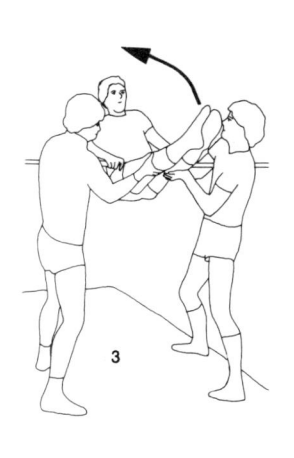

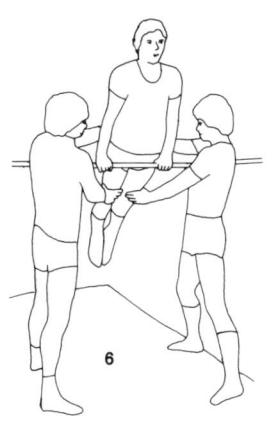

Backward Hip Circle

Spotting
1. Two spotters are preferable. They can provide support for this skill standing in front or to the rear of the bar.
2. The spotter's main duty is to cradle the performer and to make sure that his legs are brought up and over the bar (illustrations #1-4). Notice the strong cradling position (illustration #3) and the stabilization given in the final front front support position.

SKILL	TEACHING TECHNIQUES AND OBSERVATION POINTS

Common Errors:
Errors in Performance:
1. Prematurely falling backward and dropping away from the bar. *Correction:* Wait until the thighs make contact with the bar before leaning backward into the skill. The legs should be rising in front of the bar as the upper body drops backward. Hold the bar against the legs.
2. Not leaning backward when the hips contact the bar. *Correction:* This error usually occurs because the performer is apprehensive about the backward rotation. Spotters should initially cradle the performer through the motion slowly in order to develop his confidence. By cradling strongly below his body, they will be able to hold the performer to the bar and slowly rotate him through the skill. This develops orientation and confidence.
3. Piking the body and bending the legs and arms. *Correction:* It is not altogether wrong for a beginner to pike at the waist and bend at the arms and legs during initial attempts. As confidence develops, the skill can be performed faster and the legs and arms kept straight. With practice the pike action can be reduced until it is minimal.

Errors in Spotting:
1. Not moving fast enough from supporting the performer below the bar to stabilizing him in front support. *Correction:* A quick hand change is necessary to move from one support position to the next. Concentrate on shifting quickly from supporting below the bar to gripping the performer's upper arm in the final front support position. This will be necessary to stop any further rotation occurring at the completion of the back hip circle.

7. Underswing Dismount

This skill leads to:
1. straddle sole dismount (pages 189-190)
2. The underswing action is used as a means of generating high amplitude swings on the full height horizontal bar.

Lead-up skills:
1. front support swings and cast (pages 173-174)
2. back hip circle (pages 179-180)
3. glide swing and return (pages 181-182)

Teaching Points for the Skill:
1. Jump to front support (overgrip).
2. Pike at the waist and lift the legs high in front of the bar. Simultaneously drop the upper body backward. Keep the arms straight and hold the hips against the bar.
3. Extend the hips up and forward and push the bar back behind the head by extending the arms (illustrations #2-4).
4. From an extended position in front of the bar, drop the legs downward and bring the arms forward and upward for the dismount (illustrations #3-5).
5. Once some of the initial confidence has been gained in this skill, begin the underswing dismount with a cast or swing away from the bar. As the body returns to the bar pike at the waist and lift the legs high in front of the bar.

Safety and Spotting:
1. Use chalk to improve the grip, and place a mat under and also ahead of the bar for the landing.

Spotting
1. Spotters place one hand behind the performer's back and the other to the rear of the knee (illustration #1).
2. The spotters then give the performer a cradling support through the extension away from the bar. Spotting is simple and easy to perform.

| SKILL | TEACHING TECHNIQUES AND OBSERVATION POINTS |

Underswing Dismount

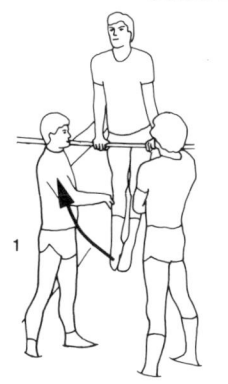

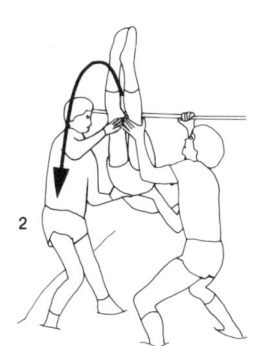

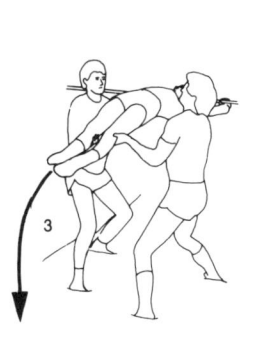

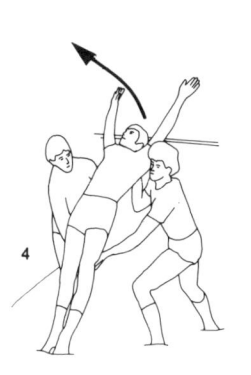

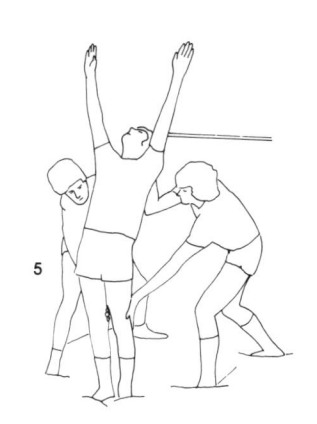

Common Errors:

Errors in Performance:
1. The performer's body (or hips) drop away from the bar immediately after the cast. *Correction:* The performer's hips must come back to the bar as his shoulders drop backward. The initial cast and backward rotation of the underswing dismount is similar to the back hip circle. Spotters can assist by providing strong support during the "drop" backward and the extension into the underswing dismount.
2. The chin is pressed onto the chest, causing the flight to be long and low in the dismount. *Correction:* Keep the head back and attempt to drive the body up into an arc in front of the bar.

Errors in Spotting:
1. Not stepping with the performer during the extension of the dismount. *Correction:* Spotters should allow for distance and flight in the dismount. To support the performer during this action they must move in unison with him away from the bar.

8. Glide Swing and Return

This skill leads to:
1. the glide kip on the horizontal bar (pgs. 190-1)
2. the glide kip on the parallel bars (pgs. 163-5)
3. pike swing to rear support (pages 191-193)

Lead-up skills:
1. all forms of abdomen strengthening exercises (pages 14-18)
2. lead-up activities outlined in Teaching Points for the Skill

Teaching Points for the Skill:
1. With the bar set at chest height, begin by standing in a semi-piked position (illustration A#1). "Run" under the bar to the full extended position (illustration A#4) and "run" back again. Aim at stretching as far out in the extended position as possible. Do not attempt any form of glide.
2. Attempt the glide swing without a return. Assume the starting position, jump upward and pike the legs forward. If the legs cannot be kept straight then bend them a little. Stretch out in the extended position (illustration B#4). Try to avoid having the feet hit the floor midway through the swing. Walk back to the starting position
3. Attempt a full glide and return with straight legs throughout. Jump as high as possible at the rear of the bar (illustration B#2). Pike forward strongly and glide forward without the feet hitting the floor. Extend outward (try to touch a mark set just ahead of full extension), pike back to the return position without the feet hitting the floor.

Safety and Spotting:
1. Set the bar at chest height. Use chalk to improve the grip.

SKILL	TEACHING TECHNIQUES AND OBSERVATION POINTS

Lead-up
Run Out to Extension-Run Back

(illustration A)

2. A thin resilite mat is all that is required below the bar. Thick matting or crash pads may hinder the performance of the glide swing.

Glide Swing & Return

(illustration B)

Spotting
1. Spotting is not essential, although spotters can be used to elevate the performer's legs during the glide. For this form of spotting see pages 190-191.

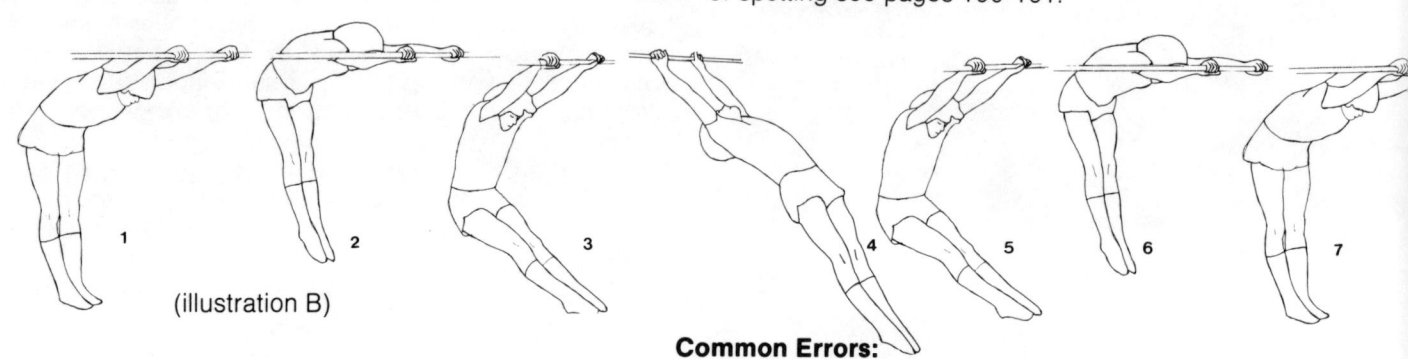

Common Errors:
Errors in Performance:
1. Inability to stop the feet from hitting the floor during the glide.
   Correction: There is no short term correction for this fault, since it indicates lack of abdominal strength. The performer should continue to practice a "run" under the bar, and work to improve abdominal strength (pages 14-18).

Level III Skills

9. Stride Inverted Swings (With Assistance)

This skill leads to:
1. stride inverted hang position and the stride inverted swings are important orientation activities
2. forward and backward stride circles (pages 184-185)
3. glide-stride inverted swing to stride support (pages 187-188)

Lead-up skills:
1. stride inverted hang (pages 172)

Teaching Points for the Skill:
1. Begin by jumping to front support position and straddle one leg over the bar (page 173). Change from overgrip to undergrip
   (*Note:* Although this hand change is not absolutely necessary for the stride inverted swings, it is required for a related skill, the forward stride circle, and needs to be remembered).
   With spotters assisting, lower backward into the stride inverted hang (illustration A#1-3). Hold the stride position throughout. The performer can also climb into the stride inverted position, but this does not give the opportunity of practicing the shift from front support to stride support, or the maintenance of the stride position.
2. To initiate the swings, hold the *back* of the leading or

SKILL

(illustration A)

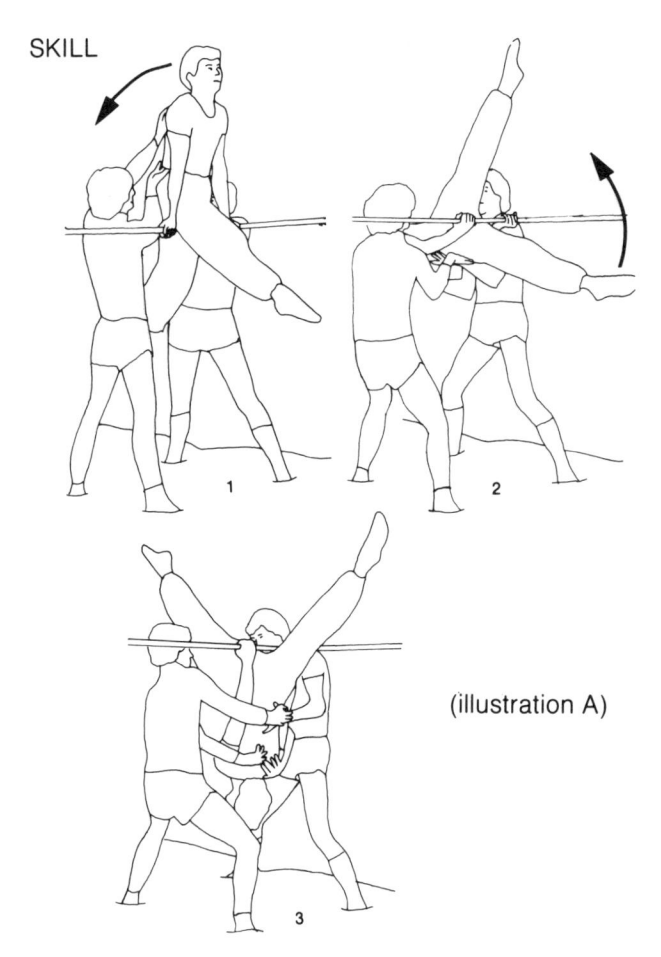

Performer Being Lowered into Stride Inverted Hang from Stride Support

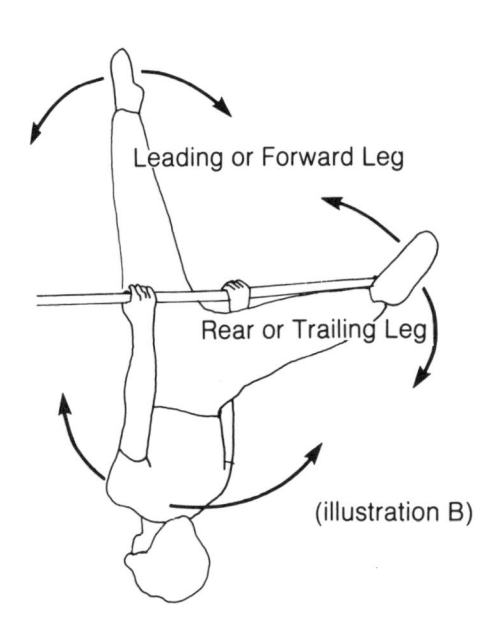

Stride Inverted Swings

(illustration B)

Leading or Forward Leg
Rear or Trailing Leg

TEACHING TECHNIQUES AND OBSERVATION POINTS

forward leg against the bar and press downward with the rear leg (illustration B#1). Pull with the arms. Press the leading leg against the bar.
3. As the return swing occurs, relax the arms.
4. Keep the legs in a wide stride position throughout and hold the upper body as straight as possible.
5. Spotters can assist in initiating the swinging motion, particularly as most beginners will have trouble in becoming oriented to swinging in an inverted position.
6. Spotters *must* elevate the performer back to stride support (which is an excellent orientation practice for the forward stride circle), or the performer can climb out of the stride position.

Safety and Spotting:
1. Place a crash pad or good matting below the bar. Set the bar low. Use chalk to improve the grip.
2. Rubber cushioning can be placed around the bar beneath the performer's legs.
3. The pull on the hands in the inverted position will be considerable. Beginners should swing back and forth two or three times and dismount. Then repeat the skill.

Spotting
1. Spotters cradle behind the back as they lower and elevate the performer. Because of the difficulty in performing this skill alone spotters must assist in initiating the swings. This is done by pushing down on the appropriate leg, or to the rear of the body (illustration A#3). Additional assistance can be given by holding the performer at the wrist.
2. It is important the performer hold the stride position as he is being lowered down into the stride inverted hang. This makes it much easier for the spotters to provide assistance.

Common Errors:
Errors in Performance:
1. Failure to maintain a good stride position. *Correction:* The performer should not bend or pike at the waist. The back must be kept straight and the legs held wide in the stride position. The neck is extended. Do not tuck the chin in.
2. Inability to initiate the piked inverted swings. *Correction:* The swings are initiated by pressing down with the rear leg and simultaneously pulling slightly with the arms. The pull with the arms acts as a pumping action to the swings. Beginners will find this action difficult first, because orientation is distorted by being upside down, and second, because beginners usually have insufficient strength to flex the arms while hanging in an inverted position.

SKILL	TEACHING TECHNIQUES AND OBSERVATION POINTS

10. Forward Stride Circle (also known as a Front Stride Circle)

This skill leads to:
1. more advanced rotational skills on the horizontal bar, such as seat circle forward or backward

Lead-up skills:
1. stride inverted hang and stride inverted swings (page 183)
2. the lead-ups outlined in Teaching Points for the Skill and shown in illustrations A#1-3 and B#1.

Teaching Points for the Skill:
1. Practice stride inverted swings (page 183).
2. Learn to hold a good Y-shaped position from below the bar and into stride support above the bar. (Spotters provide assistance. Notice the undergrip-illustration A#1-3)
3. With a spotter assisting, lift off the bar and lean forward toward the lead leg. Hold the head forward and press the chest down toward the leg (illustration B#1).
4. Attempt the forward stride circle with two spotters:
    a) Lift the front leg up and forward as much as possible with the chest forward and head held up. Step out and aim for as much forward and downward speed as possible (illustration C#2).
    b) Once underneath the bar, begin to extend the body.
    c) On the return to stride support position, extend the body as much as possible and grip tightly on the bar. This will slow down rotation (illustrations C#1-5).

Lead-up
Stride Inverted Hang To Stride Support

(illustration A)

Lead-up
Lift off the Bar, Step Forward, and Press the Chest Forward

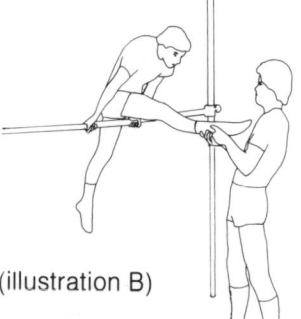

(illustration B)

Safety and Spotting:
1. Set the bar at chest height, use chalk to improve grip and be sure to use an undergrip on the bar.

Spotting (illustrations C#1-5)
1. Spotters stand in front of the bar and prepare themselves to assist in elevating the performer in the second half of his rotation (illustration C#1).
2. One or both hands are placed behind the performer's back and he is boosted upward at the back of the bar (illustrations C#2-4).
3. Both hands are then used to stabilize the performer in the final stride support position (illustration C#5).

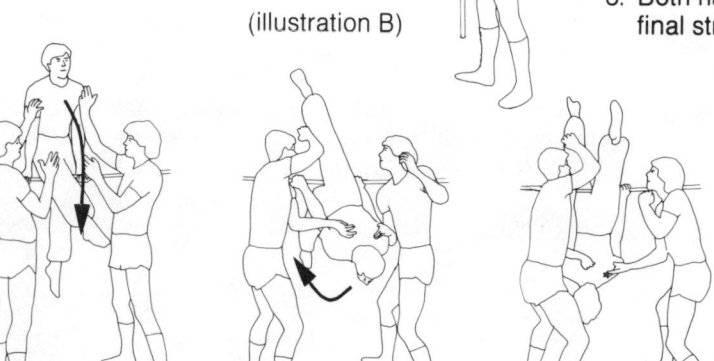

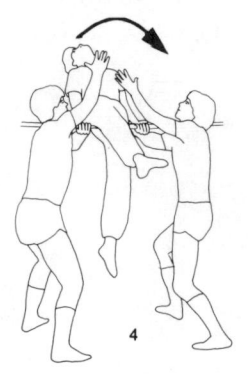

Forward Stride Circle (illustration C)

SKILL	TEACHING TECHNIQUES AND OBSERVATION POINTS

Common Errors:

Errors in Performance:

1. The initial position is incorrect. (the lead leg is held too low, the back is curved, and the arms are bent). *Correction:* The lead leg must be held out forward and parallel to the floor. The chest is well forward and the arms are straight.
2. The performer fails to allow the hands to rotate around the bar causing the arms to bend and the body to bend forward. *Correction:* This problem is caused partially through anxiety and partially through a desire to "fight" back to stride support position. Re-practice the lead-ups, particularly stride inverted hang to stride support with assistance.

11. Forward Hip Circle (also known as a Front Hip Circle)

This skill leads to:
1. more advanced rotational skills on the horizontal bar. It is also used frequently as a connecting move between other skills.

Lead-up skills:
1. forward roll dismount from front support position (pages 174-175)
2. forward stride circle as orientation to forward rotation (pages 184-185)

Teaching Points for the Skill:
1. Begin by practicing the forward hip circle with bent legs (illustrations A#1-5). This makes the skill a little easier.
2. Stretch up high above the bar in front support position (illustration A#1). Push the chest forward and keep the head back.
3. Generate as much downward speed as possible until the body is parallel to the floor (or in a horizontal position). At that point pike strongly at the waist and drive the upper body toward the legs. Keep the bar tight against the body.
4. Rotate the hands until the wrists are above the bar (illustrations A#3-4).
5. Straighten up into front support position (illustration A#5).

Safety and Spotting:
1. Although more difficult than the back hip circle, the forward hip circle is a very safe skill to practice. The bar should be set at chest height, chalk used to improve grip, and a mat set below the bar.

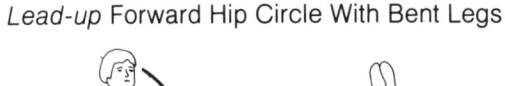

Lead-up Forward Hip Circle With Bent Legs

(illustration A)

Spotting
1. Whether assisting from in front or to the rear of the bar, spotters must concentrate on cradling the performer when he is below the bar (illustrations A, B, C#3)
2. Support under the thighs and back helps to elevate the performer upward as he rises to the rear of the bar. See also illustrations B#1-5 and C#1-5.

SKILL	TEACHING TECHNIQUES AND OBSERVATION POINTS

Forward Hip Circle (Spotting in Front of Bar)

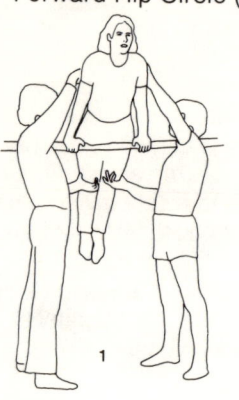

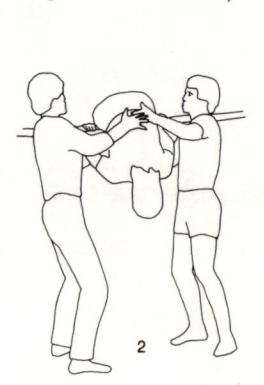

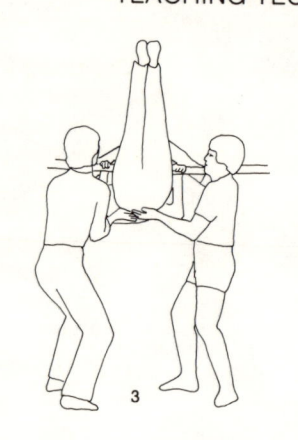

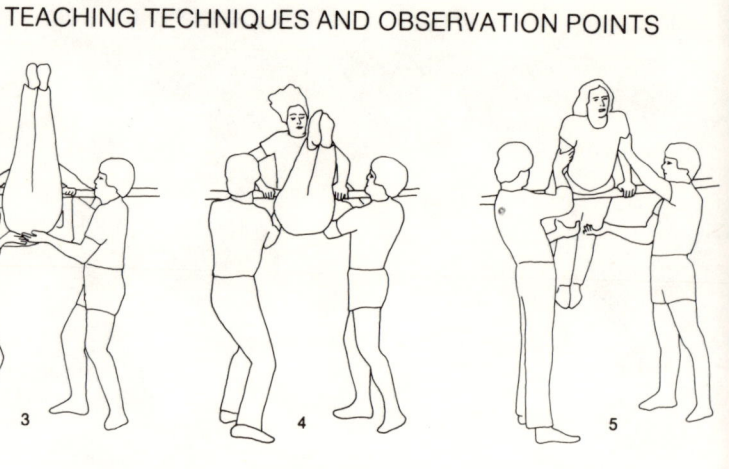

(illustration B)

Common Errors:

Errors in Performance:

1. The body is not extended as the performer enters the skill. *Correction:* The performer must stretch up and extend so that there is more of his weight above the bar than below. This will speed up the entry to the skill.
2. The pike is initiated either too soon or too late. *Correction:* Only practice will indicate the correct timing for piking at the waist. The performer should attempt to reach a horizontal position (body parallel to the floor) or slightly beyond, before piking.
3. The hands are not rotated around the bar so that a re-grasp can be made for the front support position. *Correction:* As the pike action is made, the hands must be shifted quickly around and "ahead" of the body so that the wrists are above the bar in preparation for front support.

Forward Hip Circle (Spotting to Rear of Bar)

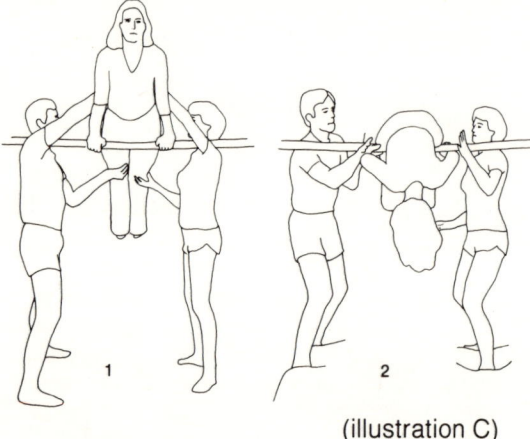

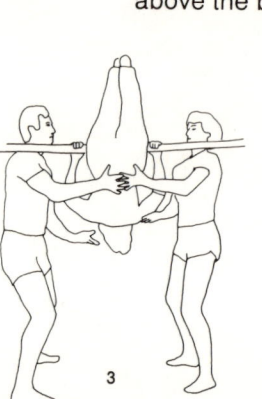

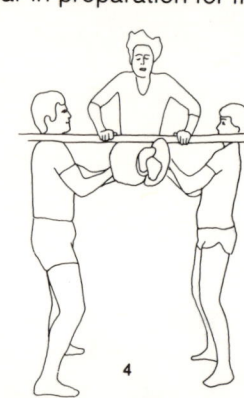

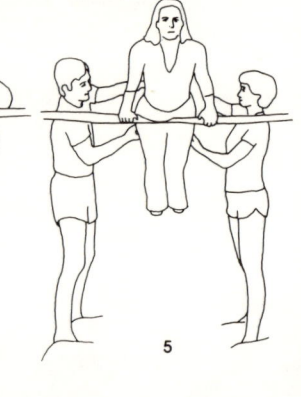

(illustration C)

Errors in Spotting:

1. Spotters are too slow in their assistance. *Correction:* There are two important actions to make in the spotting:
   a) support under the performer's body as he passes under and around the bar.
   b) stabilize the final front support position.

   Because the forward hip circle is performed quickly, spotters must move fast from one support position to the next. Spotting in front and to the rear of the bar is equally efficient.

| SKILL | | TEACHING TECHNIQUES AND OBSERVATION POINTS |

12. Piked Inverted Swing

This skill leads to:
1. piked swing to rear support (page 192)
2. seat circle forward and backward
3. glide-piked inverted swing to rear support (pages 191-193)

Lead-up skills:
1. piked inverted hang (page 173)
2. stride inverted swing (pages 182-183)
3. good physical preparation - strength work on the shoulders, arms and abdomen (pages 13-18)

Teaching Points for the Skill:
1. Begin in the piked inverted hang position (illustration #a).
2. With spotting assistance (optional), lift the legs upward and press the arms back toward the seat (illustrations #a-b).
3. Quickly close to a piked position again and press the arms toward the feet (illustrations #a-c).
4. After the body has swung back under the bar, reverse the process. Lift the legs and press the arms back toward the seat (illustrations #a-b).
5. Rest and repeat.

Safety and Spotting:
1. Set the bar at waist height. Use chalk to improve the grip and place a mat below the bar.

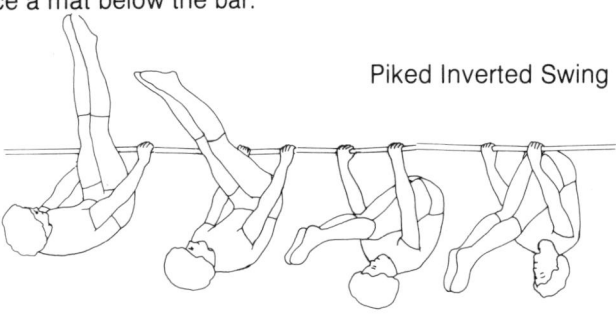

Piked Inverted Swing

Spotting: (b) ← (a) → (c)
1. Spotters can assist by standing either side of the performer and holding the performer's upper arm and around the knee. They pump the performer back and forth, opening and closing the pike at the waist and pressing the performer's arms in the correct direction.
Note: This skill is very tiring and the performers will have great trouble in orienting themselves to the correct movements. Each attempt should be for a short time period. Rest and then repeat the practice.

Common Errors:
Errors in Performance:
1. The legs are too low or too high. *Correction:* Note that the legs in the initial position are parallel to the ground and the chest is angled at approximately 45 degrees to the arms. This is the correct position for piked inverted hang.
2. Lack of orientation and timing in the swings. *Correction:* This error occurs because the performer is upside down and his bodyweight resists the initiating of the swings. Use spotter assistance to gain an understanding of the correct action and work for small periods of time until technique and endurance improves.

Level IV Skills

13. Glide-Stride Inverted Swing to Stride Support

This skill leads to:
1. glide piked inverted swing to rear support (pages 191-193)
2. the glide-stride inverted

Teaching Points for the Skill:
1. Begin by running out to full extension (see illustrations A#1-7, page 182).
2. At full extension, flex one leg at the knee and bring it back between the arms. With practice, attempt to do this with a straight leg flexing only at the hips.

| SKILL | TEACHING TECHNIQUES AND OBSERVATION POINTS |

swing to stride support can be immediately followed by forward or backward stride circles

Lead-up skills:
1. glide swing and return (pages 181-182)
2. single leg swing up (pages 176-177)
3. forward stride circle (optional lead-up, pages 184-185)
4. stride inverted swings (pages 182-183)

3. On the return swing, press down vigorously on the bar with straight arms. This helps to elevate the body up to stride support (illustrations #4-6 below).
4. If this skill is to be followed without a pause by a forward stride circle, the glide-stride inverted swing to stride support must be performed in undergrip (more difficult than in overgrip)

Safety and Spotting:
1. Set the bar at head height, use plenty of chalk and place mats below the bar.

Spotting
1. Spotters allow the performer to run out or glide out below the bar without any assistance. The performer also flexes his leg and brings it back between his arms without spotting assistance.
2. As the performer drives himself up at the rear of the bar to stride support, spotters assist by gripping the upper arm and elevating him upward. They then stabilize him in stride support position.

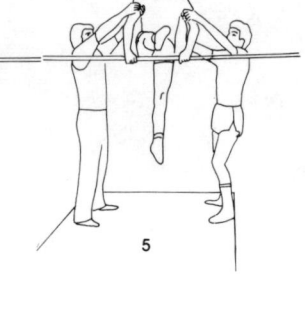

Glide-Stride Inverted Swing to Stride Support

Common Errors:
Errors in Performance:
1. Attempting to bring the leg back between the arms before reaching full extension. *Correction:* Whether the performer initiates the Stride Inverted Swing to Stride Support by "running under the bar" or by gliding under the bar, he must reach full extension at the end of the run or glide before bringing the leg back between the arms. At full extension the arms should stretch above the head and form a straight line with the upper body. Any position less than this makes it more difficult to bring one or both legs back between the arms. It is much easier to bring a bent leg back between the arms than a straight leg. The remaining part of the Glide-Stride Inverted Swing to Stride Support repeats the latter half of the forward stride circle (see pages 184-185).

Errors in Spotting:
1. Overspotting. *Correction:* Spotters must take care that their support of the performer is not too vigorous. Their duty is simply to elevate the performer upward at the rear of the bar and then stabilize him in stride support. They should not "throw" him up into stride support so that the performer over-rotates beyond it.

SKILL	TEACHING TECHNIQUES AND OBSERVATION POINTS

14. Cast-Straddle Sole Dismount

This skill leads to:
1. advanced mounts onto the bar from a cast action, such as cast to squat, stoop, or straddle-sit.

Lead-up skills:
1. Hang under the bar in a bent-legged straddle sole position. Two spotters "pump" swing the performer upward to the rear of the bar. The performer then swings forward under the bar for the dismount. The dismount can also be assisted in the manner shown in illustrations A#3-4.
2. Using a low box, jump to a bent-legged straddle sole position on the bar (illustrations A#1-2). Allow the body to swing under the bar and extend out for the dismount (illustrations A#4)
3. Repeat the skill and with each attempt mount the bar with straighter legs (illustration B). Keep the feet close to the hands. *Do not straddle too wide.*

Teaching Points for the Skill:
1. Begin the straddle sole dismount from front support. Cast back, lifting the hips up and away from the bar (illustrations C#1-2).
2. Pike strongly and straddle the soles of the feet onto the bar (illustrations C#2-3). Swing under the bar and bring the legs together for the dismount and landing.

Safety and Spotting:
1. Set the bar at head height, use plenty of chalk to improve the grip, and place mats well out in front of the bar to cushion the landing.

Spotting
1. Spotters cradle under the back and knee for the pump swing dismount. There is usually no need to give assistance for the dismount in this practice.
2. When the performer jumps to a straddle sole position from a box, spotters concern themselves with giving assistance for the swing under the bar and the dismount (illustration A#3).
3. Once the performer has learnt to "hang on" during the swing under the bar, there is usually no need for assistance.
4. If the decision is to give assistance, spotters should remember the following:
   a) It is very difficult to spot this skill if the performer mounts the bar in a *wide* straddle position.
   b) The speed of swing under the bar becomes greater the closer the performer places his feet to his hand positions on the bar. In this case it is almost impossible to move fast enough to be of assistance.

Lead-up
Jump to Bent-Legged Straddle Sole Dismount

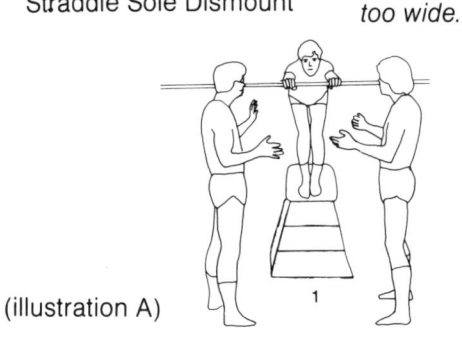

(illustration A)

Lead-up
Jump to Straight-Legged Straddle Sole Dismount

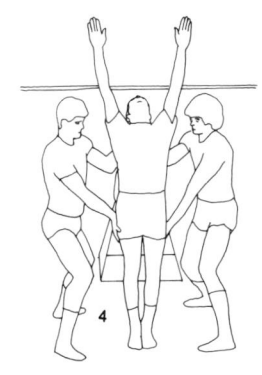

(illustration B)

| SKILL | TEACHING TECHNIQUES AND OBSERVATION POINTS |

Straddle Sole Dismount

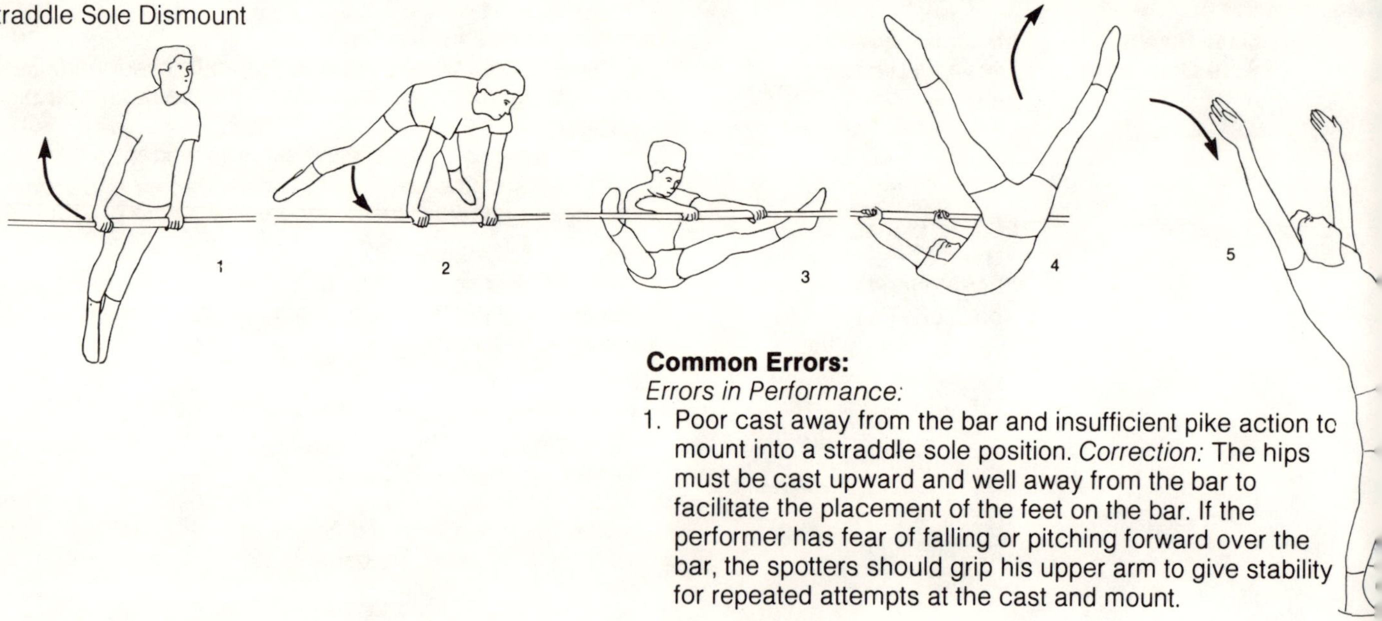

Common Errors:
Errors in Performance:
1. Poor cast away from the bar and insufficient pike action to mount into a straddle sole position. *Correction:* The hips must be cast upward and well away from the bar to facilitate the placement of the feet on the bar. If the performer has fear of falling or pitching forward over the bar, the spotters should grip his upper arm to give stability for repeated attempts at the cast and mount.

Errors in Spotting:
1. See items #3 and #4 in Spotting.

15. Glide Kip

This skill leads to:
1. advanced kipping skills on the horizontal bar, parallel bars and rings. See drop kip on the parallel bars (pages 165-166).

Lead-up skills:
1. glide swing and return (pages 181-182)
2. forward stride circle (pages 184-185)
3. single leg swing up (pages 176-177)
4. forward hip circle (pages 185-186) (optional lead-up)

Teaching Points for the Skill:
1. Practice the lead-ups listed in Lead-up skills. This will establish a good feeling for elevating the body at the back of the bar.
2. Practice the glide swing. Return by bringing the legs back and upward to the bar (illustrations #1-3).
3. Attempt the complete skill with two spotters assisting. The performer should glide out as far as possible so that the body is fully extended (illustration #2). At this point there is a strong pike action at the hips and the legs are brought back to the bar (illustration #3). As the return swing occurs there is a strong downward strike with the legs coupled with a downward push of the arms. This brings the performer up to front support (illustrations #4-5)

Safety and Spotting:
1. Set the bar at head height. Use chalk to improve grip and place a mat below the bar (the mat should not hinder the glide action).

Glide Kip

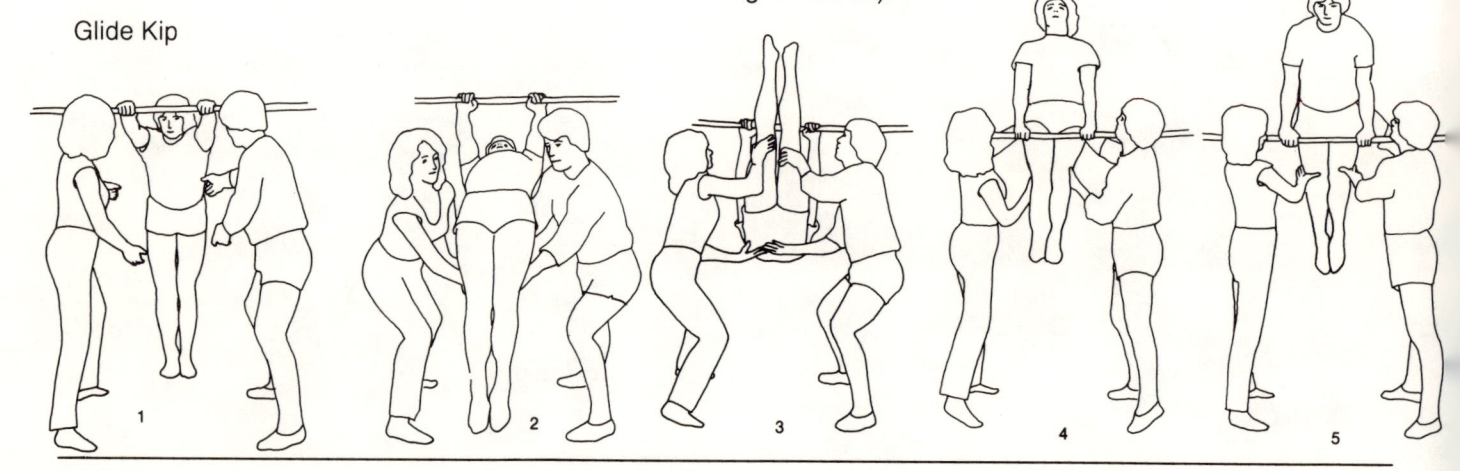

SKILL	TEACHING TECHNIQUES AND OBSERVATION POINTS

Spotting
1. Spotters stand ahead of the bar and assist the performer by:
   a) cradling him out into a full extension at the end of the glide (illustration #2)
   b) bringing his legs back to the bar to initiate the pike at the hips (illustration #3)
   c) driving the performer's body upward at the rear of the bar (illustration #4)
   d) stabilizing him in front support (illustration #5).

Common Errors:
Errors in Performance:
1. The pike at the hips is initiated too late. *Correction:* The pike action must occur when the body is fully extended and not when the return movement is already underway.
2. The extension at the hips is initiated too early so that the hips are driven downward. *Correction:* After he has performed the pike action at the hips the performer must "wait" momentarily until the backswing is carrying his body backward and upward. At that point a vigorous extension at the hips occurs in unison with the press downward with the arms. Spotters can assist in timing this action.
3. The arms bend during the phase when the body is rising upward at the back of the bar. *Correction:* This is a common error among beginners attempting to bully their way up to the front support position. Use spotters to assist in establishing the correct timing for the complete skill. Accurate timing of all actions will remove the need to bend the arms.

16. Glide-Piked Inverted Swing to Rear Support

This skill leads to:
1. further advanced skills on the horizontal bar which incorporate the glide and piked inverted swing.
2. The glide-piked inverted swing to rear support can be followed by forward or backward seat circles

Lead-up skills:
1. glide stride inverted swing to stride support (pages 187-188)
2. piked inverted swing to stride support (illustrations A#1-5)
3. glide kip (pages 190-191)
4. all hip flexibility exercises (see pages 19-20)

Teaching Points for the Skill:
Lead-up: Piked inverted swing to rear support (illustrations A#1-5)
1. Begin in piked inverted hang and *with assistance* begin swinging back and forth (illustrations A#1-2).
2. On a pre-determined count, the spotters elevate the performer at the rear of the bar and into rear support (illustrations A#3-5).
3. During the skill the performer holds the piked position until his body has risen well up at the rear of the bar (preferably to horizontal or above)
4. The arms are kept straight and press downward on the bar as the performer rises upward (illustrations #3-4).
5. When the shoulders have risen well above the horizontal plane of the bar, the performer extends out of the piked position and lowers the legs into rear support (illustrations A#4-5).

| SKILL | TEACHING TECHNIQUES AND OBSERVATION POINTS |

Piked Inverted Swing to Rear Support (With Assistance)

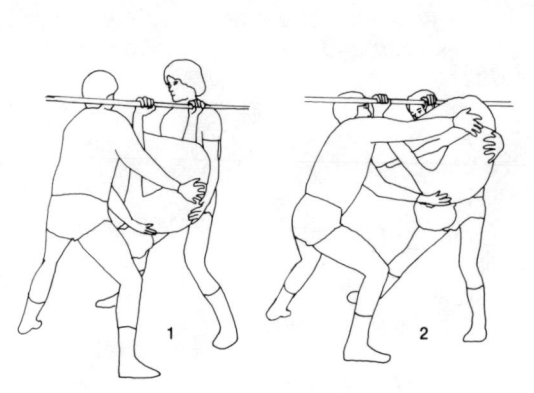

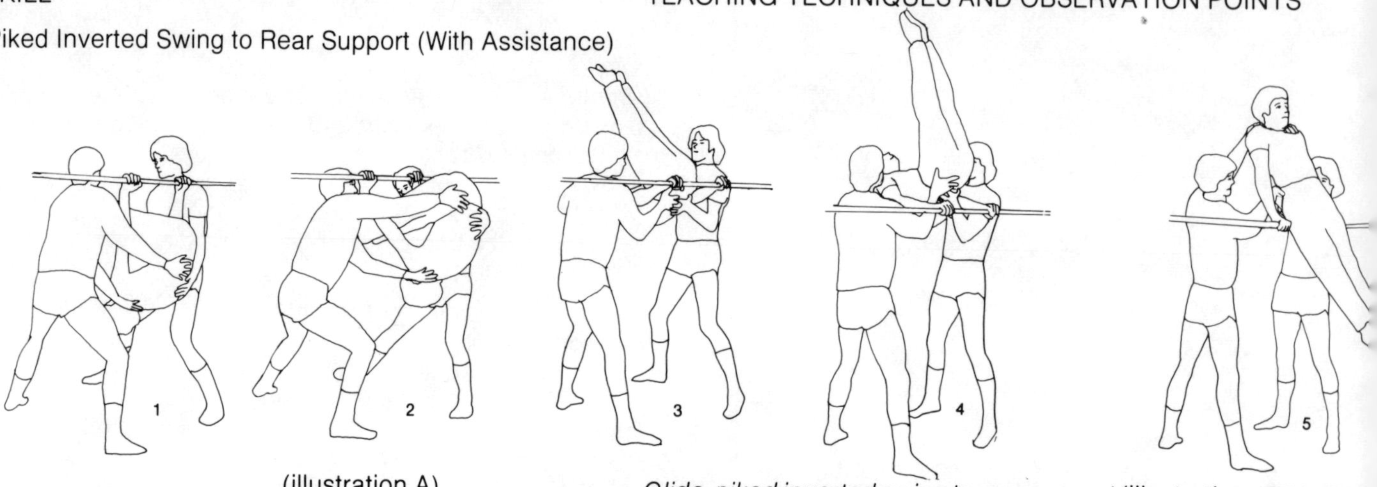

(illustration A)

Glide-piked inverted swing to rear support (illustrations B#1-5)
1. Once oriented to the piked inverted swing to rear support, the performer now initiates the same skill with a glide or with a run under the bar to full extension.
2. For those without sufficient hip flexibility, the legs will be brought back between the arms in a flexed position (that is, bent at the knees).
3. The performer must glide or run out to full extension and immediately pike vigorously at the hips. Both feet are brought back under the bar and between the arms.
4. On the return swing, the performer holds a strong piked position and presses down on the bar with his arms to help elevate his body upward to the rear of the bar..
5. When the performers body has risen above the horizontal plane of the bar, he then extends the legs downward in order to assume the rear support position.

Glide Piked Inverted Swing to Rear Support

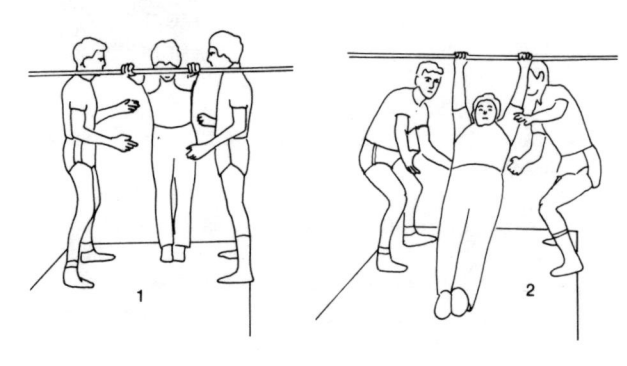

(illustration B)

Safety and Spotting:
1. Set the bar at head height. Use chalk to improve the grip and place a mat below the bar.
2. The performer should be familiar with a dismount from rear support.

Spotting
1. Spotting for this skill is exactly the same as for the glide-stride inverted swing to stride support.
2. Spotters grip the performer in a squeeze grip around the upper arm and help to elevate the performer upward at the rear of the bar and into rear support.

SKILL	TEACHING TECHNIQUES AND OBSERVATION POINTS

3. No assistance is given in the glide or in bringing both legs back between the arms for the double leg shoot-through.

Common Errors:

Errors in Performance:
1. Inability to bring both legs back under the bar and between the arms. *Correction:* Do not initiate the double piked inverted swing to rear support with a glide but run under the bar to *full extension*. Flex both legs as much as necessary to bring the feet back under the bar. Practice this action finishing in piked inverted hang. With spotting assistance, add the remaining part of the skill to finish in rear support.
2. Allowing the legs to drop down toward the floor at the rear of the bar rather than driving up and over the bar into the rear support. *Correction:* This is a potentially hazardous error since the performer drops into a dislocated position. Spotters can counteract this action by making sure that the performer's upper body continues its movement upward toward rear support. The performer should spend more time working on the lead-up practicing of swinging with assistance from piked inverted hang into rear support.

Errors in Spotting:
1. Overspotting. *Correction:* As with the glide-stride inverted swing to stride support, spotters must control the amount of assistance given to the performer. They should take care not to lift the performer up too high above the bar, so that he then drops down on it, or to throw the performer forcefully into the rear support position.

17. Combinations and Routines

(Horizontal bar chest height throughout)
The routines listed in this section are almost exclusively made up of skills taken from Levels I-IV. The instructor should feel free to adjust and modify these routines to the needs of students. Skills not listed in Levels I-IV but with which the instructor is familiar, should be included to make routines more attractive. Assistance should be given by spotters where necessary.

Level I Skills:

1. Jump to front support—front support swings (three times with minimal amplitude)—push back from the bar to dismount
2. Jump to front support—front support swings (three times with minimal amplitude)—cast backward strongly from the bar to dismount
3. Jump to front support—cast away from the bar (twice with moderate amplitude-each time returning to front support—forward roll dismount
4. Jump to front support—front support to stride support and return to front support (right leg)—front support to stride support and return to front support (left leg)—forward roll dismount
5. Jump to front support—front support to stride support—drop back to hock swing and return to stride support (single knee swing up)—return to front support—forward roll dismount.

Level I and Level II Combined:

1. Pullover mount—front support swings—forward roll dismount
2. Jump to front support—front support to stride support—single leg swing up—return to front support—forward roll dismount
3. Pullover mount—backward hip circle—underswing dismount
4. Glide swing and return—jump to front support—backward hip circle—underswing dismount

TEACHING TECHNIQUES AND OBSERVATION POINTS

5. Pullover mount—backward hip circle—shift to stride support—single leg swing-up—return to front support—cast backward and push away from the bar to stand.

Level I, II and III Combined:

1. Pullover mount—forward hip circle—underswing dismount
2. Pullover mount—shift to stride support (change grip)—forward stride circle (change grip)—single leg swing-up—shift to front support—forward roll dismount
3. Jump to front support—forward roll—(no dismount)—pullover—backward hip circle—forward hip circle—underswing dismount
4. Glide swing and return—jump to front support—forward roll with straight legs—touch floor and immediately pull into a pullover mount with straight legs—backward hip circle—underswing dismount
5. Pullover mount with straight legs—front support to stride support (change grip)—forward stride circle—return to front support (change grip)—backward hip circle—forward hip circle—underswing dismount

Level I, II, III, IV Combined

1. Glide kip—forward hip circle—cast straddle sole dismount
2. Glide-piked inverted swing to rear support—half turn on the bar to front support—forward hip circle—underswing dismount
3. Glide-stride inverted swing to stride support—(change grip)—forward stride circle—(change grip)—single leg swing up—return to front support—backward hip circle underswing dismount (make the motion from the backward hip circle to the underswing dismount continuous)
4. Pullover mount—backward hip circle—forward hip circle—cast straddle sole dismount
5. Glide-piked inverted swing to rear support—half turn on the bar to front support straddle leg to stride support—(change grip)—forward stride circle—return to front support—(change grip)—backward hip circle—forward hip circle—cast-straddle sole dismount

Chapter Four
Planning the Program
(A Co-Educational Approach)

A. How to Progress to Group Activities (Stations)

The gymnastic instructor often has problems with insufficient apparatus and too many students. This handbook emphasizes men's artistic gymnastics; however, frequently the class is mixed (co-ed), which results in the use of an increased variety of apparatus accommodating no more than one or two students at a time.

To avoid a situation where large numbers are standing inactive, it is essential to progress from activities where the class works as a unit, to stations where groups work independently. This chapter offers suggestions on how to resolve these problems. The characteristics of women's artistic gymnastics apparatus (beam, vault, uneven bars), have been discussed here, so that the instructor using this apparatus and faced with a co-ed class will be assisted in his planning. An instructor teaching an all-male class is recommended to follow the planning suggestions in this chapter, substituting men's apparatus for women's apparatus when necessary.

1. Introducing Apparatus

Which apparatus should be introduced first, second, third, and so on? Two factors must be considered:
  a) Will the apparatus allow fairly large numbers to use it without too much waiting in line?
  b) Will the apparatus accommodate a mixed group?

Apparatus that accommodates large numbers of both sexes should be introduced early in the gymnastic program. It gives the instructor flexibility in planning, and permits the development of a foundation of activities on which to draw later when the class is divided into groups. Each piece of apparatus must be considered from this standpoint, and also assessed for any other unique characteristic which may influence the planning of the program.

The following list outlines the major characteristics of each piece of apparatus strictly from the point of view of the influence they have on planning and organization.

The apparatus is listed in the order in which it would be introduced to a mixed class. For an all-male or all-female class, the planning options are more flexible.

a) Floor Exercises and Tumbling (i.e., the floor area)
This activity always begins the program.
The floor area is the most important "piece of apparatus" available to the instructor. Floor exercises and tumbling skills are the foundation of gymnastics and provide the building blocks for apparatus skills. The floor area allows the whole class to work together—male and female—and with a little effort, inactivity and waiting in line can be cut down to a minimum. Because floor exercise and tumbling are the keystone to any gymnastics program, they must be introduced first and take precedence over all other activities.

b) Vaulting
Vaulting apparatus should be introduced early in the program because it can accommodate a large mixed group and offers the opportunity for a good level of activity.

A single vaulting station can accommodate up to eight students in a mixed group. The speed of change-over from waiting in line to performing is rapid, and active involvement of students as spotters means few are uninvolved in the performance. If other apparatus is also used for vaulting, the instructor has the possibility of teaching vaulting to the whole class as a unit.

c) The Low Horizontal Bar
Basic skills on the low horizontal bar lead to uneven bar skills for females and high bar skills for males. Because this apparatus accommodates a mixed group, ideally six students at a time, it should be introduced early.

The horizontal bar offers the possibility of active involvement of spotters, and the speed of change-over from performer to spotter, and from spotter to "spectator" can be quite rapid. Many skills allow two performers on the bar at once.

d) The Uneven Bars
The uneven bars can be used for a mixed group (using the lower bar only) or for female performers only. The characteristics of this apparatus are the same as those of the horizontal bar. Because it will take a mixed group, the uneven bars should be initially introduced as a low horizontal bar.

e) The Parallel Bars
Whether this apparatus is introduced prior to the horizontal bar depends on instructor preference.

Some parallel bars are built to use as uneven bars and this feature gives the instructor added flexibility in planning. Used as parallel bars, this apparatus will accommodate six to seven students. For many elementary parallel bar skills, it is possible to work in stream along the apparatus, or to have one student working at one end and one at the other. Spotters are also actively involved in assisting the performer. This apparatus should be used first as a low horizontal bar (one bar removed) and then introduced later as parallel bars for teaching an all male group.

f) The Beam

The beam is usually considered as apparatus for women. It comfortably allows six to eight individuals to work on it as a group activity. There are possibilities of stream movement along the beam from one end to the other and two to three students can perform static or slow-moving skills on it without hindering each other. There also can be active involvement of spotters in assisting the performers.

Skills performed on the beam are in essence floor activities performed at height and in a straight line. This means that if the gymnastic class were all female beam activities could follow as a group activity directly after floor exercises and tumbling.

With the beam set low—with assistance from spotters—and with little to no run-up, it is possible to practice many elementary vaults, such as front, flank, squat, and straddle. If the beam is used this way, it can be added to the existing vaulting apparatus and used by a large mixed group, possibly the whole class.

g) The Pommel Horse

This apparatus should be introduced after students have benefited from the upper body activities on the low horizontal bar, parallel bars and rings. However, some instructors may prefer to introduce the pommel horse prior to the rings because it is stable apparatus, and requires no inverted or swinging skills.

The pommel horse will accommodate four to five students in a group, but with only one working on it at a time. Because of the physical demands of pommel horse skills there is a quick change-over from performer to "spectator." Usually a "male" piece of apparatus, it is very safe and generally needs no spotting. However, this means that those watching and waiting their turn are doing nothing.

h) The Rings

A single set of adjustable rings will comfortably accommodate five to six male students. Like the pommel horse, the physical demands of the skills are considerable. This means that there is a fast change-over from performer to spotter. Many elementary rings skills are duplicated on the parallel bars. These should be taught first because the parallel bars offer greater stability. The ropes can be used as a separate station (leading to the rings) or as part of a station

2. From Floor to Apparatus

Taking into consideration the apparatus characteristics just outlined, the following plan (see pages 197-198) is suggested as one way in which a mixed class could progress from working as a unit on floor exercises and tumbling to groups working at stations on apparatus. In this plan, STEP 1, STEP 2, STEP 3, etc., indicate stages in the development of the gymnastic program. *Each step may be a single lesson or a series of lessons depending upon the rate of progress of the class.* Irrespective of the stage of development, the class always warms up together under the guidance and leadership of the instructor. This also gives the instructor the opportunity to teach the whole class specific activities (which for the greater part of the plan will be floor exercises and tumbling).

B. Sample Lesson Plans

A series of eight lesson plans (pages 199-208) follows the Progressing to Group Activities Plan (pages 197-198), and is directly related to it. Each of the sample lesson plans illustrates one possible lesson from those that could be taught in each of the steps outlined in the plan. Each skill listed in these lesson plans is accompanied by page numbers indicating where lead-ups and teaching techniques can be found in this handbook.

These sample lesson plans are designed with the following conditions in mind:

1. Class size 24-28, male and female, with a single instructor.
2. Each lesson approximately 45 minutes to one hour.
3. Changing clothes, organization of equipment and warm-ups take approximately one quarter of the total class time. As the program progresses, students learn their equipment duties by heart and the time taken for shifting equipment is cut to a minimum.
4. The instructor will use a station approach for teaching apparatus skills. When the class is divided into stations, students will work at differing levels according to their individual levels of ability. The instructor will give individual instruction as he or she moves from station to station.
5. Audio visual aids (wall charts, pictorial skill sequences continuous film loops, etc.) will be used to assist the instructor, particularly when the class is divided into groups.

PROGRESSING TO GROUP ACTIVITIES PLAN
A PLAN FOR PROGRESSING FROM THE WHOLE CLASS
ON FLOOR EXERCISES TO GROUPS ON APPARATUS

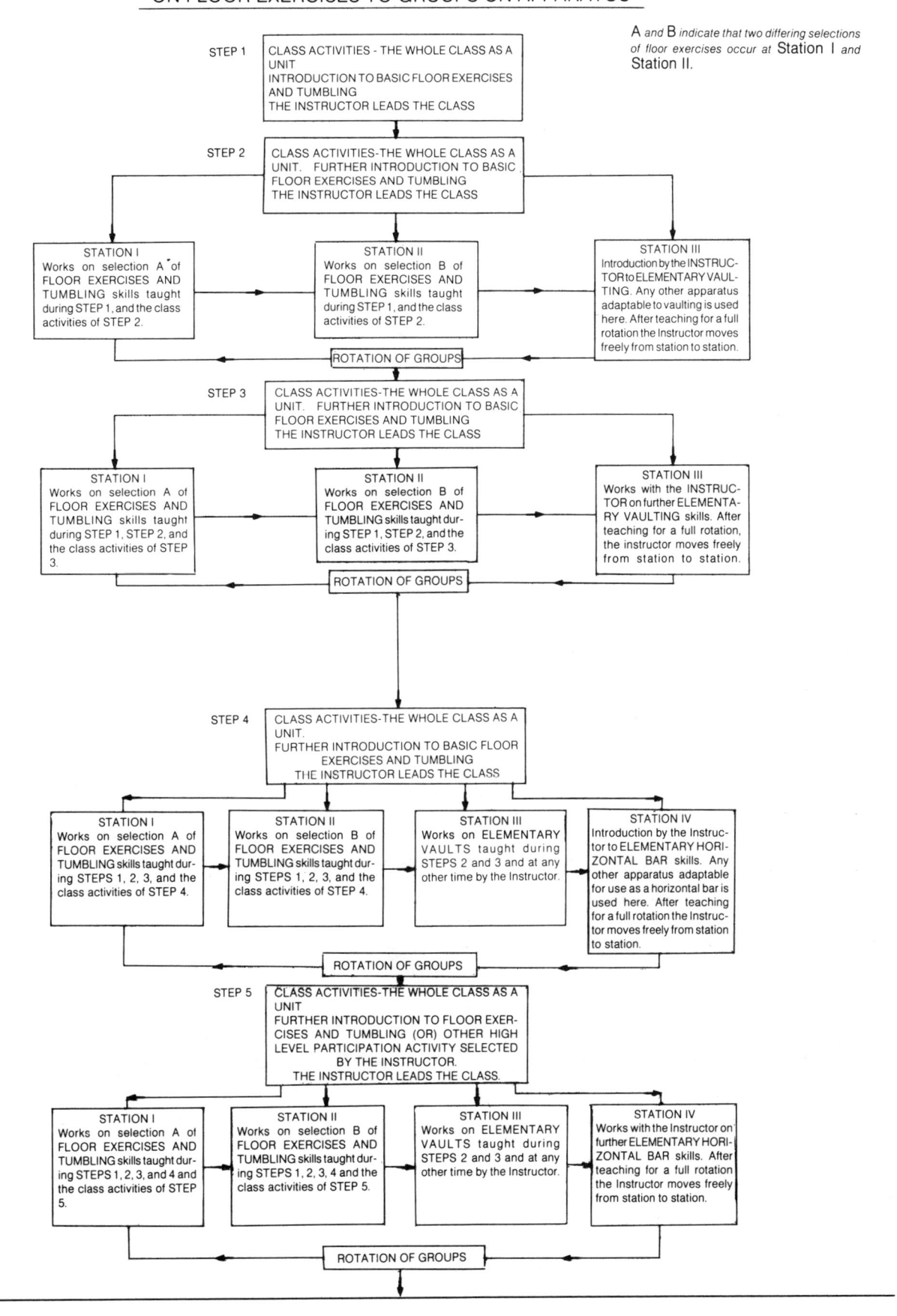

A and B indicate that two differing selections of floor exercises occur at **Station I** and **Station II**.

STEP 1 — CLASS ACTIVITIES - THE WHOLE CLASS AS A UNIT
INTRODUCTION TO BASIC FLOOR EXERCISES AND TUMBLING
THE INSTRUCTOR LEADS THE CLASS

STEP 2 — CLASS ACTIVITIES-THE WHOLE CLASS AS A UNIT. FURTHER INTRODUCTION TO BASIC FLOOR EXERCISES AND TUMBLING
THE INSTRUCTOR LEADS THE CLASS

- **STATION I**: Works on selection A of FLOOR EXERCISES AND TUMBLING skills taught during STEP 1, and the class activities of STEP 2.
- **STATION II**: Works on selection B of FLOOR EXERCISES AND TUMBLING skills taught during STEP 1, and the class activities of STEP 2.
- **STATION III**: Introduction by the INSTRUCTOR to ELEMENTARY VAULTING. Any other apparatus adaptable to vaulting is used here. After teaching for a full rotation the Instructor moves freely from station to station.

ROTATION OF GROUPS

STEP 3 — CLASS ACTIVITIES-THE WHOLE CLASS AS A UNIT. FURTHER INTRODUCTION TO BASIC FLOOR EXERCISES AND TUMBLING
THE INSTRUCTOR LEADS THE CLASS

- **STATION I**: Works on selection A of FLOOR EXERCISES AND TUMBLING skills taught during STEP 1, STEP 2, and the class activities of STEP 3.
- **STATION II**: Works on selection B of FLOOR EXERCISES AND TUMBLING skills taught during STEP 1, STEP 2, and the class activities of STEP 3.
- **STATION III**: Works with the INSTRUCTOR on further ELEMENTARY VAULTING skills. After teaching for a full rotation, the instructor moves freely from station to station.

ROTATION OF GROUPS

STEP 4 — CLASS ACTIVITIES-THE WHOLE CLASS AS A UNIT.
FURTHER INTRODUCTION TO BASIC FLOOR EXERCISES AND TUMBLING
THE INSTRUCTOR LEADS THE CLASS

- **STATION I**: Works on selection A of FLOOR EXERCISES AND TUMBLING skills taught during STEPS 1, 2, 3, and the class activities of STEP 4.
- **STATION II**: Works on selection B of FLOOR EXERCISES AND TUMBLING skills taught during STEPS 1, 2, 3, and the class activities of STEP 4.
- **STATION III**: Works on ELEMENTARY VAULTS taught during STEPS 2 and 3 and at any other time by the Instructor.
- **STATION IV**: Introduction by the Instructor to ELEMENTARY HORIZONTAL BAR skills. Any other apparatus adaptable for use as a horizontal bar is used here. After teaching for a full rotation the Instructor moves freely from station to station.

ROTATION OF GROUPS

STEP 5 — CLASS ACTIVITIES-THE WHOLE CLASS AS A UNIT
FURTHER INTRODUCTION TO FLOOR EXERCISES AND TUMBLING (OR) OTHER HIGH LEVEL PARTICIPATION ACTIVITY SELECTED BY THE INSTRUCTOR.
THE INSTRUCTOR LEADS THE CLASS.

- **STATION I**: Works on selection A of FLOOR EXERCISES AND TUMBLING skills taught during STEPS 1, 2, 3, and 4 and the class activities of STEP 5.
- **STATION II**: Works on selection B of FLOOR EXERCISES AND TUMBLING skills taught during STEPS 1, 2, 3, 4 and the class activities of STEP 5.
- **STATION III**: Works on ELEMENTARY VAULTS taught during STEPS 2 and 3 and at any other time by the Instructor.
- **STATION IV**: Works with the Instructor on further ELEMENTARY HORIZONTAL BAR skills. After teaching for a full rotation the Instructor moves freely from station to station.

ROTATION OF GROUPS

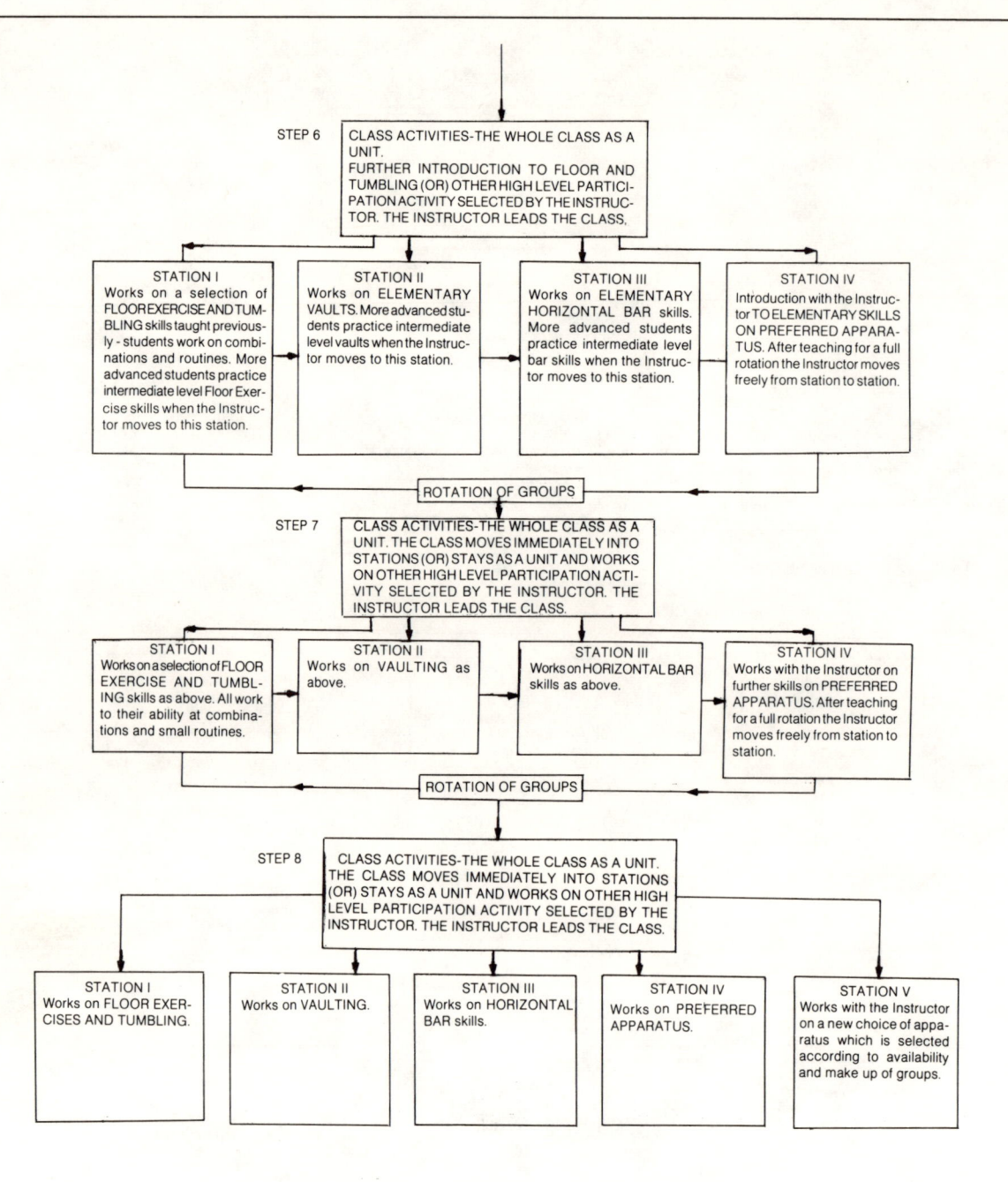

STEP 6 — CLASS ACTIVITIES-THE WHOLE CLASS AS A UNIT.
FURTHER INTRODUCTION TO FLOOR AND TUMBLING (OR) OTHER HIGH LEVEL PARTICIPATION ACTIVITY SELECTED BY THE INSTRUCTOR. THE INSTRUCTOR LEADS THE CLASS.

STATION I — Works on a selection of FLOOR EXERCISE AND TUMBLING skills taught previously - students work on combinations and routines. More advanced students practice intermediate level Floor Exercise skills when the Instructor moves to this station.

STATION II — Works on ELEMENTARY VAULTS. More advanced students practice intermediate level vaults when the Instructor moves to this station.

STATION III — Works on ELEMENTARY HORIZONTAL BAR skills. More advanced students practice intermediate level bar skills when the Instructor moves to this station.

STATION IV — Introduction with the Instructor TO ELEMENTARY SKILLS ON PREFERRED APPARATUS. After teaching for a full rotation the Instructor moves freely from station to station.

ROTATION OF GROUPS

STEP 7 — CLASS ACTIVITIES-THE WHOLE CLASS AS A UNIT. THE CLASS MOVES IMMEDIATELY INTO STATIONS (OR) STAYS AS A UNIT AND WORKS ON OTHER HIGH LEVEL PARTICIPATION ACTIVITY SELECTED BY THE INSTRUCTOR. THE INSTRUCTOR LEADS THE CLASS.

STATION I — Works on a selection of FLOOR EXERCISE AND TUMBLING skills as above. All work to their ability at combinations and small routines.

STATION II — Works on VAULTING as above.

STATION III — Works on HORIZONTAL BAR skills as above.

STATION IV — Works with the Instructor on further skills on PREFERRED APPARATUS. After teaching for a full rotation the Instructor moves freely from station to station.

ROTATION OF GROUPS

STEP 8 — CLASS ACTIVITIES-THE WHOLE CLASS AS A UNIT. THE CLASS MOVES IMMEDIATELY INTO STATIONS (OR) STAYS AS A UNIT AND WORKS ON OTHER HIGH LEVEL PARTICIPATION ACTIVITY SELECTED BY THE INSTRUCTOR. THE INSTRUCTOR LEADS THE CLASS.

STATION I — Works on FLOOR EXERCISES AND TUMBLING.

STATION II — Works on VAULTING.

STATION III — Works on HORIZONTAL BAR skills.

STATION IV — Works on PREFERRED APPARATUS.

STATION V — Works with the Instructor on a new choice of apparatus which is selected according to availability and make up of groups.

Possible Options for Choice of Apparatus at Station IV and V, Steps 6, 7 and 8.

1. Introduce the parallel bars to males or remove one bar and introduce further low horizontal bar skills to females.
2. Introduce uneven bar skills to females or use the lower bar of the uneven bars for further horizontal bar skills for males.
3. Introduce pommel horse skills to males or remove the pommels and use this apparatus as an additional vaulting station for females.
4. Introduce the beam to females and use this apparatus for further practice on elementary vaults for males.

Lesson One - Introduction of Floor Exercises and Tumbling

1. Introduction

In this lesson, participants will be introduced to basic floor exercises and tumbling, the foundation of gymnastics. The class stays as a unit throughout this lesson. This lesson occurs in Step 1 of the Program to Group Activities Plan.

Equipment needed: mats and benches.

Advance preparation:
  a) Check to see that the equipment is in good repair.
  b) Have prepared the names of students to bring out equipment.
  c) Plan the best arrangement for partner activities.
  d) Plan the gymnasium lay-out for the best use of equipment (maximum activity, minimum of waiting in line).

Class preparation:
  a) Supervise the lay-out of equipment.
  b) Bring the class together. Explain the goals of the gymnastic bloc, the methods of instruction and grading. Outline the requirements relating to attendance, dress and basic safety.

2. Objectives

By the end of this lesson, participants will have been introduced to the following skills:
  a) Tip-up (elbow balance, page 31).
  b) Headstand (pages 31-32).
  c) Tucked forward roll (pages 37-38).
  d) Front scale (page 36).
  e) Forward roll-jump-pirouette (pages 44-45).
  f) Headstand-forward roll (pages 41-42).

DIAGRAM 1

Suggested plan for warm-up (all students in front of the instructor).

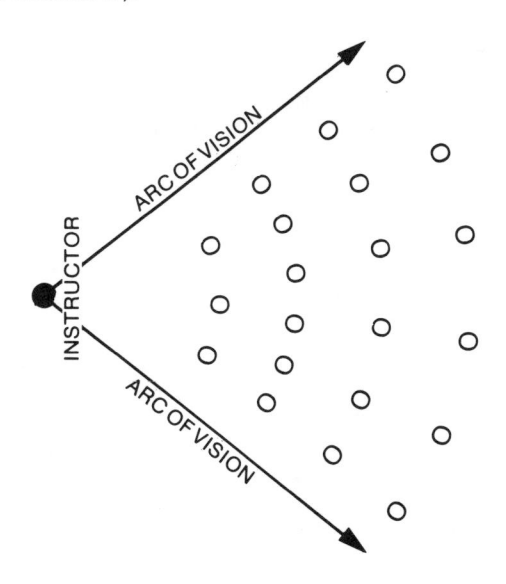

DIAGRAM 2

Suggested lay-out for Floor Exercises and Tumbling. Students work across the mats.

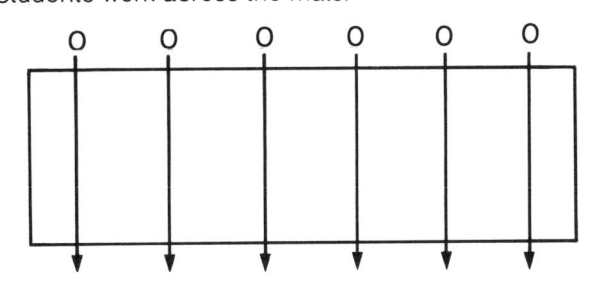

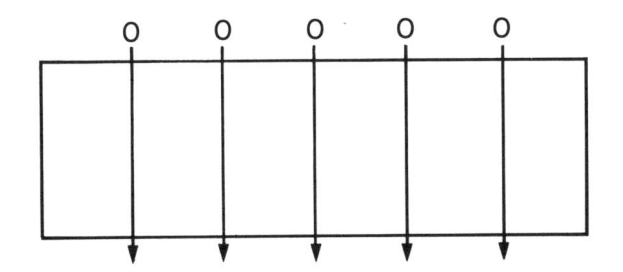

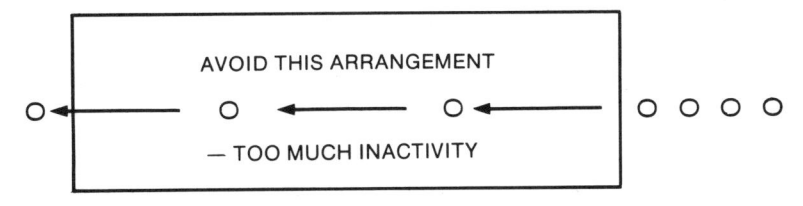

AVOID THIS ARRANGEMENT
— TOO MUCH INACTIVITY

3. Warm-Up

  a) Begin with a fast moving activity to generate excitement and interest. Emphasize individual activity. *Avoid* any activity that demands waiting in line.
  b) Commence warm-up activities (single and partner). Emphasize first easy rhythmic movements, then move to specific flexibility activities (pages 19-20). Include some non-exhaustive power activities (see pages 14-18).
  c) Work on balance and coordination. Experiment with balancing on: (i) one foot; (ii) one hand and one foot; (iii) two hands and one knee; (iv) one knee and one hand. Have the class attempt simple scales (straddle scale and front scale). Try the front scale with (i) arms down; (ii) both arms held out to the side; (iii) both arms forward.
  d) Emphasize orientation and control. (Jump to half and full pirouettes on the spot).
  e) Include some fun partner activities of a light combative nature (pulling, pushing, and lifting each other). This will get the students used to each other's weight both in a static and moving situation. This will be important for later spotting activities.

4. Review

There will be nothing to review in the first lesson.

5. New Material

Floor Exercises and Tumbling (all skills performed *across* the mats).
- a) Introduction to the tucked forward roll: (pages 37-38)
  - i) Practice the tucked forward roll from a kneeling position on benches (to raise the hips).
  - ii) Remove the benches—enter the tucked forward from (a) a squat; (b) a crouch; (c) one foot forward and one foot back; (d) straddle stance (legs brought together entering the roll).
  - iii) The class learns to come out of the roll with: (a) a push from the floor; (b) a push from the floor and a jump upward; (c) without a push off (with or without a jump upward); (d) with the arms stretched forward.
  - iv) A half pirouette is added at the end of the roll, i.e. tucked forward roll, jump, half pirouette.
  - v) A three quarter pirouette and a full pirouette are added at the end of the roll.
  - vi) Spotting is used where necessary and demonstrations are given.
- b) Introduction to the headstand (tucked and extended) (pages 31-32).
  - i) Instructor shows hand and head positioning for headstand.
  - ii) The instructor demonstrates the tucked headstand and the spotting methods used.
  - iii) The class is taught the following variations of a headstand: (a) tucked, (b) extended (legs straight upward), (c) legs straight up and straddled, (d) legs straight up and in stride position, (e) legs straight, together and semi-piked, (f) legs straight, together, and parallel to the floor, (g) legs straight, straddled and parallel to the floor.
- c) A forward roll is added to the headstand (leading into and leading out of the headstand) (pages 41-42).
  - i) Students practice: (a) tucked forward roll-pause-headstand (the instructor shows how the spotters must allow for the distance covered in the roll), (b) tucked forward roll-tip-up (and with assistance from a spotter), kicking from the floor into a headstand.
  - ii) The instructor demonstrates a headstand with a forward roll out.
  - iii) Spotting is shown. The class practices the skill.
- d) Combinations
  - i) Students are challenged to make up their own variations of the skills taught above. The instructor demonstrates a sample combination, e.g. tip-up-headstand-forward roll-jump-pirouette-pause-front-scale-stand.
  - ii) A student is chosen to attempt the same sequence. The instructor shows how the spotter must move from one skill to the next in order to assist.

6. Culmination

- a) The class is brought together. The instructor comments on the efforts of the class. Requirements for the next lesson are outlined.
- b) The instructor reminds those chosen to put apparatus away of the required methods for carrying and stacking the apparatus.
- c) The apparatus is put away. The instructor supervises.

Lesson Two - Floor Exercises and Tumbling Continued

1. Introduction

This lesson will continue the introduction of floor exercises and tumbling. The class stays as a unit throughout this lesson. This lesson occurs during *STEP 1* of the Progressing to Group Activities Plan.

Equipment needed: mats and crash pads (if available, but not absolutely necessary).

Advance preparation:
- a) Check equipment.
- b) Have prepared teams to bring out and return mats and crash pads.
- c) Recheck the arrangement for partnering students. Re-arrange if necessary.
- d) Plan the gymnasium lay-out.
- e) Prepare a tape of slow beat popular music with gaps on the tape which are long enough to allow for demonstration and explanation of flexibility and rhythmic exercises.

Class preparation:

Lay out the mats as per the diagram in Lesson One. If crash pads are available set these at the side of the gymnasium until required.

2. Objectives

By the end of this lesson, participants will have been introduced to the following skills:
- a) Handstand (pages 33-35).
- b) Handstand-forward roll (pages 45-46).

3. Warm-Up

- a) Explain the object and method of warm-up. (This will be a trial use of music for flexibility exercises. If it is successful the instructor will use the method again in future lessons. Exercise and rhythmic demands will be changed frequently to maintain interest.)
- b) Play the tape and work through the flexibility activities. Use light stretching exercises. No vigorous ballistic movements (see page 19).
- c) Demonstrate two examples of partner flexibility exercises. Explain the technique of stretching preferred and the responsibilities involved.

4. Review

Practical review of skills taught previously. Refresh technical aspects of skills and spotting.

5. New Material

a) Introduction to the handstand: (pages 33-35)
  i) Work through momentary tucked handstand with a two footed take-off (often called "rabbit hops," see page 33). Demonstrate the skill and challenge participants to see how long they can hold a tucked handstand position. Spotters are used where required.
  ii) Move to "Kick and point" (page 34) Demonstrate the skill and emphasize correct leg action.
  iii) Demonstrate a momentary handstand with a one footed take-off. Kick the legs back and forth vigorously in the air. Challenge participants with "How many kicks can you manage in the air?"
  iv) Move to partner-assisted handstands (pages 34-35). Demonstrate correct technique for the performer and assistance from one or two spotters.
  v) Have performers initially step back down out of the handstand.
  vi) Demonstrate a forward roll out of a handstand (pages 45-46). Emphasize how the spotters hold the ankles and lower the performer into the roll (page 45).
  vii) If a crash pad is available, have performers kick into a handstand and roll forward onto the crash pad. Spotters assist at the side of the performer.

b) Combinations of skills
  i) Demonstrate a front scale and lower the hands and kick into a handstand. Have performers attempt the skill with assistance.
  ii) Demonstrate a combination of a tucked forward roll-step-kick to handstand-forward roll Emphasize how the spotters must shift their positions to help the performer. Challenge the students to make up combinations according to their individual ability. Stress team work between performer and spotter.
  iii) Complete the instruction with a short informative talk on the importance of form and style in gymnastics. Indicate briefly how an Olympic performance is scored and what causes the score to be reduced. Illustrate with correct and incorrectly performed skills.

6. Culmination

a) The class is brought together. Requirements for the next class are outlined. Those participants chosen to bring out new apparatus (e.g. vaulting equipment) are warned of their duties and what is required of them.
b) Those putting apparatus away are reminded of the correct method for carrying and stacking equipment.
c) The apparatus is put away. The instructor supervises.

Lesson Three - Introduction to Vaulting

1. Introduction

This lesson will introduce the skills of vaulting. The class stays as a unit for the warm-up and floor exercise skills then divides into three groups—STATION I - Floor Exercises, STATION II - Floor Exercises, STATION III - Vaulting. This lesson would occur during Step 2 of the Progressing to Group Activities Plan.

Equipment needed:
a) Floor exercise mats and crash pads (if available).
b) Vaulting apparatus (mats, box or horse, and take-off apparatus). Also any other apparatus that can be used for introductory vaulting, i.e. the beam or pommel horse with pommels removed.)

Advance preparation:
a) Check apparatus. In particular check the vaulting horse to see that legs extend and retract *easily*. Make sure that the take-off apparatus is in good order.
b) Organize teams to bring out the equipment.
c) Plan the gymnasium lay-out (see suggested lay-out diagram below).
d) Plan how the class will be split into three groups. Consider the benefits of various group arrangements and pick the system best suited to the needs of the class.
e) Prepare skill lists on clipboards to be set by Stations I & II. Make sure that there is enough variety and challenge in skills to satisfy a group shifting from one floor exercise station to another.

DIAGRAM 1

Suggested lay-out of the gymnasium. Instructor should be positioned to oversee complete class.

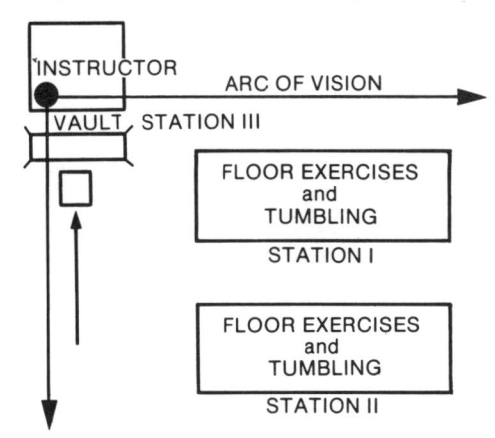

Class preparation:
a) Supervise lay-out of equipment. Make a mental note of "snags" that cause delays. Consider solutions to these problems so that the equipment can be brought out quickly but safely on the next occasion.

2. Objectives

By the end of this lesson, participants will have been introduced to the following skills:

Floor
  a) Tucked backward roll (pages 38-39).
  b) Straddle backward roll (pages 40-41).

Vaulting
  a) Orientation to apparatus (see pages 124-125).
  b) Front vault (pages 127-128).
  c) Flank vault (pages 129-130).

3. Warm-Up

a) Bring the class together in the floor exercise area and begin warm-ups. Emphasize hip and shoulder flexibility (pages 19-20)
  i) Use a selection of elementary floor exercise skills as part of the warm-up.
  ii) Introduce at least one partner flexibility exercise. Stress responsibility and correct performance in partner exercises (pages 19-20). Control the time spent on partner activities. Do not allow this to become excessive.

4. Review

For this lesson, skills already introduced are reviewed as part of the warm-up.

5. New Material

Whole class as a unit working across mats.

Floor Exercises and Tumbling

a) Introduction to the tucked backward roll.
  i) Introduce the tucked backward roll and its related lead-ups, e.g. "the rocking horse" (pages 38-39).
  ii) Demonstrate the skill and the manner in which it is spotted.
  iii) Emphasize correct placement of hands either side of the head.
  iv) Begin the tucked backward roll from: (a) sitting and rolling back, (b) squatting, (c) crouching.
  v) Working back and forth across the mats, add an additional skill to the tucked backward roll (use assistance throughout where necessary), e.g. (a) forward roll-pause-backward roll; (b) tip-up-headstand-forward roll-pause-backward roll; (c) handstand-forward roll-pause-tucked backward roll.

b) Straddle backward roll
  i) Demonstrate the "rocking horse" action on the floor from a straddle sitting position. Emphasize correct hand placement.
  ii) Demonstrate the straddle backward roll.
  iii) Demonstrate the spotting. Emphasize the quick actions used by the spotter to follow the performer and lift at the hips (page 40).
  iv) Demonstrate the straddle backward roll from standing. Work first on sitting backward in a straddle position with the hands cushioning the landing. Then add the complete roll action.

  v) Add additional skills to the straddle backward roll, in the same manner as for the tucked backward roll. Performers make up individual combinations.

The class is divided into three groups — Station I, Station II, and Station III.

Station I - Floor Exercises and Tumbling.
Work on combinations of the tucked and straddle backward roll with skills taught previously. Performers work in pairs across the mats or lengthwise if the number of mats allow this to occur *without line-ups*. The skills required are listed on a clipboard which is posted near to Station I. With the exception of the tuck and straddle backward roll, skill requirements differ from those listed at Station II.

Station II - Floor Exercises and Tumbling.
Work on combinations of the tucked and straddle backward roll with skills taught previously. Performers work in pairs across the mats or lengthwise if the number of mats allow this to occur without line-ups. The skills required are listed on a clipboard which is posted on the wall near Station II.

Station III - Introduction to Vaulting - With the instructor
  a) Orientation to vaulting
    i) Use of the take-off apparatus without a horse.
    ii) Orientation to the horse.
    iii) Orientation to the horse and the take-off apparatus combined.
  b) Introduction to the front vault
  c) Introduction to the flank vault

Note: Rotate groups from station to station as far as time will allow. The completion of a full rotation may occur in subsequent lessons. The instructor uses any occasion when the vaulting group is working well to move to other stations.

6. Culmination

a) The class is brought together. The instructor comments on the standard of work at each station. Requirements for the next class are outlined.

b) The instructor reminds those chosen to put apparatus away of the correct methods of carrying apparatus, i.e. vaulting horse. The positioning of apparatus in the storage room is supervised by the instructor.

Lesson Four - Continuation of Instruction in Vaulting

1. Introduction

In this lesson, new floor and vaulting skills will be introduced. The class stays as a unit for the warm-up and floor exercise skills and then divides into three groups — Station I - Floor Exercises, Station II - Floor Exercises, Station III - Vaulting.

This lesson would occur during *Step 3* of the Progressing to Groups Plan.

Equipment Needed:
a) floor exercise mats and crash pads (if available)
b) vaulting apparatus (mats, box, horse, take-off apparatus, and any other apparatus to be used for vaulting)
c) clipboards with skills listed for Station I and Station II
d) taped music to accompany flexibility exercises

Advance Preparation: (This is similar to the preparation for Lesson Three.)
a) Check vaulting apparatus.
b) Organize teams to bring out equipment.
c) Plan the gymnasium lay-out.
d) Prepare new skill lists on clipboards to be placed by Station I and Station II. These will be based on the progress made in previous lessons.

Class Preparation:
Lay out the equipment as before (Lesson Three).

2. Objectives

By the end of this lesson, participants will have been introduced to the following skills:
Floor
a) Piked backward roll (pages 43-44).
b) Press to headstand from straddle stand (pages 42-3)
Vaulting
a) Rear vault (pages 130-131)
b) Squat vault (pages 132-133)

3. Warm-Up

a) Bring the class together and begin flexibility exercises to music. Participants will be familiar with six to eight flexibility exercises. Gaps in the taped music allow sufficient time to name the exercise and demonstrate it once through. New music of a slightly faster beat is used. Ballistic movements are avoided.
b) The taped music is kept relatively short and time allows for some partner activities for developing pulling and pushing power. These are competitive, challenging but at the same time, fun. Activities are chosen that are agreeable to both sexes.

4. Review

Whole class as a unit working across the mats.
Review previous floor skills, emphasize the headstand, and tucked and straddle backward rolls. Demonstrate kicking into a headstand from a bent and straight legged straddle position. Show spotting.

5. New Material

Floor Exercises and Tumbling

Whole class as a unit working across the mats.
a) Piked backward roll
   i) Introduce the piked backward roll from sitting. Demonstrate the skill and show the spotting. Have the class practice the skill with one or two spotters assisting.
   ii) Add an additional skill to the piked backward roll, working back and forth across the mats, e.g. piked backward roll-jump-half pirouette-tucked backward roll. Include a straddle press to headstand to various combinations of skills. Spotters assist throughout.
   iii) Demonstrate the piked backward roll from standing (page 43). Use soft mats to cushion the initial efforts at sitting backward.
   iv) Add an additional skill to the piked backward roll from standing (working back and forth across the mats), e.g. piked backward roll-pause-kick to handstand-forward roll to stand. Emphasize how the spotters shift to assist in these skills.

b) The class is brought together and divided into groups in the same manner as for Lesson Three.

Station I
Works on the straddle press to headstand, the piked backward roll, and combinations with other skills taught previously. These are listed on a clipboard set up near Station I. With the exception of the straddle press to headstand and the piked backward roll, skills listed at Station I differ from Station II.

Station II
Works on the straddle press to headstand, the piked backward roll, and combinations with other skills taught previously. These are listed on a clipboard set up near Station II.

Station III - With the instructor
a) Review of the front and flank vaults.
b) Introduction to the rear vault (page 130) and the squat vault (page 132). Demonstration of skills and spotting. The run-up is kept to a minimum and change-over from performer to spotter is made as rapidly as possible.

Note: Rotate groups from station to station as far as time will allow. The completion of a full rotation may occur in subsequent lessons. The instructor uses any occasion when the vaulting group is working well to move to other stations.

6. Culmination

a) The class is brought together. Requirements for the next class are outlined. Participants who are chosen for bringing out new apparatus such as the horizontal bar are warned of their duties.
b) The instructor supervises the storage of equipment.

Lesson Five - Introduction to the Low Horizontal Bar

1. Introduction

In this lesson, skills on the low horizontal bar are introduced. The class stays together as a unit for the warm-up and the floor exercise skills and then divides into four groups — Station I - Floor Exercises, Station II - Floor Exercises, Station III - Vaulting, Station IV - Low Horizontal Bar.

This lesson would occur during *Step 4* of the Progressing to Group Activities Plan.

Equipment needed:
- a) floor mats and crash pads
- b) vaulting apparatus
- c) low horizontal bar apparatus (use other apparatus that can be used as a low horizontal bar, i.e. the low bar of the unevens, a single bar of the parallel bars, and the horizontal bar set at chest height - i.e. average chest height of the students in the class)
- d) clipboards with skills listed for Station I, Station II, and Station III

Advance Preparation:
- a) Check equipment (particularly the apparatus to be used for the low horizontal bar). Remember chalk for the bar.
- b) Carefully organize the teams to bring out equipment. Aim for minimal delay, maximum control and safety.
- c) Plan the gymnasium lay-out.

Diagram I.
Suggested lay-out of the gymnasium. Instructor should be positioned to oversee complete class.

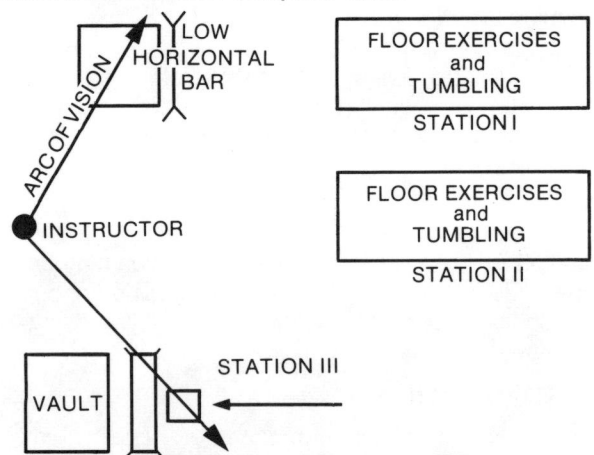

- d) Prepare the skill lists to be placed by Stations I, II, and III. These skill lists will be based on progress made in the previous lessons.
- e) Plan the division of the class into four groups, one at each station. Have prepared the best possible arrangement of students in these groups.

Class Preparation:
Lay out the equipment. Supervise the setting up of the low horizontal bar and any other apparatus being used for the same purpose. (Re-check the bite on turnbuckle threads to make sure that it is adequate.)

2. Objectives

By the end of this lesson, participants will have been introduced to the following skills:

Floor
- a) The cartwheel (pages 47-50)

Low Horizontal Bar
- a) Orientation to the apparatus and basic positions (pages 170-173)
- b) Front support swings and simple cast (pages 173-174)
- c) Front support-forward roll dismount (pages 174-175)
- d) Pullover mount (pages 177-178).

3. Warm-Up

Begin the warm-up. Work through a series of the most important flexibility exercises only. Eliminate other activities to allow as much time as possible for the remainder of the class.

4. Review

Review the handstand and its lead-ups.

5. New Material

Whole class as a unit working across the mats.

Floor Exercises and Tumbling
- a) Progress from the handstand to the cartwheel. Use whichever lead-up method brings the greatest success (see pages 47-49)
- b) Demonstrate the cartwheel and show the preferred spotting technique. Emphasize the importance of the hips passing over the hand positions on the floor.
- c) The class is brought together and is divided into four groups, one at each station.

Station I - Floor Exercises and Tumbling
Work further on the cartwheel and add the cartwheel to a selection of skills previously taught. These are listed by the instructor on a clipboard near Station I.

Station II - Floor Exercises and Tumbling
This group also works on the cartwheel but joins it to a different selection of skills previously taught. These are listed by the instructor on a clipboard placed near Station II.

Station III - Vaulting
Work on front, flank, rear, and squat vaults.

Station IV - Introduction to the Low Horizontal Bar with the instructor.

If there is only one bar then two performers are put on the bar at one time (single spotters assist from the outer side of each performer).
- a) The instructor demonstrates all the basic static positions and each performer practices these positions.
- b) The instructor demonstrates and each individual

works through the following sequence of skills
  i) Jump to front support (overgrasp)-two low amplitudes swings-dismount.
  ii) A cast backward to stand is added to the above, i.e. jump to front support-low amplitude swings-cast backward to stand.
  iii) The forward roll dismount is demonstrated from front support. Each performer begins in front support and practices this action with *as much control as possible.* Spotting positions are shown.
  iv) A pullover mount is demonstrated. The spotting is shown and the importance of the final stabilization of the performer is stressed. All practice.
  v) Sequences are then made up of the above skills, e.g.
    - jump to front support-cast (with assistance)-return to front support-cast backward to stand
    - jump to front support-three low amplitude swings-forward roll-pullover mount (from a kick)-forward roll dismount
    - pullover mount with straight legs-(with assistance)-three low amplitude swings-cast backward to stand.
  vi) - The instructor then challenges the performers to make up variations of the above skills (using assistance where necessary). He demonstrates the following: jump to front support-three swings with low amplitude-forward roll dismount-kick through a pullover mount-front support swings-cast backward to stand
  vii) - While performers are working on the above skills, the instructor moves to other groups or stays at the low horizontal bar and verbally instructs performers in other groups.

Note: Rotate groups from station to station as far as time will allow. The completion of a full rotation may occur in subsequent lessons. The instructor uses any occasion when the low horizontal bar group is working well to move to other stations.

6. Culmination
  a) The instructor brings the class together, comments on their efforts at their respective stations and outlines the requirements for the next class.
  b) The apparatus is put away. The instructor supervises.

Lesson Six - Low Horizontal Bar continued

1. Introduction

In this lesson, instruction on the low horizontal bar continues. The class stays as a unit for the warm-up and floor exercises and tumbling and then divides into four groups — Station I - Floor Exercises, Station II - Floor Exercises, Station III - Vaulting, Station IV - Low Horizontal Bar.

This lesson would occur as part of *Step 5* of the Progressing to Group Activities Plan.

  Equipment needed: (as for Lesson Five)
  a) floor mats and any available crash pads
  b) vaulting apparatus
  c) low horizontal bar apparatus

  Advance Preparation:
  a) Use the same sequence of actions for checking on equipment, teams and gymnasium lay-out as for Lesson Five.

  Class Preparation:
  Lay out the equipment. This is the same as for the previous lesson. It is expected that less time will be taken in setting it up.

2. Objectives

By the end of this lesson, participants will have been introduced to the following skills
  Floor
  a) Standing dive roll (pages 52-53)
  Low Horizontal Bar
  a) Front support to stride support (page 175-176)
  b) Single knee swing up (pages 176-177)
  c) Backward hip circle (pages 179-180)
  d) Underswing dismount (pages 180-181)
  e) Glide swing and return (pages 181-182)

3. Warm-Up

Work through a selection of flexibility exercises and a new partner flexibility exercise. Introduce some new partner activities for developing power.

4. Review

Review a selection of previously-taught skills that need extra work.

5. New Material
  a) Lead from the warm-up activities directly into floor exercises.
  b) Work through the lead-ups for the standing dive roll (see pages 52-53). Emphasize the sequence necessary for cushioning the roll. As an additional lead-up, review the handstand forward roll with spotting assistance. Move to the dive roll using two spotters (if crash pads are available have performers roll across them).
  c) The class divides into four groups, one at each station.

Station I
Work on a selection of floor exercise and tumbling skills (and combinations of skills) listed by the instructor on the clipboard set at the station. The standing dive forward roll is included as one of these skills.

Station II
Work on a selection of floor exercises and tumbling skills (and combinations of skills) listed by the instructor on the clipboard set at the station. The dive forward roll

is included as one of the skills. With the exception of the standing dive roll, skills at Station I differ from Station II.

Station II

Work on vaults previously taught. If time permits, the instructor will move to this group and show the lead-up skills for the straddle vault.

Station IV - With the instructor

Further progress on the low horizontal bar.
  a) Performers review previous skills.
  b) The instructor demonstrates how to shift from front support to stride support (pages 175-176). Spotting is shown.
  c) From stride support performers are shown how to drop (with assistance) to a single knee swing and how to return to front support.
  d) The pullover mount is reviewed as orientation to the backward hip circle (pages 177-178). The cast entry is practiced and a slow backward hip circle is practiced with full assistance from two spotters.
  e) A sequence of skills is given to the performers, i.e. pullover mount-front support to stride support-single knee swing up-return to front support-forward roll dismount.
  f) The glide swing and return and its related lead-ups are shown to the group. Performers begin with the run out to extension and run back (pages 181-182). Performers run out and run back and then try to glide out and glide back. (While this and other risk free skills are being practiced, the instructor moves to other stations.)
  g) The underswing dismount is demonstrated. Performers practice this skill without any cast action and initially with two spotters.
  h) Combinations are made up of the skills taught relative to the individual's level of performance.

Note: Groups rotate from station to station as far as time will allow. The completion of a full rotation may occur in subsequent lessons. The instructor uses any occasion when the low horizontal bar group is working well to move to other stations.

6. Culmination

  a) The class is brought together. Requirements for the next class are outlined. Participants who are chosen to bring out new apparatus such as the parallel bars are warned of their duties.
  b) The instructor supervises the storage of equipment.

Lesson Seven - Introduction to Parallel Bars (Males) — Further Work on the Low Horizontal Bar (Females)

1. Introduction

In this lesson the class will stay together for warm-ups and then divide into four groups of single sex—Station I - Floor Exercises and Tumbling, Station II - Vaulting, Station III - Low Horizontal Bar, Station IV - (a) further Low Horizontal Bar skills for females (a different selection from Station III), (b) Parallel bar skills for males.

This lesson would occur during *Step 6* of the Progressing to Group Activities Plan.

Equipment needed:
  a) Mats and crash pads if available.
  b) Vaulting, low horizontal and parallel bar apparatus

Advance Preparation:
  a) Check equipment, particularly the parallel bars. Check castors and transporter.
  b) Organize the teams to bring out and set up the equipment.
  c) Organize four groups—each group single sex.
  d) Plan the gymnasium lay-out.
  e) Prepare the skill lists to be set near Stations I, II, and III. These skill lists will be based on progress made in previous lessons.

Class Preparation:

Lay out equipment. Supervise personally the placement of the parallel bars and check the low horizontal bar.

2. Objectives

By the end of this lesson, participants will have been introduced to the following skills:

Parallel Bars (males)
  a) Basic static positions (page 148)
  b) Cross support hop travel (page 149)
  c) Cross support swings (pages 149-150)
  d) Dismount from a forward swing (pages 150-151)
  e) Other elementary skills which can be used to make up simple combinations, e.g. straddle travel.

Low horizontal bar - (females)

Further practice on single bar skills in preparation for work on the uneven bars.

3. Warm-Up

  a) Work through a series of important flexibility exercises.
  b) Use a short selection of floor exercise skills as part of the warm-up.

4. Review

Review is combined with warm-up for this lesson.

5. New Material

The class is divided into four new groups—single sex.

Station I - Floor Exercises and Tumbling

This group works on skills and combinations previously taught. These are listed and posted by the station. Performers work according to ability.

Station II - Vaulting

Practice front, flank, rear, squat, and the lead-ups to the straddle vault. Requirements are listed at the station. Performers work according to ability.

Station III - Low Horizontal Bar

Work on low horizontal bar skills previously taught.

Skills and combinations are listed at the station. Performers work according to ability.

Station IV - with the instructor - Parallel bar skills (males) - One bar of the parallel bars is removed for low horizontal bar skills (females).

Parallel Bars (males)
a) Introduction to basic static positions. Two (occasionally three) performers are on the bars at one time for this practice.
b) Introduction to simple travels.
   i) Cross support hop travel (with no swing).
   ii) Cross support hop travel with a low swinging action. Emphasize shift on front swing.
   iii) Straddle travel the length of the bars.
c) The instructor demonstrates and has performers practice low amplitude swings. Emphasize swinging from the shoulders. One performer is placed at either end of the bars. The method of assistance is shown.
d) The lead-ups to the dismount from a forward swing are demonstrated and practiced.
e) Performers work through the full skill.
f) The group practices small combinations of skills, e.g. straddle travel (twice)-hop travel (twice)-dismount from a forward swing.

Low Horizontal Bar skills (females)
Further practice on single bar skills in preparation for work on the uneven bars e.g. orientation to forward stride circle.

Note: Rotate groups from station to station as far as time allows. The completion of a full rotation may occur in subsequent lessons. The instructor uses any occasion when Station IV is working well to move to other stations.

6. Culmination
a) The class is brought together. The instructor comments on the efforts of the class. Requirements for the next class are outlined. Performers who are chosen to bring out new apparatus are warned of their duties.
b) The instructor supervises the storage of equipment.

Lesson Eight - Introduction to New Apparatus

1. Introduction

In this lesson, beam skills will be introduced for females (all skills performed on benches), and rope and low ring activities will be introduced for males. The class stays as a unit for the warm-up and then divides into five groups (each group is single sex) — Station I - Floor Exercises and Tumbling, Station II - Vaulting, Station III - Low Horizontal Bar, Station IV - Parallel Bars, i.e., parallel bars for males and single bar skills for females. Station V - Rope and Ring skills for males. Beam skills for females.

This lesson would occur during *Step 8* of the Progressing to Group Activities Plan.

Equipment needed:
a) mats for floor exercises
b) vaulting apparatus
c) low horizontal bar (use other available bars)
d) parallel bars
e) benches or beam, ropes and rings.

Advance Preparation:
a) Careful planning of groups (each group single sex).
b) Planning of teams to bring out and put away apparatus.
c) Planning the gymnasium lay-out.

Diagram I
Gymnasium Lay-Out

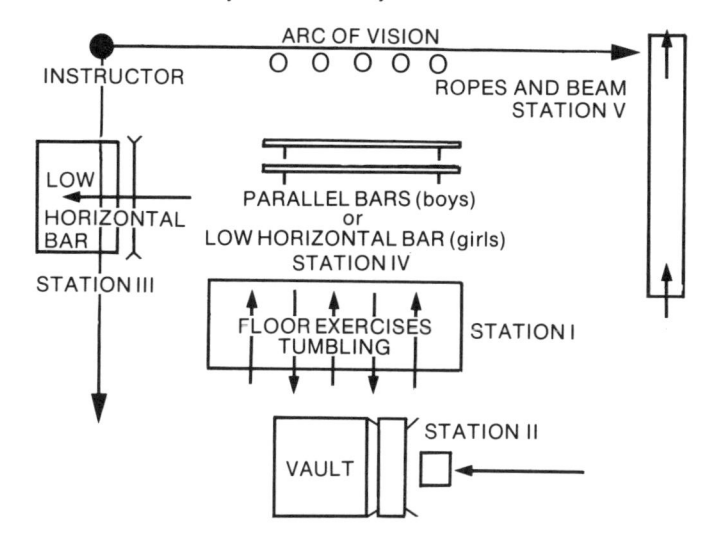

d) Prior check of all equipment
e) Lists of skills on clipboards for Stations I-IV.

Class Preparation:
Lay out equipment. Instructor supervises throughout.

2. Objectives
By the end of this lesson, participants will have been introduced to the following skills:

Beam
a) Basic locomotor patterns back and forth on the beam—poses, pirouettes, balances, simple mounts and dismounts.

Ropes (and adjustable rings)
a) Static positions (pages 102-103)
b) Climbing and traveling and making fast (page 101)
c) Tuck support (pages 106-107)

3. Warm-Up
Bring class together and begin warm-up activities. Work on specific major flexibility exercises, emphasize squatting, stooping, and straddling actions as preparation for vaulting.

4. Review
Review is combined with warm-up for this lesson.

5. New Material

Organize five new groups—single sex.

Station I - Floor Exercises and Tumbling

Work on a selection of skills listed on a clipboard at the station. Performers work on combinations and short routines using assistance where necessary.

Station II - Vaulting

Group works on front, flank, rear, squat, and straddle. Performers practice squatting on and jumping off—each time extending the legs further (lead-up to the stoop vault, pages 136-138).

Station III - Low Horizontal Bar

The group practices skills taught in previous lessons and make up combinations of these skills. The glide swing and return is added to the beginning of the routines in the following manner: glide swing and return-jump from floor to front support-forward roll-pullover mount-cast back and dismount.

Station IV - Parallel Bars (males) - One bar removed for single bar skills (females)

This group works on skills taught previously. The emphasis in this group is on perfecting these skills and putting them together in *two* and *three* skill combinations.

Station V - With the instructor
  a) If a female group rotates to this station, the instructor works with them on basic beam skills.
  b) If a male group rotates to this station the instructor works with them on the low rings and the ropes (or ropes alone).
     i) Static positions are introduced (piked inverted hang, straight inverted hang, cross support (in low rings). Each position is shown and performers rotate through practicing skills with assistance.
     ii) Climbing, traveling from one rope to the other and making fast is taught and used as power activities as preparation for the rings.
     iii) Skin-the-cat is shown and attempted in the ropes and rings. Spotting is also demonstrated and practiced.
     iv) The tuck support is demonstrated (from a hang in the ropes and from cross support in the rings).
     v) Performers are challenged to make up small combinations of skills using assistance where necessary. The instructor demonstrates one example in the ropes, e.g. hang-lift the legs to momentary tuck support-lower the legs and using the floor kick up to a straight inverted hang-lower to piked inverted hang-lower the legs forward and dismount.

Note: Rotate groups from station to station as far as time will allow. Complete the rotation in subsequent lessons.

6. Culmination
  a) The class is called together and the requirements for the following class are outlined.
  b) The instructor supervises the storage of equipment.

Chapter Five
Evaluation

A. Individual Evaluation

The conditions under which gymnastics is taught differ from one school to another. Apparatus, available time, the make up of the class, student skills level and rates of progress vary widely. These factors force the instructor to consider individual differences throughout a program. In essence, every class is a multi-level class.

Variables such as these create a difficult situation for the instructor not only in class organization and teaching, but also in attempts to measure student progress. However, gymnastics differs little from other sports in that ultimately each student is evaluated in relation to:
1. the level at which the individual starts in the program
2. the progress the student makes during the program

Final evaluations should reflect a student's progress in relation to the goals that the instructor has set for the program. These goals have to be reasonable. It is obviously unrealistic to expect all students to perform Level IV skills and to join a gymnastic club as a result of their school gymnastic experience. It is equally unrealistic to expect that no student will progress beyond the skills in Level I. Within these extremes a realistic range of expectations must be found. The method of evaluation used should then demonstrate as accurately as possible where the student lies in relation to these expectations.

Whatever format the evaluative process takes, it must stimulate and challenge the students and be part of an overall experience which is positive rather than negative.

With this in mind the following suggestions are made:
1. Avoid any system of evaluation which takes up an inordinate amount of time that could better be spent on teaching.
2. Try to develop an on-going evaluative system rather than a single shot (one try only) method. Have this begin during the latter half of the gymnastic bloc after a foundation of skills have been taught, and preferably after the class has been divided into stations. This is better than having a single, and often long, testing session at the end of the bloc.
3. In order to relieve some of the pressure on the instructor, consider the possibility of a simple scoring system carried out by other students such as group leaders. Spot checks are then made by the instructor.
4. When a station approach is used, set up clip-boards listing names and basic skills at each station. A check-off system would mark success and progress from one skill to the next.
5. Booklets which list events and point scores for each skill could also be used. These would be given out at the start of the lesson and collected at the end. The complexity of the scoring would depend upon the instructor and the teaching situation. Group leaders could assist in the scoring.
6. In order to emphasize good safety habits and to maintain interest among students of lesser ability, the following is also recommended:
    a) Let regular attendance and visible effort be worthy of a positive evaluation in the class.
    b) Reward a skill performed alone only slightly higher than the same skill performed with spotters.
    c) Use a system which will give a positive evaluation in the class even with the majority of skills assisted by one or two spotters.
    d) Allow more than one attempt at a skill or combination of skills. This removes the fear of testing and encourages continuous improvement.
    e) Discourage students from performing skills alone with poor technique.
    f) For those who cannot attempt the skills, consider the possibility of awarding scores for active involvement as spotters and for knowledge of teaching progressions and spotting techniques.
    g) If students cannot participate they should be able to achieve a positive assessment through cognitive and affective evaluation in such areas as teaching progressions, spotting techniques and leadership ability.
    h) As a fun finale to complete a gymnastic bloc, consider the possibility of an inter-station competition where scores for single skills or combinations of skills result from the combined efforts of spotters and performer. In this situation the efforts of performer and spotters count equally in the overall performance of members of the group.

B. Program Evaluation

Ultimately the instructor must evaluate the total gymnastic program to see whether the objectives are being achieved. The instructor must ask:
1. Are the objectives reasonable given the conditions and limitations under which the program is taught?
2. Are the methods used the best for achieving the desired objectives, or should some adjustment be made?

If the instructor feels that the objectives of the program are reasonable and yet students fail to meet them, then each part of the program must be assessed for weakness and improvements made. There are

numerous variables which will influence the quality of a gymnastic program. A selection of the most important are as follows:
1. The instructor's own knowledge and ability to teach gymnastics.

    Too frequently other aspects of the program are blamed for lack of progress in gymnastics. Yet often the problem stems from the instructor's limited background in gymnastics, and the fact that there has been no effort to upgrade the instructor's teaching ability in this sport. This causes either of two situations to occur:
    a) The instructor avoids gymnastics and teaches sports which are less stressful in terms of organization, control and teaching ability.
    b) The instructor attempts to teach gymnastics using haphazardly chosen skills and poorly constructed teaching progressions.

    In both these situations the students are ultimately the losers.
2. Conditions and apparatus

    An excellent gymnastic program can be taught with very little apparatus but it is also true that lack of time, apparatus, and space present great handicaps. Program objectives must be adjusted accordingly.
3. Organization and management

    Few sports so seriously test the organizational and logistical ability of the instructor as does gymnastics. The nature of the equipment and the wide range of student abilities all demand careful planning and well conceived teaching progressions. The instructor must question whether any short comings in the program are due to poor planning or possibly to the sequence in which skills have been introduced. Often a re-organization in this area can do much to upgrade the quality of the program.

Finally, in assessing the components of a gymnastic program, the instructor must always keep in mind that the program must be directed towards:
1. A pleasurable experience

    Above all else the gymnastic class must be enjoyable. If it is fun for the students, the teaching situation becomes more effective and the chance of realizing objectives becomes greater.
2. General physical development

    The rate of progress in learning gymnastic skills is linked with an improvement in such areas as flexibility, coordination, power, and endurance. A general improvement in these areas makes skill learning so much easier and the achievement of objectives much more rapid.
3. The fundamental of gymnastics

    If students enjoy gymnastics, they learn faster and they are likely to spend more time with the sport. If they are in good condition it will be much easier to teach them the fundamentals of gymnastics. A pleasurable experience in learning the fundamental skills in Levels I and II leads to the additional excitement and challenge of Levels III and IV, possibly even beyond.

Appendix I
Reference Material

A. Books

Canadian Gymnastics Federation Development Program.

Book I Participation (Red-White-Blue Levels).

Book II (Men's) Achievement (Merit-Bronze-Silver-Gold Levels).

Book III (Women's) Achievement (Merit-Bronze-Silver-Gold Levels).

Coaching Certification Manual, Level I. T. Kinsman (ed.), CGF, 1977

Coaching Certification Manual, Level II. T. Kinsman (ed.), CGF, 1978.

Carr, Gerald A., *Safety in Gymnastics. A manual of safety and spotting techniques for elementary and intermediate gymnastics.* Hancock House Publishers, #10 Orwell Street, North Vancouver, B.C. V7J 3K1, 1980.

Gymnastic Safety Manual. Eugene Wettstone (ed.), United States Gymnastics Safety Association, 17241 Dulles International Airport, Washington, D.C. 20041. 1977.

Hartley, Sandra. *Training, Conditioning, Flexibility Work for Women's Competitive Gymnastics.* Coaching Association of Canada, 333 River Road, Vanier City, Ontario K1L 8B9, N.d.

Holt, Laurence. *Scientific Stretching for Sport.* The Coaching Association of Canada, 333 River Road, Vanier City, Ontario K1L 8B9, N.d.

Kaneko, Akitomo. *Olympic Gymnastics.* Sterling Publishing Co., Inc., New York, 1977.

Kos Bohumil, Teply, Volrab. *Gymnastik, 1200 Ubungen.* Sportverlag Berlin (East), 1971. (No knowledge of German necessary, 1200 conditioning exercises of every type.)

Nett, Toni. *Kraftubungen zur Konditionsarbeit.* Verlag Bartels und Wernitz, 1 Berlin 65, 1970. (No knowledge of German necessary—strength and power exercises illustrated.)

Ryan, Dr. Frank. *Gymnastics for Girls.* Penguin Books and Viking Press, U.S.A., 1977.

Schmid, Andrea Bodo and Blanche Drury. *Gymnastics for Women.* Mayfield Publishing Company, 1977.

Spackman, Robert. *Conditioning for Gymnastics.* Springfield, Illinois: Chas. C. Thomas Publishers, 1970.

Taylor, Bryce, B. Bajin and T. Zivic. *Olympic Gymnastics for Men and Women.* Englewood Cliffs, N.J.: Prentice-Hall, 1971.

B. Films

8mm, 16mm, loop and strip films can be obtained from the following sources.

The Sport Information Center of the Coaching Association of Canada, 333 River Road, Vanier City, Ontario K1L 8B9.

The Sport Information Center provides loop films and reels of world and Olympic championships, Olympic champions on specific events, and teaching progressions for specific skills. (See following information on the Coaching Association of Canada.)

The Athletic Institute, 705 Merchandise Mart, Chicago, Illinois 60654.

This institute provides loop films of routines and individual skills.

Frank Endo, 12200 S. Berendo Avenue, Los Angeles California 90044.

Frank Endo sells loop films and reels of World and Olympic Championships. He is also an important source of the latest Japanese gymnastic material - text books, gymnastic clothing, equipment.

C. Journals

International Gymnast, Sundby Sports Publications, P.O. Box 110, Santa Monica, California.

Contains information on all areas of gymnastics—competitions, club news, up-coming clinics, teaching and coaching. Each issue contains a giant fold-out of a gymnastic star. These photographs are excellent for use on bulletin boards and as wall posters.

D. Wall Charts

Wall charts can be obtained which offer diagrams of gymnastic skills, apparatus, and spotting techniques. Progression charts are also available. These are visual reminders of correct teaching progressions and act as a warning against by-passing essential lead-ups.

AMF American Athletic Equipment Division, 2000 American Avenue, Jefferson, Iowa 50129.

Nissen Corporation, 930 - 27th Avenue S.W., Cedar Rapids, Iowa 52406.

WM Productions, P.O. Box 10573, Denver, Colorado 80210.

A large gymnastics rules posters (stressing safety rules and regulations concerning dress, equipment, and skills progressions) is available from *The United States Gymnastics Safety Association,* 17241 Dulles International Airport, Washington, D.C. 20041.

E. The Coaching Association of Canada

The Coaching Association of Canada (CAC) is a national, non-profit organization. Its major aims are to increase coaching effectiveness in all sports and to encourage the development of coaching by providing programs and services at all levels. There are several important programs that the CAC has developed in cooperation with the National Sporting Bodies. The following are of particular importance to the instructor and coach of gymnastics.

1. *The National Coaching Certification Program.*
This program organizes courses in each of the provinces to certify coaches. Those interested in certification should contact any of the following three agencies:
   a) CAC offices - 333 River Road, Vanier City, Ontario K1L 8B9.
   b) The Canadian Gymnastic Federation offices - address as above.
   c) For British Columbia - The BCGA, 1200 Hornby Street, Vancouver, B.C.

2. *The Audio-Visual Department*
Gymnastic loop films of all types are produced by this department and published in the catalogue of the Sport Information Center of the Canadian Coaching Association.

3. *The Sports Information Resource Center*
This is a national sport library and documentation center that possesses the largest computerized data base on sport in the western world. By joining the Coaching Association, members are able to purchase—often at special rates—films, texts, and print-outs on texts and research that are carried in the *Sport Information Catalogue.*

4. The Coaching Association of Canada publishes material relating to physical education, coaching and teaching. This appears bi-monthly in the *Coaching Review.*

How to join the Coaching Association of Canada:
Write: The Coaching Association of Canada, 333 River Road, Vanier City, Ontario K1L 8B9.

Appendix II
Glossary

Amplitude:	Degree or amount. Low amplitude swings are swings that move only a few degrees back and forth from the vertical position.
Backhandspring:	Also called flick flack or flip flop.
Back Salto:	Also called back somersault, back sommie, back flip. A rotational skill performed backward in the air.
Bridge:	Also called back bend, back arch or crab stand.
Beat board:	Also called Reuther Board. The springboard used for competitive vaulting.
Buck:	A short vaulting horse often equipped with pommels.
Cheating:	Changing the body position slightly to make the skill easier to perform.
Crash pad:	A large mat filled with a block of foam rubber and used for cushioning dismounts.
Cross support:	Supported on and across the apparatus by the arms. (This does *not* mean "in a cross shape.")
Cross box:	Also called side box (e.g. vaulting across the width of the box rather than lengthwise).
Dished position:	Concave. A dished body position is one where the chest is pulled in so that there is a slight concave shape from the shoulders to the waist.
Dismount:	The finishing skill in a gymnastic routine. This term also applies to floor exercise routines. The performer does not necessarily have to be dismounting from apparatus.

Extended:	Stretched out or straight.	**Straddle:**	With the legs straight and apart in a sideways direction.
Feint:	Used on the pommel horse, this is a preliminary motion in one direction used to generate momentum in the opposing direction.	**Torque:**	Twisting or turning motion.
		Trampette:	A small trampoline used for acrobatic, tumbling and vaulting skills.
Flex:	To bend.	**Tucked:**	In a ball shape with the knees and hips flexed.
Front Salto:	Also called front somersault, front sommie, front flip. A rotational skill performed forward in the air.	**Undergrip:**	Reverse grip.
Horizontal Bar:	The high bar or low bar (i.e., the horizontal bar set at chest height).		
Inverted:	Upside down.		
Lay-out:	An extended or straight body position.		
Lead-up:	A series of skills (or a single skill) in a teaching progression.		
Mount:	The first in a series of skills. The beginning of a gymnastic routine. This term also applies to floor exercises. The performer does not have to be getting on apparatus.		
Orientation:	Knowing where you are—getting to know the "feeling" for a skill.		
Parallettes:	Small parallel bars built close to the floor and used for practicing handstands and related parallel bar skills.		
Pirouette:	Rotation around the long axis of the body (from head to feet).		
Piked:	A body position with the hips bent (i.e. flexed) and with the legs straight.		
Pommel horse:	Also called side horse.		
Pull up:	Chin up		
Push up:	Press up.		
Skill:	Also called stunt or trick.		
Spotting:	The act of providing assistance to the performer.		
Spotting block:	A large cube shaped block on which the spotter stands to give assistance for skills performed well above the floor.		
Stride:	With the legs straight and apart in a forward and backward direction.		

Notes

Notes

hancock house

Sports Handbook Series

Tennis Handbook
Graphics illustrate grips and strokes in this compact guide to a popular sport. Everything necessary to teach - and play - is tucked between the covers.
ISBN 0-88839-049-1

Folk Dance Handbook
The fascinating complexities of this activity are set out in a clear, easy-to-follow format that should bring the delights of folk dance within the reach of everyone.
ISBN 0-88839-044-0

Soccer Handbook
Skills and how to teach them; drills and when to use them; plus detailed plans for sequential teaching of the game. Compact yet comprehensive.
ISBN 0-88839-048-3

Field Hockey Handbook
Concise, clearly illustrated, a useful guide to learning and teaching a fast-growing sport.
ISBN 0-88839-043-2

Basketball Handbook
Rules and activities are clearly illustrated to make this guide indispensable to anyone coaching or teaching the game.
ISBN 0-88839-042-4

Badminton Handbook
A well-illustrated guide to all the basics of the game, this also includes a discussion of teaching strategies when player skills vary widely.
ISBN 0-88839-041-6

Men's Gymnastics Handbook
Teaching sequences for the six Olympic events of men's artistic gymnastics are explained in detail, with precise information on spotting and safety techniques providing valuable guidance for the instructor.
ISBN 0-88839-046-7

Women's Gymnastics Handbook
A detailed guide to the teaching of gymnastic skills for women, including lesson plans and methods for evaluating performers.
ISBN 0-88839-045-9

Orienteering Handbook
The rapidly-growing interest in this activity makes the publication of this book particularly timely. It includes detailed information on basic concepts, setting a course and organizing a meet, as well as addresses for obtaining equipment and other resources.
ISBN 0-88839-047-5

ALSO AVAILABLE

Safety in Gymnastics by Gerald A. Carr Phd. A comprehensive guide to spotting and safety techniques in the gymnasium. 600 sequential illustrations. ISBN 0-99939-054-8 $12.95.

Curling Handbook by Roy D. Theissen. The history of the game, complete, detailed. ISBN 0-919654-71-1 $5.95

Tennis: The Decision-Making Sport by Josef Brabenec. Think your way to victory on the court with Canada's national tennis coach. ISBN 0-88839-052-1 $9.95